Praise for
Donald L. Maggin and *Dizzy*

"Maggin brings the multifaceted man, the marvelous music, and Dizzy's rich and fascinating life into full and clear view. A fine job of research and writing."

—Dan Morgenstern, Director of the Rutgers Institute of Jazz Studies and author of *Living with Jazz*

"An important biography. . . . An inclusive, well-documented, and honest analysis of Gillespie's work and place in American music. Highly recommended."

—*Library Journal* (starred review)

"Don Maggin has written a biography both informative and knowing. He has given a line, with peaks and valleys, to the life of his subject, who was a genius, an organizer, a leader, a virtuoso, a clown, a scrapper, a venturesome intellectual, an aristocrat, and a man of the people. Maggin has done a superb job of orchestrating the craft, the drama, the humor, and the complexity of an extraordinary man's life. Ever the insider, Maggin also offers shrewd insights into the serpentine nature of the music business and what it demands of those who enter it. Dizzy Gillespie would surely have loved it."

—Stanley Crouch

"Maggin, in this long-overdue, full-dress biography, reestablishes Gillespie's premier role in not one but two jazz revolutions. . . . He capably traces Gillespie's life. . . . The full force of Gillespie's mercurial personality shines throughout this important contribution to American musical history."

—Bill Ott, *Booklist*

"Maggin provides an enlightening view . . . framed by the intimate details of a fascinating life in jazz. He has done extensive research . . . and he has scoured every other imaginable source of material. . . . [*Dizzy*] reads as something far more compelling than an aggregation of research. Maggin uses his data to create a foundation of time, place, and attitude for every stage of Gillespie's journey. . . . The complete package is persuasive, for the musical as well as nonmusical reader, in part because of Maggin's apparent desire . . . to remain out of the picture as much as possible, allowing his extraordinary subject to take center stage."   —*Los Angeles Times*

"Richly detailed."   —*New York Post*

"Authoritative . . . explains Gillespie's musical innovations in precise language that doesn't confuse novices or alienate knowledgeable players and fans. . . . *Dizzy* carefully traces Gillespie's two major legacies. . . . Maggin's book effectively documents the many changes pioneered by Gillespie, who never lost contact with either the experimental or traditional wings of the jazz world."   —*BookPage*

"Engrossing. . . . Maggin does a fine job of noting the social changes that helped shape [jazz's] historical arc. . . . An inspiring account of what genius and conviction can do."
                                                    —*Publishers Weekly*

"Maggin has ample fun with Gillespie the prankster but tells the more enlightening story of Gillespie the pioneer. . . . Maggin serves up delicious anecdotes."   —*Baltimore Sun*

"Excellent . . . accessible [and] well researched. . . . [An] invaluable portrait of the artist and his life and times in an America sometimes driven by racism." —*Hartford Courant*

"Solid. . . . Mr. Maggin has fashioned a very readable narrative that charts the genesis of the new music from the meeting of Gillespie and drummer Kenny Clarke in 1938. . . . Maggin well describes the collaborations between Gillespie, Clarke, guitarist Charlie Christian, pianist Thelonious Monk, and, especially, alto saxophonist Charlie Parker. . . . [Maggin] has fashioned Gillespie's career into an exciting narrative." —*New York Sun*

"A beautiful study. . . . A book that is and will be authoritative." —*JazzMan* (Paris)

"[Maggin] unveils a more complex life story of Dizzy Gillespie beyond the upturned trumpet, beret, bulging cheeks, and clowning demeanor." —*The Black World Today*

"Dizzy Gillespie was a complicated man, and this fine book helps us appreciate his many achievements." —*Open Book*

"[A] most entertaining and interesting biography. . . . The whole book is full of fascinating disclosures about Gillespie and his fabulous career. . . . Hopefully it will serve as an eye opener to the many obstacles that a young man in his position had to face to get anywhere. . . . The book is a cracker. Get it if you possibly can. Thoroughly recommended, and very well written." —*Crescendo & Jazz Music* magazine

Godlis

About the Author

DONALD L. MAGGIN is the author of *Stan Getz: A Life in Jazz*. A writer and businessman, he has produced jazz concerts by such artists as Max Roach, Sonny Stitt, James Moody, Roland Hanna, Eubie Blake, Roberta Flack, and Dizzy Gillespie. He was a board member of the American Jazz Orchestra, served in the Carter White House for three years, is an editor of the literary journal *The Reading Room*, and is a trustee of the Cathedral of St. John the Divine in New York.

DIZZY

**ALSO BY
DONALD L. MAGGIN**

Bankers, Builders, Knaves, and Thieves
Stan Getz: A Life in Jazz

DIZZY

THE LIFE AND TIMES OF JOHN BIRKS GILLESPIE

DONALD L. MAGGIN

Harper

An Imprint of HarperCollinsPublishers

A hardcover edition of this book was published in 2005 by HarperEntertainment, an imprint of HarperCollins Publishers.

HarperCollins books may be purchased for educational, business, or sales promotional use. For information please write: Special Markets Department, HarperCollins Publishers, 10 East 53rd Street, New York, NY 10022.

FIRST HARPER PAPERBACK PUBLISHED 2006.

Designed by Jeffrey Pennington

The Library of Congress has catalogued the hardcover edition as follows:

Maggin, Donald L.
    Dizzy : the life and times of John Birks Gillespie / by Donald L. Maggin.—
    1st ed.
    p. cm.
    Includes bibliographical references (p.) and index.
    ISBN 0-688-17088-9
    1. Gillespie, Dizzy, 1971–1993. 2. Jazz musicians—United States—Biography.   I. Title.

ML419.G54M34 2005
788.9'2165'092—dc22   2004059789
[B]

ISBN-10: 0-06-055921-7 (pbk.)
ISBN-13: 978-0-06-055921-2 (pbk.)

06 07 08 09 10 ❖/RRD 10 9 8 7 6 5 4 3 2 1

To the memory of my uncle, Dr. Nathan Winter.

PERMISSIONS

CONTENTS

DIZZY

INTRODUCTION

Improvisation, the instant creation of melody, is the essence of jazz. Dizzy Gillespie, one of the greatest improvisers of the twentieth century, fashioned an utterly distinctive style, as original and American as Hemingway's or Motherwell's; when you hear one of his phrases on trumpet, you know instantly who is performing.

Dizzy made his greatest artistic contributions as a revolutionary. As a creator of the bebop and the Afro-Cuban revolutions, he twice fundamentally changed the way jazz improvisation was done. It was as if Monet had been in the vanguard of both Impressionism and Cubism.

With bebop during the late 1930s and early 1940s, Dizzy and four colleagues—Charlie Parker, Kenny Clarke, Thelonious Monk, and Charlie Christian—radically expanded the rhythmic and harmonic foundations of jazz. Their innovations were akin to moving classical music from Brahms to Bartók in five years.

Dizzy and Mario Bauzá led the Afro-Cuban revolution of the late 1940s when they brought complex, exciting African polyrhythms into jazz and recast and enriched what was essentially a monorhythmic music. In doing so, they introduced a second pure African element into jazz roughly sixty-five years after the first, the blues, made its entrance. For decades, Dizzy worked tirelessly and successfully to expand the revolution to encompass the Afrocentric music of Brazil and other nations of the Southern Hemisphere.

Dizzy was drawn to rhythmically rich Afro-Cuban music because, for him, rhythm ruled supreme. As he reflected:

The basic thing about jazz music is putting the notes to rhythm, not the other way around. . . . I think up a rhythm first and then I put notes to it to correspond with the chord. You can play very, very beautiful notes and if it doesn't have any rhythmic form, it doesn't amount to anything. Don't lose sight of the rhythm in the music, because that's the most important part. Even more than the notes, because you can take just one note and put all kinds of different rhythms to the note and with just that one note everybody is clapping their hands and dancing and shouting.[1]

Dizzy came to maturity during the World War II heyday of the big bands, and he loved the music of that era. He endured financial hardship to make an essential artistic statement when he created a big band during the late 1940s, a time when such groups were collapsing left and right; he took bebop and Afro-Cuban jazz, which had evolved primarily in smaller groups, and brilliantly adapted their aesthetics to that of the big bands, forever changing the genre. The critic Gene Seymour has commented on Dizzy's innovative vision: "It is still possible to listen to the powerful recordings made by Dizzy Gillespie and his Orchestra in the late 1940's and feel everything around you transformed. What Orson Welles did for movies with 'Citizen Kane,' Gillespie did for big band jazz."[2]

A self-taught virtuoso, Dizzy could execute with ease all the dazzlingly complex and high-velocity concepts that his revolutions called for. He possessed incredible rhythmic acuity, achieving perfect tonal articulation and accuracy at tempos exceeding three hundred beats per minute, and he had complete control of his instrument throughout its range and particularly in the higher octaves. A few may have equaled his jazz technique on trumpet—Wynton Marsalis comes to mind—but none have outdone him.

Dizzy was born black in Cheraw, South Carolina, at the bottom of the American social and political ladder on October 21, 1917. After his father died of asthma when he was nine, his family became so poor that they hid from neighbors at Easter time, ashamed of their threadbare clothing. And they were subject to the relentless, brutal racism of their time and place; a member of Dizzy's high school band was lynched for allegedly being a Peeping Tom, and other indignities were endured almost daily.

The love given to Dizzy by his mother and the structure and discipline imparted by his father gave him a sense of comfort with the world and an unassailable feeling of self-worth. Thus armed, he fought racism his entire life without self-lacerating bitterness or rage.

Dizzy combined youthful energy and focus with a one-in-a-million natural talent and a furious drive to succeed, and he taught himself well enough to achieve a high level of competence by the time he moved north in 1935 at age seventeen. He began his revolutionary musical activities three years later, and he was still going strong fifty-one years afterward when he recorded his fourth Grammy-winning album at age seventy-one in 1989 with his last big band, the United Nation Orchestra.

By the time of his death on January 6, 1993, the Cheraw native had been showered with accolades—among them, eighteen honorary degrees, the James Smithson Medal, a Commandership in the French Academy of Arts and Letters, and America's highest award for the performing arts, a Kennedy Center Honor.

Dizzy was among a handful of jazz stars who brought humor to his performances as he combined a nonthreatening zaniness with a Chaplinesque sense of timing to keep his audiences laughing. Purists complained that he diluted his art with his routines, but he couldn't help it; he simply could not curb his comedic bent.

Over the decades, Dizzy grew spiritually as he tamed a youthful pugnacity to become what the writer Gene Lees has called "the most benign of men." He embraced at the age of fifty the Baha'i faith, whose major tenet, the unity of mankind in brotherhood, conformed to beliefs he had held since childhood. Baha'is believe in an evolving religion revealed progressively by God to mankind by messengers such as Krishna, Moses, Buddha, Christ, and Muhammad.

Like one of God's prophets who enlightened mankind, Dizzy saw himself as a link in a chain of messengers who similarly transformed the art of jazz. For him, the path ran from giants such as Louis Armstrong, Duke Ellington, Coleman Hawkins, and Roy Eldridge to him and his contemporaries, and from them to Lee Morgan, Jon Faddis, Paquito D'Rivera, Arturo Sandoval, and other younger musicians.

Dizzy showed how deeply he cared about carrying this evolution forward by teaching what he called "our music" to any and all who were interested. He enthusiastically imparted his knowledge to thousands in seminars and workshops and to those who worked with him, and he added a home telephone line during the 1970s for those who wished his musical guidance.

Dizzy's generosity of spirit and his warm, infectious openness brought forth a full measure of love from Lorraine, his wife of fifty-three years, his nephew Boo Frazier, and from friends such as Mike Longo, James Moody, Dave Usher, Lalo Schifrin, John Motley, and Jon Faddis. Deep personal failure found him only once—in the relationship with his out-of-wedlock daughter, Jeanie Bryson.

The author Nat Hentoff has described Dizzy's unique personal aura:

Dizzy reached an inner strength and discipline that total pacifists call "soul force." He was always a presence. Like they used to say of Fats Waller, whenever Dizzy came into a room, he filled it. He made people feel good, and he was the sound of surprise, even when his horn was in its case. . . . Seeing Dizzy, however casually, was like coming into sunlight.[3]

As he lay dying, Dizzy told a little girl, "It's been a great gig." It was. The poor black kid from Cheraw grew to enjoy more than his share of love and adulation, and he used his immense talents to create a music that seems always fresh and electric and beautiful—"honey mixed with liquid fire,"[4] as Langston Hughes has written. It swept the world, and it endures, thriving everywhere today.

BATHED IN MUSIC 1

JOHN BIRKS "DIZZY" GILLESPIE ALMOST VOMITED FROM exhaustion as he picked cotton for the first time outside his hometown of Cheraw, South Carolina, in the summer of 1928. He was ten years old, and he hated it.

Those close to him called him John Birks, John, or sometimes Birks. To the world at large, he was Dizzy, a nickname he acquired, as I will describe, when he was eighteen. To keep things simple, I will call him Dizzy throughout this book.

Cheraw is surrounded by a fertile, nearly flat plain 150 miles inland from the Atlantic Ocean and just south of the North Carolina border. Cotton was planted on more than 75 percent of the land in 1928, and the landscape was dominated by its large white fields, which were separated at intervals by stands of commercial pine. Working those fields was a rite of passage for Dizzy and other southern blacks in an era when cotton was king.

Blacks represented roughly 1,300 of Cheraw's 3,700 citizens, and picking cotton was almost the only private employment available to them. A few labored in sawmills or brick factories, fewer still were artisans or owned food stores and other small businesses, and some of the women found employment as domestics in the homes of wealthy whites.

The only form of public employment for blacks was teaching, because the white power structure monopolized jobs with the police and fire departments, the road-maintenance gangs, and the court system. Ten blacks taught at the town's segregated Robert Smalls School. Cheraw spent roughly forty dollars per year educating each white student and less than ten dollars on each black.

If you were strong and worked for ten hours, you could pick 150 pounds of cotton, and during the 1920s your labor would net you seventy-five cents.

Dizzy was a short, skinny kid when he joined his large and robust older brother Wesley in the fields that late summer day in 1928. Following the lead of the other field hands, Dizzy got down on his hands and knees to pull the white blossoms from their pods and in a continuous motion toss them into a sack that was strapped across his chest and hung down his back. He soon felt nauseous crawling in the ninety-five-degree heat, inhaling and coughing up dust laden with bits of fertilizer and insecticide. He gulped water, poured some over his head to cool off, and lay down to rest.

After he went back to work, he came close to crying as he cut his hands several times on the sharp, rigid fronds that encased the blossoms. The nausea returned. He lay down again. Got up and worked. Lay down. By midafternoon, he was exhausted and totally miserable.

When your sack was full, you emptied it into a larger one and went back to picking. Dizzy never filled his sack. His harvest was 15 pounds, which garnered him a measly eight cents. He was furious at the world, at himself, and at Wesley who had gathered a respectable 125 pounds and had earned more than sixty cents.

After they returned home, Dizzy told his mother, "I wasn't cut out for picking cotton. Someday I'm gonna be a musician, and you'll be proud of me."[1]

Becoming a musician was not a far-fetched ambition for the boy, because he had been bathed in music from birth. His father, James, who had died from a sudden asthma attack the year before when Dizzy was nine, was a bricklayer who also led a dance band.

Music was an important emotional and creative outlet for the black families of Cheraw, and many of them, including Dizzy's, laboriously saved their dimes and quarters to buy pianos and other instruments. Dizzy's boyhood friend John Motley, who went on to become the accompanist of contralto Marian Anderson and a distinguished choir director, remembered, "We couldn't vote; we couldn't use the library. And they drummed into us that menial labor was our lot. All we had was school, the church, and music. And our black public school didn't really meet our needs because it ended in the ninth grade; the whites' schools went on through the twelfth. So it was the church and music."[2] Motley's aunt, Lucile McIver, confirmed his sentiments: "When Dizzy and John came along, every parent had a teacher give their child music lessons. You were in a hopeless condition and that lifted your spirits—the songs and the music and whatnot. It was part of your spiritual life. Everybody could play a piano and everybody had a piano. Every house. You would go out to parties, and you would sit around and entertain yourselves."[3]

James Gillespie purchased an upright piano so large that he had half the side of his home torn out to bring the instrument in, and Dizzy loved to sit on the floor and look up at his dad pounding out piano choruses as he ran his band through rehearsals. The house was full of instruments—a drum set, a mandolin, a guitar, a clarinet, and a bass fiddle—because James was fearful that his musicians might pawn them between gigs. James spent every spare penny on his instruments, and though he led his band from the piano, he taught himself to play all the others.

Dizzy enjoyed fondling the dark burnished string bass and the shiny guitar, and at age three he was already exploring melodies on the piano and playing precise rhythmic patterns on the drums. James was pleased because Dizzy was the only one of his seven children who exhibited any musical talent.

Dizzy's parents were serious Christians, and almost from birth he imbibed music in large quantities at two nearby black churches. The Gillespies worshipped at United Methodist, a large red brick structure that Dizzy could reach by running through a backyard, and he was an almost obsessive visitor at the small, wooden Sanctified Church eight doors from his home on Huger Street.

In the century between the Civil War and the civil rights revolution, whites monopolized almost all power in the South, ceding control in just one area: the black church. The historian Albert Raboteau emphasized the importance of this institution:

> As the one institution which freed blacks were allowed to control, the church was the center of social, economic, educational, and political activity. It was also a source of continuity and identity for the black community. In their churches, black worshipers continued for decades to pray, sing, preach, and shout as they or their parents had during slavery. . . .
>
> The spread of Baptist and Methodist Evangelicalism between 1770 and 1820 changed the religious complexion of the South by bringing unprecedented numbers of slaves into membership in the church and by introducing even larger numbers to at least the rudiments of Christianity.[4]

By the time of Emancipation, the black South was at least as Christian as the white South. And this black Christianity was powerfully and insidiously subversive, burning into the black man's consciousness a conviction of his worth before God and man. He was taught as a fundamental truth that Christ, who preached the sacred humanity of each person, was a Master who reigned above his earthly master, the white man.

James Gillespie and his family took this message of self-worth seriously. Two of his brothers were forced to leave Cheraw as antiwhite troublemakers, and at the open-coffin wake for one of them in Georgia, angry whites spat tobacco juice on his face. Young Dizzy thoroughly absorbed the lessons of his family; he never felt inferior to anyone and often fought fiercely against racist bullies.

The new black Christianity had a number of distinctive features, and Dizzy was exposed to them several times a week as he attended United Methodist with his family and the Sanctified Church on his own.

Most important, worship was centered on improvised communal dance and song. While whites sat quietly during sermons and sang their hymns as they were written, blacks participated in a spirited call-and-response with their preachers and improvised wildly in song.

Spirituals went on as long as the communicants felt the spirit, and they were never sung the same way twice; typically, a worshipper would improvise a line in the middle of a chorus, others in the congregation would pick it up, and the song would continue in a new direction. Frequently the rhythm of the spiritual inspired foot-stomping and hand-clapping counterrhythms as an ecstatic response was built with people shouting, dancing, and testifying.

United Methodist offered rousing services, but they were pale copies of what Dizzy took part in at the Sanctified Church. African religion emphasized the experience of the divine within the worshipper, the presence of the spirit in all things, and this doctrine pervaded all of black Christianity. But it was far more important among the Sanctified than among the Methodists.

Sanctified (also known as Holiness or Pentecostal) churches were created in the early twentieth century by blacks who wanted to be possessed by pure spirit, who wished to be "saved, sanctified, and filled with the Holy Ghost."[5]

For Sanctified congregants, music was an essential element in welcoming the Holy Spirit. While United Methodist employed a lone pianist, the Sanctified Church was rocked by a raucous band that included a piano, drums, trumpets, saxophones, tambourines, and guitars.

Dizzy was transported emotionally by the fervent spirituality and the rhythmic power of the Sanctified services. He recalled that the preacher's four sons formed a rhythm section, playing the snare drum, the cymbal, the bass drum, and the tambourine.

They used to keep at least four different rhythms going, and as the congregation joined in, the number of rhythms would increase

with foot stomping, hand clapping, and people catching the spirit and jumping up and down on the wooden floor, which also resounded like a drum. . . . Even white people would come and sit outside in their cars just to listen. . . . Everybody would be shouting and fainting and stomping. . . . The Sanctified church's rhythm got to me as it did to anyone else who came near the place. People like James Brown and Aretha Franklin owe everything to the Sanctified beat. I received my first experience with rhythm and spiritual transport going down there to the well every Sunday, and I've just followed it ever since.[6]

The young boy was so fascinated by Sanctified rhythms that he created his own percussion instrument to perform alongside the preacher's sons during the services. He attached a wire brush to the handle end of a mallet, and with his right hand held the shaft in the middle so that with wrist movements he could hit the bass drum alternately with the mallet and the brush. He also strapped a cymbal to his left hand and created polyrhythms by bringing it down on another cymbal mounted to the top of the bass drum while he alternated right hand strokes on the drum with the brush and the mallet. His fellow congregants marveled as he carried off sophisticated syncopations and complex cadences such as five beats against two and four against seven. He had found within himself an extraordinary rhythmic talent that would blossom spectacularly when he became an adult.[7]

While Dizzy was being transported by the spirited music at the Sanctified Church in 1928, trumpeter Bubber Miley called as he improvised and the Duke Ellington band responded with multirhythmic riffs. That same year Louis Armstrong and Earl Hines improvised a sinuously rhythmic musical conversation on "Weatherbird," and Bessie Smith sang the first ten beats of a sixteen-beat blues line and trombonist Charlie Green improvised a response in the last six. What Bubber, Duke, Louis, Earl, Bessie, and Charlie were doing had deep roots in the soil of black Christianity. With minimal access to a phonograph or a radio, young Dizzy knew virtually nothing about these pioneering artists, but he was drinking from the same well they frequented.

The compelling spirits of black music had entered his blood-stream at birth. When musical opportunity beckoned less than a year after his failure as a cotton picker, he was ready to grab it.

But before we explore how this happened, let us trace the stories of black and white Gillespies and Powes (Dizzy's mother's family) in a drama of blood and race. This drama created a happy confluence of genes that produced a boy of tremendous talent in a most unlikely place, a small South Carolina town.

2
BLACK AND WHITE IN SOUTH CAROLINA

JAMES GALESPY (HE LATER CHANGED THE SPELLING TO Gillespie) and his family became in 1730 the first whites to settle in Cheraw, a clearing in the wilderness on the banks of the Pee Dee River.

An enterprising emigrant from Northern Ireland, he was attracted to the site because the river represented an outlet to the Atlantic for a large and potentially fertile inland area. To the north of Cheraw, the Pee Dee was too narrow and shallow for commercial shipping, but to the south it became a deep and navigable highway to the ocean.

In rapid succession, Gillespie established a boating business, a trading post, and a cotton plantation. The indigenous people, members of the Cheraw and Pee Dee tribes, grew corn and other crops nearby. They had for several decades enjoyed peaceful relations with whites on the Atlantic coast to the south and presented little threat to Gillespie. He traded with them, frequently buying their pelts, and with the whites who soon moved into the area.

The British government strongly desired to colonize the region and in 1736, six years after Gillespie's arrival, granted substantial bounties plus 173,840 acres to a community of Welsh Baptists who lived in Pennsylvania. After the Welsh moved their entire settlement to this large tract, Gillespie applied to them for 300 acres directly across the river from Cheraw in a town now called Wallace; his request was quickly granted.

The Welsh were soon joined by English, Scotch, and Irish settlers; they brought with them smallpox and other white man's diseases that almost wiped out the native peoples.

By the 1750s, Gillespie's ships were moving cargoes to and from Charleston on the Atlantic, and his businesses thrived as the surrounding land yielded profitable crops of hemp, flax, wool, cotton, and, above all, indigo. In 1742, one of the settlers traded three wagonloads of indigo for twenty slaves.

The Revolutionary War was fought with particular brutality in the Cheraw area, and Gillespie's son, James Jr., distinguished himself as a soldier. The shipping business gave the Gillespies a great commercial start, but their cotton plantations made them wealthy in the decades following the Revolution.

Cotton became king in the south in 1800 and held sway over the black population for more than 150 years. Two inventions bracketed his reign: the cotton gin, introduced in 1795, and the harvester, which changed everything in the early 1950s; the latter could do the work of fifty field hands and drove six million blacks off the land in what is now called "the Great Migration."

Cotton thrived in the heat and the rich moist soil of the South, but before the gin (the word is shortened from engine), most of the crop was useless because removing the multitude of small seeds ripped the fibers. The gin scraped the seeds out with minimal damage to the fibers, and in the five years between its arrival and 1800, the American harvest increased by more than 400 percent.

Cotton with lightning speed became the South's principal revenue producer, replacing the previous mainstay, rice. The hugely profitable and labor-intensive cotton bonanza changed the course of American history by creating a tremendous demand for new slaves; hundreds of thousands of acres were freshly planted in the old seaboard colonies such as South Carolina and Georgia, and vast tracts were opened westward from Alabama to Texas. The South's desire to feed the boom by maximizing the number of new slave states dominated American politics from 1800 to 1861. With cotton driving the economy, the southern slave population grew from 658,000 in 1790 to almost 4,000,000 in 1860.[1]

When the first steamboat arrived in Cheraw in 1819, it brought the town a period of unprecedented prosperity that lasted until the start of the Civil War in 1861. The steamers, pulling eight to ten barges, could haul up to eight hundred bales of cotton per trip and sparked a bonanza; brokers and bankers flocked to Cheraw to service the burgeoning trade, and during the selling season, downtown streets were chockablock with bales awaiting sale.

By 1830, Samuel Gillespie, a grandson of James the original settler, had become rich enough from his cotton plantations to build an opulent mansion in Wallace, which he called Rose Hill. Today it faces U.S. Highway 1, and a cemetery for white Gillespies, overgrown with weeds, sits across the way.

The earliest records we have regarding the black Gillespies concern Dizzy's grandfather, Wesley, who was born a slave around 1850 on the prosperous Gillespie plantation. He married Lucy McIntosh, also born a slave, and they had two daughters and five sons. Dizzy's father, James Penfield Gillespie, born in 1882, was the youngest. Grandfather Wesley lived into the 1920s, but Dizzy had no recollection of him.

The end of Reconstruction in 1876 brought forth in South Carolina a virulent racism whose effects rivaled the oppression of slavery. The most powerful southern leader and a figure of great national political importance was "Pitchfork Ben" Tillman, one of South Carolina's senators, whose ideology dominated the South Carolina polity from 1876, when he began his career, until the civil rights revolution of the 1960s, decades after his death in 1918. It was based on two tenets:

1. *The white race, guardian of civilization, was superior to all other races.*

2. Any level of violence, including murder, was justified in maintaining the status of the white race at the top of the heap.

"The negro," Tillman said, "must remain subordinate or be exterminated."[2]

He launched his career in 1876 as Reconstruction ended and the federal power structure, which had held southern racism in check, was dismantled. He led his Red Shirts, an organization similar to the Ku Klux Klan, as they participated in the Hamburg Massacre, the cold-blooded murder of a dozen blacks (five of them captives) in a South Carolina hamlet. No one was prosecuted for the crimes, as Tillman and his allies overthrew the elected Republican government of South Carolina the following year.

Tillman always gloried in the killings; he stated years later in 1909, "I have nothing to conceal about the Hamburgh [*sic*] riot. [We] had to shoot negroes to get relief from the galling tyranny to which we had been subjected."[3] He became governor in 1890, and two years later, while holding the office, pledged that he would lead the lynch mobs in cases where black men were *accused* of raping white women.[4] He entered the U.S. Senate in 1894, and in 1895 ran a state convention that disenfranchised black voters.

Tillman was contemptuous of all black leaders, even the more conciliatory ones like Booker T. Washington. When Washington dined with Teddy Roosevelt at the White House in 1901, Tillman commented, "The action of President Roosevelt in entertaining that nigger will necessitate our killing a thousand niggers in the south before they will learn their place again."[5]

Tillman defined the victorious ideology of race in South Carolina from 1876 until 1960, and legions of white South Carolinians lived his doctrines in their daily lives. In death, he was held in such high esteem that an imposing statue of him was erected at the South Carolina statehouse in 1940 and a U.S. Navy destroyer was named for him in 1941.

The industrious Powe family, which arrived in Cheraw in the early 1760s, created great wealth from the cotton bonanza and by the early nineteenth century owned the largest plantations and the most slaves in the area. Suffering setbacks during Reconstruction, they prospered again during the long era of Tillman's hegemony.

The Powes have left a strong architectural imprint on Cheraw; three commodious homes they built between 1790 and 1822 still adorn the town. Since the early 1930s, members of the family have lived in another dwelling, a handsome Italianate residence situated on Kershaw Street near the center of Cheraw.

Dizzy was familiar with the house as a child, because he visited it with his mother, Lottie, when she was working there as a domestic for James Powe, a plantation owner and cotton broker and one of the town's leading citizens. When visiting Cheraw during the 1940s and early 1950s, Dizzy liked to stop by and chat with James. In those days, blacks were enjoined to enter a white home by the rear entrance, and he complied.

Lottie's maiden name was Powe, and Dizzy learned about her ancestry when he visited James in the Kershaw Street house in March 1959. Cheraw was honoring its most illustrious son with a "Dizzy Gillespie Day" marked by the town's first ever integrated concert, and he decided he would drop in on Mr. Powe.

For the first time Dizzy was determined to enter by the front door. Powe was a symbol of the old order that the Gillespies had fled to find a better life up north, and Dizzy wanted to assert his status as a hero of Cheraw and to gauge Powe's reaction to it.

After blustering his way past Mrs. Powe and through the front door, Dizzy was welcomed by Mr. Powe, who was seventy-five at the time and ill. Powe told Dizzy that all of Cheraw was proud of him because of his good character and achievements and added that Dizzy's great-grandmother would have been proud of him too. Then Powe asked him if he knew the real story of his great-grandmother; Dizzy answered no, and Powe proceeded to tell him. Dizzy remembered the conversation in 1976:

> He told me that my great grandmother was the daughter of a chief. Immediately, I told him, "Well, say, call me, Your Majesty, then!" He laughed this off.
>
> These people, the Powes, they heard about her and they needed somebody to run the house, not as a field hand like most of the slaves were in those days, so they went down [to Charleston] and they bid on her and brought her back to Cheraw. He said, "Well, we named her Nora."[6]

Neither Dizzy nor anyone else in his family had heard this story previously, and subsequent research by him revealed that Nora was Yoruba, a people who had created a highly urbanized civilization in what is now Benin, Togo, and southwestern Nigeria. The majority of today's inhabitants of Lagos, Nigeria's capital, are Yoruba.

The purchaser of Nora was Dr. Thomas Powe, James's grandfather, a man who played many roles—the town's leading physician, the owner of a grand plantation with 134 slaves, a state senator, a magistrate. Nora had two sons by white men: Hampson "Yank" Powe, Dizzy's grandfather, and William. Dizzy's family had long been told that Hampson's father was a Yankee from up north, but as James talked about Nora, Dizzy began to have serious doubts about this genealogy.

> Sitting there in Mr. Powe's living room, putting two and two together, something dawned on me. If Grand No' was strictly a house slave, owned by Mr. Powe's [grandfather], who wouldn't allow for any contact between her and the black males on the plantation, then who was most likely to be the father of her children? The implications were enough to knock me off my feet, and I reared back in my seat on the sofa laughing.[7]

Dizzy left James Powe's house strongly convinced that Lottie, his mother, and James were first cousins who shared a grandfather, Dr. Thomas Powe. Subsequent research by Dizzy's cousins serves to confirm this.

Nora, who was probably born around 1840 in the United States, was purchased by Dr. Thomas Powe during the late 1850s, and gave birth to his son Hampson during the last years of slavery in the early 1860s. Hampson's daughter (Dizzy's mother), Lottie Powe Gillespie, was born in 1885.

In 1962, James's sister, Charlotte Powe Kittrell, presented vivid glimpses of Nora when she wrote a letter to the Cheraw newspaper about the "colored people" of her youth:

> This William and Hamp's mother was our own dear Nora, or "Nonie," as we always called her, one of our grandfather's slaves.

In her youth she was untamed, but once during a revival meeting she became converted. "Got religion," as it was then called.
Next morning she came to our home, and as she'd see each one of
us she'd grab us, hug us tightly, and jump up and down. She really
was a changed person the remainder of her life and we loved her
truly. . . .

As long as she was able to walk, she came in winter to "polish
our hearths" and to polish the brass andirons on Saturdays and in
summer to sweep the yards. She was truly a rare character.[8]

Dizzy was bitter about the exploitation of slave women by
white men, but he realized that he was dealing with a common-
place event in the antebellum South, and he believed that Nora
had made the best of a perverse situation. He was especially
proud of his connection to Yoruba royalty, and he was delighted to
discover that most of the basic rhythms of his beloved Afro-
Cuban music came from Yoruba rituals.

Nora was snobbish about the light skin of her offspring, and
when Lottie was being courted by the dark-hued James Gillespie,
Nora objected. Dizzy remembered:

She didn't have *nothing to do with no nigguhs!* . . . My mother
said my great grandmother took one look at my father, nappyhead
and real dark, and she said, "If that black nappyhead nigguh cross
that door sill one more time, I'm gonna put *both* your asses out of
here!" Of course, nothing happened cause my mother went on and
married my father.[9]

EARLY DAYS 3

JAMES PENFIELD GILLESPIE, DARK AND NAPPY-HEADED, and Lottie Powe, of a much lighter hue, were married in 1899 when he was seventeen and she was fourteen. They had nine children, seven of whom survived infancy, and Dizzy, born on October 21, 1917, was the youngest. He and his siblings Sonny, Mattie, James Penfield Jr. (known as J.P.), Hattie Marie, Eugenia (known as Genia), and Wesley all inherited James's rawboned facial structure and wide mouth, and the color of their skin was considerably lighter than his.

Dizzy knew Sonny, born in 1900, only slightly. He left home in 1923 when Dizzy was six, and they never saw each other again; Sonny died up north in 1935. Mattie, J.P., and Hattie Marie, teenagers as Dizzy was growing up, were almost of another generation, but the three youngest siblings formed a close group. Genia was the resident babysitter for her younger brothers, and Dizzy, a bright child, caught up to Wesley—two years his senior—in the second grade and spent eight years in the same class with him.

James found his calling as a young man when he became a bricklayer and joined one of Cheraw's modest industries. The exploitation of nearby deposits of kaolin, a clay used extensively for bricks, had helped fuel Cheraw's economic recovery at the start of the twentieth century. The town vigorously boosted this home industry as brick storefronts replaced wooden ones, substantial brick homes and commercial buildings were erected, and even sidewalks were laid with brick.

James helped build his own church, the imposing all-brick United Methodist, and other local structures, and when times were slack in Cheraw, he worked with construction crews in northern cities. His trade had kept him out of the cotton fields, but he needed the income from his second job as a bandleader to provide adequately for his large family.

Cheraw was laid out in 1768 in a grid running west from the Pee Dee River and roughly a mile and a half square, and the handsome streets are one hundred feet wide. The Gillespies' modest home on Huger Street was near the middle of the grid, a half mile or less from every building of importance in Dizzy's young life. Water was drawn from a communal well about one hundred yards away, and the toilet facilities were outside.

Dizzy's maternal grandfather, Hampson, an affectionate and amusing man who worked in a restaurant, lived in a small house at the end of the Gillespies' backyard. He introduced his grandson to show business when, after a few nips, he would perform comic routines out on Huger Street and get all the neighbors laughing.

These performances made a deep impression on the boy. When Dizzy saw how deeply comedy and music moved people, it stirred in him the desire to be a *performer*, to mount a stage and transform the emotions of an audience. He copied some of his grandfather's routines and invented some of his own as he strove from an early age to amuse people with his antics.

His urge to perform was strongly reinforced by having witnessed many times the high opera of the preacher at the Sanctified Church. Albert Raboteau describes the dynamic of what he calls the "black folk sermon":

> It is not, then, merely the word as spoken—much less as read— but the word as *performed* that must be taken into account if the sermon is to be adequately understood. . . .
>
> The preacher begins calmly, speaking in conversational prose; he then gradually begins to speak more rapidly, excitedly, and to chant his words in time to a regular beat; finally, he reaches an emotional peak in which his chanted speech becomes tonal and merges with the singing, clapping, and shouting of the congregation. . . . Ideally, the preacher's delivery will ignite the congregation's vocal response, which will, in turn, support and push him further.[1]

Dizzy's lifetime desire to ignite an audience was born early on Huger Street in the ecstatic services at the Sanctified Church and in his grandfather's comedy.

The appropriate twenty-first century adjective to describe Dizzy as a young child is hyperactive. When he wasn't darting around the neighborhood climbing trees, telling jokes, exploring abandoned houses, or scrapping with Wesley, he was burning energy on his father's piano and drum set.

The first adult to channel this energy was a neighbor, a retired schoolteacher named Amanda Harrington, whose husband owned a shoe shop and an ice cream parlor. Her house held two attractions for the child at the age of four: a piano and an icebox filled with ice cream. Dizzy, who throughout his life had a huge appetite, scarfed down large quantities of Harrington ice cream, and for half an hour at a time pounded out on the piano "Coon Shine Lady," the only tune he knew,

Mrs. Harrington, tired of hearing "Coon Shine Lady" and recognizing the intelligence of her charge, devised a private preschool program for Dizzy and had him counting to one hundred and reading simple texts by the time he was ready for kindergarten the next year.

James brought discipline, structure, music, and, unfortunately, a touch of sadism to the raising of his sons. He never hit his daughters, but he whipped his boys with a belt every Sunday on the premise that they had done something bad during the week even if he did not know the details.

After repeated beatings, J.P. ran away in 1922 when he was sixteen, because he was afraid his anger would drive him to violence against his father. Dizzy was reunited with J.P. in New York in 1937.

Lottie was a loving and attentive mother. And the combination of her warmth and James's sense of structure and discipline produced seven children who led productive lives.

His parents gave Dizzy an unalterable sense of self-worth that led to a happy and stable marriage of fifty-three years, a tremendous drive to define and achieve his goals, and a number of deep long-term friendships. Dizzy's musical talents were a one-in-a-million gift of nature, but the uses to which he put them were a reflection of the nurturing he received from his parents.

Dizzy later commented on the fractious streak engendered by his father's thrashings: "He treated us that way because he wanted us all to be tough and he turned me into a tough little rebel, very early, against everyone but him."[2]

The upside of this contrary spirit was Dizzy's rebellion against the musical materials he inherited to create two revolutions that fundamentally changed the course of jazz. The downside was an anger that could boil over aggressively when he was crossed and that he did not bring under control until well into adulthood.

Because Mrs. Harrington had prepared Dizzy well with his reading and his numbers, he was bored on the first day of kindergarten and began whistling during class. His teacher responded by whipping him around the legs, and Dizzy bolted and ran home.

Dizzy's father beat his boys when he believed they had done something wrong, but he came strongly to their defense when he was convinced they were in the right. After he heard about the incident at the kindergarten, James stormed over to the principal's house and harangued him about punishing his small son on the first day of school before he knew the rules. Dizzy had followed him at a discreet distance and, listening to his tirade from a hiding place, felt proud and reassured that his father had supported him so strongly.

Always in a hurry, Dizzy usually arrived at school late and out of breath, with the bottoms of his knickers, the schoolboy's trousers of his era, hanging down around his calves. During the first two grades his energy was expended mostly in mischief and scrapping with other kids, but all this changed in 1925 when he found an important mentor, his third grade teacher, Miss Alice Wilson. John Motley remembered her: "She was the mother of the town for the black kids. She gave us lots of affection in a gentle way and a sense of purpose. We used to congregate at her house and talk and listen to her play the piano and sing."[3]

Miss Wilson soon found that Dizzy's piano at home took precedence over school, and she encouraged his musicality while making sure that he scraped by academically. She recalled, "He first came to my classroom in third grade . . . fidgety, and a little frisky fellow. Anything that he liked he would stick to. . . . He wouldn't study, he didn't care about anything but music. He was always more interested in music than he was in academic work. But he got it. He got enough to pass."[4]

James was making a decent living in 1926, and that summer he felt affluent enough to send Lottie, Wesley, and Dizzy on a northern vacation trip. They spent most of the time in Philadelphia with James's sister Rose and her family and ended the summer with a short tourist's excursion to New York.

Dizzy, age eight, was in a high state of excitement throughout. He was impressed by the affluence of his relatives, and he particularly remembered a charity picnic where smiling whites served him food, white and black children played freely together, and for the first time in his life he could eat enough of everything he wanted, particularly ice cream. He resolved then that he would come north again, perhaps to stay.

Death came swiftly to James one June morning in 1927. After he suffered a severe asthma attack in front of the house, Dizzy helped Wesley and Lottie carry him to his bedroom. Dizzy went back outside, and when he heard his mother crying a few minutes afterward, he knew his father had died.

Dizzy raged at James's death. After destroying the belt his father had used to whip him and Wesley, he embarked on an orgy of fistfights. The only kid he never bested was Wesley.

When James died, the family was thrown from relative comfort into deep poverty, as Lottie and the four children still living at home scrambled to keep food on the table. Lottie, who had never before held a job, became a seamstress, took in washing, and worked as a domestic for white families and earned about two dollars per week. All the children picked cotton, but Dizzy augmented his meager income from the fields with more imaginative forms of employment.

Cheraw had separate black and white swimming pools, and Dizzy became an attraction at the white one where he performed one and a half gainers and other fancy dives from a height of forty feet. His compensation came from the coins spectators threw into the water.

He also danced for coins. Nurtured by the rousing and intricate cadences he had absorbed at the Sanctified Church, Dizzy's rhythmic sense was to become as acute as that of any musician in jazz history, and his talents as a dancer blossomed early. He was a fixture at local white parties and dances, wowing his audiences with a specialty he called "snake hips."

Dizzy worked another job for payments in kind instead of cash. He had became a film buff early on, and he hung around the local movie house, the Lyric, so often that the owner let him in for nothing in exchange for keeping other people from sneaking in. Dizzy's film favorites were the heroes of Westerns—stars such as Tom Mix, Ken Maynard, and Yakima Canutt—and he also thrilled to the weekly serials with their cliffhanger endings.

His work at the Lyric reinforced the knowledge that he could never escape the imperatives and humiliations of southern racism in the age of segregation. One day he ejected a white teenager who had sneaked in, and soon after the boy and six other whites met up with him and two of his cousins, cursing them as niggers and threatening mayhem. He and the boy fought while the others circled round, and Dizzy knocked him down. As the boy's friends edged forward to enter the fray, Dizzy and his cousins threatened them with rocks, and they ran away.

There were other reminders of racism. By ironbound custom, white and black children could only play together until they were ten or eleven, and soon after James' death, Lottie was forced to tell her son that he could no longer play with a white pal, John Duvall. Dizzy later remembered, "We was tight, very, very, very tight, inseparable. . . . I was shocked. We were both shocked. And mad."[5]

The economic health of the Gillespie family worsened considerably a year after James died; the nest egg for which he had laboriously saved disappeared in 1928 when the president of the local bank absconded with its assets and bankrupted the institution. The family was so impoverished that they hid in the woods at Easter time, because they felt ashamed that they had no new clothes to wear.

As 1929 dawned, Dizzy was an angry, unfocused, and despairing eleven-year-old. All that would change a few months later, when Alice Wilson recruited him for the Robert Smalls band.

BECOMING A MUSICIAN 4

MISS ALICE WILSON, ACCOMPANIED BY THE PRINCIPAL OF the Robert Smalls school, walked into Dizzy's fifth-grade class-room one day in the spring of 1929 and asked, "Who would like to join a band?"

Only Dizzy's hand shot up, and he was told to gather with other interested students in a nearby room where an array of mu-sical instruments was laid out. The principal had bought the in-struments with special funding from South Carolina's education department.

Dizzy soon realized that he was five years younger than any of the other volunteers, and when it was his turn to take an instru-ment, he found that the older children had left him with only one, a slide trombone. The school officials did not want him to have it, because he was so small that his arm could not extend the slide to the farthest positions, the sixth and seventh. But he clutched it closely to him and yelled, "I can play it. I can learn it. Give me a chance. Give me a chance." Faced with such fierce passion, the officials gave in.

Dizzy could not wait to start making good on the promise he had made to his mother the previous summer, that he would become a musician and make her proud, and he was ecstatic as he rushed home with the gleaming horn.

He practiced incessantly and enjoyed playing so much that it imposed a discipline on his life that had been missing since his father's death nearly two years before, and Miss Wilson soon recruited him for the five-piece school band that she was leading from her piano chair. She could not read music and only played in the key of B-flat, so the students were forced to train themselves by ear to find the correct notes in her arrangements.

Dizzy was at home practicing the trombone one afternoon soon after Christmas in 1929 when he heard the pure tones of a trumpet coming from the neighboring Harrington home. He rushed over and found that the Harringtons had given their son, Brother, a trumpet for Christmas.

When Brother showed Dizzy how to play a B-flat scale, he fell in love with the instrument and spent the rest of the afternoon and the evening taking turns practicing with Brother. Almost every day that winter, Dizzy would work out on the trombone for an hour and then join Brother for several hours on the trumpet at the Harringtons' or at his own home. When their mothers grew tired of the blasting, they would banish the boys to a field out of earshot. Brother gave Dizzy the benefit of lessons he was taking, and by the spring of 1930, Dizzy was proficient on trumpet and, handicapped by his size, passable on trombone.

Miss Wilson was pleased with his progress and found a battered cornet (a smaller cousin of the trumpet with a warmer tone) for him to play; she recruited another boy, Bill McNeil, to replace him on trombone. Dizzy carried his cornet everywhere and practiced constantly—as he walked to school with Wesley trailing and carrying their books, during recess, at all hours at home and at the Harringtons'.

In his spare time, he became a rhythm consultant to the band at the white high school, introducing them to the use of counter-rhythms and to a smooth four-beats-to-the-bar pulse for dancing. This was a true testament to his rhythmic acuity, because it was highly unusual for Cheraw whites of that era to seek help from blacks for anything.

Miss Wilson had, for several years at the end of each spring semester, produced a minstrel show for which she accompanied the performers on piano. Because her student quintet had become quite proficient, she changed that practice in May 1930 and enlisted them to play an overture and accompaniments that she had created.

Eager to perform for an audience, to strut his stuff, Dizzy practiced even more intensely than usual. One day during a rehearsal, he was so immersed in running scales that he drowned out Miss Wilson's instructions about a scene, and she angrily knocked his horn from his mouth. Despite this contretemps, she remembered her young performer with affection:

> He was a mess, but he was a loving child. All the children loved him, and so did the teachers that had anything to do with him. In a sense he was comical. Course we didn't call it that way then; we'd say he was "crazy"! . . . He was always full of fun.
>
> Yet he had his own individual style with everything. . . . He'd try to hold [his horn] with one hand. Anything to show off. He's a show-off. That's the best way I can say it. Yeah, he was a real show-off, but he was a good one.[1]

Dizzy, aged twelve, performed in public for the first time in Miss Wilson's band at the minstrel show. They played everything with gusto in B-flat and captivated the audience.

He left the performance feeling euphoric about his musicianship, but he soon experienced a comeuppance that brought him back to earth. When Sonny Matthews, a Cheraw native who had become a professional pianist up north, came home to visit his mother, he heard about the hot young horn player in town and asked Dizzy over to his house to play some tunes together. Sonny started performing "Nagasaki" in the key of C, and Dizzy quickly lost his way and broke down crying. He had discovered the hard way that there were other keys besides B-flat.

The sting and humiliation of this incident immediately drove Dizzy to increase his musical knowledge; he practiced intensively in different keys, took lessons in reading music from Norman Powe, a cousin who played the trombone, and began at twelve a lifelong exploration of harmony on the family piano.

The success of the Robert Smalls band at the minstrel show brought the group local notoriety and with it the opportunity to go commercial. Miss Wilson dropped out reluctantly, because she realized the band had to play in more than one key; she was replaced by Bernis Tillman, a Robert Smalls student and a seasoned pianist. She also found a trumpet for Dizzy, and he left the cornet behind.

Miss Wilson helped the band members add a bassist, a clarinetist/saxophonist, and a singer for their first paying gig, a dance at the white high school. It was a major success and soon the group was performing at parties and dances not only in Cheraw but in several neighboring towns in North and South Carolina.

As the months flew by, the band prospered and improved and Dizzy became its undoubted star. Their prospects for an unblemished future were destroyed in 1931 when their trombonist, Bill McNeil, was lynched for allegedly being a Peeping Tom; his murderers dumped his body outside of Cheraw by the railroad tracks.

The doctrines of Ben Tillman were thus in full force in South Carolina more than a decade after his death. Because Tillman, more than anyone, created the mind-set of white South Carolinians during the first half of the twentieth century. It was Tillman who said: "The poor African becomes a fiend, a wild beast, seeking whom he may devour, filling our penitentiaries and our jails, lurking around to see if some helpless white woman can be murdered or brutalized. We realize what it means to allow ever so little a trickle of race equality to break through the dam."[2] And it was the ordinary white citizen who took his words to heart and acted on them.

It is highly doubtful that McNeil's lynching made the official list that Tuskegee Institute compiled between 1882 and 1962, because the institute required a very high degree of documentation (for example, police and eyewitness reports). Tuskegee recorded thirteen lynchings in 1931. As he would recount years later, Dizzy was deeply shaken:

Bill's murder tore me apart inside, made me literally sick. He was a fun-loving guy, full of life. A good musician with a fiery style. He went down helpless at the hands of those rednecks.

We were so sad and burning with anger, but we had to resign ourselves, because we knew that all of us blacks in Cheraw were fair game for this kind of brutal stuff. We wanted to get far away from Cheraw, and we talked about becoming better musicians so some big-time national band would hire us.

My cousin Norman Powe took Bill's place, but the band never was the same. Some spiritual thing was missing.

I learned a lesson from Bill's murder; I began to carry a knife for protection.[3]

The band soldiered on through 1932, and Dizzy earned his certification as a local star one night early in 1933, when he was fifteen. A good black professional touring outfit was playing a dance at the Elks Hall, and he went there with his horn hoping they would ask him to join in. He sought the opportunity because, like every jazz musician of worth, he wished to prove himself in the heat of battle. The band wanted to accommodate him, but there was a hitch: he was too short to read the scores on the music stand. After they found a box for him to stand on, he excelled, sight-reading smoothly and improvising with imagination. He was overjoyed at this confirmation of his talent.

Except for the relatively scant instruction he received from Brother Harrington and Norman Powe, Dizzy was entirely self-taught. One consequence of this was that he allowed his cheeks to puff out when he played—a taboo for every established trumpet teacher in the world. But Dizzy became so comfortable with the practice while performing with the Cheraw band that he decided early on that he would not change over to the conventional style. In later life, his cheeks became a visual symbol, a trademark, but he discounted their importance in his playing. As he told me in 1990, "You start by tightening your ass, your butt muscles, and build your foundation from there. Then the stomach muscles. If you don't start from the bottom, your diaphragm will never contract and push that air up and out. You finally control the stream of air with your lips. The cheeks have a minor role; they're just a way station."[4]

Dizzy faced a dreary prospect as May 1933 approached. He would graduate that month from the ninth grade at Robert Smalls, and the ninth grade was where public school ended for Cheraw's black kids. The black Presbyterian church ran a private school for black children that continued through the twelfth grade, but the tuition was well beyond the means of the Gillespies.

Dizzy hoped to make it as a professional musician sometime in an uncertain future, but his prospects for the next several years were bleak as he could only foresee a regimen of manual labor in the cotton fields and on road gangs to augment his sporadic earnings from his band. His fortunes changed with great suddenness when a young Cheraw woman named Catherine McKay found for him a rich new opportunity.

Black educational institutions had found that music could be a powerful fund-raising tool during the 1870s, a time when the Jubilee Singers of Fisk University began earning large amounts of money for the college on the international concert circuit. The Laurinburg Institute, a coed black boarding school just twenty-eight miles from Cheraw in North Carolina, was one of the institutions that followed Fisk's lead; it developed two first-class commercial bands that built solid fan bases in the Carolinas. The school faced a mini-crisis in June 1933, because its best trumpet player and trombonist had graduated and were on their way to college.

McKay, who was a student nurse at Laurinburg and a band enthusiast, stepped in and lobbied the school all summer on behalf of Dizzy and Norman Powe—both penniless—as replacements for the departed musicians. She argued persuasively because, just before the new semester started in September, the institute gave the two boys full scholarships.

Dizzy had been transformed during his years under the tutelage of Miss Wilson. He was no longer an angry, drifting child; absorption in music had helped him heal the hurt and loss occasioned by his father's death and had given him a career goal. He could now allow himself to hope that performing and studying at Laurinburg might put the cotton fields behind him and open a clear path to that goal.

LAURINBURG 5

Newlyweds Emmanuel and Tinny McDuffie, their clothes stained with sweat and red dirt, trekked with purpose across the Deep South in September 1904. They rode behind mules on creaky wagons, hoboed in railway cars, and walked carrying their small suitcase six hundred miles from Tuskegee across half of Alabama and all of Georgia and South Carolina until they arrived in Laurinburg just over the North Carolina border five days after they had set out.

They were stopped more than once by Ku Klux Klan toughs who wanted to know what they were doing in "furrin" parts, and they always answered politely and went quietly on their way. The Klan had been encouraged by publications such as North Carolina's widely read *Progressive Farmer*, which earlier that year called for a "rural police force" to protect white women "against the reckless, roving element of blacks." And Ben Tillman had begun agitating for a federal passport system, enforced by white men on horseback, to control travel by blacks.[1]

Emmanuel and Tinny found it safer to move at night and relied on the kindness of black sharecroppers who put them up in ramshackle cabins and barns and fed them biscuits and gravy, fatback pork, and greens.

Emmanuel, age seventeen, and Tinny, age eighteen, were missionaries of education, filled with zeal and faith. They were the children of former slaves and disciples of Booker T. Washington, founder of the Tuskegee Institute, the most prestigious black university in the United States, an adviser to President Theodore Roosevelt, and in 1904 the most influential black man in America.

The McDuffies had recently graduated from Snow Hill, a high school affiliated with Tuskegee, and they were filled with the desire to work for their less fortunate black brethren. They had hoped Washington would send them from their native Alabama to less racist precincts such as Chicago or Toronto, but when their charismatic leader told them they were needed in rural North Carolina, they could not refuse him.

A black Laurinburg landowner, Walter Evans, and a group of sharecroppers had written to Washington asking for help in educating their children, explaining that their all-black public schools were subpar and provided no classes after the second grade. They assured him that they had saved enough money to start a modest institution.

The McDuffies arrived to a joyous welcome in Laurinburg on September 15, 1904, with seventy-five cents in their pockets. They wasted no time getting to work, because they wanted to have a school up and running before November first. The cotton-picking season had just ended, so they knew they had an adequate pool of workers for the tasks at hand.

Conferring with Evans, they settled on a practical initial strategy—obtain approval from the white power structure and then proceed. So, a few days after his arrival, Emmanuel, wearing his only suit and tie, visited Billy McLaurin, a former Confederate colonel whose family had given Laurinburg its name, and asked for his protection for the planned private school and for the opportunity to buy land in the town.

McLaurin quickly gave the project his imprimatur and offered to sell Emmanuel three acres of his own land. Most of it was a creek-bottom swamp, but this didn't daunt the McDuffies and their allies, because they noted that several sturdy trees stood tall in the marshy waters.

They bought the plot and immediately organized their charges. Slip-sliding in the mud and bedeviled by mosquitoes and leeches, men, women, and children cut trees out of the steaming swamp, hauled them up to high ground, and laboriously built a log cabin classroom.

By late October, the McDuffies were teaching twelve boys and girls there in what they called the Laurinburg Institute. Emmanuel and Tinny had resolved to turn no child away; some parents paid nothing, and others made tuition payments in kind—cabbages, a small wagon, firewood, a hog.

During the first academic year the McDuffies taught only vocational subjects—carpentry, farming, metalworking, masonry, animal husbandry—and they started a farm. They wanted to build a firm economic base before they launched an academic curriculum, and their program was solidly grounded in the philosophy of Booker T. Washington; he preached that as a first priority blacks should acquire skills that would assure them a degree of self-sufficiency in an essentially hostile America.

When Dizzy arrived twenty-nine years later in 1933 with one change of underwear, a toothbrush, a towel, and the clothes on his back, the Laurinburg Institute had blossomed into a community of fifteen hundred persons spread over sixty-five acres. He found classroom buildings, a working farm, dorms for boys and girls, athletic fields, an administration hall, and a hospital.

Emmanuel and Tinny were still in charge, and they ran a tight ship. Church and Sunday school attendance were compulsory, and all the students were given work assignments—duties such as washing dishes, mowing lawns, cleaning the dorms, or growing crops. Thanks to a white ancestor who had provided a modest financial patrimony for his slave progeny, Tinny grew up in a relatively prosperous middle-class home, and she demanded that her students adopt such middle-class virtues as good table manners, personal cleanliness, and proper dress. Students were fined for wiping their hands on their clothes, walking on the grass, or listening to the radio during study hours. Whippings were meted out for more serious offenses.

Students were held to high academic standards from the first grade onward, and the curriculum was so enriched that the school was permitted to award high school diplomas after the eleventh grade.

Laurinburg was the right place at the right time for Dizzy. The school freed him of financial anxiety for the first time since his father's death, and it gave him the time, the resources, and the encouragement to raise his musical skills and harmonic knowledge to a truly professional level. What is more, he found in Emmanuel McDuffie a role model and a surrogate father who, unlike his real father, provided discipline and structure without sadism, and who inspired him to direct his abundant energies toward viable, concrete goals. Dizzy spoke about the school in 1990:

> Laurinburg was a little paradise for me. . . . I had security *and* serenity. No more cotton picking, no more scuffling.
>
> They lent me a raggedy trumpet and they had a piano which I could work out on for hours at a time.
>
> Mr. McDuffie was a dignified man, and he represented strength and idealism to me. He made us feel good about ourselves. If a guy like him, the son of slaves, could create such a terrific institution in the racist Carolinas, there was hope for a poor black kid like me. He got me thinking real seriously about making a future for myself as a musician.
>
> Norman Powe and I roomed with a rich boy from New York. Thank God he was generous and the same size as me. I might have froze to death if it weren't for the clothes he lent me.[2]

The enhancement of Dizzy's wardrobe was topped by the improvement in his diet; the food at Laurinburg was far better than anything he had eaten before. After he noticed that the athletes received extra rations, he decided to join the football team. The coaches told him he was too small to play, but, in a reprise of the scene with the trombone at Robert Smalls, he pleaded his case passionately and after a turbulent half hour, the coaches relented. Dizzy made up for his lack of size with a determined pugnacity and became a passable football player.

Dizzy and Norman performed in the school's dance orchestra and in a marching band, and they received small stipends for playing in the dance group. Norman remembered:

> The marching band was super-sharp, and the dance band swung. We checked out all the professional groups that came through our area, and we could hold our own with any of them.
>
> For dancing, we had no written arrangements, just head arrangements that we made up. We played popular songs of the day like "I Can't Give You Anything But Love," Glen Gray's "Casa Loma Stomp," and "St. Louis Blues." For marching, we played a lot of music by John Philip Sousa.
>
> Overnighters were out, because we were due back at two or three a.m. But like all musicians, we made out pretty well with the girls—despite the curfew.

And, as Norman recalled, the boys had chosen musical role models:

> We didn't have a phonograph at Laurinburg, but we listened to Ellington and Calloway regularly on the radio. They were our big influences at the time. Not Basie or Roy Eldridge. The Eldridge influence on Dizzy came later. Once we saw Ellington and his men in a movie dressed very elegant up there on the screen.
>
> And of course, there was Louis Armstrong. Everybody wanted to play like him—especially trumpet players.[3]

Dizzy received little instruction as a horn player at Laurinburg. The school did not have a full-time teacher until his second year, but he progressed rapidly working on his own during his first year and the following summer while he worked at the school's farm to fulfill his scholarship obligations.

"Shorty" Hall, an accomplished musician who had directed the future novelist Ralph Ellison in the band at Tuskegee, arrived at the end of that summer (1934) and quickly recognized Dizzy's talents. However, after convincing him to abandon football because of the potential damage to his lips and giving him pointers on classical technique, Hall decided he had little more to teach Dizzy and turned his attention to his less advanced students. According to Norman Powe, Hall was motivated in part by jealousy: "Hall became jealous of Dizzy, because the kid could play everything on both trumpet and trombone—all that classical stuff, those marches, and the dance arrangements. He was miles ahead of everybody. Dizzy had become very popular, and Hall didn't care too much about that."[4]

Dizzy added piano and harmony lessons to his workload, but he did it surreptitiously. Because he wanted to maintain a macho football-player image with peers who considered the piano an effete instrument, he sneaked up the back stairs of a dorm twice a week to study with the McDuffies' daughter, Verdell.

For Dizzy, the piano was a means to an end: the exploration of a subject, the principles of harmony, which fascinated him the way other teenagers might be fascinated by the latest dance step, math conundrums, or shooting a basketball. Dizzy became one of the major harmonic innovators in jazz history, and the piano was his indispensable tool in this area. His reliance on the instrument was unusual; few jazz musicians have used it this way.

At Laurinburg, the rebelliousness inculcated by his father surfaced in a desire to improve on the harmonic materials he had inherited, and he spent countless hours experimenting with chords (three or more notes played simultaneously). He discussed this in 1990:

> I can play only one note at a time on the trumpet, but I can play as many as ten on the piano and hear the beautiful sounds they can make together.
>
> I must have worked through every chord sequence in western music on that Laurinburg piano. Even invented a few myself. And with gusto I dissected individual chords, turned them inside-out, upside-down. I gradually began to realize that the harmony in our

popular music was pretty limited . . . and I started to think that I
could create something much richer than that.[5]

Course work mattered less to him at Laurinburg than the almost unlimited opportunity to develop his art:

The great benefit for me in music came from the atmosphere at
Laurinburg, the quiet and serenity of being in the country. . . . I
practiced constantly, until all times of the night, anytime I wanted.
I'd practice the trumpet and then the piano for twenty-four hours
straight if they didn't come around and shut me up when they
checked the locks every night. I developed a very serious attitude
about music, and music was the only thing I was serious about.[6]

Joseph Campbell, the eminent philosopher of myth, advised his
students that to find satisfaction in their careers, they should "follow their bliss." Dizzy had found and was following his bliss at
Laurinburg.

Although serious about music, Dizzy never stopped clowning
or finding mischief at the school. He performed part of a prom
gig from a tree limb, was caught in an off-limits girls' dorm and
received a whipping from Mr. McDuffie for it, and was frequently
disciplined for fighting.

He escaped punishment on one occasion when he pulled his
knife to scare off a bully who outweighed him by a hundred
pounds; using all his histrionic skills, he made a passionate speech
that convinced Mr. McDuffie that he had acted in self-defense.

Forty years later, in a joint interview with Dizzy, Tinny Mc-
Duffie complained about his antics: "I got so tired of that little
Gillespie boy. I got so tired of him." Then she turned to her former student and said, "We had patience with you. If we hadn't,
you wouldn't be where you are today, brother."[7]

Because he missed his mama and because he continued to earn
decent fees playing with his hometown band, Dizzy leapt at every
opportunity to hitchhike home on the rutted dirt roads connect-
ing Laurinburg and Cheraw.

As he was leaving a convenience store on one such excursion, he came face-to-face with a redneck pointing a pistol at him. Dizzy stopped immediately as his antagonist demanded: "Nigger, do you know how to dance? I hear you niggers have a lot of rhythm. Show me." Without warning, he began spraying bullets into the dust at Dizzy's feet, forcing him to "dance" an impromptu jig to avoid harm. After he emptied his weapon, the redneck said, "I guess you can dance," and abruptly left.

Dizzy sat down in the dirt, his body quivering, and half an hour passed before he could regain his composure. His desire to leave the South, formed after the lynching of Bill McNeil, turned now into steely resolve.

Dizzy's mother Lottie, his brother Wesley and his wife, and his sister Genia moved in March 1935 to Philadelphia to join his sister Mattie and her husband, Bill, a prosperous barber, in an apartment there. They found work almost immediately, a testament to both their initiative and their luck in the midst of the Great Depression. Lottie managed the home, Wesley became a chef, and his wife and Genia joined Mattie performing piecework jobs in a factory.

The racial situation they encountered in the North was light years ahead of what they had endured in South Carolina, but it was far from paradise. On March 19, 1935, during the week the Gillespies arrived in Philadelphia, a race riot in New York's Harlem killed one, injured more than 100, and resulted in 121 arrests. A few weeks previously, after months of boycott and protest, the first blacks were hired in the stores of 125th Street, Harlem's main drag. The new employees were only four in number and very light-skinned. Philadelphia's racial climate was slightly worse than New York's, because the Philadelphia police were particularly hard-nosed in dealing with blacks.

Dizzy had wanted desperately to go north with his family, but his mother insisted that he wait three months until he had won his Laurinburg diploma. Their departure threw him into a depressed funk, and his grades suffered. He failed physics and, facing another summer on the school farm followed by a makeup semester, he decided to move on. He quit school and hung out with Norman Powe in Cheraw until, a short time later, he was able to hitch a ride to Philadelphia with a neighbor.

Laurinburg changed the course of Dizzy's life in ways that cannot be overestimated. The school was his Oxford, his Harvard, his Heidelberg. And he didn't need teachers; all he required was the secure environment, the abundant time, and the tough love and inspiration that the McDuffies provided. His energy, a fanatical dedication toward solving musical problems, and his natural talents allowed him to transform himself radically there. He entered as a fifteen-year-old cotton picker with musical promise, and he left, three years later, a first-class harmonic theoretician and a technically adept, improvising musician ready and able to enter the professional ranks. Roughly eighteen months after leaving Laurinburg, he established his professional credentials when he began earning the then princely sum of forty-five dollars per week with an excellent band; first-rate legal secretaries made twenty-five dollars at the time.

6
BECOMING DIZZY

DIZZY'S MAMA, WHO BELIEVED HER SON WAS STILL AT school in Laurinburg, was surprised and overjoyed when he walked into her Philadelphia parlor in late June carrying all his belongings in a knapsack. After a tearful welcome, Dizzy began to make himself at home as the seventh resident of the family's three-and-a-half-room flat, located at 627 Pine Street in the city's teeming black "South Philly" district.

Conditions were spartan. The rooms formed a row from front to back like railroad cars, and the makeshift walls were paper-thin. The only fresh air had to enter through the front and back windows, so cooking odors lingered and clung tenaciously to the upholstery. Fire prevention consisted of two small water buckets hung from the wall of the hallway.

Dizzy found that he had little privacy as the family slept on a catch-as-catch-can array of beds, cots, mattresses set on the floors, and couches. Summer temperatures approaching one hundred degrees added to their discomfort as they fought the heat with a patchwork of feeble solutions—positioning a fan to blow air over a large chunk of ice, taking turns sleeping near the windows, bathing two or three times a night.

The view from the Gillespies' backyard was dominated by the 549-foot tower of city hall at the epicenter of the city. In fact, it was impossible to ignore this behemoth from anywhere in their segregated neighborhood, which formed a mile-square rectangle less than a half mile south of it. Until larger skyscrapers were built after World War II, the tower of city hall totally dominated the Philadelphia landscape; it remains a commanding presence to this day.

The streets of black South Philly, chockablock with three-story tenements, were a far cry from the quiet, leafy, hundred-foot-wide expanse of Huger Street back in Cheraw; they were so narrow that trolleys were barely able to pass between the flanking rows of parked cars and horse-drawn wagons, and they were eternally noisy. Dizzy's ears were assaulted from all sides with the clanging of the trolleys, the cries of street-corner blues singers, the shouts of vendors, and the blare of swing music blasting from the record stores. It was summer and there was no home air-conditioning in 1935; the sidewalks and building stoops were filled with people talking, smoking, playing cards, sipping beer and soda pop, shooting craps.

Most important for Dizzy, the streets of his neighborhood were dotted with saloons and nightclubs that beckoned with the promise of employment. But first he had to have a trumpet. Fortunately, Bill, his barber brother-in-law, was a generous man and bought him—on Dizzy's second day in town—a $13 horn (worth roughly $150 in today's dollars) on credit at a local pawnshop. Unfortunately, Bill could not afford a case, so Dizzy was forced to carry his trumpet around in a paper bag.

Armed with his new instrument, Dizzy auditioned and won a job two days later at a rowdy joint called the Green Gate Inn seven blocks from his home. That night Dizzy joined a trio with a drummer and a piano player at eight dollars per week (about ninety dollars today) and played in the style of the long-reigning king of jazz, Louis Armstrong. The club was the site of almost nightly brawls, and during World War II, the level of violence there earned it the nickname "Pearl Harbor."

With his first earnings, Dizzy headed directly for a clothing store and, for $1.50 down, bought on installments three draped pinstripe suits. He was delighted to throw his raggedy southern clothes in the trash, and he felt a rush as he sauntered through the crowded streets in his sharp new duds; he had found in the city a natural habitat, a place whose noisy kinetic energy excited him and matched his own. Throughout his life, Dizzy loved to "hang out"; he felt fidgety and bored at home or in hotel rooms on tour and would quickly flee their confines for the comradery of the streets, the greasy spoons, the clubs, the barbershops, and the saloons.

Five weeks after he was hired at the Green Gate Inn, he secured another local gig at twelve dollars per week and started giving his mama some money for household expenses. He also joined the union, an all-black offshoot of the white local; it was founded by Frankie Fairfax, a trombone player and leader of one of Philadelphia's best black bands. Fairfax had secured a coveted long-term gig as the house band at the Strand Ballroom, Philadelphia's equivalent of the renowned Savoy Ballroom in New York. It was a magnet for both black and white dancers, and it was located where the main drag of black South Philly, South Street, met Broad Street, the city's principal north-south artery.

As knowledge of Dizzy's talent spread among local musicians, he came to the attention of Fairfax, who offered him a tryout. Dizzy had boasted that he could read a speck of fly shit on a musical score, so he felt no trepidation as he approached his audition. But he ran afoul of a conspiracy.

Joe Facio, a trumpeter with the band, had heard of his prowess and feared that, if hired, Dizzy would take all the solo spots away from him. Facio plotted with pianist Bill Doggett, who ran the audition, to provide Dizzy with scores in a squiggly, unorthodox style of notation favored by Fairfax. Dizzy became thoroughly confused, and afterward Doggett told everyone, "You know that little dizzy cat, the one who carries his horn around in a paper bag.

He can't read worth a damn." Dizzy had failed the audition but gained a nickname.[1]

Doggett had chosen the sobriquet because of the paper bag, but Dizzy's kinetic energy and penchant for comic antics ensured that it stuck.

DIZZY'S SWING 7
INHERITANCE

AT ABOUT THE TIME DIZZY FAILED HIS AUDITION WITH Fairfax, a momentous event occurred in American popular culture; on the night of August 21, 1935, the Swing Era was born when the Benny Goodman band played a tumultuously successful gig at the Palomar Ballroom in Los Angeles.

Swing joyfully dominated American pop culture for more than a decade following the Palomar engagement. Hundreds of big bands flourished, record sales skyrocketed, and for the only time in our history, improvised jazz and popular culture were one. As the composer and scholar Gunther Schuller has written:

> Through the proliferation of recordings and the growth of the recording industry, the development of network radio and its nightly broadcasts of jazz groups from hotels and ballrooms all over the land—jazz suddenly seemed to be everywhere. . . . In the

process a style and aesthetic of jazz were forged which reflected a
preponderance of American popular taste. It is undoubtedly the only
time in its history when jazz was completely in phase with the social
environment, and when it both captured and reflected the broadest
musical common-denominator of popular taste in the nation.[1]

Dizzy thus came of age professionally at the wonderful moment when jazz, in its big band incarnation, had become America's popular music. He reveled in the opportunities it provided,
and unlike many important contemporaries such as Charlie
Parker, Thelonious Monk, and John Coltrane, he became totally
hooked on the big band aesthetic pioneered by Fletcher Henderson, Don Redman, and Louis Armstrong; it remained central to
his endeavors until the end of his life in 1993.

Swing music, as distinct from the Swing Era, was created in
1923 and 1924 by Fletcher Henderson and his all-black orchestra.
It became very popular within the black community and with sophisticated whites during the next decade, but it did not become a
mass cultural phenomenon until Goodman, a white musician,
fired up millions of young white people in the mid-thirties.[2]

Henderson, who had extensive classical piano training as a
child, came to New York in 1920 at age twenty-three to pursue a
master's degree in chemistry at Columbia University. He was soon
earning lucrative fees performing at parties and clubs, and he
proved so talented that he gave up chemistry in 1921 to become
the musical director of Black Swan, the first black record company.

By the summer of 1923, Henderson had made more than one
hundred records. He had also organized a seasoned recording
band from among the gifted black musicians who played a new
kind of music, jazz, and who had been drawn to Harlem, the new
Afro-American mecca, after the war.

The explosion of Harlem's black population during the
1920s spawned a vital nightclub and theater scene where dance
bands flourished and musicians thrived. By 1923 important venues like the Cotton Club, Connie's Inn, the Bamville Club, the
Renaissance Ballroom, and the Lafayette Theater were doing
excellent business. The commercial possibilities for large dance
orchestras were considerably greater than for the newly popular

New Orleans style of small-group polyphonic jazz, and Henderson seized the day by creating a ten-piece jazz dance band from the talented musicians in his recording group.

Swing's birth can be traced to January 1924, when Henderson brought his "Recording Orchestra" down from Harlem to begin its first public engagement at the Club Alabam in midtown Manhattan. The group included Don Redman, an innovative arranger/saxophonist, and the master saxophone soloist Coleman Hawkins.

In the standard dance bands before Henderson, the brass and reed instruments were blended together in soupy, homogenized arrangements, the beat was weak and monotonous, and there were few, if any, improvised solos. But Henderson was dealing with a new breed of musician; his bandmates liked to improvise and they played with an incisive beat and attack, and he and Redman devised a new kind of music to accommodate and celebrate them. Excellent record sales showed that a significant public liked what they were doing.

The basic idea that the two men developed was to divide the band into three sections—reeds (saxophones and clarinets), brass (trumpets and trombones), and rhythm (drums, bass and/or guitar, piano)—and give each a distinctive role. The arrangements would feature the masses of reeds and brasses harmonizing crisply and powerfully as separate units, a driving beat created by the tightly knit rhythm section, and exciting interplay between improvising soloists and the band as a whole. This music, made by black men, was infused with a blues and gospel aesthetic, and it involved a goodly amount of call-and-response among the sections and the soloists.

The three-section-plus-soloist formulation was the first of two key concepts that defined big band swing. The second was swing rhythm, a hard thing to define; the central idea is to move from one beat to the next in a relaxed, propulsive way so as to carry the listener irresistibly forward.

The man who created swing rhythm, this second ingredient, was Louis Armstrong, a genius.

Henderson had the good sense to pluck Armstrong, age twenty-three, from relative obscurity in Chicago and bring him to

New York in October 1924 soon after the band moved from a successful run at the Club Alabam into the much larger Roseland Ballroom, a midtown spot that drew crowds of white dancers.

Armstrong turned the whole world on to his swing rhythm and his magical improvising from the Roseland stage, and he converted Hawkins and the other soloists and Henderson and Redman to his gospel. By the end of Armstrong's tenure with Henderson thirteen months later, the band had found a swing groove. And the improvisers, learning from Armstrong every night, were playing far more expressively. His revolutionary musical contributions helped turn what was to be a relatively short engagement for the band at Roseland into a five-year residency there.

The big band principles of Henderson, Redman, and Armstrong have remained basically unchanged during the eight intervening decades and are still defining the genre; they were valid with Frankie Fairfax's band in Philadelphia in 1935, and they are valid with major twenty-first-century aggregations such as the Lincoln Center Jazz Orchestra, the Danish Radio Orchestra, and the Village Vanguard Orchestra.

Despite Redman's departure in 1927, the band continued to improve; Gunther Schuller's comments about the 1932 version attest to this: "The band's sound was unique: light, buoyant, airy, loose, and yet remarkably cohesive. And its swing was superb, total and collective in a way that perhaps no other band of the period equaled. Form and content, style and arrangement were truly one."[3]

During the late 1920s and early 1930s, other great black orchestra leaders—Ellington, Lunceford, Carter, Webb, Calloway—built on Henderson's foundation to create the world that Dizzy aspired to when he came north to Philadelphia. The big bands were "where it was at" for a black jazz musician in 1935. Ironically, Henderson had no band to lead at that time. A feckless businessman, he had gone bust in November 1934. His fortunes improved when clarinetist Benny Goodman, then twenty-five, solicited his help soon after.

During the early 1930s, Goodman had built a solid reputation as a freelance musician in New York, playing in pit bands for Broadway shows, leading ad hoc groups for recordings and club dates, backing crooner Russ Columbo, and jobbing with studio orchestras in the burgeoning radio industry.

A month before Henderson threw in the towel, Goodman—almost by default—was given six weeks to organize a band for *Let's Dance*, a Saturday-night NBC radio show sponsored by Nabisco; its premiere was set for December 1, 1934. Ross Firestone, Goodman's biographer, describes the hiring process:

> The show . . . called for a swing band, but where were such bands to be found? The racism pervading the radio networks at the time meant that none of the magnificent black orchestras playing around New York—Duke Ellington, Fletcher Henderson, Benny Carter, Jimmy Lunceford, Chick Webb, and so on—could even be considered for the spot. That left only the smallest handful of white possibilities. [NBC] tried to interest the Dorsey Brothers, but they were busy working at the Rockland Palace. The Casa Loma was also tied up. Benny was almost the only choice they had left.[4]

Let's Dance featured three bands alternating in short segments: Goodman's for hot jazz, Xavier Cugat's for rumbas and other Latin rhythms, and Kel Miller's for "sweet" dance tunes. (Miller's real name was Murray Kellner; this was considered too Jewish for the radio public, and the producers made him change it.)[5] The show gave its audiences three hours of live music in each of the four U.S. time zones, and this meant that the musicians were obliged to work for five consecutive hours in New York.

Goodman was woefully short of material for the broadcasts and reached out to a number of writers. Several responded, including Henderson, who ultimately provided the arrangements that proved to be crucial to Goodman's success.

Goodman started *Let's Dance* by using existing Henderson arrangements and then drove Henderson to produce three new ones each week during the show's six-month run. Ross Firestone recognized the importance of their partnership: "Through no fault of his own, Benny was the beneficiary of a dozen years of experimentation, development, and gradual perfection of a style of big band arranging that was to give him the identity he needed."[6]

To his credit, Goodman never stinted in his praise of Henderson. More than a half century later, in 1985, he dedicated his last television special to his long-deceased colleague, saying, "The fascination with his arrangements was endless. I really thought he was a genius."[7]

The *Let's Dance* broadcasts were abruptly canceled in late May 1935, because a strike had closed down all the Nabisco factories. In a desperate move to keep the band alive, Goodman's managers booked for him an August engagement at the Palomar Ballroom in Los Angeles with one-nighters and a four-week stay in Denver along the way. The pay was so low that the band could not afford a bus, and the musicians were forced to drive their own cars. Most of the ballroom owners insisted that Goodman emphasize his romantic "sweet" arrangements, and the tour was a dismal flop; Benny almost closed it down in Denver.

The band played to a surprisingly full house at its first California stop in Oakland, and then moved on to the Palomar. The audience was apathetic during the first set as the band played "sweet" arrangements requested by the ballroom owners. Then sparks began to fly. Ross Firestone describes what happened:

> The band was still dying, slowly this time, by inches. As they prepared for the next set, one of the sidemen—it might have been Bunny Berigan or maybe Gene Krupa—told Benny, what the hell, as long as they were going down, they might as well go down swinging. Benny nodded his head and broke out the Fletcher Henderson arrangements. Benny recalled, "To our complete amazement half of the crowd stopped dancing and came surging around the stand. . . . That was the moment that decided things for me. After traveling three thousand miles, we finally found people who were up on what we were trying to do, prepared to take our music the way we wanted to play it. That first big roar from the crowd was one of the sweetest sounds I ever heard in my life, and from that time on the night kept getting bigger and bigger."[8]

Three reasons, all rooted in the radio medium, account for the Palomar success. First of all, *Let's Dance* started in prime listening time—9:30 p.m.—on the West Coast, an hour earlier than in the other time zones. Secondly, the band was loose and thoroughly warmed up when it started performing for Pacific audiences two hours after it began playing its East Coast segment. And finally, popular California disc jockeys had been ardently plugging records that the band made just before it left New York. In other words, radio had created, without the band's knowledge, an army of California fans before they had arrived.

The explosion at the Palomar propelled Goodman forward on an astonishing arc of success as his "swing music," a PR man's term, swept the country, and he became a cultural liberator of major proportions. Like Elvis Presley a generation later, he brought to the kids of straitlaced, white middle America a hot, orgiastic black music that drove them wild—something the racial mores of the times would not allow a black man to do. Unlike Elvis, Goodman was the least likely candidate one could imagine for an American pop icon—an introverted, absentminded, bespectacled, Jewish musical perfectionist. But he loved hot music and he could play it to a fare-thee-well, and that was all that mattered.

Soon after Dizzy arrived in Philadelphia as the gospel of swing was sweeping the country, he found a mentor and an idol. Dizzy had been playing, like all young jazz trumpeters of the era, in the prevailing Armstrong style, when he became entranced with something fresh and different—the music of the electrifying swing horn man Roy Eldridge, who was beginning at age twenty-four to receive wide exposure on radio and on record. Eldridge's first broadcast—with the Teddy Hill big band—aired on June 22, 1935, as the first show of a three-times-per-week NBC series from New York's Savoy Ballroom; and later in the summer his first recordings, also with Hill's band, were released.

Eldridge, a bantam rooster at five feet five and 115 pounds, was ebullient, passionate about music, anxiety prone, and fiercely competitive. Unlike hundreds of 1920s trumpeters who aped Louis Armstrong, Eldridge found his main inspiration elsewhere—in the speedy, legato phrasing of saxophonists. Jazz scholar John Chilton has observed: "He found the fast-running intricacies of Coleman Hawkins' saxophone lines much more appealing [than Armstrong's], and the transference of saxophone phrasing on to trumpet was to be the basis of Roy's revolutionary style. He began to string together long legato phrases, switching from register to register like a top saxophonist."[9]

It is difficult to articulate fast patterns on the trumpet, because the player must carefully coordinate lip movements with finger movements. The saxophonist has an easier task, because he simply blows a steady column of air into his instrument as he pushes down the keys with his fingers. By a sheer effort of will, Eldridge taught himself to play the trumpet like a saxophone.

After he completed his apprenticeship with an array of traveling carnivals and regional big bands, Eldridge arrived in New York in late 1930 at age nineteen and quickly secured a job at Small's Paradise, a fifteen-hundred-seat Harlem nightspot where he worked for two and a half years.

Despite a supple imagination and great technical prowess, Eldridge did not become a complete improviser until 1932, when he began to listen carefully to Armstrong. Armstrong's solos exhibited intense emotion and high drama, because, more than anyone else before him, he told stories with them; they had shape—beginnings, middles, and ends. Eldridge achieved musical maturity when he imbued his solos with Armstrong's deep sense of structure. But Eldridge took little else from him as he pioneered a new way of playing jazz trumpet.

As we have seen, the Eldridge style was based on the saxophonist's linked, serpentine lines instead of the cleanly articulated patterns of Armstrong and his followers on trumpet. But the differences between the two men went deeper than that.

Armstrong built tension by creating tantalizing spaces between his phrases and by playing slightly behind the beat and then catching up to it. Eldridge typically hit the middle of the beat and created tension by pouring out an insistent, headlong cascade of fiery notes. Armstrong would reach selectively into the upper register for dramatic effect. The upper register was Eldridge's natural habitat; he was the first major jazz trumpeter to play entire choruses there. Armstrong's sound was magisterial, soulful; it entered your chest cavity, became your breath. Eldridge's sound crackled, ripped, and popped with nervous intensity; it picked you up and drove you inexorably forward.

In addition, Eldridge pushed jazz harmony into exciting new realms. Gunther Schuller described this in his comments about a July 1935 recording, "It's Too Hot for Words":

In just four bars—the introduction to the song—Eldridge calls forth a new melodic/harmonic world that Armstrong could certainly not have envisioned. . . . Melodically/linearly Roy's intro is laden with tritones which fellow musicians found "eccentric" or "weird." And in truth, not only were they entirely new as melodic or intervallic material, but they landed at odd places in the phrase, creating strange little harmonic collisions and unexpectedly sharp-cornered contours. Even more significantly, they were "flatted" notes, a tendency which Eldridge was to develop into a distinctive hallmark of his style, and which players younger than Roy, like Howard McGhee and Gillespie, were to take up and eventually develop into an entire tritone-dominated new language.[10]

Dizzy, who had absorbed well the basic tenets of Armstrong's aesthetic, was enamored with what was new and fresh about Eldridge—the harmonic and rhythmic daring, the fiery headlong passion which imbued everything he played, and the incredible technical facility (particularly in the highest reaches of the trumpet's range).

It is a popular but false cliché of jazz history to say that Eldridge was the conscious link between Armstrong and Dizzy in the development of jazz trumpet. Eldridge himself scoffed at the notion: "I was never trying to be a bridge between Louis Armstrong and something. I was just trying to outplay anybody and to outplay them my way."[11]

In the spring of 1933, six months after absorbing Armstrong's lessons, Eldridge moved six blocks north on Lenox Avenue from Small's Paradise to the Savoy Ballroom for a short stay with Teddy Hill's big band.

The Savoy, an interracial dance palace, had quickly become a Harlem institution after opening in 1926 on the second floor of a newly constructed, block-long building. Known as "the home of happy feet" or "the Track," it drew an international crowd to watch some of the best dancers in the world—the masters of the Lindy Hop—toss their partners through the air in heart-stopping arabesques at furious tempos. (The Lindy Hop was named for Charles Lindbergh's 1927 transatlantic flight.) The Savoy boasted a 50-by-250-foot hardwood dance floor, which was worn down every three years by the pounding of those happy feet.

The undisputed king of the Savoy was Chick Webb, the great, innovative swing drummer whose orchestra was a leading attraction there from 1932 until his death in 1939; his reign was crowned by the hiring in 1935 of Ella Fitzgerald, who became a national star under his aegis. Webb's achievements were remarkable, because tuberculosis of the spine had made him a hunchback.

Dancing was continuous at the Savoy, and other bands were needed to spell the Webb aggregation; Hill's band—built around a number of good soloists—frequently played this role.

Eldridge began a second stint with Hill in January 1935 as the band started a long engagement at the Savoy. On February 26, they cut four 78 sides; this marked Eldridge's recording debut less than a month after his twenty-fourth birthday.

Dizzy heard the 78s following their release six months later, and he and the rest of the jazz world were particularly excited by a track called "Here Comes Cookie," in which Eldridge burst on the scene by erupting in a sinuous, daredevil break with unexpected rhythmic and harmonic twists; he followed this with three joyously free improvisations in a call-and-response chorus with the band. Dizzy memorized every note of the solo.

Soon after, he heard Eldridge in the flesh when the Hill band played a gig at Philadelphia's Pearl Theater; Ellington's orchestra was in town at the same time, and Eldridge dazzled Dizzy at an after-hours jam session where he bested Ellington's Rex Stewart in a furious trumpet duel and made Stewart cry.

Dizzy was ready to follow his idol anywhere. But first he had to figure out what Eldridge was doing with his horn.

MAKING IT

8

DIZZY WOULD HAVE TO WAIT SEVERAL MONTHS, UNTIL January 1936, before he found the opportunity to unlock Eldridge's secrets. In the meantime, he kept busy.

He was not unduly discouraged by his failure at the Fairfax audition, because he found plentiful employment in several Philadelphia clubs. He soon reconciled with Bill Doggett, one of his Fairfax nemeses, and found that he shared with him a desire to explore the mysteries of harmony. Dizzy leapt at the opportunity to continue the studies he had begun at Laurinburg as the two men met often to practice and to experiment with new musical ideas. Doggett remembered their encounters:

> Dizzy was going to be something, because he had a tremendous conception. . . . His execution was always there, and with his knowledge of chords on the piano, he could play anything that he

imagined in his mind. . . . We would take a tune like "I Can't Get Started," . . . and we would try to make different chords off of almost every note. We would play the introduction, make a change there, make a change on the next melody note. . . .

The third and fourth bars practically had the same chords. We were fooling around and we found out that we could go from a B-minor seventh to the regular seventh, back and forth, four times. In other words, we'd make eight chords off of this one note, and these were the types of things we were into.[1]

While these creative sessions were taking place, Doggett was engineering a mutiny against Fairfax by convincing most of his musicians that Fairfax was embezzling salary money from them. Doggett quickly organized a new band with these men and headed to Atlantic City for an extended engagement as the defections caused Fairfax to lose his regular gig at the Strand Ballroom. Doggett offered Dizzy a job with his group, but Dizzy wanted no part of the mutiny and turned him down.

Soon after, in late November 1935, Fairfax formed a new band and hired Dizzy, who was happy to join a first-class outfit and leave his freelancing behind him. The group regained its niche at the Strand and then took a five-week leave of absence for a southern tour with Tiny Bradshaw, a nationally known bandleader and an excellent, hard-swinging vocalist. Fairfax had rented the group to Bradshaw, which was a fairly common practice during the 1930s. During the trip, the nickname Dizzy became permanent as fellow trumpeter Palmer Davis insisted on using the sobriquet at every turn.

When they came under Bradshaw's aegis, the Fairfax musicians felt certain that they had arrived in the big time. Instead of traveling in two ancient Packards, they rode in a Greyhound bus with "Tiny Bradshaw's Orchestra—New York" painted on both sides and were served by a road manager and a valet. After two successful weeks in Baltimore and Washington, DC, however, disaster struck in Richmond, Virginia, as several future bookings were canceled. Bassist W. O. Smith remembered, "On the days when we didn't have a hotel, the bus was our hotel. When the motor wasn't running, there was no heat. There was a daily collection of assets so that we could have food. . . . When we were lucky enough to make a gig, we could rent two rooms in a hotel. The fourteen of us often had to sleep in shifts with three or four in the bed crosswise."[2]

The band struggled through three weeks in Richmond and the Carolinas, and in Charlotte, North Carolina, Dizzy saved Palmer Davis's life when he came upon him unconscious from gas that had leaked from the heater in his room. Dizzy, who weighed 145 pounds at the time, needed all his strength to lug the 300-pound Palmer to safety. The musicians returned sadder and wiser to Philadelphia in late January.

As the band regrouped in Philadelphia, Fairfax hired two first-rate New York musicians—Charlie Shavers and Bama Warwick— to join Dizzy in the trumpet section. Shavers always described Warwick, who was not a blood relative, as his brother, because from early adolescence Warwick had lived with the Shavers family. No virtuoso, Warwick was a solid professional who became the anchor of many trumpet sections. He rarely soloed. The two trumpeters had heard Roy Eldridge many times in Harlem and were die-hard fans.

Shavers, just two months older than Dizzy, had been a prodigy as a child and had developed a virtuoso technique second only to that of Eldridge when he joined Fairfax at age nineteen. He had assiduously analyzed Eldridge's improvisations and was eager to share his knowledge, and Dizzy at last had an opportunity to study Eldridge seriously. Dizzy recalled bonding with Shavers and Warwick:

Charlie, Bama, and I were the Three Musketeers of Philly, getting into mischief everywhere, and Charlie opened new horizons for me. He had figured out how Roy Eldridge got his effects, and had memorized every one of Roy's solos. Damn—did I pick up on that! I had been stumbling around before, and now I had it made. I memorized the solos too, and for the first time I had a good feeling for what Roy was doing.[3]

The Three Musketeers, as a matter of course, followed closely the progress of Eldridge's career. In October 1935, Fletcher

Henderson organized a new band, and one of his first moves was to attempt to lure Eldridge away from Teddy Hill. Eldridge made, as a condition of his employment, the hiring of his pal Chu Berry, an outstanding saxophonist, and Henderson acquiesced. The band completed successful runs at Roseland, Harlem's Apollo Theater, and other East Coast venues before moving in January 1936 to Chicago's Grand Terrace Ballroom and a nightly NBC radio show.

They soon had a nationwide hit, "Christopher Columbus," a riff tune written by Berry. (A riff is a catchy melodic phrase that is repeated several times during the course of a song.) The band recorded "Christopher Columbus" on March 27, 1936, along with three other titles, and the Three Musketeers listened to the sides for hours and memorized every nuance of Eldridge's improvisations.

Eldridge and Berry won national exposure as "Christopher Columbus" became Henderson's nightly NBC theme song, the 78s flew off the record store shelves, business at the Grand Terrace improved by more than 50 percent, and several other bands made cover versions.

The star status of the two men was confirmed when *Downbeat* magazine, which quickly became the bible of the pop music industry after its founding in 1934, published in July 1936 the results of a musicians' poll for an "All-Time Swing Band." Armstrong, Eldridge, and the deceased Bix Beiderbecke were selected on trumpet, and Hawkins, Berry, and Jimmy Dorsey were the winners on saxophone.

The School of Eldridge was not Dizzy's only academy; the Fairfax band also proved to be an excellent conservatory. In particular, the scholarly clarinetist and trumpeter Jimmy Hamilton (who later became a star with Duke Ellington), Shavers, and bassist W. O. Smith provided intellectual stimulation for him. After gigs, they often lingered until dawn in bars and greasy spoons discussing musical problems.

Band morale was high, and the musicians usually arrived for rehearsals well ahead of time. To sharpen their mental and physical agility, they would pick challenging tunes with difficult chord changes, play them in the original key and then proceed a half step up in each chorus until they returned to the original key.

The Fairfax band made extensive use of "head" arrangements, arrangements created spontaneously by the musicians themselves in a technique made widely known by Count Basie's great aggregation. This practice requires a high degree of musicality, and Dizzy loved the challenge and took an active part in the process. Smith described what happened:

> We built up a repertoire in which no written music would be in sight. . . . Somebody starts off a riff (straight out of the black church or a blues pattern) and goes not more than a couple of bars when he is picked up by the rest of the members in his section— we'll say it's the saxophone section—and within the space of two bars or less, the riff is harmonized with each saxophonist instinctively grabbing his part, usually with the correct notes.
>
> Then the trumpet section, at the correct instant, plays a counter riff, something like the call and response pattern of the black church. This, too, is instantly harmonized in three or four parts, depending on the number of trumpets. Mind you, everybody has different but effective notes. The trombone section, not to be outdone, then plays a counterpoint to the whole arrangement.
>
> From the very beginning, the rhythm section realizes harmonic patterns or chord changes implied by the first riff, and the result is a new addition to the repertoire.[4]

Amid the talent in the Fairfax band, Dizzy stood out. Smith recalled:

> My first impression [of Dizzy] was that he was one of those walk-loud, talk-loud characters. Certainly, he was brash, forthright, and mercilessly honest, but I found out eventually that despite the nickname "Dizzy" he was anything but dumb. Beneath that sometimes humorous exterior was a cool, calculating, and analytical mind. . . .
>
> Dizzy always had an acute sense of harmony. He would change the chordal background of a stock or standard tune until it fit his higher harmonic sense. To play with Dizzy was an aesthetic experience in that we basically had to relearn a standard tune like "Body and Soul" to conform to his musical requirements. His reaction to

a mistake was immediate. He would yell out his correction at the danger spot even while soloing.[5]

The Fairfax band prospered during 1936 as it alternated engagements at the Strand and other Philadelphia clubs with tours to nearby communities in Pennsylvania, New Jersey, Maryland, and Delaware. Occasionally the trips were marred by encounters with institutionalized racism; in Hagerstown, Maryland, for example, four band members were arrested when they innocently violated an 8:00 p.m. curfew for blacks.

Dizzy had a more violent racial encounter one night as he walked home from an engagement. He remembered:

In South Philly there were a lot of gangsters who used to grab little colored guys off the street and beat 'em up and throw 'em out in the woods half dead. One time . . . three white guys in a car pulled up close to me and say, "Comere, boy." I just kept walking. . . . I used to carry a knife all the time in those days and I got it out— ready. . . . The car pulls alongside the curb and one of these guys reached out the car and *grabbed* me. . . . When he grabbed me, I almost cut his arm off (with the knife). Listen, his arm was hangin'! Then I tore out running! They turned the wrong way on a one way street chasing after me, and I could hear this guy going, "Naw, naw, leave him alone. To the hospital, the hospital!"[6]

At about this time, Dizzy had his first romantic encounter with a white woman, a short affair that he could not enjoy because the potential consequences of an interracial romance scared him too much.

In the autumn of 1936, Tiny Bradshaw lured Shavers and Warwick away from Fairfax with salary increases. They tried to convince Dizzy to join them, to keep their clique intact, but he wasn't yet ready to leave his mama and the security of his family. With Shavers gone, he became Fairfax's leading soloist.

Roy Eldridge went into Chicago's Three Deuces Club with his own stellar nine-piece band in September 1936 and four months later reached a new peak when his group recorded seven tracks;

one ("After You've Gone") is a masterpiece, another ("Heckler's Hop") comes close, and the rest are well above average.

Eldridge began "After You've Gone" with a melody statement that contained a serpentine break that presaged the incredible energy to be released in his improvised choruses. The intensity level was lowered during Gladys Palmer's undistinguished vocal, but quickly rocketed skyward as Eldridge returned to build his two-chorus improvisation around three incendiary breaks that top each other in heat and invention; the climax occurred in the final break as he snaked downward through four clusters of notes and slowed the tempo. He rounded out the solo with a bravura flourish. On "After You've Gone," Eldridge reached new peaks of trumpeting passion as he carried the listener forward on a journey of joyous audacity. His first chorus on "Heckler's Hop," a riff tune taken at a brisk tempo, provides a supple, harmonically fascinating lead into the second, where Eldridge piles climax upon climax in two blood-curdling excursions into the upper register.

Dizzy listened to the records almost every day following their issue in April 1937, and, as he practiced, he attempted to bring to his playing more of Eldridge's scalding intensity. His first recording the following month demonstrates that he made great progress in this direction.

In early 1937, the Fairfax organization moved several rungs up the professional ladder when it became the house band at the Nixon Grand Theater in west Philadelphia. The Nixon Grand was a huge, ornate movie palace built for white audiences but abandoned by them as the black population expanded into the surrounding area during the early 1930s. First-run movies alternated three times a day with stage shows featuring a chorus line, novelty acts, stand-up comedians, dancers such as Bojangles Robinson, and, at times, top-drawer bands such as the Lunceford, Waller, Basie, and Ellington aggregations.

Each of the Fairfax musicians earned forty-five dollars per week, and sometimes they made their money without playing a note. When a major orchestra such as Ellington's or Lunceford's headed the bill, the Fairfax group had to be on hand but were not always required to perform.

On March 3, 1937, the Swing Era reached a new level of intensity when, during Benny Goodman's first show at New York's Paramount Theater, hundreds of screaming spectators left their seats to dance in the aisles. *Variety* called the outburst "tradition-shattering in its spontaneity, its unanimity, its sincerity, its volume, in the child-like violence of its manifestations." The hysteria continued throughout 1937 and 1938 as screaming and dancing in the aisles became a liberating ritual for middle-class kids throughout the United States.[7]

During Goodman's two-week run at the Paramount, Shavers and Warwick left Tiny Bradshaw for better paying jobs with Lucky Millinder's very popular orchestra. They soon set about convincing Millinder that he should replace the group's third trumpeter, the excellent Harry "Sweets" Edison, with Dizzy. When Millinder made a halfhearted commitment, they thought they had a deal, but they were mistaken. Dizzy moved to New York around March 15 and was paid by Millinder for a few weeks, but he never performed with the group as the bandleader refused to fire Edison.

The Fairfax musicians envied Dizzy's move to New York, not realizing that it would result in disappointment. W. O. Smith remembered, "Being sent for was every musician's dream; it was recognition and status. Usually it meant New York with a nationally known outfit. . . . We were traumatized when we lost Dizzy Gillespie. . . . The trauma pointed up everybody's desire to get better and hope somebody would notice. New York was the end of the rainbow."[8] Dizzy decided to stick it out at the end of the rainbow. As he later told a journalist, "There was no question of going back to Philadelphia. I was much too ashamed to show my face after a failure like that."[9]

Frugality was not one of Dizzy's virtues, and his finances were precarious when he arrived in New York. He stayed initially with cousins in semisuburban Queens but wanted to be in the middle of the action in Harlem and soon moved into a one-room apartment there with J.P., the older brother who had run away from Cheraw and their father's anger fifteen years before. J.P., who was in his early thirties, was earning $12.50 per week as a busboy in a midtown restaurant. He allowed Dizzy to board rent-free in the $6.50 per week flat on 142nd Street, and he gave him thirty-five cents a day, which was enough for a big meal at a nearby restaurant.

Dizzy scuffled hard, as, with the help of Shavers and Warwick, he threw himself into the seething jazz life of New York, earning fees wherever he could. While meeting musicians such as Kenny "Klook" Clarke and Mario Bauzá, who would later play important roles in his career, he performed at after-hours clubs such as George's in Greenwich Village and Small's, Monroe's Uptown House, and Wells's in Harlem. He became a fixture at the Savoy with Chick Webb, where he sat next to Bauzá in the trumpet section, and with the Teddy Hill, Claude Hopkins, Savoy Sultans, and Willie Bryant orchestras. Webb, who rarely allowed outside musicians to play in his band, was strongly impressed by Dizzy's talents; when he encouraged him to take solos, word spread in the jazz community that Dizzy was a comer.

After his gigs, Dizzy usually arrived at J.P.'s apartment around 5:00 a.m. with a young woman on his arm. His brother would give him the room and sit in a nearby park until 7:00 a.m., when it was time to board the subway to work.

In late April 1937, Dizzy heard that Teddy Hill was seeking a replacement for trumpeter Frankie Newton, who eighteen months previously had taken the Roy Eldridge chair when Roy left Hill to join Fletcher Henderson. Hill was committed to a European tour that Newton did not want to join because he was rehearsing a group of his own for a nightclub engagement in Greenwich Village.

Hill had heard Dizzy perform in Philadelphia in late 1935 and was impressed by his talents when he sat in at the Savoy with Hill's band and with Webb's. And he was particularly intrigued by the closeness of Dizzy's style to that of the very popular Eldridge.

Hill, a middling saxophone player, had built a solid dance orchestra from 1932 onward and by 1937 was meeting the exacting standards of the Savoy crowd six months a year; the rest of the time, the band performed at the top black East Coast theaters, venues such as New York's Apollo, Philadelphia's Lincoln, and

Washington's Howard. His 1937 unit boasted top-drawer soloists in trombonist Dicky Wells, multireedman Russell Procope, saxophonist Howard Johnson, and trumpeter Shad Collins.

Forever the clown, Dizzy performed his audition for Hill in early May in gloves and an overcoat; unsuspecting, he had walked into a wasp's nest of opposition.

A clique of Hill veterans led by Wells and Collins were pushing their own candidates for the Eldridge/Newton position, and they resented Dizzy's precocious talent and were put off by his clowning. These feelings were exacerbated when, for the audition, Hill asked Dizzy to replace Collins in the second trumpet chair, which was awarded the lion's share of the solos, and moved Collins to the third chair, where he was relegated to less demanding ensemble work. The old-timers were hostile as Dizzy improvised in the Eldridge manner, but the more they taunted him, the better he played.

Several of the veterans threatened to quit when Hill decided to hire Dizzy in the second trumpet slot at forty-five dollars per week while working in the United States and seventy dollars per week during the European tour. But Hill called their bluff, and they soon backed down. During the second week of May 1937, only eight weeks after his discouraging arrival in New York, Dizzy had made it to the big leagues. He was not yet twenty.

9
SEEDS OF REBELLION

THE TEDDY HILL BAND THAT DIZZY JOINED WAS CONSIDERABLY better than the group that featured Roy Eldridge and Chu Berry two and a half years earlier. The 1937 group evidenced a more precise and cohesive attack, a fuller ensemble sound, and a more powerful swing than the earlier aggregation.

All agree that by 1937 the Duke Ellington Orchestra was in a class by itself, attaining a level of creativity beyond the reach of any other late-1930s group. The Hill band was just a step behind the great black orchestras who were on the rung below Ellington—Webb, Lunceford, Calloway, and Carter.

Dizzy quickly discovered that his work with Frankie Fairfax had not brought his skills to the level that Hill demanded. He could read and improvise well, but he was deficient in such subtleties of big band trumpeting as creating a consistent vibrato, phrasing and attacking in unison with the other brass players, and sustaining long tones.

Bill Dillard, in the first trumpet chair, was responsible for the performance of the three-man trumpet group, and he became Dizzy's tutor in big band technique. Dizzy improved rapidly under his tutelage and in later years always heaped praise on Dillard for his help. Adding to the pressure on Dizzy was the hostility of the Wells-Collins clique. Collins interpreted his new assignment as third trumpet as a demotion, and he and his pals openly and constantly derided Dizzy, who contained his anger as he concentrated on improving his craft.

In the midst of this melodrama, Dizzy had to prepare for a May 17, 1937, recording session at the end of his first week with the band, and to deal with a mini-crisis concerning his passport.

Time was short, because the band was scheduled to leave for Europe on May 27, and the passport office was demanding that Lottie Gillespie sign several documents for her son, who at nineteen was still legally a minor. Dizzy was forced to break away from much-needed rehearsals to travel with Hill to Philadelphia to ensure that she do this properly.

The May 17 session, which marked Dizzy's recording debut, took place in New York and produced six tracks: four insipid pop tunes sung by Dillard and two rousing instrumentals, "King Porter Stomp" and "Blue Rhythm Fantasy." Dizzy soloed on both of the instrumentals and two of Dillard's songs, and he did not forget that Hill had hired him because he sounded like Roy Eldridge. Rising above his travails, he improvised with both verve and imagination and performed competently in the ensemble passages.

On Dillard's vocal feature, "I'm Happy, Darling, Dancing with You," Dizzy swung a melodic eight-bar break with the assurance of a veteran, and when he followed the singer on "Yours and Mine," he used a burnished tone to create a tingling urgency in his improvisation. Dizzy began his half chorus on the brooding "Blue Rhythm Fantasy" with powerful phrases punched out in the middle register and followed them with a typical rising and descending Eldridge figure; but he failed to finish the solo with a flourish, and it ended in an almost inaudible two-bar flurry. The listener is left wishing that the recording engineer had asked for another take.

These three solos were but preludes to Dizzy's main contribution to the session, his extended work on "King Porter Stomp," a jazz perennial that Jelly Roll Morton wrote in 1902. The first score that Fletcher Henderson delivered to Benny Goodman for the *Let's Dance* radio show was his arrangement of "King Porter Stomp," and Goodman's recording, made in June 1935, was his first megahit. A cheerful but somewhat plodding affair with fine solos by trumpeter Bunny Berigan and Goodman, the record became an aural icon for masses of Swing Era fans. Henderson himself recorded the tune four times, and his group's 1933 version, featuring trumpeter Henry "Red" Allen, is arguably the best rendition of the piece.

Hill's version, noticeably superior to Goodman's, was loosely based on Henderson's arrangement and was set up to showcase Dizzy's talents. He played the Berigan/Allen role but was given considerably more solo space than the other two men, who were established stars when they interpreted the tune; the quality of his improvisations, though derivative of Eldridge, is at least equal to theirs. Following a short introduction, Dizzy entered with a powerful half chorus punctuated by fiery Eldridge licks. When he returned midway through the recording, he built his solo from an insistent, nagging phrase in the middle register to a bristling high-note climax, and then drove the entire band for two rollicking "out" choruses to complete a confident, uninhibited performance.

Dizzy's phrasing came from Eldridge, but his sound was very different. Eldridge cultivated a raspy, buzzy tone that heightened the emotional intensity of his playing. In contrast, Dizzy's tone, like Louis Armstrong's, was clean and pure. It was slender, however, with nothing of the breadth and buttery richness that Armstrong achieved. As Dizzy's career progressed, he added considerable heft to his sound.

Dizzy continued to work intensively on technique with Dillard as the band headed for France in late May on the *Île de France*, a premier ocean liner. The Hill group was part of a show-biz extravaganza called The Cotton Club Revue, which was scheduled to perform for six weeks in Paris and, possibly, for several additional weeks in the British Isles. A French promoter had booked the revue into Paris to coincide with Exposition Internationale 1937, a major cultural and commercial fair that attracted thirty-one million spectators.[1]

The revue was put together by the man who had produced and directed the show at the Cotton Club in New York, and he employed sixty-two entertainers; in addition to the thirteen-piece Hill band, the package included the outstanding singer Alberta Hunter, the dancer Bill Bailey (Pearl Bailey's brother), who performed the tap routines Bill "Bojangles" Robinson had made famous, a "tramp" band comprising two kazoo players and a four-man rhythm section featuring a washboard artist, the acrobatic Berry Brothers dance team, several novelty vaudeville acts, a troupe of Lindy Hoppers, and a bevy of chorines. With the exception of a thirteen-year-old Berry brother who traveled with his mother, Dizzy was the youngest of the performers.

Many of the *Île de France* passengers enjoyed a daily treat as they watched the revue's entertainers polish their acts in one of the ship's ballrooms. The Hill band participated in every rehearsal, as they were required to accompany all the acts and play for dancers as well. Dizzy had musical energy to burn and spent his spare time jamming with members of the tramp band.

The show opened on June 11, 1937, with a week at Les Ambassadeurs cabaret, and then moved on to Le Moulin Rouge, the large and famous nightclub, for five successful weeks.

The enthusiastic patrons, who had never seen Lindy Hoppers before, made the spectacular dancers their favorites and tried, tentatively but energetically, to emulate them when they took their turns on the dance floor. Leonard Feather, the British writer, waxed enthusiastic in *Melody Maker*, England's equivalent of *Downbeat*: "This band, with the whole superb Cotton Club revue at the Moulin Rouge, defies any brief description. For the present, let it be said that no greater band, except Ellington's, has ever come to Europe."[2] Hughes Panassié, who, with his good friend Charles Delauney, operated France's first important jazz magazine, *Jazz Hot*, and its first jazz record label, Swing, agreed: "Besides Duke Ellington's Orchestra, this is the best band which ever came to France."[3] He also noticed Dizzy: "John Gillespie has a tremendous swing: his style, very much like Roy Eldridge's, is not my ideal, but he is so sincere I like him a lot."[4]

Although Dizzy began every day by listening to Eldridge's recording of "After You've Gone," discerning listeners recognized that he was beginning to move out from the shadow of his idol as he experimented with new harmonic concepts and developed a more varied rhythmic attack.

Bill Dillard found Dizzy's approach to improvising foreign to anything he had experienced previously, and French jazz critic Maurice Cillaz wrote: "He was already playing in a way which differentiated him from Roy Eldridge. He had a varied and powerful style."[5] Buddy Johns, the pianist and leader of the tramp band, practiced with Dizzy during afternoons at Le Moulin Rouge and remembered that Dizzy insisted on inserting fresh chord progressions into standard tunes. Johnson found the new harmonies somewhat unsettling, but Dizzy could not stand still; he was heeding a revolutionary urge, an inner imperative to expand the boundaries of jazz.

On July 7, 1937, Panassié organized a recording session that, under Dicky Wells's leadership, brought together members of the Hill band with one of its former stars, Bill Coleman, a graceful and lyrical trumpet player who had moved from New York to Paris in 1935. Gypsy guitarist Django Reinhardt, Europe's greatest jazz musician, also participated.

Panassié had two main aims: to feature Dicky Wells, who at age thirty had become a master trombone improviser, and to create a happy reunion for Coleman and his old colleagues.

Dizzy was very angry that he was not invited, but he had to know that his feud with Wells and Shad Collins precluded his participation. In addition, the bandstand was crowded. Panassié wished to provide solo space for Wells, three trumpeters, and Reinhardt, and the three-minute limit of standard 78 rpm recordings could not comfortably accommodate another improviser.

The results were spectacular, as the men created six sunny Swing Era gems. Reinhardt swung the group seemingly without effort, the ensemble passages were performed with élan, and all five soloists sparkled. A follow-up quintet session by Panassié on July 11 showcased Wells's talents.

Dizzy let neither his deep resentment against the Wells-Collins clique nor his lack of opportunities to jam with local musicians cramp his style in the City of Lights. He began a lifelong infatuation with photography there, and, when not working to push jazz in new directions or performing, he and Hill's guitarist, John Smith, spent many hours partying in the whorehouses and sightseeing.

Union and Ministry of Labour restrictions made British work permits for foreign musicians difficult to come by, and permission from the British officials for the Cotton Club Revue was not granted until well into the Moulin Rouge engagement. The British allowed the Hill musicians to perform only as accompanists, and their bodily movements were restricted to what was necessary to play their instruments.

The show was immediately booked into London's Palladium Theater for a four-week engagement starting July 26, 1937. As the correspondent for *Melody Maker* reflected, the band and the show excited the crowds: "When it goes to town, it is something like a real Harlem band. The dizzy speed of the dancing, the garish colors of the settings and costumes, the restless music and whirling movement of the whole production appeared to leave the public in a daze as they walked out."[6] Overflow crowds caused the Palladium to exercise an option for an additional week, and the revue completed the junket with bookings in Dublin and Manchester. Dizzy relished the opportunity to jam with local musicians in both London and Manchester.

He had curbed his temptation to spend money during the tour by lending small sums to his fellow musicians, but his resolve broke down in London as he splurged in the whorehouses and invested in a magnificent twin-breasted, green tweed overcoat and a homburg hat.

Soon after his return to New York on September 21, Dizzy received depressing news: the musicians' union, citing an arcane regulation, ruled that his trip to Europe had invalidated his transfer from the Philadelphia local to the one in New York. As a consequence, the union limited him to one-night gigs in New York or short out-of-town tours as it barred him for ninety days from steady employment with Hill or any other band. For any work outside New York, he had to obtain permission in advance from an official of the local. He suffered true privation as he was forced to scramble for work until well into January 1938.

Dizzy's place in musical history rests firmly on his crucially important role in two upheavals that radically changed and enriched the art of jazz: the bebop revolution and the Afro-Cuban revolution.

Ironically, it was during this ninety-day stretch of economic hardship that the seeds of these revolutions were planted and nurtured; during that short period, he discovered Afro-Cuban music, began to work with the drummer Kenny "Klook" Clarke on the rhythmic foundations of what would become bebop, and met the woman who would provide him with the support that allowed him to pursue his revolutionary aims—Lorraine Willis.

As he struggled to make ends meet, Dizzy found that his best meal ticket was Cass Carr, a West Indian performer whose specialty was the musical saw. Carr had built a following among the Communist faithful and played at their functions in varied venues in New York City and its suburbs. Dizzy believed that currying favor with them would help him get gigs, and he was for a brief time a card-carrying member of the party.

Dizzy found occasional employment outside New York with a band led by Edgar Hayes, an accomplished pianist, composer, and arranger. Hayes had organized his band in early 1936 at age thirty-two after a five-year apprenticeship as musical director of a fine New York group, the Mills Blue Rhythm Band. He hired a solid assortment of soloists and sidemen who recorded prolifically during 1937, producing what Gunther Schuller has described as "some of the brightest, smartest, and expertly swinging jazz to be found in Harlem." One of his stars was Kenny Clarke, whom Dizzy had met soon after arriving in New York seven months earlier.

Dizzy turned as well for sustenance to Mario Bauzá, the Chick Webb trumpeter who had also befriended him during his first

days in New York. Bauzá, a black Cuban, was able to secure for
Dizzy gigs with salsa bands in East Harlem, and Dizzy experienced an epiphany as he heard for the first time the passionate
and intricately twined percussion lines laid down by the conga,
bongo, and timbale players. As he told me in 1990:

> Africa hit me all at once in those little clubs in Spanish Harlem. Got
> right into my marrow. I found my musical heritage, my roots there.
>
> African slaves in America were not allowed to practice their
> own religions or to use the drum, their main instrument for com-
> munication and ceremony. In places like Cuba and Brazil, slaves
> could keep their drums and their cultural and religious roots with
> Africa. They could continue their tradition of talking to each other
> with the drums.
>
> The Africa they wouldn't let us have in South Carolina I discov-
> ered for myself in East Harlem in 1937. I began a lifelong crusade to
> make that Afro-Cuban stuff part of our music.[7]

After his East Harlem experience, the seeds of two musical passions began to grow simultaneously in Dizzy. The first one, which
had taken root at Laurinburg and which continued to germinate in
Paris, was to take the inherited harmonic and rhythmic materials
of swing and to transform them into something more profound
and exciting, something that later came to be called bebop.

East Harlem confirmed for Dizzy the strength and truth of a
second passion—the African rhythmic heritage that he had always felt deeply and that he shared with people as diverse as the
folks in the Sanctified Church on Huger Street, Brazilian *sam-
baistas*, Cuban *congeros*, James Brown, and Louis Armstrong. The
power of this heritage would infuse everything he did thereafter.

Dizzy met Lorraine Willis on an occasion when he sneaked a
gig in Washington, DC, with Edgar Hayes without getting permission from the union. A young widow, she danced in a chorus
line on the TOBA circuit—a group of black theaters in major
cities in the East, the Midwest, and the South. TOBA stood for
Theater Owners Booking Association but was known among the
entertainers as Tough On Black Asses; the pay was low, the conditions spartan, and the hours long.

Dizzy was impressed by Lorraine's beauty and her values. She preferred knitting in her hotel room to hanging out in bars and after-hours joints, she read her Bible, and she did not sleep around as many of the chorus girls did. At first she paid little attention to the notes and telephone messages he left for her, but another dancer, Alice Lyons, convinced her that Dizzy was a serious young man, and she agreed to date him.

Soon after he met Lorraine, Dizzy hit rock bottom financially. His brother J.P. had instantly doubled Dizzy's rent by moving out of their apartment without notice, and the gigs dried up completely.

When Lorraine saw him begging backstage at the Apollo for fifteen cents to buy a bowl of soup, she began to help him in earnest. He discovered later that she had been giving her mother, for household expenses, ten dollars from her weekly twenty-two-dollar salary. When the older woman perceived that a romance was budding, she told Lorraine to spend the ten dollars on her new beau and herself. The relationship became considerably more serious when Lorraine moved in with Dizzy soon after. Thus began more than fifty-five years of support and sustenance.

10
DIZZY AND KLOOK: THE BIRTH OF BEBOP

THE FIRST MUSICAL FRUITS OF LORRAINE'S SUPPORT WERE the radical innovations Dizzy fostered in the new year, 1938, when he helped drummer Kenny "Klook" Clarke to inaugurate the bebop revolution.

As Bill Dillard, Maurice Cullaz, and Buddy Johnson testified in Paris, Dizzy had already begun in 1937 to forge a revolutionary style of improvising. But he had been on his own. For the first time, during his short engagements in late 1937 with the Hayes band, he found a true collaborator and kindred spirit in Clarke. The drummer, like Dizzy, was driven by a strong inner force he could not contain, an urge to transform and enrich his art.

The bebop revolution radically recast both the rhythmic and the harmonic bases of jazz, and the men who made it were very serious about their music. It is ironic, therefore, that its name was constructed from two nonsense syllables. Among the many myths about the origin of the word, the most plausible involves Dizzy's interview with a journalist in 1944. The writer asked him about the cadence of one of Dizzy's tunes, and Dizzy sang, "bebop-a-rebop-a-bebop." The reporter replied, "Oh. You play bebop music," and the name stuck. The practitioners of bebop preferred to use a more serious name for their music, modern jazz.

Clarke's innovations were an outgrowth of advances made previously by Chick Webb and Count Basie's drummer, Jo Jones.

Webb wrought a fundamental change in jazz percussion during the early 1930s. He eschewed the drummer's traditional function as an accompanist and became a conductor, leading his band from center stage with a mesmerizing power, intensity, and virtuosity that drove audiences wild. Webb established the basic rhythm with the foot pedal of his bass drum, and almost all of his work had a two-beat feel; that is, he emphasized beats two and four in the normal swing four-beat measure, and legions of percussionists followed his lead. Webb's brilliant solos exploited the entire dynamic range of the jazz drum set, which is illustrated, from the drummer's point of view, in figure 1 (next page).

Jo Jones, while with Basie in 1934, pioneered a major change that differentiated him from Webb and the other drummers of his time. Instead of laying down the basic rhythm with his right foot on the bass drum, he created it by moving his right arm across his body to strike the hi-hat cymbal, which, as we can see in figure 1, sat to his left. While doing this, he would—for tonal emphasis at appropriate moments—open and close the hi-hat's two opposing plates with his left foot. He reinforced the hi-hat beats by striking the snare drum with the stick in his left hand and by employing subtle strokes on the bass drum. Occasionally he would play rhythmic counterpoints between his foot on the hi-hat and his right stick on the ride cymbal to his right. And he frequently substituted an even, four-beat pulse for Webb's more insistent two-beat rhythm.

By replacing the insistent pounding of the bass drum with the metallic, legato hiss of the hi-hat cymbal, Jones created a more fluid pulse and a more compelling, relaxed, and subtle swing. As

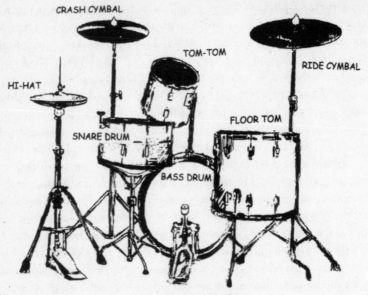

Figure 1: Jazz Drum Set

the scholar Albert Murray has written, "Sometimes, indeed, it was as if Jo Jones only whispered the beat."[1]

Jones and the Basie band had arrived in New York from its Kansas City base in late 1936. After a faltering start, they redeemed themselves with a highly professional March 1937 engagement at the Apollo and prospered on the New York scene thereafter.

Jones became the king of jazz percussion when he bested Webb in an epic drum battle at the Savoy on January 16, 1938. The entire Goodman band was there and Duke Ellington sat in as thousands attended and thousands more were turned away by the police. Webb's "hometown" Savoy fans had idolized him for years and secured for his band a victory over the Kansas City up-starts in the printed ballots that were a Savoy tradition. But the critics, who had consistently sided with Webb in previous band battles, now sided with Basie and Jones.

Bill Rowe of the influential black newspaper the *Pittsburgh Courier* saw Basie "as the close winner," and the writer from Harlem's *Amsterdam News* also leaned slightly toward him: "Chick took the aggressive, with the Count playing along easily, and, on the whole, more musically, scientifically. Undismayed by Chick's forceful drum beating, . . . the Count maintained an attitude of poise and self-assurance. He constantly parried Chick's thundering haymakers with tantalizing runs and arpeggios."[2]

What is more, the reviewer from the established industry magazine *Metronome* came down firmly for Basie. Under the headline "Basie's Brilliant Band Conquers Chick's," he wrote:

> Basie had everything that night. Seldom has any band, any place, cut loose with such unmitigated swing. . . . The battle was one of solid swing versus sensational swing. . . . Basie's band devoted its attack to the body, to the heart . . . with a steady rhythmic attack (led by Jones) that was truly devastating. . . . All the men settled into one unbeatable groove after another and were held fast by the stupendous drumming of Jo Jones. . . . Chick, on the other hand, suffered from an inability to settle into a rhythmic groove.[3]

Even as Jo Jones was being anointed the new monarch of jazz drumming, Kenny Clarke was beginning to subvert his reign.

Clarke, who was born into a musical family in Pittsburgh in 1914, played the organ at church at age twelve, took up the drums in junior high, and dropped out of high school at age fifteen in 1929 to become a full-time professional. During the next six years, he sharpened his percussion skills and learned to play the vibraphone in bands in Pennsylvania, Ohio, West Virginia, and Missouri. This apprenticeship included an eighteen-month stint with another Pittsburgh native, Roy Eldridge, whom he idolized.

Clarke decided in late 1935 to test himself in New York's competitive jazz cauldron, and his talents soon brought him success with a trio in a Harlem club. He was featured on both vibes and drums, and his brother Frank played bass. Soon after, the saxophonist Lonnie Simmons hired the brothers for his sextet at the Black Cat Club in Greenwich Village for an engagement that would last for almost a year. The Black Cat combo included such outstanding performers as guitarist Freddie Green and trumpeter Bobby Moore, who both later found acclaim with Count Basie, and it played at a level high enough to draw serious attention from both Benny Goodman and Basie.

Goodman, Basie, and Goodman sidemen Gene Krupa, Harry James, Lionel Hampton, Teddy Wilson, and Vido Musso often visited the Black Cat to sit in and jam with the house band—sometimes till 10:00 a.m. John Hammond, a Vanderbilt heir who had just embarked on a remarkably successful career as a record producer and who was a Goodman adviser, was so impressed by the sextet that he paid their union dues.

Clarke respected greatly the way Chick Webb and Jo Jones created the dynamic rhythms that drove their bands. But he wanted to take the drums further; he wanted to make them an improvising, melodic voice in the ensemble, an equal partner with the other instruments. This is the key concept that drove all his revolutionary explorations.

Clarke's aesthetic was rooted in melody from the age of five, when he sat for hours on his mother's lap as they played tunes together. And this aesthetic became more firmly entrenched as he performed on the organ as a child and mastered the vibraphone as an adult.

At the Black Cat, he started to implement his ideas by breaking up the steady swing pulse to insert original rhythmic patterns that related to and reinforced the melody played by the other instruments. One of these phrases, which sounded like "klook-a-mop," was later shortened to "klook" and earned him his nickname. Clarke worked especially hard with Green in developing his new concepts. "Freddie Green and I got something new going with Lonnie's band . . . long before the new rhythmic approach to playing drums was noticed. We'd come to the job early—at least 45 minutes before the other players—and work out patterns. The results were swinging."[4]

The sextet broke up in February 1937, but Clarke found a sympathetic climate for continuing his innovations when he joined Edgar Hayes's band during the same month.

As we have seen, Dizzy, newly arrived in New York, met Clarke just weeks after Klook joined Hayes—a critical juncture in the drummer's career. Hayes and his main lieutenant, Joe Garland, a saxophonist who was an excellent arranger and composer, recognized Clarke's promise and encouraged him to develop his groundbreaking percussion ideas. Clarke remembered, "That was the university for me. . . . They taught me everything. . . . The band gave me a chance to try all my possibilities, all the things I thought I was capable of doing."[5]

Garland commissioned Clarke to write new arrangements and also encouraged him to insert his ideas into existing arrangements:

> I began to change my style about 1937. . . . I was trying to make the drums more musical instead of just a dead beat. . . . The usual way of playing drums had become quite monotonous. Around this time, I began to play things with the band, with the drums as a real participating instrument with its own voice. I'd never heard anyone else do it before.
>
> Joe Garland . . . would write out a regular trumpet part for me to read. That's where I hit upon the idea of playing like that all the time. He'd just leave it to my own discretion to play the things out of the part that I thought the most effective. . . . I played rhythm patterns, and they were superimposed over the regular beat.[6]

As Gunther Schuller has pointed out, Clarke's work on a series of Hayes's recordings during 1937 and 1938 was truly revolutionary.

> While most drummers were converting to the ride and sock [hi-hat] cymbals by 1937, Clarke, a long-time admirer of Chick Webb, remained loyal to the snare drum and bass drum, using both instruments . . . to evolve a new style of drumming that integrated the drums much more into the arrangements and soloists' work. By participating in the orchestra's rhythmic figures as a full-fledged ensemble instrument, as well as injecting independent snare-drum figures increasingly into the accompaniments to soloists, the result was suddenly a true musical dialogue between drums and orchestra, a discourse lifting the drums (at least partially) out of their limited role as a mere provider of rhythmic substructures. . . . Clarke's

timing and sense of balance were superb, especially considering that he was pioneering a whole new concept of big-band drumming. . . . Here we have the beginnings of modern drumming.[7]

While Clarke was thriving with Hayes, Dizzy was scratching out a living with Hill and other bands in the New York area. Dizzy had returned to Hill with his new union card in January 1938, and he was happy to find that his nemesis, Shad Collins, was gone. Collins and Bill Dillard had been replaced by Al Killian and Joe Guy, young trumpeters sympathetic to Dizzy's modernist ideas. Recognizing that Dizzy had quickly mastered Dillard's teaching, Hill promoted him to the first trumpet chair vacated by his mentor. Hill also welcomed Dizzy into his family: "Dizzy made my home his home. He'd come in almost every day. He was very fond of my little daughter Gwendolyn, who was five or six years old; he'd wallow all over the floor, tell her candy wasn't good for her, then eat it all himself. Still a big kid."[8]

Tempering Dizzy's happiness with his promotion and his closeness to the Hills was the knowledge that the bandleader was now unable to provide steady employment. On his return from Europe, Hill was forced to scuffle because his group had lost its place as a house band at the Savoy, where it had been performing for six months every year. Dizzy found work with other groups to put bread on his table, and chief among them were the Savoy Sultans, a hard-swinging outfit that now occupied Hill's preeminent niche at the Savoy.

Dizzy and Clarke were reunited in late April 1938, four months after they had performed briefly together in the Hayes band. The occasion was an extended Hayes versus Teddy Hill "battle of the bands" tour of the South.

As the tour progressed, Clarke saw that there was something special about the man whose rhythmic precocity had dated back to his childhood experiments at the Sanctified Church on Huger Street in Cheraw.

I noticed something unique about Dizzy's playing, that's why I was hanging out with him. His approach to modern harmonies, but rhythms, mostly. He could take care of all that harmony, but his rhythms interested me real profoundly, and I just had to find out about that gift he had hidden in him, the gift of rhythm. It wasn't only his trumpet playing, he was doing a lotta other things that some people didn't see, but I saw the rhythmic aspect of it. The way he played and the way he would hum time and things like that. I knew it was avant-garde, ahead of time, so I just fell in line with what was going on.[9]

And Dizzy reciprocated the compliments:

By far, the most important thing that happened to me musically during this period (1938–39) was my friendship and association with the great drummer, Kenny Clarke. . . . Kenny was modifying the concept of rhythm in jazz, making it a much more fluid thing, and changing the entire role of the drummer, from just a man who kept time for dancers to a true accompanist who provided accents for soloists and constant inspiration to the jazz band as a whole. . . .

Kenny initiated a new language into the mainstream of jazz drumming. . . . He infused a new conception, a new language, into the dialogue of the drum, which is now *the* dialogue.[10]

The two men began experimenting rhythmically as they jammed together in their spare time on tour, and Dizzy was over-joyed when he saw an opportunity in July to put Hill's shaky prospects behind him and to work with Clarke full-time. When Hayes became exasperated with a trumpeter who continually messed up the band's more complicated arrangements, Clarke en-thusiastically championed Dizzy for the job. Hayes's trombonist Clyde Bernhardt remembered the audition and Dizzy's impact on the band:

"Goddamn, there he is," shouts Kenny. "This here boy'll play your goddamn music, and he'll take it apart. . . ."

Wasn't but a minute that the band lit out on *Bugle Call Rag*. Old Diz played every damn note that was written there. Edgar [Hayes] started laughing. "Take it down again for me." . . . Dizzy played flawlessly again.

"Fess," said Dizzy, "take it down again for *me*." . . . Now Dizzy turned his back to the music and played the entire number from memory. Everybody about fell out. . . .

Everybody got to like Diz, kept a lot of life in the band. Diz was a born comedian. . . . One time during a number he slid off his seat and sat on the floor, blowing and turning his horn all kinds of funny ways.

Another time, he rose from his chair while playing, came down, and pushed Hayes halfway off the piano bench. With his right hand he chorded some extra harmony, then slowly walked back to his seat and sat down, not missing a note the whole time.

"That's the biggest fool I ever saw in my life," Hayes said. But the audience loved it, thought it was part of the act, and had a good laugh.[11]

Dizzy and Clarke performed together with Hayes for about two months until Clarke left to join the Claude Hopkins Orchestra in September 1938. The bebop revolution was born during those sixty days as the two men began to work on the rhythmic concepts that would lead to seminal breakthroughs several months later when they renewed their experiments with Teddy Hill.

Dizzy remained with Hayes until mid-November 1938, when he left to perform his first extended Latin jazz engagement with the band of Cuban flautist Alberto Socarrás, a first-rate group that was good enough to perform at the Savoy opposite Chick Webb.

With Socarrás, Dizzy confirmed what he had discovered in the salsa bands of East Harlem the previous year: he had a deep subconscious affinity, not only for the rhythms but also for the chords, scales, and harmonies of Latin music. In contrast, he knew that his soul made little connection with the same elements in the blues, another African-derived music:

I don't consider myself a blues man. . . . When I hear the blues, I hear Lips [Page] play the blues, and it's different from me. Mine ain't the real blues with toe jam between your toes, come in and bend a note around the corner. . . .

In our music we've got different strains. I worked on developing modern jazz of a different kind, more like mixing hot peppers in a dish of black-eye peas or macaroni. . . . I was influenced by Latin. If you play any of my tunes in Latin countries, they understand it. I was always more of a Latin player. . . . I don't know where it comes from, because my early training was to sit and listen to music in the Sanctified church, and I've always said that spirituals were blues too. You need a psychiatrist to figure that one out.[12]

Socarrás, an esteemed veteran, confirmed that Dizzy, the South Carolina neophyte, had Latino musical blood running through his veins. The bandleader commented that Dizzy's "style was very Cuban" and that he "phrased his solos marvelously" in the Cuban idiom.[13]

Teddy Hill's fortunes had revived by early 1939, and he was able to hire Dizzy full-time as the lead trumpet player when the Socarrás engagement ended. Dizzy immediately lobbied Hill to hire Clarke away from Claude Hopkins, and by April 1939 he had succeeded. At this point, Clarke was frustrated; he had progressed since 1937 on making the drum set a melodic voice and a force for rhythmic freedom, but he couldn't yet create physically everything he heard in his head. He lacked the technical means to achieve his goals. During a few short months with Hill, he solved, with Dizzy's help, his technical problems.

Clarke's discoveries, two in number, laid the rhythmic foundation for the bebop revolution and set a standard for jazz percussion that prevails to this day. Look again at figure 1 (page 78) to visualize what he did.

His first discovery involved his right arm. Bringing his right arm across his left arm to play the pulse on the hi-hat cymbal in the accepted Jo Jones manner severely restricted what Clarke could do with his left arm. So he opened his body and extended his right arm in the opposite direction to create the pulse on the ride cymbal. He recalled the transformation:

Everyone wanted me to play like Jo Jones, but I didn't want to play like that. I changed over to the top (ride) cymbal, which gave me the freedom of my left hand. Because Jo, he was cramped. . . .

I wanted to do something completely different. Freeing my left hand. My idea was to never leave your left hand idle. It's like a one-handed piano player. I began to work on it. . . . I talked to Diz about it, and he said, "That's a perfect combination. Now you have the whole thing working."

Dizzy understood, being a rhythmical musician. All kinds of rhythms fascinated him. I used to write out little things, and Dizzy was right behind me. I would write out a little thing and I would hand it back to him. I'd say, "Hey, Diz, how do you think this would sound." He'd say, "Well, try it."[14]

And there was an additional benefit. By moving the beat to the ride cymbal, Clarke created a wash of sound, a more fluid, shimmering swing than could be achieved on the hi-hat: "I found out I could get pitch and timbre variations up there, according to the way I struck the cymbal, and a pretty sound. The beat had a better flow. It was lighter and tastier."[15] The lighter, tastier cymbal sound soon became the standard for jazz rhythm that has persisted to this day.

Clarke's second important discovery happened fortuitously. It involved the bass drum, whose function until then was to provide a steady beat. One night, when the Hill band was performing "Old Man River" at an ultrafast tempo, Clarke's right leg became so tired playing the unswerving beat that he switched to playing creative accents at appropriate moments. He found that the practice released so much creativity that he adopted it thereafter.

The fruit of these discoveries is what Clarke called "coordinated independence." By this he meant that his four limbs undertook independent roles that, when coordinated by his mind, created a unity, a melodic ensemble voice. His right hand played the basic beat on the ride cymbal, his right foot made comments on the bass drum, his left hand ranged over the snare, the tom-tom, and the crash cymbal to create a continuing stream of melody, and his left foot reinforced on the hi-hat the ride cymbal rhythm.

In other words, the right hand and the left foot set the rhythmic pulse while the right foot and, most important, the left hand were given freedom to fashion percussive melodic patterns of any length or shape; the two limbs became creative forces, commentators, improvisers. In short, Clarke had elevated the drums from a time-keeping role to an improvising voice in the ensemble on an equal footing with the other instruments.

This appealed tremendously to Dizzy, who felt severely constricted by the steady swing band rhythms. As he matured as a musician, his natural propensity was to create phrases of varied length, phrases that began and ended at odd places in the bar. Clarke's revolutionary drumming was the ideal inspiration for him to develop to great heights the rhythmically free and asymmetrical style of improvising that felt so natural to him. Dizzy felt proud to have been a helpmate in Clarke's discoveries, and he would make great use of them as he moved to the forefront of the bebop revolution in the years ahead.

Clarke's first opportunity to consolidate his advances in percussion came at the 1939 New York World's Fair. The Hill band opened on the fair's first day, April 30, just two weeks after he had come on board. The group alternated with Chick Webb's band backing a Lindy Hopper dance troupe at the Savoy Pavilion, a rough facsimile of the Savoy Ballroom located in a honky-tonk amusement area called Freedomland; the concession was managed by the owners of the Savoy. Clarke and Dizzy had plenty of opportunity to collaborate, because they were required to play ten shows a day.

The death of Webb at age thirty on June 16 cast a pall over the entire proceedings. He succumbed following an operation for his worsening spinal tuberculosis, and his last words were, "I'm sorry, but I've got to go." Ella Fitzgerald, his star singer, kept the band intact for two years following his passing.

Hill's musicians were never happy with the World's Fair engagement, because the union had decreed a lower than normal pay scale for the grueling gig. When Hill backed his men strongly in a confrontation with Savoy management in early July, the entire band was fired. Hill had lost both the fair gig and his foothold at the Savoy and was forced to scramble for bookings; when he was idle, Dizzy and Clarke found sporadic employment with Edgar

Hayes's group.

Dizzy had become so fond of Lorraine Willis that he began to have fantasies about marrying her. She, however, felt wary about hooking up with someone whose income flow was as uncertain as his. Her job in the Apollo chorus line was their main source of income, and they were barely able to make ends meet.

When she heard that a trumpet chair in Cab Calloway's orchestra had been vacant for several weeks, she began a campaign to find Dizzy a job with the group, one of the nation's highest-paying bands. She secured help from two people: Mario Bauzá, who was performing with Calloway at the Cotton Club, and Calloway's valet, Rudolph. Bauzá feigned sickness one night in late July and sent Dizzy in as his substitute. Dizzy recalled what happened: "He told me to let Lamar Wright take all the first parts and then, when it came to take a solo, to blow. Cab didn't even know me, and I didn't even report—just put on the uniform and sat down!"[16]

Dizzy's performance impressed Cab, and now Lorraine asked Rudolph to push for Dizzy when a new hire seemed imminent. During the week of August 13, when Dizzy was performing with Hill at the Apollo, Rudolph called him and told him to report that evening to the Cotton Club with his horn. He donned a uniform and joined the trumpet section without ever meeting Calloway or knowing what his salary would be. He soon discovered that Cab was paying him $80 per week while in New York and $120 per week while touring. He knew that a career in jazz was a precarious one, and he was delighted that, with Lorraine's help, he had put scuffling behind him for the time being.

Dizzy performed that first night with a deep cut on his right hand, the result of a childish fight with Edgar Hayes over money that was rightly his and that Hayes was holding back.

The great initial bebop experiments ended as Dizzy moved on and Clarke remained with Hill. But the revolution was just beginning. Let us now explore its rhythmic and harmonic foundations.

11
BEBOP RHYTHM/
BEBOP HARMONY

THE SOUNDS OF SWING AND BEBOP ARE UNMISTAKABLY
different. A listener will quickly recognize, for example, that
Dizzy's May 1945 quintet recording of "Salt Peanuts" with Charlie Parker exists in a different musical realm from the July 1945
Benny Goodman quintet recording of "Rose Room."

The two genres diverge, because they are based on different
rhythmic and harmonic principles. Two concepts distinguish bebop from swing: linearity and chromaticism. The first is vital to
both bebop rhythm and harmony, while the second is a purely
harmonic formulation.

The development of bebop from the application of these two
concepts resulted in its most important legacy to future generations—
a radical expansion of the resources available to the improviser.
Taboos were erased and new vistas were opened as the beboppers
greatly expanded both the rhythmic and harmonic options available

for self-expression in jazz. Let us deal with linearity and chromaticism in turn.

The beboppers were not comfortable with the predictable strong-beat, weak-beat rhythms of swing where the strong beats, the downbeats, usually fell on two and four.

They felt rhythms differently from their predecessors; their imaginations teemed with irregular rhythmic patterns, and they thought linearly. They loved to spin out *lines* of notes, melodic statements of odd lengths that ignored the boundaries of bars and floated over the insistent swing beats. And these linear statements usually started and stopped in unexpected places.

For Dizzy and his cohorts all beats were equal, including the upbeats—the "ands" in the *one-and-two-and-three-and-four-and* cadence. They achieved equal status with the downbeats—the *one, two, three, four*—and frequently served as the downbeats; the beboppers were fond of beginning and maintaining melodic statements on the "ands." On an occasion when Charlie Parker was persistently emphasizing the "ands" in a solo, drummer Max Roach switched *his* downbeats to them, but Parker, wishing to highlight the contrast in accents, quickly waved him off.

Rhythm ruled supreme for Dizzy, who said:

> The basic thing about jazz music is putting the notes to rhythm, not the other way around. . . . I think up a rhythm first and then I put notes to it to correspond with the chord. You can play very, very beautiful notes and if it doesn't have any rhythmic form, it doesn't amount to anything. Don't lose sight of the rhythm in the music, because that's the most important part. Even more than the notes, because you can take just one note and put all kinds of different rhythms to the note and with just that one note everybody is clapping their hands and dancing and shouting.[1]

In other words, the shape of the rhythm profoundly influenced the shape of the melody for Dizzy. The importance of rhythmic contours was equally pronounced in the improvised and written melodies of the three other men who joined Dizzy and Kenny Clarke as the founding fathers of bebop: Charlie Christian,

Charlie Parker, and Thelonious Monk. Because bebop melody grew out of bebop rhythm, its rhythmic innovations were more important than its harmonic innovations.

A comparison of the first eight bars of the Gillespie-Parker composition "Anthropology" with the first eight bars of "I Got Rhythm," the swing tune that provided the chord sequence for "Anthropology," illustrates clearly how far the irregular rhythmic

Figure 2: Scores: The First Eight Bars of "Anthropology" and "I Got Rhythm"

patterns of bebop had moved from the rhythmic practices of swing. The respective scores are shown in figure 2.

The "I Got Rhythm" sequence consists of four statements. The first three are four-note, six-beat passages with identical rhythmic contours; each begins on a second beat and ends on a third beat. The notes of the first statement ("I got rhythm") are the same as those of the third ("I got my gal"). The fourth statement ("Who could ask for anything more") has a different contour, starting on a fourth beat and lasting for eight.

"Anthropology," on the other hand, is made up of five differently shaped statements of varying lengths. As can be seen in figure 2 and in the array below, each begins with an offbeat at a different place in the bar.

STATEMENT	STARTING POINT	LENGTH
I Got Rhythm #1	Two (Bar #1)	6 beats
I Got Rhythm #2	Two (Bar #3)	6 beats
I Got Rhythm #3	Two (Bar #5)	6 beats
I Got Rhythm #4	Four(Bar #6)	8 beats
Anthropology #1	Four-and (Pre-bar #1)	4½ beats
Anthropology #2	Two-and (Bar #2)	2½ beats
Anthropology #3	One-and (Bar #3)	5½ beats
Anthropology #4	Four-and (Bar #4)	7 beats
Anthropology #5	Three-and (Bar #6)	8½ beats

Joining spiky melodies like "Anthropology" with the free percussion voicings of Kenny Clarke created a fresh sound and feeling—the rhythmic basis for a new jazz genre more imaginative, more complex, more difficult than what had come before: bebop.

Western music is based on a scale of twelve notes; on the piano they appear as seven white and five black ones. A chord contains three or more notes, and a song's chord sequence provides the spine or structure of its harmony. When a chord is notated on sheet music, it says to the interpreter that its tones will be the mellow, "comfortable" ones until the next chord appears. If it is a three-note chord, then the other nine notes in the twelve-note scale are in varying degrees dissonant or "uncomfortable." For example, a D-flat played against a C-E-G chord sounds far more dissonant than a B-flat played against the same chord. The chords are thus an essential guide for the improviser when he or she chooses what notes to play.

Lester Young was the first great linear improviser in jazz. Instead of moving up and down each chord vertically, he would create an independent melodic line that he fashioned to fit *over* the chords, a horizontal flow of notes that he made sure would agree with what the chordal harmony was doing. Young's brother Lee talked about his approach: "He would say it confines you too much if you know it's a D flat 7. You start thinking of only the notes that will go in that chord, and he'd say that's not what he would hear. He wanted to play other things and make it fit. And he did."[2] Young would speak in musical sentences of varying lengths as he perfected a narrative style rooted in the storytelling southwestern blues culture that nurtured him.

Improvising linearly gives the musician more harmonic latitude while, at the same time, providing greater opportunities for rhythmic freedom and innovation. As we have seen, the improviser can spin out statements of any length, statements that have a rhythmic logic of their own and can stop and start anywhere within the bar lines.

The beboppers made this rhythmic-harmonic concept of Young's their own, and by 1939, Dizzy, Parker, Christian, and Monk were teaching themselves how to integrate it into their improvisations. The younger men, while taking so much from Young, were at the same time moving into harmonic territory that he did not wish to explore. Young was wedded to diatonic harmony, and Dizzy and his confreres were opting in 1939 and 1940 for a fresh jazz concept, chromatic harmony.

Harmony presupposes movement, and the movement of a song is created by "magnetic" forces that pull chords toward resolution into other chords. One can say that the harmonic function of a particular chord is to resolve into another chord. The listener feels satisfaction whenever resolution occurs; it releases tension and sounds "right." In Western harmony, a song's chord sequence carries the listener through a series of these satisfying resolutions to its ultimate destination—the tonic chord, the chord that names the key (in the key of C, it is a chord with C as its root). The beboppers thrived on harmonic movement and, to achieve this, they frequently added chords to the sequence of a tune.

Diatonic harmony, the prevailing system of the Swing Era, is based on seven of the twelve available notes, the do-re-mi-fa-so-la-ti major scale that many of us learn as kids. The five nonscale notes are used only as embellishments. Chords are built only on the seven scale tones (for example, in the key of C, one can build a chord on the note A, but not on A-flat, a nonscale note).

Dizzy and the beboppers found this very limiting and turned to chromaticism, which widened the harmonic palette by treating the nonscale notes as equals to the scale notes. In chromaticism, chords can be built on all twelve of the notes, not just seven. This greatly expanded the improviser's resource and made his or her task considerably more complex.

The path into the chromatic universe was discovered by moving up into the second octave past the second "do" of the do-re-mi-fa-so-la-ti-do sequence. There one found the "higher intervals"—the ninth, the eleventh, and the thirteenth—of the chord.

The crucial interval for Dizzy, Christian, Parker, and Monk—the key that unlocked the door to chromaticism—was the eleventh, which, to avoid dissonance, was sharpened. The sharp eleventh is the seventh note in the second octave and, technically, it can be called a sharpened fourth; for reasons lost to history, Dizzy and his colleagues habitually used the note's other name, the flatted fifth.

Dizzy discovered the magic of the interval in 1938, and he remembered that Rudy Powell, one of Edgar Hayes's saxophonists, was the catalyst:

Rudy wrote this arrangement for Edgar Hayes that had this weird change, an E-flat chord built on an A, the flatted fifth. When I ran across that in the music, it really hit—boom! The flatted fifth. Oooo, man! . . .

He had an E-flat chord in there, and I heard this A concert going up a scale, and I played it, and I played it again, played it again, played it again. I said, "Damn! Listen at this shit. Listen at this, man!" That's when I became aware that there was a "flatted fifth." Before that time, until 1938, that was not a part of my musical conception.[3]

Charlie Parker achieved a similar epiphany in New York in December 1939 when he was jamming with guitarist Buddy Fleet at Dan Wall's Chili House in Harlem. He described it in 1949:

> Now I'd been getting bored with the stereotyped changes that were being used at the time, and I kept thinking there's bound to be something else. I could hear it sometimes but I couldn't play it. Well, that night I was working over "Cherokee," and, as I did, I found that by using the higher intervals of a chord as a melody line and backing them with appropriately related changes, I could play the thing I'd been hearing. I came alive.[4]

The flatted fifth divides the octave exactly in half; for example, a G-flat is equidistant from the two Cs that frame its octave. It is three whole tones away from both the C below and the C above, and is commonly referred to as a tritone. Slotting a chord from the scale of the flatted fifth into a tune's sequence is called a tritone substitution. The beboppers discovered that

- *any major scale built on a note a flatted fifth away from another contains all five of the chromatic notes missing from the first scale and vice versa, and*
- *using the scales in partnership makes fully harmonic the five notes that were nonharmonic in the diatonic system.*

In other words, *using the flatted fifth to find two scalar routes to the same resolution enables the improviser to build chords on all twelve notes of the octave instead of just seven.* The improviser now had a full rainbow of musical colors to work with instead of just the basic hues.

Less than a month after joining Cab Calloway, Dizzy used bebop concepts in a recorded solo for the first time. It occurred at a session organized by Lionel Hampton.

NEW DIRECTIONS 12

CALLOWAY CLEARLY RECOGNIZED THE EXTRAORDINARY talents of his new trumpet man. When he took his band into a recording studio to cut four tracks on August 30, 1939, less than two weeks after Dizzy joined the group, he gave him all the trumpet breaks and the lone trumpet solo. Dizzy, who continued for the next eighteen months to be Calloway's only trumpet improviser, was in fast company; his saxophone soloist counterpart was the redoubtable Chu Berry.

The great majority of the vehicles for jazz improvising have been thirty-two-bar popular songs with an AABA structure (where the B segment is commonly called the bridge) and the twelve-bar blues with an ABC structure. I will discuss in this chapter several recordings; all of them involve tunes of the AABA variety.

Dizzy soloed on only one number on August 30, a tune featuring bassist Milt Hinton called "Pluckin' the Bass." His effort is tentative; he seems not yet comfortable in his new surroundings and attempts nothing ambitious as he engages in an energetic, Eldridge-tinged swing exercise. Calloway gave him another go at "Pluckin' the Bass" on November 20, 1939, and the results are much better. He was far more at ease as he created a distinctly linear improvisation with an inventive melodic fragment in the B (bridge) section.

On September 11, soon after his first Calloway session, Dizzy felt decidedly uneasy when he arrived for a freelance record date convened by Lionel Hampton, a featured soloist at the time with Benny Goodman. Dizzy's hands were, in fact, shaking as he took his trumpet from its case. His nervousness grew from a fervent desire to succeed, because at age twenty-one he was going to solo in the company of jazz royalty; his invitation to participate had been a stunning vote of confidence.

Dizzy was not the first choice for the single trumpet spot, but Hot Lips Page and Charlie Shavers, who were favored, were unavailable. He was hired because Calloway bandmates, bassist Milt Hinton and drummer Cozy Cole, had lobbied strongly for him after they had heard that Hampton had been favorably impressed by Dizzy during his August 1939 Apollo engagement with Teddy Hill.

At the session were four giants of the saxophone (Coleman Hawkins, Ben Webster, Chu Berry, and Benny Carter), Hampton on vibraphone, and Benny Goodman's sensational new hire, Charlie Christian, on guitar. Christian, who took no solos, was joined in the rhythm section by Cole, Hinton, and pianist Clyde Hart.

The older musicians were welcoming, and, once the group began to rehearse, Dizzy calmed down. Four tracks were cut; three featured Webster, Hawkins, and Carter, respectively, and the fourth, "Hot Mallets," put the spotlight on Dizzy, Berry, and Hampton. Dizzy soloed with a mute on the three eight-bar A segments of the tune, as Benny Carter performed the B segment. Although he used a couple of swing licks, Dizzy was clearly moving in new harmonic directions as he unfurled two fast, descending chromatic runs and fashioned bristling horizontal lines over the chord sequence. Hampton later remarked that Dizzy's harmonic

daring had deeply impressed him and that he immediately understood that the young trumpeter was forging a fresh approach to
jazz improvisation.

Dizzy's solo was good enough to merit his first mention in the
American jazz press; a *Metronome* reviewer noted that "C.[*sic*]
Gillespie emits some neat muted trumpeting on 'Hot Mallets.' "[1]

Dizzy recognized Christian as a fellow pioneer at the Hampton session, and soon the two musicians were jamming together at
late night spots all over town. The guitarist had ample opportunity to explore the New York scene because a painful back condition afflicting Benny Goodman severely limited the band's travel
from its base in the city. This provided Dizzy with many chances
to hang out with him, as Calloway's touring schedule allowed the
two men to be in New York simultaneously for fourteen months
before Christian left Goodman's band in June 1941.

Christian, the third founding father of bebop, did not venture
as deeply into chromaticism as his colleagues, but he led the way
in his explorations of linearity. He was an absolute master of the
linear, creating with ease chorus after chorus of free-flowing,
melodic delight.

Musicologist Scott DeVeaux has described Christian's rhythmic legerdemain:

> Christian's lines dissolved the usual hierarchical distinction be-
> tween strong beats and weak beats (and strong and weak parts of
> the beat), allowing him to shift effortlessly between sharply con-
> trasting rhythmic grooves. . . . (He) treated the rhythmic flow as an
> undifferentiated stream of eighth notes that could be shaped in-
> stantaneously into unpredictable patterns.[2]

These patterns were constructed from an array of phrases that
tumbled ceaselessly from his fingers—headlong multibar runs,
bluesy scales, ingenious riffs, tension-building pauses, ascending
and descending chromatic sequences, strummed chords. And he
pulled it all together with relentless musical logic.

Goodman had plucked Christian from obscurity during the
same week in August 1939 when Calloway hired Dizzy. John

Hammond, who launched the careers of such great artists as Billie Holiday, Count Basie, Bob Dylan, and Bruce Springsteen, discovered Christian at the Ritz Café in Oklahoma City. He recalled, "He was great. He was unique. . . . He phrased like a horn, which no other guitar did in those days. . . . He was endlessly inventive. As with every other great musician I have 'discovered,' there was never a moment's doubt. . . . Lights flash. Rockets go off."[3] Hammond arranged for Christian to audition with Benny Goodman in Los Angeles, and Benny quickly hired him at $120 per week; Christian had been working three nights a week for $2.50 per night at the Ritz.

As with Dizzy, Christian had been bathed in music from birth. His father, a blind guitarist, was a full-time musician who led a family band that included Charlie and two of his brothers. He became a professional at age sixteen in 1932 and, despite chronic respiratory problems, toured throughout the Southwest with several excellent bands before Hammond discovered him.

Christian and his family feared in 1939 that his already precarious health would be compromised by travel; he accepted Hammond's ticket to California with reluctance. Upon joining Goodman, however, he put his fears aside and embarked on a cross-country tour that ended at the New York World's Fair a few days before the Hampton session. Word of his prowess traveled fast, and he was already a star when he arrived in New York less than a month after joining Goodman.

As Dizzy and Christian made the New York jam session scene, one of their frequent companions was Kenny Clarke; he had remained with Teddy Hill until November 1939, when he was fired for being too radical. A clique of older musicians led by Hill's right-hand man, trombonist Henry Woode, convinced the bandleader that Clarke was disrupting the band unduly with his unorthodox percussive accents. They had wanted a steady 2/4 or 4/4 beat, and they won out. Clarke settled down in New York, finding plentiful work there with Roy Eldridge, New Orleans star Sidney Bechet, and the house band at the Apollo.

Dizzy, Christian, and Clarke frequently greeted the dawn at Clark Monroe's Uptown House, Manhattan's prime venue for jam sessions and a place that had welcomed Dizzy from his first days in New York in 1937. Monroe's was an after-hours club that began to heat up only after 4:00 a.m., the legal closing hour for New York's saloons. Clark Monroe stayed in business by making discreet payoffs to the powers that be; as a formality, the police would periodically raid the club, but it would always reopen a day or two later. The saxophone player Cecil Payne, a longtime collaborator of Dizzy's, once had his instrument confiscated during a raid at Monroe's and was forced to retrieve it sheepishly the next day from the police.

New visitors needed to know the club's address in advance, because there were no signs indicating its location in a basement on Harlem's West 134th Street at Seventh Avenue. The place seated about one hundred and attracted hip blacks drawn mostly from the entertainment world and a mix of white celebrities and socialites that included Lana Turner and several Woolworths. The music was continuous as a procession of dancers and singers (including drag queens) accompanied by a house band alternated with ad hoc groups of visiting musicians. Presiding over the festivities was Monroe, a convivial former tap dancer. Bassist Leonard Gaskin remembered the man who was known in Harlem as "the Dark Gable": "He was an outspoken, dapper, colorful dude, and one that the women loved, because he was a handsome guy. He had a way about him. He was really a ladies man. The fellows seemed to like him too."[4]

Charlie Parker jammed frequently at Monroe's in late 1939, but his path did not cross Dizzy's at that time. Among the established stars who sat in with the young boppers were Hot Lips Page, Ellington's outstanding bassist Jimmy Blanton, saxophonist Don Byas, and Dizzy's old friends Charlie Shavers and Roy Eldridge. The show usually ended with an extended jam session around 7:00 a.m. The sessions at Monroe's provided a happy, creative release for Dizzy, because his parts in the Calloway shows were precisely written and provided him with little opportunity to improvise.

Calloway had been a star for nearly a decade when Dizzy joined his band. And he had been a fixture at the Cotton Club for almost as long. As Duke Ellington was planning to embark on a long tour in September 1930 after a spectacularly successful three-year run at the club, Owney Madden and Big Frenchy Le-Mange, the two vicious mobsters who controlled the place, asked Ellington and his manager, Irving Mills, for the name of an appropriate fill-in. They chose the twenty-two-year-old Calloway, whose singing and showmanship had recently caused a sensation at the Savoy Ballroom and whose orchestra had bested Ellington's in a "battle of the bands" there one month before.

To secure his new position, Calloway was forced to give up a hefty share of his income for several years to Ellington, Mills, and Mills's lawyer, but he prospered nonetheless. The Cotton Club, as the nation's number one nightspot, boasted a coast-to-coast radio hookup, and the wide exposure it afforded catapulted the singer to national stardom. He was soon earning fifty thousand dollars per year at the bottom of the Depression. Calloway alternated with Ellington at the club for several more years and gradually took over as the main attraction when Ellington and his aggregation found wider horizons as a touring band.[5]

The shows at the Cotton Club rivaled the top Broadway musicals in talent and extravagance, featuring stars such as Bill Robinson, Ethel Waters, and the dancing Nicholas Brothers and music by songwriters such as Ellington, Jimmy McHugh, Dorothy Fields, Harold Arlen, and Ted Koehler. The club, which was originally located at 142nd Street and Lenox Avenue in Harlem, moved to Forty-eighth and Broadway in 1936. At both locations, a whites-only customers' policy was enforced, and the stage was a replica of the veranda of a southern mansion; a painted backdrop pictured the cabins of black field hands.

Calloway built a wildly successful career on two assets: his voice and an extravagant, attractive persona. Gunther Schuller has described Calloway's vocal instrument:

> Calloway had a phenomenal voice. Its range is extraordinary: from low B . . . to the highest tenor range and, by means of excellent "mixing" and falsetto, even quite beyond that into the soprano range. . . . But his technique extends beyond timbre to a perfectly controlled coloratura, quite natural and impeccable breath support, and above all incredible diction.[6]

The persona that Calloway created was outsize, like that of David Bowie or Elton John of the rock era, and it was complex. He was the handsome sex symbol who made women swoon when he sang love songs such as "I'll Be Around" and "My Gal"; the black faux primitive who titillated whites with frenzied scat vocals and hip-gyrating dances to "jungle" music; the street-smart sophisticate who was hip to all the current trends in language, the arts, and fashion; the raffish comedian who cavorted in outlandish zoot suits; and the guide to the drug world when he sang about "The Wail of the Reefer Man" and "Cokie" Joe who liked to "kick the gong around" (a euphemism for smoking opium).

His revues were meticulously choreographed to burnish all the elements of his multifaceted personality, and Dizzy was deeply impressed by his performances. He studied them with great care and later incorporated important elements of Calloway's show business character into his own public persona. Dizzy became a master at creating costumes both iconic and amusing; he often danced provocatively; he projected himself as totally hip; and he frequently joked about reefer and other drugs in his between-numbers patter.

Calloway's revue was in 1939 by far the country's highest-grossing black entertainment package, and his entourage of fifty traveled in private Pullman cars with a special compartment for his dark green, four-door, convertible Lincoln coupe. The Pullmans enabled them to escape the indignities visited on black performers when they toured the South and spared the entertainers the often cramped and fatiguing bus rides from town to town. When Dizzy embarked in late September 1939 on his first road trip with Calloway, the Cotton Club Revue included the talented gospel/jazz singer Rosetta Tharpe, the Three Choclateers dance act, the comedians Apus and Estelle, sixteen "tall, tan, and terrific" chorus girls, and six chorus boys.

Buoyed by his successful innovations with Clarke and Christian, Dizzy continued to experiment with fresh harmonies and rhythms and was forever urging his Calloway colleagues to join him in his voyages of discovery. He found only one willing acolyte, bassist Milt Hinton. Although Hinton was seven years older than Dizzy, he had been the "baby" of the band before

Dizzy arrived, and he had been frustrated by his colleagues' lack of creative spark. Prosperous and satisfied, they had settled into a comfortable routine, because the Calloway show varied little from night to night. Hinton was musically adventurous, but he realized that Dizzy had advanced far beyond him, and he was delighted to have the opportunity to learn from him.

The Cotton Club occupied the second floor of a two-story building that included a spiral staircase leading to the roof. Dizzy would conduct seminars there for Hinton after helping him lug his cumbersome instrument up the stairs. Guitarist Danny Barker was intrigued by their efforts but lacked the energy to participate:

> Dizzy and Milt Hinton, between those two-and-a-half-hour shows at the Cotton Club (and they were very strenuous shows) would re-tire to the roof. Dizzy would blow his new ideas in [chord] progressions, and he and Hinton would experiment on different ideas and melodic patterns, and they would suggest that I come up and join them. But after that two-and-a-half-hour show, sometimes I would go up and sometimes I wouldn't. Because what they were doing called for a lot of mental concentration on harmonies. It was very interesting, but I couldn't see going up there and wasting energies on something not commercial. . . .
>
> Dizzy would take his solos and Hinton would follow his patterns harmonically, would follow the changes that Dizzy was making. Often, what Dizzy was playing would be contrary to the arrangement. But Hinton would look at me, and I'd bend the chord so it would fit in. It sounded interesting and beautiful to me, but it annoyed Cab and three or four of the guys in the band.[7]

Following the Cotton Club shows, Dizzy would frequently take Hinton up to Monroe's to continue their explorations.

A gregarious southerner like Dizzy, the Mississippian Hinton hit it off with his new colleague immediately, and the two men formed a deep, lifelong friendship. Their bonds were reinforced by the warm relationship that grew between Lorraine and Hinton's wife, Mona. The families socialized frequently over the decades, and the childless Gillespies doted on the Hinton children.

Another force binding the two men together was their joint

passion for photography. Hinton had become an accomplished photographer during the 1930s and always carried a camera with him; the thousands of pictures he created are an invaluable documentary resource of the jazz life over seven decades, and the best of his images were published in two excellent books. Over the years, he and Dizzy bought each other equipment and constantly swapped technical information and advice.

Calloway, who respected Dizzy's writing skills, organized on March 8, 1940, the first recording of songs written and arranged by him: "Paradiddle," a feature for drummer Cozy Cole, and "Pickin' the Cabbage," a Latin jazz piece. On the former, Dizzy shares composer credit with Cole. The arrangements are highly professional; Dizzy exhibits both an original flair and a mastery of the fundamentals as he transforms his straightforward swing tunes into treats for the ear.

Cole's unimaginative soloing consumes two of the three minutes of "Paradiddle," but Dizzy gets to shine with a bold full-band statement of the tune and with three short interludes that punctuate Cole's choruses. He achieves his best effects with momentum-building rhythmic accents and a series of descending flatted fifths in the trumpet voicings.

Dizzy was motivated to make "Pickin' the Cabbage" authentically Latin, because he was disgusted with Calloway's previous foray into the genre, an October 1939 recording of Mario Bauzá's "Chili Con Conga." The bandleader had assumed that American audiences were not yet ready for complicated Latin rhythms, and he forced Bauzá to serve up a tepid, watered-down version of the real thing. Calloway agreed to reverse course after Dizzy forcefully pleaded his case for authenticity.

"Pickin' the Cabbage" shows Dizzy moving deeply into chromatic harmony as he begins his arrangement with a series of four parallel eleventh and thirteenth chords; Gunther Schuller has pointed out that Duke Ellington was the only other jazz composer of the time who would have attempted anything as chromatically daring.

The recording has become a landmark in Latin jazz. Dizzy placed a strong repeated bass pattern under his minor-key tune and, in a departure from the practices of the day, used the baritone saxophone to reinforce the rhythm section. He deliciously dislocated the 4/4 rhythm of the A segments by making the first beats in the measures weak ones and by having the baritone sax and Cozy Cole alternately emphasize and anticipate (with accents on "three-and") every fourth beat. Weak first beats are characteristic of much Latin music, and as Dizzy later commented, he was looking forward here to the rhythmic complexity of fully mature bebop and to his groundbreaking integration of Latin rhythms into jazz:

> A careful listening to "Pickin' The Cabbage" will show you the musical direction I'd follow for the rest of my career. It's a real beginning of Latin jazz and possibly the first use of polyrhythms in our music since the very beginning of jazz. All of the elements for fusing and synthesizing Afro-American swing with the various Latin and Caribbean beats are right there in that one composition.[8]

Unfortunately, Dizzy's solo on "Pickin' the Cabbage" was not as adventurous as his writing; he played a standard swing chorus. *Downbeat*'s reviewer was turned off by Cole and was not quite ready to accept Dizzy's modernist "weird" harmonies: "Cozy Cole runs rampant on 'Paradiddle' . . . pounding himself into a frenzy of technical show-offs. . . . The obvious result is a disappointing feeling on the part of the listener. . . . ['Cabbage'] is better with Dizzy Gillespie's trumpet taking the go parts. The theme is weird and at times smacks of the Duke."[9]

In mid-March 1940, Dizzy received the disturbing news that Charlie Christian had been hospitalized in Chicago with tuberculosis. He had fainted during a concert and was admitted with a temperature of 104. The guitarist had been reveling in a life of late-night jam sessions, reefer smoking, headlong touring, and frantic partying, and he was badly worn down. On his release, his doctor advised him to slow the pace and get more rest, but Christian never heeded him, and his health remained precarious.

When Dizzy began to earn a decent salary with Calloway, he talked Lorraine into leaving the fatiguing grind of the Apollo chorus line, and he took her on the road with him. They had been together for almost two and a half years when the band began a six-week engagement in Boston in April 1940, and Dizzy felt increasingly sure that he and Lorraine could make a success of marriage. He proposed in early May and Lorraine accepted immediately; on May 10 they went down to the central Boston courthouse and were married by a clerk with a stranger as their witness.

The marriage was a fruitful one until Dizzy's death fifty-three years later, and Lorraine attributed their happiness together to the respect they maintained for each other. She strongly believed that love had little meaning if it was not accompanied by respect.

In later years, Dizzy carried his marriage certificate in his wallet. He told me that he frequently looked at it to remind himself where his life's anchor lay. And in 1979, he wrote the following dedication to his autobiography:

To my wife
LORRAINE

Her love, help, humor, and wisdom
Her unselfish and unswerving
devotion made me the man
and musician I wanted to be

DIZZY

Allowing for some hyperbole, this statement contains a good deal of truth. Dizzy was a freelance artist whose grueling professional life was a constant scuffle for gigs; into his seventies he traveled more than two hundred thousand miles per year, and early in his career he carried an added burden, because he was preaching a radical musical message that frequently met with hostility and derision. He was out there on his own, without the luxury of the institutionalized backing that exists today for musicians in ensembles such as the Lincoln Center Jazz Orchestra and the Danish Radio Jazz Orchestra.

In the midst of all this striving and hustle, Lorraine created an oasis of stability and calm for Dizzy. And she did more; she curbed his penchant for careless spending and, as he often pointed out, she was the main reason he did not succumb to the drug epidemic that destroyed so many of his colleagues.

Lorraine knew that Dizzy wasn't a saint as she began her successful lifelong campaign to keep his appetites in check. Dizzy never came close to being addicted to any substance, but he enjoyed alcohol, large cigars, marijuana, aromatic pipe tobacco, and an occasional hit of cocaine. Marijuana abetted his robust appetite for food and contributed to the considerable girth he acquired in middle age, and, into his fifties, he became seriously drunk on relatively small amounts of alcohol. In his autobiography, published in 1979, he stated that he used both marijuana and cocaine.

Lorraine's strength derived mostly from her grandmother; her childhood was divided between her grandmother's home in Darlington, South Carolina (only thirty-five miles from Cheraw), and her mother's apartment in New York City. The older woman—strict and demanding and a much stronger presence than her mother—was the primary influence on her childhood and helped mold a girl who became a practical, determined woman with a strong moral compass. Fortunately, Lorraine found her professional calling early; she developed a passion for dancing at age six, and the lessons she took from that time until her early teens prepared her for her vocation as a chorus girl.

She had been married as a teenager to a young South Carolinian who worked as a chauffeur for wealthy whites. After he died of a brain tumor during their first year of marriage, she pursued a dancing career in earnest and found employment on the TOBA theater circuit where she met Dizzy in 1937.

Six weeks after he married the woman who had sustained him since she saw him begging for fifteen cents at the Apollo, Dizzy would meet the man who would affect his career more profoundly than any other—Charlie Parker.

ENTER BIRD 13

On May 30, 1940, Dizzy and his new bride embarked with the Calloway troupe on a six-week tour of the Midwest that took them to Kansas City's Fairyland, a family-oriented amusement park, for a show on June 23. That night, $1.10 would buy you a double treat: a cooling swim in an outdoor pool plus the Calloway revue.

Buddy Anderson, a friend of Dizzy's and a trumpeter with the Jay McShann band that currently featured Charlie Parker, attended the Calloway performance and was "knocked out" by Dizzy's advanced ideas. Anderson wanted very much for Dizzy to hear Parker perform, and after the show he took Dizzy and other Calloway musicians to a jam session where Parker was expected to participate; they were disappointed when he did not show up.

Fortuitously, Anderson and Dizzy ran into Parker the next day, and the three men agreed to jam together at the headquarters of AFM Local 627, the black musicians' union. Anderson and

Parker happened to have their horns, and Dizzy, who was without his, suggested that he accompany them on the piano. The only room in the building that housed a piano reeked of dog shit, because the union chief frequently kept his hunting animals there. The men persevered, however, and Parker blew Dizzy away: "He provided the missing link which made bebop whole—his *phrasing*, the way he moved from one note to the other. It was liquid, quicksilver, sinuous. He wove his advanced harmonic ideas seamlessly through a succession of offbeats, microscopic delays, strong beats, smears. That became the model for our *style*."[1]

In his autobiography, Dizzy had more to say:

> I was astounded by what the guy could do. . . . The moment I heard Charlie Parker, I said, there is *my* colleague. . . .
>
> I never heard anything like that before. The way that he assembled notes together. That was one of the greatest thrills because I had been a Roy Eldridge fan up until then, but I was definitely moving on into myself. Charlie Parker and I were moving in practically the same direction too, but neither of us knew it.[2]

Dizzy's perception was correct: the two men were indeed moving in the same direction, and the journey had begun for Parker in Kansas City, Kansas, on August 29, 1920. His mother, Addie, brought him up alone after his father, a sometime vaudeville dancer and singer who was a severe alcoholic, drifted away to take a job as a Pullman railway chef when the boy was about nine. Addie, who supplemented her income as a charwoman by taking in boarders, lived for her son and spoiled him totally. They moved from Kansas City, Kansas, to the much larger and more sophisticated Kansas City, Missouri, in 1931; the two cities are contiguous.

In 1933, at age thirteen, Parker found his calling when he joined his high school marching band; he was uncomfortable, however, with his assigned instruments, the tubalike baritone horn and the clarinet, and quickly moved to the alto saxophone. He was soon practicing obsessively.

Parker's musical horizons expanded immeasurably when he began listening to the great musicians performing in the maze of jazz and blues clubs that were clustered around Twelfth and Eighteenth streets—areas less than a mile from his home. In 1934, Addie took a midnight-to-eight job as a charwoman in an office building, and most evenings after she left, Charlie headed straight for those clubs with his horn under his arm.

During the 1930s, Kansas City attained a place alongside New Orleans, Chicago, and New York as one of the truly seminal cities in jazz history, and it was mostly due to Tom Pendergast, the city's rough-hewn political boss who reigned from the Prohibition days of 1928 through the Depression decade that ended in 1939.

He brought a high degree of prosperity to his town by opening it to an array of around-the-clock bars, cabarets, dance halls, whorehouses, and gambling halls where booze flowed like a river, marijuana (which was legal until 1938) was smoked everywhere, and the music never stopped. Most of these establishments were controlled by the mob, and Pendergast gave them free rein to develop a flourishing narcotics trade. John Hammond remembered his first night in Kansas City when he heard Count Basie's band at the Reno Club: "There was a whorehouse upstairs . . . and there was a window in the back of the bandstand . . . People used to just shovel up pot through the back window, and it didn't seem to affect the guys at all. It (the Count Basie band) was still the best band I had ever heard, and without that kind of stimulus they couldn't have done it."[3]

Kansas City was a major commercial city, a market center for the southwestern and midwestern grain and cattle industries, and it drew a continuing stream of big spenders. For many Kansas City jazz musicians, almost all of whom were black, the Depression never happened. A brilliant array of talent gathered there in joints with names like the Reno, the Hey-Hay, Piney Brown's Sunset, the Subway, the Wiggle Inn, and the Hi-Hat to create a hard-driving, blues-tinged, strongly improvisational form of swing that later rocked the world.

The greatest of the Kansas City musicians was Lester Young, and he was joined by a once-in-a-century constellation of stars: Jo Jones, Charlie Christian, Count Basie, Jay McShann, Ben Webster, Mary Lou Williams, Herschel Evans, Joe Turner, Pete Johnson, Buck Clayton, Buddy Tate, Walter Page, Jimmy Rushing, Oran "Hot Lips" Page, Buster Smith, Budd Johnson, and Tadd

Dameron. Parker heard them all, and, in addition, listened to the stars of touring bands such as Ellington, Calloway, and Goodman when they came through Kansas City.

Biographer Ross Russell has described how Parker, age fourteen, would sit in the balcony of the Reno Club and emulate Young, his idol:

> Charlie would hear the fat, airy notes, the long flowing lines, the big grunting sounds and the light tripping ones. Then he would remove his own horn from its case, adjust the neck-strap and place his fingers on the keys. The reed would be in his mouth but no sound would come out. Charlie wasn't putting any air into the horn. He was playing along with Lester, only in his head, his fingers moving on the keys the way Lester's fingers moved, hearing the long flowery line, imagining that he was shaping the notes in the same way.[4]

Night after night, Charlie would creep into bed at 5:00 a.m. with the sounds of Young and the other great soloists ringing in his ears.

Heroin was plentiful around Twelfth and Vine, and Charlie probably became addicted to it in 1935 at age fifteen. He later told a friend that the rush of ecstasy from his first hit hooked him for life. He would never truly escape his slavery to heroin until his death at age thirty-four.

As the pianist Jay McShann has attested, Parker had attained musical maturity by 1937.

> He was a teenager, barely seventeen. . . . He had a tone that cut. Knew his [chord] changes. He'd get off on a line of his own and I would think he was headed for trouble, but he was like a cat landing on all four feet. A lot of people couldn't understand what he was trying to do, but it made sense harmonically and it always swung.
>
> Musical ideas, that is what jam sessions were really about. Charlie was able to hold his own against older men, some of them with years of big band experience. He was a strange kid, very aggressive and wise.[5]

Parker's addiction deepened as he performed in the Kansas City bands of McShann and Buster Smith until early 1939. After he stabbed a cab driver in an altercation about a fare and served a short jail sentence as a result, he lit out for Chicago and New York.

While forced to wait out a union probation period with the New York local, he could not legally work as a musician and took a job as a dishwasher at Jimmy's Chicken Shack, a popular Harlem club. He earned nine dollars per week and all he could eat and the privilege of listening every night to Art Tatum, who many consider the greatest jazz pianist who ever lived and whom Dizzy idolized.

Tatum was more harmonically advanced than any other jazz musician of the time, and his technical skills were at such a high level that they mesmerized Vladimir Horowitz, the great classical piano virtuoso. One night when Tatum walked into a club where Fats Waller was performing, Waller stopped playing and announced, "God is in the house."

Parker was too shy to introduce himself to the great man, but he listened hungrily to every note. Tatum's three-month engagement was like a PhD course for the precocious eighteen-year-old.

Parker ignored his union probation as he took part in jam sessions all over Harlem and became a regular at Monroe's. Following Tatum's departure in June and armed with his union card, he landed a regular job at the Parisien, a Times Square dime-a-dance hall. It was during this engagement that he experienced his epiphany about chromaticism and the "higher extensions of a chord" while jamming at Dan Wall's Chili House in December 1939. Soon after, he rejoined McShann's band in Kansas City and remained with him for two and a half years. He was four months into that engagement when he met Dizzy.

There are several conflicting stories about how Parker acquired his widely used nickname, Bird, but the most probable one concerns a Nebraska road trip soon after he joined McShann. The bandleader related that, after one of the group's drivers ran over a chicken, Parker retrieved the "yardbird" from the road and had it cooked for dinner at the band's boardinghouse that evening. Most of Parker's friends shortened the sobriquet to Bird, but Dizzy preferred to call his colleague Yardbird or Yard.

On the evidence of his first recording in May 1940, Parker had moved much further into the linear, chromatic universe than had

Dizzy at the time; in fact, the disc shows that at age nineteen he had become a master of the new rhythmic and harmonic language.

Parker performed alone on a privately made recording, improvising on "Honeysuckle Rose" for two minutes and fourteen seconds and "Body and Soul" for a minute and twenty-five seconds. The disc, one of the most fascinating documents in jazz history, heralded an amazing new talent and was made roughly one month before he met Dizzy; it is known to scholars as "Honey and Body."

Unaccompanied, he played "naked." There was no drummer to provide a propulsive beat and no bassist or pianist to underpin the chordal harmony. Yet he swung with ease and brought a fully mature creativity to the harmony.

Parker's phrasing was liquid, varied, and free as he improvised three and one-half linear choruses on "Honeysuckle Rose" at a medium tempo; he stated the tune in one short fragment only. He pulled off several intricate chromatic runs, and on two occasions he daringly moved the harmony a half step away from the chords and maneuvered brilliantly to resolutions (musicians soon began to call this practice "running out of the key").

Bird performed one ballad chorus of "Body and Soul" at a slow tempo. He adhered closely to the melody, rephrasing and embellishing it as he wove in and out of the harmony. He used a tritone substitution in each of the A sections and created a striking descending chromatic phrase in the B section. "Honey and Body" demonstrates that Bird had left the Swing Era behind him and was ready to lead the jazz world into rich new territory.

In contrast, Calloway recordings from the May–August 1940 period portray Dizzy as a musician in transition, a soloist who was gradually leaving the swing idiom to follow the modernist instincts that he first displayed with "Hot Mallets" and were further influenced by his first encounter with Parker.

His improvisations in May on two takes of "Calling All Bars" are essentially diatonic with the exception of rising chromatic figures in the last A sections, and his "Hard Times (Topsy Turvy)" outing from the same date is a well-crafted swing improvisation with a distinct blues feel.

However, at the session of June 27, three days after his meeting with Parker, Dizzy soloed on two takes of "Bye Bye Blues" (an AABA pop tune and not a blues) and became an apostle of linearity as he articulated a series of stunning rhythmic variations reminiscent of Christian. And his July and August versions of "Cupid's Nightmare" are quite boppish as his solos contain daring chromatic lines. An August recording of "Boo-Wah Boo-Wah" finds him following sixteen bars of diatonic swing with eight bars of nearly pure chromaticism.

Three weeks after the Parker encounter, the Calloway band returned to New York from the Midwest, and soon after Dizzy and Lorraine rented a small apartment in a "musicians" building in central Harlem on Seventh Avenue between 121st and 122nd streets; jazzmen Erroll Garner, Billy Eckstine, and Clyde Hart also lived there.

World War II intruded on Dizzy's world when the Selective Service Act was passed by Congress in September 1940 as England was fighting alone against the Axis powers. The act required that all males between the ages of twenty-one and thirty-five sign up for the draft by October 21; Dizzy registered on October 17. He later claimed that he was interviewed on that day by a selective service board and avoided a call-up by stating an aversion to fighting in a white man's war; in this instance, however, his memory failed him. Surviving records show that he was not summoned to his first interview until May 1941.

If he inveighed against the white man's war at that time, it had no palpable effect; he was classified 1-A (fit for duty). He was reclassified 4-F (unfit for duty) in May 1943. Unfortunately, the reasons for his reclassification cannot be ascertained, because all relevant records were destroyed in 1980.[6]

On October 24, one week after Dizzy answered his draft call, the bebop revolution moved into a higher gear as Teddy Hill became the manager of a Harlem club called Minton's.

MINTON, MONK, AND MONROE

14

TEDDY HILL'S BAND NEVER RECOVERED FROM ITS leader's dispute with the Savoy Ballroom management when the band was fired from its Savoy Pavilion engagement at the 1939 World's Fair. With the powerful Savoy people against him, Hill stumbled along until September 1940 when, faced with very sparse bookings, he disbanded.

Hill wasn't idle for long. Within a few weeks, he was hired by Henry Minton to build up the dwindling customer base at Minton's Playhouse, his supper club on West 118th Street near Seventh Avenue in Harlem. The place, whose capacity was about seventy-five, sported a bar in front and a back room for music with a small bandstand that could comfortably house a rhythm section and five or six horn men. The decor never rose above adequate.

Minton, a former saxophone player who wielded power as the only black delegate to New York's musicians union, was a gregarious man with a wide circle of friends; two years after he had taken over a dilapidated ground-floor space and brought it up to a minimum standard of comfort, he decided to stimulate his business by making the club a gathering place for musicians. This made sense, because musicians and their show-business friends formed an oasis of solvency in a Harlem where the unemployment rate hovered around 25 percent. Minton felt sure that Hill, a popular man with a decade of experience near the top echelons of black music, knew how to draw them in.

Minton endeared himself to his musical clientele on two counts; he set a good table (delicious dinners cost seventy-five cents), and he encouraged sitting in by those who liked to jam. Union rules prohibited musicians from jamming because they were not usually paid at the sessions; agents diligently patrolled other New York clubs to fine performers who sat in, but Minton used his union clout to keep them from enforcing the rules in his own bailiwick.

Hill was unimpressed by the house band, a Dixieland-cum-swing outfit, because he believed that he could best create a "buzz" for the club by hiring from the pool of exciting young musicians who had recently been expanding the stylistic boundaries of jazz. The man he chose to form the new band was Kenny Clarke, whom he had fired a year earlier for upsetting his bandmates with his radical rhythmic ideas. Together they decided that a horn-plus-rhythm-section quartet, which could easily be expanded for jam sessions, was the right size for the core group.

Clarke wanted Dizzy for the horn spot, but he couldn't convince his friend to give up the first-class salary and the recording opportunities that he was enjoying with Calloway. Clarke then turned to Joe Guy, who had been Dizzy's associate and admirer in the trumpet section of the Hill band: "If I chose Joe Guy, it's because he was an old-timer of Teddy Hill's orchestra. When Teddy left his orchestra, mainly because he didn't like the impresarios and agencies, he thought that he owed us something. By taking the organization of Minton's into his own hands, he thought he could help some of the musicians and asked me to hire Joe Guy."[1] Guy's playing was rooted in Roy Eldridge, but he was beginning to integrate Dizzy's harmonic concepts into his solos.

Clarke then chose Nick Fenton, a friend of Guy's who possessed

an impeccable sense of time, to play bass. After trying unsuccess-
fully to fill out the quartet by hiring Sonny White, another ex-Hill
sideman and Billie Holiday's pianist, Clarke was forced to settle for
a little-known, twenty-dollar-per-week scuffler who had impressed
him on the jam session scene, Thelonious Sphere Monk.

Once when asked "What is jazz?" Monk replied, "New York,
man. You can feel it. It's around in the air."[2] Monk was a quintes-
sential New Yorker, although native to Rocky Mount, North Carolina. He was born there just eleven days before Dizzy, on
October 10, 1917, and his family moved to New York when he
was four. They settled in San Juan Hill, the neighborhood in
Manhattan's West Sixties that had been the center of New York
black life before Harlem became preeminent in the 1920s.

Monk took up the piano when he was thirteen and was so precocious that, within four years, he had won so many amateur contests at the Apollo that he was banned from further competitions.
Soon after, he dropped out of high school to join, with his
mother's encouragement, the Reverend Graham, also known as
the "Texas Warhorse," a female preacher, gospel singer, and faith
healer who had come out of the Sanctified Church. He followed
the gospel road with her all over the United States for two years.
His jazz playing was limited to sporadic jam sessions in towns
along the way, as he absorbed the bedrock black culture of gospel
and its close secular cousins, rock and roll and rhythm and blues.

He later remembered that he scuffled as a musician for three
years after returning to New York in late 1936: "I tried to find
jobs . . . nonunion jobs, $20 a week, seven nights a week, and then
the man might fire you anytime and you never got your money. . . .
I've been on every job you can think of all over New York. I really
found out how to get around this city. Dance halls. Every place."[3]

When Monk wasn't scuffling, he found time to practice and
compose at home and to participate in the city's teeming jam session scene. One of the session musicians who respected his gifts
was Kenny Clarke, who brought him into the circle that created
the bebop revolution.

Hill quickly found success at Minton's when he established
"Celebrity Nights" on Monday, the entertainers' night off, and
invited the entire cast of the show at the Apollo Theater, only

seven blocks away on 125th Street, for free food and liquor (paid
for by the owners of the Apollo as a goodwill gesture). Minton's
soon became packed on Mondays, as singers, dancers, and comedians joined musicians on the bandstand for impromptu turns.

When musicians heard about the high quality of the music demanded by Clarke in the jam sessions, the other nights of the
week, which were devoted only to music, became almost as popular as Mondays. At first it was the swing elite who crowded in;
bandleaders such as Basie, Goodman, Ellington, Shaw, and
Hampton lent their prestige to the scene, and great soloists such
as Chu Berry, Lester Young, Coleman Hawkins, Don Byas, Ben
Webster, Benny Carter, Hot Lips Page, Roy Eldridge, Charlie
Shavers, and Mary Lou Williams also made it to the bandstand.
Often the modernists accommodated them with uncomplicated
rhythms and diatonic harmony, but gradually their resolve stiff-
ened, and the music became more demanding. Some of the swing
soloists adapted, others dropped out.

Ralph Ellison wrote eloquently of the spirit of the Minton's
patrons who, listening to the sessions,

> were pressed in the crowds beneath the dim rosy lights of the bar
> in the smoke-veiled room, and who shared, night after night, the
> mysterious spell created by the talk, the laughter, grease paint,
> powder, perfume, sweat, alcohol, and food—all blended and sim-
> mering, like a stew on the restaurant range, and brought to a sus-
> tained moment of elusive meaning by the timbres and accents of
> musical instruments locked in passionate recitative. . . . Those
> who shared in the noisy lostness of New York, the rediscovered
> community of the feasts, evocative of home, of South, of good
> times, the best and most unself-conscious of times, created by the
> generous portions of Negro American cuisine—the hash, grits,
> fried chicken, the ham-seasoned vegetables, the hot biscuits and
> rolls. . . . They were gathered here from all parts of America and
> they broke bread together and there was a sense of good feeling
> and promise.[4]

The singer Carmen McRae took a more prosaic view of the
proceedings: "Minton's was just a place for cats to jam. People

didn't pay too much attention to what was going on. I mean those people there that weren't musicians. So when you went in you'd see cats half-stewed who weren't paying much mind to what was happening on stage. But the musicians were."[5]

Dizzy was based in New York roughly 80 percent of the time during late 1940 and all of 1941 and therefore had many opportunities to sit in at Minton's. But he jammed at Monroe's more often, because a number of his Calloway engagements took him past the 4:00 a.m. Minton's closing time. At Monroe's he was welcomed by kindred modernists such as the bandleader and pianist Al Tinney, trumpeter Vic Coulsen, and saxophonist Kermit Scott. And he almost always found that the Minton's gang had migrated there after Minton's had shut down.

Minton's was slightly more important than Monroe's at this stage of bebop's development, and for two reasons: one of the core revolutionaries, Kenny Clarke, was in charge, and instrumental music was the top priority there. At Monroe's, the instrumental jams were constantly interspersed with features for dancers and vocalists.

If Dizzy hadn't had enough music by breakfast time, he would invite his pals to his apartment (a ten-minute walk from Monroe's) and ask Lorraine to put ham and eggs, biscuits, and grits on the table as they gathered around his upright piano. Frequently he and Monk would sit side by side, jamming and working out harmonic problems, as Christian took soft solos on acoustic guitar, Clarke beat out rhythms with brushes on a table top, and the sax and trumpet players tried to whisper on their horns to avoid disturbing the neighbors.

Late 1940 thus marked a coming together for the first time of four of the five founding fathers of bebop—young black men from rural South Carolina, Pittsburgh, San Juan Hill in Manhattan, and Oklahoma City who were totally serious about their music and driven, to use Ezra Pound's phrase, to make it new. Clarke, the eldest, was twenty-six, and Dizzy, the youngest, was twenty-three. They would now share regularly the bandstands at Minton's and Monroe's to carry forward their revolution. Charlie Parker, who would complete the group, would not arrive until January 1942, when he blew into town with the McShann band.

Dizzy was overjoyed to work again with Clarke in an atmosphere infinitely more congenial to innovation than what they had encountered in their previous collaborations while working in the Hayes and Hill bands. The big band swing arrangements had allowed them only limited opportunities to express their creativity, and they almost always encountered hostility from the older musicians when they attempted something original. Now, with Clarke as the leader at Minton's, they were given the utmost freedom to experiment with musicians partial to their cause and in a flexible small-group setting conducive to experimentation.

As Kermit Scott remembered, Dizzy assumed a special responsibility for inculcating percussionists with Clarke's principles of modern drumming: "Diz was there *every night*. And he would get *on* drummers, man. He'd get back there—say, man, play boot-d'-ding, boot-d'-ding.' They were playing another kind of way, man, and he'll tell them how to play the cymbal because our kind of swing was a little different."[6]

Dizzy was eager to go beyond the purely rhythmic scope of his earlier innovations with Clarke and explore harmony as well. He knew that Christian would help him in this endeavor, but Monk was an unknown quantity.

He soon became for Dizzy an unexpected bonus. The pianist, who possessed a musical intelligence of the highest order, had been treading, in obscurity, the same revolutionary path to rhythmic freedom and to a linear, chromatic universe as the other bebop pioneers. He was a master of rhythm who swung mightily and punctuated his solos with rollicking Clarke-like dislocations of the beat and quirky accents. In addition, he had developed, on his own, several original and useful harmonic concepts. Among them, as Scott DeVeaux has noted, was the half-diminished chord, which brought the tritone into sharp focus:

He introduced them [the small coterie of musicians at Minton's] to the half-diminished chord, then still a "freaky sound" on or beyond the boundary of most musicians' knowledge. . . . The ultimate fascination of the half-diminished chord lay in the tritone buried in its interior. Monk's harmonic language was centered around the tritone: it showed up in his fondness for augmented

chords, whole-tone scales, and the infamous "flatted fifth." . . .
Monk's compositions isolated the characteristic sonority of the tritone more systematically than any music then in circulation.[7]

Dizzy, Christian, and Clarke were fascinated by Monk's concepts
and began spending hours with him in serious study on the bandstand and off. As Dizzy recalled, these seminars had an immediate effect on his playing: "When I first started hanging out with
Thelonious Monk, I don't think Cab could figure out at all what I
was trying to blow out of my horn on his stand. It was just the
new ideas Monk and I had worked out the night before."[8]

Monk was married to music twenty-four hours a day, and he
obeyed an inner clock whose ticking only he could hear. Teddy
Hill remembered:

> The band used to come to work at ten. He'd come in at nine, but at
> ten you couldn't find him. Maybe an hour later you'd find him sit-
> ting off by himself in the kitchen somewhere writing. . . . He'll
> come in here any time and play for hours with only a dim light. . . .
> Many times he's gone on so long I've had to come back and plead
> with him to quit playin' the piano so I could close up the place. . . .
>
> One reason for it, I guess, is that the guy was living at home
> with his own people. . . . Knowing he had a place to eat and sleep,
> that might have had a lot to do with it. Dizzy had to be on time to
> keep the landlady from saying "You don't live here anymore."
> Monk never had that worry.[9]

Not everyone who tried to sit in at Minton's and Monroe's was
a polished musician. In order to weed out the incompetents, the
insiders altered the chord progressions and the keys of the songs
that were common jamming vehicles. Clarke remembered:

> We often talked in the afternoon. That's how we came to write dif-
> ferent chord progressions and the like. We did that to discourage
> the sitters-in at night we didn't want. Monk, Joe Guy, Dizzy, and I
> would work them out. We often did it on the job, too. . . .
>
> We usually did what we pleased on the stand. There was no
> particular time we had to get on or off the stand. Teddy Hill, the

manager of Minton's turned the whole backroom over to us. As for those sitters-in that we didn't want, when we started playing these different changes we'd made up, they'd become discouraged after the first chorus and they'd slowly walk away and leave the professional musicians on the stand.[10]

Clarke also recalled the deep feelings of comradery that had developed among the pioneers:

Our unity of style came from our association; that was an unconscious thing. I have always believed that three or four musicians cannot play together if they dislike one another. We developed a style and a coordination that had never previously existed. . . .
   We hadn't really set out with the idea of developing any particular style of jazz. It just happened like that. When you think back, you tend to say, "Well, those guys were really doing something!" But it was really unconscious.[11]

Dizzy was a happy man in early 1941. He had found, with congenial colleagues, a gratifying outlet for his creative energies; he had settled into a comfortable niche with the Calloway band; and his marriage was going well. He had no inkling that trouble was coming his way. When it did, it came in the form of a genial trumpet player named Jonah Jones.

15

"CAB CALLOWAY 'CARVED' BY OWN TRUMPET MAN!!"

WHEN CAB CALLOWAY HIRED DIZZY IN AUGUST 1939 TO fill a vacant trumpet chair, Jonah Jones had been his first choice. The bandleader coveted him, because he saw strong commercial promise in the trumpeter's crowd-pleasing style, which was closely modeled on that of Louis Armstrong. In fact, from 1934 to 1936, Jones had been billed as "King Louis II."

He turned Cab down in 1939 because he preferred the extended soloing opportunities and the high salary he enjoyed in violinist Stuff Smith's popular sextet. But Cab persisted in wooing him, because he knew that Smith's leadership style was causing serious health problems for Jones, who recalled:

> I was with Stuff Smith, I was drinking whiskey and smoking pot, and I got sick. . . . Stuff would say that you didn't sound right

unless you were filled up with whiskey. One night after we had played our first number, Stuff said "That don't sound right. Jonah, are you high?" I said "No, I decided to cool it tonight." . . . Stuff said "That's no good. Anybody who ain't high on the next set gets a ten dollar fine." So the only way I could get away from that was to join a band that didn't do a lot of drinking, as the doctor had given me a year to live if I didn't give up. This is why I left Stuff and joined Cab Calloway.[1]

He came on board at the Stanley Theater in Pittsburgh on February 21, 1941.

Dizzy, who had performed all the Calloway trumpet solos during the previous eighteen months, was in a state of denial as he tried to discourage his new rival. He told Jones, "I didn't think you was coming, because you ain't gonna get nothing to play. We set up a show for a whole year and if you don't have a solo, you don't have one for a year."[2]

Dizzy soon found out that Cab was willing to rewrite the show for Jones—and more. Calloway believed that audiences would strongly prefer Jones' mellow, accessible swing to Dizzy's chromatic and frequently dissonant bebop (which the bandleader often characterized as "Chinese music"). He quickly went to work to create a starring role for Jones. First, he commissioned a tune called "Jonah Joins the Cab" and recorded it on March 5, 1941, less than two weeks after the trumpeter's arrival. Then, he invited Jones to solo on the number in front of the band instead of from within the trumpet section. No previous Calloway soloist, not even Chu Berry, had been afforded this privilege.

In addition to cutting back Dizzy's solos drastically, he asked Jones to join "The Cab Jivers," a quintet that played the role of a "band within a band" similar to Benny Goodman's quintets and sextets. This move was particularly galling to Dizzy, who felt that, since his hiring in 1939, Berry and other band veterans had unfairly prevailed upon Calloway to exclude him from the group. He had confronted Berry and Calloway several times on the issue, to no avail.

Dizzy was deeply hurt and angered by Jones's ascendancy, and he acted out with childish, disruptive pranks. He alienated several bandmates by setting fire to sheets of cellophane placed on their chests while they napped and by giving them "hot foots" (sneaking up and sticking lit matches between the soles and uppers of their shoes).

On the bandstand, he would indulge in horseplay specifically designed to anger Calloway: miming the throwing of a football, placing a hand above his eyes as if searching for a friend and then waving to the imaginary friend, shooting spitballs across the stage. Calloway would often be singing love songs during these shenanigans and would become irate when the audience laughed at tender moments. Due to their boredom with the predictable, repetitive shows, other band members sometimes participated in the pranks; Dizzy, however, was the culprit most of the time. Calloway would bawl Dizzy out about these incidents, and Dizzy would take it without reply. The situation became more explosive as the months wore on.

The Harlem jam sessions became increasingly important as outlets to assuage Dizzy's hurt. Fortunately, we have recordings that document his work at Minton's during this time of discontent. Jerry Newman, a Columbia University undergraduate and a hard-core fan of the new music, made them with a bulky recorder using acetate blanks. Despite his rudimentary equipment, he achieved decent sound quality; laughter, the hubbub of conversation, and shouts of encouragement are admixed with the music.

Newman caught Dizzy during May 1941 in two performances of "Stardust" and one of "Kerouac," a version of the popular Dorothy Fields–Jimmy McHugh tune, "Exactly Like You." Newman and Dizzy named the latter for another Columbian habitué of the Harlem clubs, Beat-novelist-in-embryo Jack Kerouac. (Dizzy had earlier vetoed naming the tune "Ginsberg" for Kerouac's pal and Beat poet, Allen Ginsberg.)

On the first version of "Stardust," Dizzy took a full thirty-two-bar chorus and then, following a solo by tenor saxophonist Don Byas, a half chorus. He articulated a wistful and harmonically advanced interpretation of the song, and created a particularly poignant phrase in the first bars of the half chorus. On the second version, performed with a group featuring the pianist Ken Kersey, Dizzy used a mute as he spun out a more lyrical and romantic interpretation of the Hoagy Carmichael standard.

The relaxed atmosphere of the jam session prevails on "Kerouac," where Dizzy alternates solos with Kersey and stretches out for a total of eight choruses as the spectators urge him on. His performance is well structured as he builds confidently to an intense climax.

The Newman recordings and his recorded work at the time with Calloway confirm that, almost a year after his encounter with Parker, Dizzy had still not achieved a mature bebop style. Remnants of swing harmony and phrasing persist, and his solos lack the rhythmic dynamism of his later work.

Newman also recorded dazzling improvisations by Charlie Christian during May 1941 at both Minton's and Monroe's. The guitarist received particularly brilliant support from Kenny Clarke on two of the Minton's tracks, "Swing to Bop (Topsy)" and "Stompin' at the Savoy"; the two men seemed to be in telepathic contact as the drummer anticipated Christian's every move with wonderfully supportive rhythmic licks. Thelonious Monk contributed a rollicking, if harmonically unadventurous, solo on "Swing to Bop (Topsy)."

Christian never recorded again. In mid-June he collapsed in Chicago and was rushed to Bellevue Hospital in New York, where his condition was described as "fair, not dangerous." When he improved slightly, he was transferred to a municipal sanitarium on Staten Island.

Dizzy never stopped pushing his bebop concepts within the Calloway band, and he even made Jonah Jones a short-term convert. It happened during the summer of 1941, shortly after the two men heard Charlie Parker with the McShann band in an Omaha nightclub. Jonah remembered:

He'd already heard Charlie and he was raving about this guy that runs the G-minor 7th against a C 7th, and that gives you your flatted fifth, your flatted seventh, your flatted ninth, and all that. . . .
So now he gets enough nerve to get up on the stand, and he

had a chorus of "Some of These Days," and he makes the [bebop] thing, and it sounded real funny. . . . And Cab said, "What the hell is that? Don't make that in my band. Don't play that, whatever it is. I don't want to hear that. Give that part to Jonah."

I started playing it, and at the same time Dizzy is showing me this thing. He's so insistent about this. . . . So I get on the stand with "Some of These Days," and I made one of these things, and Cab said, "You too? I'm going to fire both of you. I'm going to fire both of you, playing that. I won't have that in my band."

So I said, "I better stay away from this." So I went back to play-ing my old way.[3]

The long-simmering animosity between Dizzy and Calloway boiled over into violence at the State Theater in Hartford, Con-necticut, on September 21, 1941. A large spitball splatted onto a spotlight as Milt Hinton was taking a solo, and Calloway immedi-ately accused Dizzy of throwing it. For once he was not at fault; Jones was the guilty party.

The confrontation heated up as Dizzy protested his innocence, and Calloway repeatedly called him a liar. Finally, Calloway slapped him across the face. Blinded with anger, Dizzy lunged at Calloway with a knife just as Milt Hinton attempted to part them. Hinton deflected the weapon, intended for Calloway's side, and it sliced into the bandleader's buttock. Other men separated the two, and Calloway headed for his dressing room, where he discovered that blood was staining his elegant white suit. He fired Dizzy before being rushed to a hospital, where ten stitches closed his wound. Lorraine was waiting for her husband backstage, and the two quickly packed and headed by bus for New York.

When *Downbeat* reported the encounter on October 15, 1941, the headline read: "Cab Calloway 'Carved' by Own Trumpet Man!!" Dizzy and Calloway were reconciled two years after the stabbing, and Jones did not confess to throwing the spitball until decades later.

The Calloway incident was a reprise of Dizzy's childish fight with Edgar Hayes two years earlier—with consequences far more serious. Dizzy had not yet learned, at age twenty-three, to control the anger that boiled up dangerously when he felt he was wronged. The chain of events leading up to the stabbing—the juvenile acting out, the immature flaunting of authority, the destructive pranks—appears to be a continuing unconscious rebellion against the father who had whipped Dizzy as a boy every week.

To his credit, Dizzy gradually found ways to tame his anger, and, as the decades passed, he grew spiritually to become a peaceable and positive presence to everyone he encountered.

JAMMING WITH BIRD 16

JUST TWO WEEKS AFTER HIS DISMISSAL BY CAB CAL-
loway, Dizzy found almost a month's work in Boston with the
band that Ella Fitzgerald had taken over after Chick Webb died.
This October 1941 engagement marked, for Dizzy, the start of
roughly a year of freelancing during which he performed with
more than ten bands.

He endured considerable anxiety as he scuffled for work, but
later in life he would say that his firing by Calloway had been a
blessing, because during this freelance period, he began performing frequently with Charlie Parker, thereby launching one of the
most important collaborations in jazz history. In addition, he was
able to hone his skills in highly varied musical settings.

Two things in particular pleased Dizzy about the job in
Boston: Ella added "Down Under," his new tune, to her group's
repertory, and he was reunited with Kenny Clarke, who had left
Minton's late in the summer of 1941 for a short, ill-fated stint

with the Louis Armstrong Orchestra. He and Armstrong had bonded well, in large part because they shared a strong partiality to marijuana, but the band's manager felt that Armstrong needed a more celebrated performer at the drum set. Clarke was ignominiously dropped from the band in a small Georgia town at 1:30 a.m. in favor of the better-known O'Neil Spencer, who had achieved renown with the Spirits of Rhythm and John Kirby's sextet.

On October 30, 1941, Dizzy and Clarke were saddened by the news that Chu Berry was killed in an auto accident. When they returned to New York from Boston a couple of days later, Berry's widow, who lived in the same building as the Gillespies, gave Chu's piano to Dizzy, who, aided by a group of friends, lugged the instrument up several flights to his apartment.

During their Boston sojourn, Dizzy found time with Clarke to sketch out the main theme of "Salt Peanuts," which became one of bebop's most enduring anthems. As with several other bebop compositions, its harmonies were based on the chord sequence of a popular song—in this case, Gershwin's "I Got Rhythm." The two men also landed New York jobs starting on November 5, 1941, with Benny Carter's excellent sextet at a nightclub called Kelly's Stable. The beboppers would add a modernist flavor to a group that otherwise favored an advanced, sophisticated version of swing.

Benny Carter was a master of American music. Saxophonist, trumpeter, bandleader, composer, arranger, Princeton professor, creator of TV and movie scores, he would remain active as a writer and an arranger until his death at ninety-five in 2003.

Carter decided to put together a sextet in the autumn of 1941 after closing down a big band due to anemic bookings. He had participated with Dizzy in the Hampton "Hot Mallets" session in 1939 but knew little about his work until his guitarist John Collins praised Dizzy so highly that Carter had to hire him. (Dizzy knew Collins from the Harlem after-hours scene, and he and Ben Webster frequently visited Collins's apartment to jam with him.)

The other members of the sextet were Kenny Clarke, bassist Charlie Drayton, reedman Al Gibson, and on piano, Clarke's friend Sonny White. The group performed at Kelly's until December 15, took a two-week break for the Christmas holidays, and then moved to the Famous Door for a booking opposite Billie Holiday, which ran until February 4, 1942.

Dizzy and Clarke made their debuts with the band on November 5 at a concert at the Museum of Modern Art on West Fifty-third Street in New York. They worked the event with singer Maxine Sullivan, the fabulous bebop tap dancer Baby Lawrence, and the jazz harpsichordist Sylvia Marlowe, who performed "Harpsichord Blues and Boogie Woogie." After the concert (Dizzy's first), they walked a block and a half to Kelly's Stable to begin their engagement.

The pseudorustic Kelly's Stable, its floor covered with sawdust, was one of seven jazz clubs situated at the time on "The Street," the stretch of Fifty-second Street between Fifth and Seventh avenues that had become the epicenter of jazz in New York. Kelly's and the Hickory House were located between Sixth and Seventh, and the others—the Onyx, the Famous Door, the Three Deuces, the Yacht Club, and Jimmy Ryan's—were found between Fifth and Sixth.

Interspersed with the jazz clubs were a posh restaurant (the 21 Club), several small bars and eateries, a strip joint (the Samoa), and two cabarets (Jack White's Club 18 and Leon and Eddie's). The transformation of The Street from a residential enclave to a center for entertainment occurred during Prohibition when landlords discovered that speakeasies were an extremely lucrative species of tenant. The author Robert Benchley in 1932 counted thirty-eight illegal saloons on Fifty-second Street in the single block between Fifth and Sixth avenues. The speakeasy heritage ensured that there was a strong mob presence in the management of the clubs after Prohibition ended on December 5, 1933.

With the exception of the large and commodious Hickory House, the clubs were not designed for the claustrophobic. They were low-ceilinged, windowless rooms squeezed into the twenty-foot-wide ground floors of three- or four-story brownstones, and their maximum capacity hovered around 110 customers.

The bars typically ran half the length of a sidewall, and the bandstands shared the rear walls with the entrances to the restrooms. The bandstands could comfortably accommodate five or six musicians but were often required to provide space for more; when the fourteen-piece Basie aggregation performed at the Famous Door, the men were squeezed together like rush-hour subway passengers.

Fifty-second Street patrons squinted at the musicians through a haze of tobacco smoke as they sat at tables the size of large soup plates and rubbed shoulders with drug dealers, hipsters, hustlers, and pimps (customers were often serviced by prostitutes in the men's rooms). Bar customers had to hold their glasses tightly because the bartenders loved to run up their tabs by replacing half-finished drinks with fresh ones. The musicians usually drank between sets at the White Rose Tavern, around the corner on Sixth Avenue; drinks were cheaper there, and the place offered a free buffet.

If you were a fan, you endured all the aggravation because the music was so good, and you usually planned to visit more than one club. Every joint featured a star or two, and the varied musical menu ran from Dixieland to swing to modern jazz (the word *be-bop* would not enter the language until three years later).

With such an abundance of talent packed into two blocks, the musicians couldn't resist the opportunities to sit in with their peers, and they constantly crisscrossed The Street to jam with each other during their breaks. Trumpeter Shorty Rogers remembered Dizzy in 1941:

> He was playing with Benny Carter, he was a sideman in the band, and he was so obsessed thinking, "I want to play, I want to play." He'd get this hour intermission and he couldn't stand it. And I actually would see him walking down the street in the middle of the road dodging cars, with his horn, and he'd look in each club, like, "I can go in this one and sit in." And he would find a place and jam.[1]

The Street moved steadily, if slowly, toward integration at a time when the rest of the New York entertainment world outside of Harlem was segregated. It started when Art Tatum and the all-black Spirits of Rhythm celebrated the opening of the Onyx as a legal, post-Repeal saloon in February 1934. Billie Holiday and pianist Teddy Wilson performed at the Famous Door in 1935, and by the early 1940s black entertainers were being booked into all the jazz spots where they performed before mixed audiences. Writing in 1971, Arnold Shaw, The Street's historian, found this phenomenon historically significant:

> Viewed sociologically, 52nd St. is the story of how Harlem came downtown—not only its music and dances, but its chicken and rib joints and its talented people. The Street embodies the struggle of black singers and musicians to gain their rightful place in white society . . . [although] they had their problems with prejudiced New Yorkers, Southern servicemen, and the Manhattan police, The Street provided employment and a showcase for their talents, opening its doors a little more quickly than the rest of Manhattan's midtown restaurants, hotels, theaters, and even movie palaces.
>
> "Fifty-Second Street was a mother," says Dizzy Gillespie, the noted bop trumpeter. "I say mother—and I don't mean mother-fucker, though it was that too."[2]

Dizzy derived an added benefit from the Kelly's Stable gig— the opportunity to listen every night to the Nat King Cole Trio and to his hero Art Tatum, who shared the bill with Carter's sextet. Pop singers Miss Rhapsody and Billy Daniels, who served as emcee, also performed in the show.

Dizzy became fascinated at Kelly's with the challenging chord changes of "How High the Moon," a pop ballad Cole featured in his set. Cole ran down the harmony for him, and Dizzy rushed uptown to share his discovery with Monk and the other Minton's musicians. They speeded up the tempo, altered the chords, and transformed the song into a staple of bebop jam sessions. In 1946, Charlie Parker and trumpeter Benny Harris wrote a new tune, "Ornithology," over those same chords.

Dizzy composed his most famous song, "A Night in Tunisia" (originally called "Interlude"), during the Kelly's Stable engagement. It happened when he was noodling at the piano during a lull in the production of a Carter sextet/Maxine Sullivan "soundie," a short film to be used in the then-popular movie juke-boxes. He hit a thirteenth chord, and when he played its notes in sequence, he found that he had the key melodic fragment for the A section of the composition. He wrote the lilting B section soon after. As he recalled, his sophisticated bass line broke new ground:

> The melody had a very Latin, even oriental feeling, the rhythm came out of the bebop style—the way we played with rhythmic ac-cents—and that mixture introduced a special kind of syncopation in the bass line. In fact, for the first time in a jazz piece I'd heard, the bass line didn't go one-two-three-four-, "boom, boom, boom, boom." . . .
>
> The heavily syncopated rhythm in the bass line probably gave a whole lotta cats ideas.[3]

The Kelly's Stable engagement was set to end on December 15, and its last week was marked, for reasons of national security, by "blackouts" of signage on The Street as the club owners re-sponded to the December 7 attack on Pearl Harbor. Otherwise, business continued as usual.

During Carter's two-week holiday break, Dizzy worked in the popular white big band led by saxophonist Charlie Barnet. Dizzy noticed that both the phrasing by the musicians and the arrange-ments were less varied stylistically than what he had encountered in black bands, and he made use of this knowledge when he be-gan to sell arrangements to white leaders several months later. Barnet was impressed by Dizzy's musicianship but irritated by his constant horseplay.

When the Carter group started up again after New Year's at the Famous Door, they earned an excellent revue in *Metronome* from a writer who noted that "Dizzy Gillespie's trumpeting is topnotch, and . . . he fits in excellently with the Carter ensem-ble."[4] Dizzy was happily reunited at the club with Jimmy Hamil-ton, his intellectual mid-1930s colleague from the Frankie Fairfax band, who had replaced reedman Gibson.

The manager of the Famous Door complained to Carter that

his customers did not like Dizzy's strange harmonies, but Carter defied him and told Dizzy to continue playing whatever he wanted. The bandleader remembered: "When the new ideas started coming, much of what I heard sounded weird to me, because the men were experimenting. . . . I can't say that I understand everything they were attempting to do, but I could see that Dizzy, when he was with me for several months, was groping for something and he knew his music."[5]

The Carter engagement was particularly satisfying for Dizzy. Its structured environment, a perfect complement to the open-ended Harlem jam session scene, helped him toward more disciplined artistic growth. He appreciated the fact that Carter, ten years older and a swing icon, provided him with encouragement and support:

> Benny Carter, [Coleman] Hawkins, Clyde Hart, Big Sid Catlett—their music was so pure and basic that they could bridge the distance from one style to another. Benny's played with my generation, and he's right at home because he has the foundation. . . .
>
> I learned a lot from him. Playing with him was my best experience next to playing with Charlie Parker. Benny has a phenomenal knowledge of music. . . . Benny and Hawkins had the great taste in music to understand my generation and come in with us.[6]

The sextet format afforded Dizzy much more solo space than he had had with Calloway's big band, and he used it to refine both his musical ideas and his technique. He was inspired every night by Carter's mercurial improvisations and Clarke's imaginative percussion, and he found great value in a workshop that Carter created for his sidemen. He encouraged Dizzy and the other musicians to write their own tunes, and he worked with them on arrangements that the group then played; if there were rough spots, they would continue writing and performing until they were happy with the finished product. Dizzy later called his association with Carter "an extended honeymoon."

Dizzy wangled a night off from Carter on January 9, 1942, to sit in with Lucky Millinder at the Savoy Ballroom; the Jay McShann band with Charlie Parker was opening there that evening in a "battle of the bands" against Millinder, and Dizzy wanted to be in on the action.

McShann and Parker were riding a wave of success in January 1942. John Tumino, an effective manager, had guided the band for nearly two years through increasingly popular tours and had secured for them a recording contract with Decca, a newcomer label that had muscled its way into the number three spot in the industry behind Columbia and RCA Victor. The band scored a major hit with "Confessin' the Blues," which sold over three hundred thousand copies, and it earned excellent grosses on tour, breaking attendance records in places such as Houston and Oklahoma City. Tumino remembered that one of his main responsibilities was to ensure that Bird had an instrument to play every night: "Charlie Parker was always broke every morning. He was hocking his instrument every day to get the stuff. I'd have to go and get the money, get the horn, and put him to work the next night, and make him promise not to hock it before he got to work."[7]

McShann's brash and bluesy Kansas City swing easily carried the day against Millinder's smooth stylings at the Savoy, and Parker's solos on "Cherokee" and "Hootie's Blues" caused a sensation. Dizzy corralled Parker after the show and took him to Monroe's, where they jammed until breakfast. The *Metronome* writer raved about McShann's debut:

> Every once in a while, it is a reviewer's privilege to introduce a great new band to his readers. This is such an occasion. For not since Count Basie came out of Kansas City has so impressive a jazz organization made its appearance in New York City for the first time. . . .
>
> Before anything else in McShann's music is the beat. The rhythm section . . . get a colossal beat and keep it up. . . .
>
> The jazz set forth by the Parker alto is superb . . . His continual search for wild ideas, and the consistency with which he finds them, compensate for weaknesses that should be easily overcome.[8]

McShann kept his band on the East Coast until the late spring of 1942, mixing engagements at the Savoy and the Apollo with short trips to New England and the South. Dizzy couldn't get enough of Bird and sat in with McShann so often that the band-leader reserved a chair for him in the trumpet section. His part-nership with Bird had begun in earnest.

Sunday afternoon broadcasts from the Savoy brought the band and Parker, in particular, nationwide recognition. John Lewis, who became a close associate of Dizzy's and whose distinguished career included forty-five years as the leader of the Modern Jazz Quartet, was captivated by Parker's magic when he heard the pro-grams twenty-five hundred miles away in Albuquerque, New Mexico: "The alto on those broadcasts opened up a whole new world of music for me. . . . It was new and years ahead of any-body in jazz. He was in a whole new system of sound and time. The emcee didn't even announce his name . . . I didn't learn it was Charlie Parker until after the war."[9]

When the Famous Door engagement ended on February 4 and Carter began to organize a big band for an extended cross-country tour, Dizzy elected to stay in New York; he performed with Fletcher Henderson, Woody Herman, and three other bands during the next two months, and jammed in Harlem with Parker nearly every night.

He began an association on February 9 that would last a life-time when he participated in a New York record date for Decca produced by Leonard Feather, a British-born writer, impresario, and composer. Feather, who met Dizzy when the Carter sextet performed the Brit's arrangement of "Lady Be Good," was hesi-tant to hire him because he knew Dizzy for his "fascinating and nerve-wracking" bebop solos, and the session was blues-oriented.

For the date, Dizzy and Jimmy Hamilton joined a sextet led by alto saxophonist Pete Brown backing up singers Helen Humes and Nora Lee King on four numbers; three of them were written by Feather. Dizzy's only contribution, aside from the ensemble passages, is a deft, linear nine-bar obligato behind the lusty-voiced Miss King. Feather soon overcame his misgivings about "nerve-wracking" bebop and became one of its most vociferous champions.

Dizzy visited Charlie Christian whenever he could at the sanatorium on Staten Island and was saddened as the tuberculosis continued to ravage his body. Jimmy Maxwell, a Benny Goodman trumpeter, recalled the guitarist's downhill slide: "So-called friends would come by with an ounce of pot, some bottles and a couple of professional girls from uptown, thinking they were giving him a good time when they were only speeding him along on the way out. Of course, in those days, if you were black and went to one of those big county hospitals, you weren't likely to come back."[10]

Despite significant help from Count Basie's doctor, Christian failed to rally and died, at age twenty-five, on March 2, 1942. Dizzy was inconsolable for several days.

The winter of 1942 marked a major advance for bebop as Bird performed with fellow pioneers Monk and Clarke for the first time and Dizzy joined in. Minton's (where Monk was still employed) and Monroe's continued to be at the center of the action.

At Monroe's, Bird and Dizzy encountered for the first time a prodigious eighteen-year-old drummer named Max Roach. The careers of the three men became closely intertwined as Roach went on to become the greatest of all jazz percussionists. He emerged as the bebop drummer of choice after Kenny Clarke was drafted in mid-1943.

Jack Kerouac in 1957 wrote about hearing Bird, Dizzy, and Monk at Minton's fifteen years earlier:

Charlie Parker . . . talking eloquent like great poets of foreign languages singing in foreign countries with lyres, by seas, and no one understands because the language isn't alive in the land yet—Bop is the language from America's inevitable Africa. . . . Africa is the name of the flue and kick beat, off to one side—the sudden squeak uninhibited that screams muffled at any moment from Dizzy Gillespie's trumpet. . . .

Bop is here to stay . . . figure it with histories and lost kings of immemorial tribes in jungle and Fellaheen town and otherwise. . . .

Dizzy spats his lips tight-drum together and drives a high screeching fantastic clear note that has everybody in the joint look up. . . .

Monk punched anguished nub fingers crawling at the keyboard

to tear up foundations and guts of jazz from the big masterbox, to make Charlie Parker hear his cry and sigh—to jar the orchestra into vibrations—to elicit gloom from the doom of the black piano.

Dizzy screamed, Charlie squealed, Monk crashed, the drummer kicked, dropped a bomb—the bass questionmark plunked— and off they whaled on Salt Peanuts . . .

They came into their own, they jumped, they had jazz and took it in their hands and saw its history vicissitudes and development and turned it to their weighty use. . . . This man who was sent, stoned and stabbed is now . . . home at last, his music is here to stay, his history has washed over us, his imperialistic kingdoms are coming.[11]

Dizzy stayed close to the Harlem scene until March 31, 1942, when he took a high-paying job with Les Hite's California big band that was touring the East Coast. Walter "Gil" Fuller, Hite's arranger and a friend of Dizzy's who in the mid-1940s became his close associate, talked Hite into hiring Dizzy despite the bandleader's fears engendered by the stabbing of Cab Calloway. Hite was black, and his aggregation was subsidized by his girlfriend, a handsome white woman named Vera "Fluffy" Crofton. She had inherited a retail fortune and spared no expense on salaries, uniforms, transportation, or accommodations.

Dizzy's many nights jamming with Bird found fruition as he recorded, for the first time, a true bebop solo; it occurred on "Jersey Bounce" with Hite's band in mid-May 1942. The performance represents a major advance over the swing-tinged "Stardust" and "Kerouac" recorded a year earlier, and it showed that Dizzy had harnessed Parker's unique stylings to his own abundant rhythmic and harmonic talents. In the midst of Hite's flaccid two-beat rendition of the song, Dizzy unleashed a startling sixteen-bar solo replete with Parkeresque stylistic flourishes: accents between the beats and at odd parts of the beat, unexpected hesitations, startling tempo changes—with all the notes strung together in a smooth, logical structure. And the entire solo was carried off with virtuosic control; at one point Dizzy played a series of flawless ultrafast sixteenth-note triplets, unheard of in jazz at the time.

Despite his growing artistic maturity, Dizzy, at age twenty-four, had still not curbed his drive to undermine authority figures. As fellow trumpeter Joe Wilder remembered, this childish propensity led to trouble on May 19, 1942:

> We were in Washington at the Howard Theater, and Les was doing his little thing, dancing in front of the band. Dizzy is imitating every move, and the audience is hysterical, breaking up. Les has his back turned to the band, and he thinks it's him, the dance he's doing. He's just thrilled with this. When Les turned around to look at the band, Dizzy would be sitting down, the horn up. Like a saint.
>
> This went on for three days. The fourth day Les turned around quicker, and Dizzy couldn't sit down in time.
>
> Les was so mad that when he came off he said, "Two weeks notice, that's it. This band is gone." Each guy went to his office to get paid at the end of the week, and he said: "That notice is not for you. I want to get rid of Dizzy and he already cut Cab, and I'm afraid to fire him." Everybody had to wait for Dizzy to leave before they could come back to work.
>
> Except me. I took Les at his word. Before the payday meetings, I took a job with Lionel Hampton, and I was out of there.[12]

By the spring of 1942, word about the development of modern jazz (not yet called bebop) had spread in the big band business, and several orchestras wanted to keep up with the times by having at least one modernist arrangement in their books. Dizzy took advantage of this as he supplemented his sometimes erratic freelance performing income by selling arrangements at one hundred dollars each to such bandleaders as Woody Herman, Jimmy Dorsey, and Ina Ray Hutton. Herman greatly admired his work and believed that, if Dizzy had specialized in arranging, he would have become a giant of that profession. Herman's band was full of young bebop enthusiasts, and they experienced no trouble in learning Dizzy's charts, but he had to spend time tutoring the Dorsey and Hutton crews before they could master his music.

On May 24, 1942, Herman recorded a wonderfully spirited

rendition of Dizzy's arrangement of his own tune "Down Under." The lead trumpet part sounds like a Dizzy improvisation, the guitarist starts his solo with the opening phrase from "Salt Peanuts," and the ensemble passages contained subtle bebop touches. Dizzy's confidence in his modernist vision soared when he heard this first authentic big band bebop recording.

Just eleven days after he was fired by Hite, Dizzy found employment on May 30, 1942, with Lucky Millinder, the man who refused to hire him in 1937.

Millinder, a personable showman who ran a successful middle-of-the-road swing band from 1934 until 1952, had an eye for talented sidemen. When Dizzy came on board, they included pianist and deputy bandleader Bill Doggett, Dizzy's partner in harmonic study in Philadelphia in 1935, trumpeter Freddie Webster, and saxophonist Tab Smith.

Dizzy created an outstanding solo on a July 29 Millinder recording of "Little John Special," a blues composed by the bandleader. Millinder's writing was decidedly unoriginal; he stole verbatim from Count Basie a chorus from "Boogie Woogie" and a riff from "One O'Clock Jump," and in a nod to Dizzy and Kenny Clarke, he threw in, near the end of the piece, the principal four-bar riff from "Salt Peanuts." Dizzy played two twelve-bar blues choruses in succession, and his bebop inventiveness topped his work on Hite's "Jersey Bounce," offering further proof that he had left for good the world of swing.

We are fortunate to have "Little John Special" as evidence of Dizzy's artistic transformation, because, on August 1, 1942, the day after it was recorded, the American Federation of Musicians, led by James Caeser Petrillo, struck the record companies over record royalties and several ancillary issues. The union won after a bruising struggle that lasted for more than two years; Decca settled in September 1943 and Columbia and RCA Victor capitulated in November 1944. Dizzy did not enter a studio again until February 16, 1944, and Parker would not return until September 15 of the same year.

The period of the record strike was an extraordinarily fecund one for the development of bebop, and it is a tragedy that we are forced to rely on a handful of private pressings and air checks (recordings made from live broadcasts) for our aural knowledge of the era. The only extant evidence of Dizzy's work is a privately made, seven-and-one-half-minute disc of February 15, 1943 (with Parker), and a three-and-one-half-minute air check from January 1944.

Millinder was a very fickle boss; he hired and fired at will. In late September, he gave Dizzy two weeks' notice and a few days later tried to hire him back at a higher salary. But Dizzy refused the offer in early October, because he had secured his first engagement as a leader, a seven-week gig at Nat Segal's raffish Downbeat Club under the shadow of city hall in downtown Philadelphia.

Dizzy stayed with his mother and a sister in a ramshackle apartment a few blocks away and took the hour-and-a-half train ride to New York to be with Lorraine on his days off and to participate in Sunday afternoon jam sessions with Parker and others at Kelly's Stable and Jimmy Ryan's on The Street.

Dizzy's group opened a few days after his twenty-fifth birthday in late October, and Segal paid him $150 per week and covered the salaries of the pianist, the drummer, and the bass player (W. O. Smith, Dizzy's Fairfax band associate) who backed him up.

Dizzy hired seventeen-year-old Stan Levey, the first white man to play an important role in bebop, after the original drummer quit three weeks into the gig. The son of a prizefight manager, Levey dropped out of high school at fourteen and at sixteen became both a pianist at the Downbeat and a professional boxer. Inspired by Chick Webb, he practiced on a drum set at home but never played professionally.

Dizzy heard Levey beating out rhythms on a table as the group rehearsed one afternoon and was impressed. He stopped and asked the teenager if he played drums, and when Levey answered yes, he was invited to the bandstand. Dizzy showed him some basic rhythmic patterns, and Levey picked them up quickly.

He was hired ten days later. During the following weeks, Dizzy gave him an advanced course in percussion as they spent hours together at the drum set, and Levey emerged from the engagement an accomplished bebop drummer.

Dizzy's mentoring of Levey was entirely in keeping with his passion for spreading the gospel of what he called "our music." Throughout his adult life, Dizzy tirelessly taught it and proselytized for it.

Word spread within Philadelphia's jazz world that an exciting modernist was holding forth in town, and several outstanding musicians, including Tommy Dorsey, Buddy De Franco, and Charlie Shavers, dropped by to sit in. Dizzy was especially delighted to trade spirited choruses with his pal Shavers.

Another habitué was Red Rodney, a fifteen-year-old white trumpeter. The Downbeat was located on the second floor, and the youngster, barred from the club proper because of his age, would listen from the staircase until bouncers shooed him away. Rodney, who was very fair and whose hair was somewhere between blond and red, later became Charlie Parker's trumpeter. When they traveled south where integrated groups were not tolerated, he passed as a black with aberrant skin coloring and was billed as "Albino Red."

Since his dismissal by Calloway more than a year before the Philadelphia gig, Dizzy's art had advanced considerably as, with Parker's help, he had developed a genuine bebop style and left swing behind. A new chapter in his saga with Parker was written when they joined the big band led by master pianist Earl Hines in early 1943.

THE HINES BAND 17

BY LATE 1942, THE MUSIC OF DIZZY AND THE OTHER bebop pioneers was radiating outward from Harlem and finding enthusiastic listeners. One of them was singer Billy Eckstine, one of Earl Hines's major stars; he found an opportunity to fulfill a dream of working with Dizzy and Bird every night when Hines suddenly needed a trumpeter and a saxophonist in January 1943.

Eckstine, with the help of Shadow Wilson, yet another Fairfax band alumnus and Hines's drummer, lured Dizzy with the promise that Bird was about to join the band and Bird with the promise that Dizzy was going to do the same thing. The subterfuge worked; Dizzy came on board around January 15, 1943, and Parker signed up two weeks later.

Jay McShann's tolerance of Bird's addiction ended after two and a half years in August of 1942, when Bird, in stocking feet, passed out from an overdose while attempting a solo in front of the band at the Paradise Theater in Detroit. The successful resuscitation was frantic at first, because his pulse had disappeared.

He found his way back to New York, where he lived hand to mouth, joined the house band at Monroe's (which included Max Roach), and jammed at Minton's. As Monroe's bandleader Al Tinney recalled, Bird's addictive behavior continued unabated, and heroin was not its only cause:

> I saw Charlie Parker get high off of nutmeg and Coca Cola and stand up on the bandstand, and he was like out of it completely. We were off the bandstand, and Charlie was still sitting there. . . . The bass player put matches all around Charlie Parker's foot and he lit 'em up and Charlie Parker didn't do anything but scratch his face. He was that much under the spell of this nutmeg, and it made him immobile.[1]

Parker, who normally played alto saxophone, replaced tenor saxophonist Budd Johnson in Hines's band, and the leader bought him a tenor when he joined; he adapted readily to the unfamiliar instrument.

From his epochal Hot Five and Hot Seven recordings with Louis Armstrong in the late 1920s to his brilliant solo albums of the late 1970s, Hines was a towering figure who stands in the jazz piano pantheon alongside musicians such as Tatum, Monk, Bud Powell, and Bill Evans. Dizzy treated him with awe: "Earl Hines is a giant. He stands on an even level with anyone in the history of our music. The history of the piano, the history of modern piano, *is* Earl Hines. A great influence. Our music reveals itself that way, through messages to the musicians who come and create a big influence, and after they go, their stamp is on the music."[2]

What fascinated Dizzy, Bird, and the other beboppers about Hines was his mastery of rhythm, and they learned from him every night. Hines preferred conservative diatonic harmony, but he was the most daring rhythmic improviser ever to play jazz piano. The listener often walked a musical tightrope with him, wondering how he would make it home safely after a daring sally into seeming rhythmic anarchy. Hines always swung, but he could not

abide a steady tempo. He would break it up with contrapuntal figures played alongside jangling flurries, two-to-a-bar changes in
direction, swirling arpeggios against darting, stabbing phrases, or
a striding left hand blending with a fuguelike countermelody in
the right. Gunther Schuller's assessment is enlightening:

> Hines compresses more ideas into a 32-bar solo than most pi-
> anists can manage in an entire evening. . . .
>   Hines is constantly engaging both hands in competitive ex-
> changes or vigorous dialogues. His mind (*and* fingers) are continu-
> ally driven towards complexity—rhythmic and contrapuntal
> complexity. . . . Ultimately it is his mind which is to be revered, a
> mind whose imagination and fertility are seemingly boundless.[3]

Unlike Calloway, Hines encouraged bebop innovation. He bought
arrangements from Dizzy and Bird, and allowed his modernist
sidemen total freedom in their improvisations. They in turn delighted in forcing Hines to take extra choruses by delaying their
entry on ensemble passages.

Dizzy and Bird were inseparable offstage as they practiced together, working jointly on harmonic problems and jamming after
hours almost every night. Bird was a constant trial for Hines, who
fined him many times for tardiness, leaving his horn in a pawnshop, and other disciplinary infractions. On one occasion, in an
effort to be on time, Bird stayed in a theater overnight and went to
sleep in a below-stage cranny. Unfortunately, he overslept and
missed the first show.

If we are to believe a local journalist, Hines and his crew
rocked its audience on February 14, 1943, at a Chicago dance:
"It's hard to describe the band without using the word 'wild'. . . It
has an unquenchable madness in its soul that seems to exert itself
from theme to theme. Earl likes it. The fellows like it. The crowd
likes it."[4] There was madness in the soul of the audience as well
that night; three of its members were victims of shootings. The
next night, Bob Redcross, a friend of Eckstine's who occasionally
served as his valet and driver, invited Dizzy and Bird to make a
private disc recording in his room at the Savoy Hotel; Oscar

Pettiford, in town with Charlie Barnet's big band, trudged glove-less for two miles with his bass in subzero temperatures to partic-ipate in the session.

The disc, wrapped in an old *Chicago Tribune*, did not surface until 1985. The sound quality is awful, but the music is excellent. With Pettiford supplying steadfast support, the two men jammed on "Sweet Georgia Brown" for seven and a half minutes; solo time was divided almost equally. Dizzy constantly encouraged Bird, who performed on tenor, with shouts of "Go, Yard" and "Yeah, yeah" and by clapping on the offbeats. Bird's sound on tenor is more sensuous than his biting timbre on alto, and his phrasing is smoother than Dizzy's as he coolly drops in chromatic tones be-tween the beats. Scott DeVeaux's analysis of the recording is en-lightening:

> At this point Parker's and Gillespie's approaches were still quite distinct. . . . It is Gillespie who is more conspicuously and self-consciously the progressive. His improvised lines are densely packed with chromatic dissonances. . . .
>
> Peppering Gillespie's solos are flamboyant and obviously well polished gestures . . . in which chromatic dissonance is wedded to equally disruptive rhythms. These are the "hooks" of the nascent bebop style, naggingly memorable and attention-getting: off-center whole-tone scale fragments, tricky polyrhythmic alterations of adjacent notes, and Gillespie's trademark, complicated triplet patterns that fit easily into a variety of harmonic contexts. They ad-vertise both Gillespie's virtuosity and the modernity of his idiom. . . .
>
> By these standards, Parker seems more conservative. There are no startling shifts into faster rhythmic note values or polyrhythmic interruptions of the flow of eighth notes—although this may simply be a constraint of the less familiar and more cum-bersome tenor saxophone. . . . More surprisingly, there are fewer harsh, disorienting dissonances. . . . There are enough passing dissonances to give his lines both interesting shape and an extra dimension of momentum, but the dissonances are generally less ostentatious than Gillespie's flatted fifths and whole-tone scales.[5]

Eckstine, constantly scouting for talent, recruited singer Sarah Vaughan on hearing her at an "Amateur Night" competition in early March 1943 at the Apollo. He remembered:

> This little girl . . . was seventeen at the time. By the time she finished eight bars of her [first] song, I was back stage. . . .
>
> I asked Sarah to come to our rehearsal. Earl sat down at the piano and said, "Come on, let me hear you." And she started singing. It was just like one of those old-time movie things—everybody stopped and started listening. . . . Earl took her with us although we already had a girl vocalist. He made the exception because Sarah could play the piano. He put two pianos on the stage and had her sitting there in her little gown playing everything on the piano.
>
> He brought her out to sing when we went into the Apollo. She completely stormed the place. She upset that place like you never heard anybody upset a theater.[6]

Vaughan achieved equal billing with Eckstine a month after joining the band, and she quickly bonded with the band's modernist clique (which included trombonist Benny Green and trumpeter Benny Harris in addition to Eckstine, Wilson, Gillespie, and Parker) to become a confirmed bebopper. The music of Dizzy and, particularly, Bird was her Juilliard; she studied their solos intently every night and looked to Dizzy when confronted with difficult harmonic or rhythmic problems. Bird wove obbligatos behind Vaughan's ballad performances, and Dizzy wrote arrangements for her and delighted audiences when he jitterbugged with her on hot numbers.

In early May 1943, the Hines band interrupted its tour of big-city venues to play a series of engagements at army camps in the South and Southwest. The tour gave rise to an anecdote that, for reasons known only to him, Dizzy retold endlessly; it illustrates the erudite vocabulary sometimes displayed by Bird. After a redneck in Pine Bluff, Arkansas, drew blood when he hit Dizzy in the head with a bottle, Bird confronted the man and said, "You took advantage of my friend, you cur." Dizzy was continually amazed that the word *cur* had found its way into Bird's lexicon.

Back in New York, Dizzy was fortunate on May 29 to be present at the creation of the first true Latin jazz composition. Mario Bauzá had become the musical director of the Afro-Cubans, the band headed by his brother-in-law, Machito, and he invited Dizzy to attend a rehearsal in a ballroom on 110th Street in Manhattan. Author Max Salazar recounted what happened:

> Bauzá started the rehearsal by urging Varona to play some piano vamp. He then sang out what [bassist] Andino should play along with the sounds he wanted from the reeds and brass sections. The broken scale sounds soon took form as a jazz melody. Bauzá began blowing jazz riffs on trumpet on top of the melody, then nodded to his alto saxist to ad lib. At the end of two hours, Bauzá successfully merged Cuban music with jazz and a new industry came into being.
>
> Dizzy Gillespie, an onlooker, behaved madly. . . . He acted as though he couldn't believe what he had just heard. . . . Gillespie excitedly asked Bauzá what he was going to title the song. Another onlooker remarked that the sound was exciting as "Tanga" (the African word for Marijuana). The tune was thus called Tanga . . . and the new sound of Latinized jazz joined the family of Cuban rhythms . . . He [Bauzá] united Cuban music and North American jazz forever.[7]

Bauzá's creation of what was, in effect, a new genre opened Dizzy's mind to a world of stimulating musical possibilities. He studied the Afro-Cubans obsessively in performance and on record, intensified his efforts to write authentic Latin-tinged tunes, and began formulating the ideas that led to his own groundbreaking Latino work four years later.

Dizzy and the Hines orchestra were performing at the Howard Theater in Washington, DC, when the most destructive riot in Harlem history took place during the night of August 1 and the morning of August 2, 1943. The disturbance began when a policeman shot and wounded a black soldier in the shoulder after he attempted to defend a woman whom the policeman was arresting. A rumor then spread quickly that the soldier was killed, and the entire community was ignited. Six people were shot dead, over two hundred were injured, and more than one thousand were arrested; property damage was severe as fierce looting continued for ten hours.

Dizzy was able to reach Lorraine by telephone, and she stayed close to their apartment until the violence subsided thirty-six hours later. From the stoop of her building, she witnessed raids on furniture, appliance, and clothing stores, and she remembered discerning looters discarding shoes until they found comfortable fits, and a Chinese restaurant owner who posted a sign that read, "We colored too."

A government commission found the root causes of the mayhem in racial discrimination and Harlem's acute poverty, but its investigations did not result in any remedial action. Ralph Ellison, who reported on the riot for the *New York Post*, made it the climactic scene of his towering novel, *Invisible Man*.

When the riot exploded, Harlem had already declined as a center of entertainment. A year earlier the U.S. Army and Navy, alarmed by high venereal disease rates, declared Harlem out of bounds for nonresident servicemen, and in April 1943, the police closed the Savoy Ballroom for being a haven for prostitutes (Malcolm X alleged that "the real reason was to keep Negroes from dancing with white women"); it did not reopen until December. Minton's remained in operation, but Clark Monroe closed his Uptown House and came downtown to Kelly's Stable to front a group of his Harlem musicians who performed their own repertory and provided accompaniment for Coleman Hawkins and Billy Daniels. One of them was Max Roach.

Banking on a false promise of jobs with a new Billy Eckstine big band, Dizzy, Bird, Shadow Wilson, and Eckstine left Hines's employ on August 11, 1943, as Harlem was returning to postriot normalcy. They would have to wait eight months before economic conditions allowed Eckstine's promise to be realized. In the meantime, because Hines had replaced them, they scuffled.

18
DIZZY LEADS
THE CHARGE

Gillespie was probably the single musician responsible for bring-
ing it [bebop] all together: for recognizing the signal greatness
of Charlie Parker; for codifying the harmony he had worked out
with Thelonious Monk and teaching it to others; for showing
piano players how to accompany in a fresh manner; for instruct-
ing bass players in the dos and don'ts of supplying appropriate
lines; and for teaching drummers how to get a grip on the inno-
vations Kenny Clarke had brought to jazz drumming. His was
one of the great minds in all American art.

—STANLEY CROUCH[1]

THE DECLINE OF HARLEM MEANT LITTLE TO DIZZY AS HE
planned his next steps. Full of confidence after more than eighteen
fruitful months with Bird and other kindred spirits, he was convinced that the bebop movement had matured to the point where

it had outgrown the Harlem scene and was ready to seek a broader audience.

He was delighted therefore when Oscar Pettiford, the bassist who had accompanied him and Bird at the Redcross recording in Chicago, asked him to join in leading a quintet that was scheduled to open at the Onyx on Fifty-second Street on October 20, 1943 (one day shy of Dizzy's twenty-sixth birthday); they would receive second billing behind star attraction Billie Holiday and would be in residence for several months. Pettiford looked to Dizzy, five years his senior and a veteran of the New York scene, to help him put together a top-flight ensemble. The Onyx paid each leader seventy-five dollars per week.

The bassist's fortunes had risen spectacularly during 1943. In January, at age twenty, he had been plucked from a defense plant job by Charlie Barnet and found stardom immediately with the leader's popular band. He left Barnet in May to work alongside Monk at Minton's and moved soon after to the Onyx, where he joined Roy Eldridge's band and so impressed the management that they offered him the October engagement. He also impressed the critics at *Esquire* magazine, who voted him number one on his instrument for 1943, and the editors of *Metronome*; in November 1943 he became the first bebop musician to rate a feature article in that magazine. It was written by Leonard Feather.

Pettiford, the first great bebop bassist, had completed the work of deceased trailblazer Jimmy Blanton (who succumbed to tuberculosis in 1942) in transforming the bass from a mere timekeeper into an instrument for imaginative improvisation. His credentials were impressive; he was a master of chromatic harmony who possessed both a remarkably fluid sense of time and a great gift for melody. While working to organize the group, Dizzy played an aborted engagement with Coleman Hawkins' small combo at Kelly's Stable. He quit after a week when the club's management refused to pay him what he thought he deserved.

He also found a job that overlapped the Onyx gig, four weeks with Duke Ellington's band starting on October 14 at Broadway's Capitol Theater; Dizzy filled in for an Ellington trumpeter who was awaiting his union card, and he expanded considerable energy dashing between the Onyx and the Capitol, a distance of three blocks. The Ellington show, which played opposite Claude Rains in the movie *The Phantom of the Opera*, featured Lena Horne, the dancer Peg Leg Bates, and the Deep River Boys vocal group and broke all attendance records for the theater.

Ellington may have been happy about the engagement, but Dizzy was not. Cliquish veterans, some of whom had performed with the band for fifteen years, offered no help with the complicated, nuanced arrangements, and—what was worse—Ellington asked him to solo only once, on an occasion when a scheduled improviser was absent.

Dizzy felt frustration as he recruited for the Onyx quintet. He wanted Bird at his side and sent him a telegram that was never answered, but Parker couldn't have made it anyway because he needed to reregister with the New York union; Dizzy hired Lester Young in his stead. On piano he sought Bud Powell, Monk's brilliant protégé, but he could not pry him loose from Cootie Williams' big band. After he succeeded in luring Max Roach from Clark Monroe's combo at Kelly's Stable, he and Pettiford decided to start the job without a regular pianist.

Young was replaced at the end of November by swing star Don Byas, who was originally hired as a single but became so fascinated with bebop innovations that he received permission from the Onyx managers to join the Pettiford-Gillespie band. The piano chair was filled sporadically by Monk and Billy Taylor until, in December, Dizzy and Pettiford hired a shy nineteen-year-old named George Wallington, born Giacinto Figlia in Sicily. A raw talent who occasionally required on-the-job training, Wallington quickly made a positive contribution; he soloed nimbly in the linear style of Bud Powell, and his accompaniments melded quietly with the powerful playing of Roach and Pettiford.

Dizzy was correct when he later characterized the Onyx engagement as "the birth of the bebop era." The music had evolved from its formative jam session days into a true genre with its own harmonic, rhythmic, and melodic characteristics, and it was displayed at the Onyx by excellent musicians in what was to become its ideal grouping—two horns plus three "rhythm" instruments. The Fifty-second Street setting ensured a sophisticated audience and plenty of media coverage for the engagement that, in retrospect, is widely acknowledged as an historic jazz event.

Starting with the Onyx gig, Dizzy became bebop's leader during the crucial 1943–45 period when it established its position in the jazz firmament. He led by example with his trumpet and his pen, but important nonmusical skills and attributes, which probably surprised even him, also became manifest at this time: organizational ability, highly focused energy, comic showmanship, a desire to teach and proselytize, and an engaging, extroverted personality that was a PR man's dream. Dizzy received important help from Pettiford, Budd Johnson, Coleman Hawkins, Charlie Parker, and Billy Eckstine, but he led the charge.

Of the five bebop pioneers, Christian was dead; Monk was a laconic recluse when not seated at a piano; Bird, though a beacon of light while performing and highly articulate, was too focused on finding his next fix to provide significant leadership off the bandstand; and Clarke was stationed at an army camp in Alabama. As Leonard Feather has written: "Although Dizzy Gillespie was by no means the only musician who originated, developed or popularized bebop, his history, at least from 1940, is largely the history of bebop. Gillespie was so prominent in every development from that year through the entire bebop cycle that the stories of Bird, Monk, Klook, and the others dovetail into Dizzy's biography."[2]

In addition to playing the blues and standards like "I Can't Get Started" and "Honeysuckle Rose," the Onyx quintet introduced to a wider world the bebop repertory that had grown steadily during the previous five years: songs such as Monk's "'Round Midnight" and "52nd Street Theme," Bird's "What Price Love" (later called "Yardbird Suite"), Pettiford's "One Bass Hit," and Dizzy's "A Night in Tunisia" and his collaboration with Clarke, "Salt Peanuts."

While Dizzy was breaking new ground at the Onyx, Eckstine was working diligently with agent Billy Shaw to accumulate enough bookings to launch his big band; in December 1943, he made Dizzy his musical director. Dizzy took the job seriously, helping Eckstine with recruitment and with creating a "book" of scores.

Byas's place at the Onyx was taken in January by Budd Johnson, the saxophonist replaced by Charlie Parker in the Hines band. Johnson, a highly knowledgeable musician who had been Hines's musical director and who had plucked Eckstine from obscurity, had left Hines's after eight years in a dispute over money. Dizzy, who held him in the highest regard, would say: "Budd was right into it, whatever was happening. He was a genius. He taught Lester Young how to read, and he taught Ben Webster how to play. He was a grandmaster."[3]

Much of the bebop repertoire had been passed along orally and had never been properly written down, and Johnson aided Dizzy, Pettiford, Monk, and others by creating meticulous scores and arrangements of their compositions. He also played an important role in codifying the use of unison horn lines that became a hallmark of small-group bebop. He thus helped greatly in making bebop a viable commercial product, both in the clubs and in the recording studios.

The resourceful Bob Redcross made the first recording of a pure bebop band from a January 1944 Onyx radio broadcast, a four-minute fragment of "A Night in Tunisia," which begins with a Johnson solo. The sound from the disc, which came to light in 1995, is execrable. The music, however, is evidence of a remarkable advance in conception and execution beyond the Redcross Chicago recording of Dizzy, Bird, and Pettiford just eleven months before.

The presence of a full rhythm section proves to be crucial. As Pettiford laid down imaginative lines, Wallington added apt chordal punctuation, and Roach, in a virtuoso example of bebop percussion, displaced the rhythm in just the right places as he inspired both Johnson and Dizzy with rim shots and bass and snare drum flurries.

Johnson showed a fine grasp of the bebop lexicon as he unfolded a passionate solo before Dizzy followed with a magnificent, hotly urgent chorus. After a short Wallington solo, Dizzy cooled everything down as he ended the piece with an intricate, pensive coda using a cup mute.

Dizzy's next recording, with Coleman Hawkins, was a carefully planned enterprise. Hawkins, who was described by Gunther

Schuller as "obviously one of the dozen greatest artists and influences in the first half-century of jazz,"[4] was at the peak of his influence when, at age thirty-nine, he lent his prestige to the nascent
bebop movement in late 1943. His musical curiosity and absolute
self-confidence made him a champion of the new music, in contrast to his many contemporaries who feared and resented it.

Ardor and power were the landmarks of his art. A reserved intellectual (his nickname was "Bean," a stand-in for "egghead"), he
had studied classical music on his way to a mastery of harmony,
and he created an imposing musical presence with his impassioned melodicism, his virtuosity, and the magisterial tone he
achieved on his tenor sax.

Hawkins totally embraced bebop, but the beboppers did not
totally embrace his personal aesthetic. As with Lester Young, they
chose from his style what was useful to them and left the rest.
From Young, they took linear improvising and an infinitely flexible rhythmic approach, but rejected his diatonic harmony. The
opposite was true with Hawkins; they applauded his full conversion to chromatic harmony, but rejected his vertical improvising
and his stodgy rhythmic attack, which too predictably alternated
weak and strong beats.

Although they did not accept Hawkins's full musical legacy,
the beboppers enjoyed his company and remained deeply grateful
to him for championing their cause when they faced a torrent of
hostility from the swing generation. And they remained steadfast
to his memory for decades; I produced a concert for Dizzy and
Roach in 1971, and they insisted on dedicating it to Hawkins,
who had died two years previously.

While performing at Kelly's Stable, Hawkins frequently
walked over to the Onyx to hear what Dizzy and Pettiford were
doing, and he caught the attention of a *Downbeat* reader who
wrote the editor: "I noticed that Coleman Hawkins was often
present to hear Dizzy blow. Such recognition means Dizzy must
be good."[5]

A January meeting between Hawkins and Budd Johnson
sparked what would become the first bebop studio sessions. Johnson remembered:

Hawkins told me, "I've got a record date coming up. I want to know all these cats who's playing the new music, because I'm going to pick up on what they're doing."

Clyde [Hart] and I had been doing some writing together, and he [Hawkins] says, "I want you to do something, and I'm going to do some things. I want Dizzy to do something."[6]

Between Decca's capitulation to the American Federation of Musicians in September 1943 and the surrender of Columbia and RCA Victor in November 1944, more than a hundred small record companies sprang up and signed with the union. One of them, Apollo, produced the Hawkins tracks. He scheduled two days, February 16 and 22, for the recording because five of the six tunes to be used were freshly written, and he wanted to ensure a high level of competence. He composed three of the numbers, Dizzy contributed "Woody 'n You," and Johnson and Hart (who was seriously ill with tuberculosis) wrote "Buh De Dah." Dizzy helped Hawkins assemble a twelve-man orchestra for the sessions, adding Don Byas and five men from Clark Monroe's group to his own Onyx quintet with Pettiford. He also assisted Hawkins with arrangements.

Three of the six tunes, "Woody 'n You," "Buh De Dah," and a Hawkins blues, "Disorder at the Border," are significant to bebop. The others served only as vehicles for extended solos by Hawkins.

"Woody 'n You," dedicated to Woody Herman and one of Dizzy's most enduring compositions, undergirds pungent chromatic dissonance with a Latin rhythmic feeling. Dizzy followed Hawkins's heated effort with a well-constructed solo that featured a breathtaking two-octave descent from a high note and a series of serpentine, linked triplets. On "Buh De Dah," a jump tune that makes extensive use of tritone substitutions, Dizzy was limited to two eight-bar passages as the track was dominated by Hawkins. Dizzy began his "Disorder at the Border" solo in a relaxed manner and then put a fire under the listener with an eye-popping sequence of thirty-second notes. In a practice often followed by himself and Bird, Dizzy implied or "ghosted" some notes rather than playing them; as everything rushes by, the listener tends to supply unconsciously the missing tones.

Pettiford drank far too much and became belligerent when drunk. One night soon after the Hawkins session, he and Dizzy were standing at Sixth Avenue and Fiftieth Street talking to Bricktop, a red-haired black singer whose skin was very light. A redneck sailor asked, "What you niggers doing with this white woman?" and an inebriated Pettiford swung at him and landed on his chest on the pavement. Other sailors crowded menacingly around him, and as Dizzy pulled a knife to hold them at bay, Pettiford staggered to his feet.

After an abortive attempt to hail a cab, Pettiford escaped in a subway train, while the sailors cornered Dizzy in the station and dislodged his knife. He fought them off with his trumpet, drawing blood, and found safety out on the tracks, where he hid on a catwalk near the third rail. When the Navy's Shore Patrol finally rounded up the attackers, he was able to board a train for home.

Pettiford continued to drink heavily on the job, and in early March 1944, Dizzy decided he could take no more. He left the Onyx with Budd Johnson and Max Roach and walked across the street to the Yacht Club (formerly the Famous Door) and started another quintet with Clyde Hart on piano and Leonard Gaskin on bass. The group, which received second billing under Billy Eckstine, who was backed by trombonist Trummy Young's Jump Band, remained in residence until early May. During the last week of its stay, Coleman Hawkins, who had reinforced his commitment to bebop by hiring Thelonious Monk and Benny Harris, replaced Eckstine and the Jump Band.

Agent Billy Shaw aimed for a June start for the Eckstine big band as he assiduously accumulated bookings during the spring months. A new 20 percent wartime "cabaret" tax added a sense of urgency to his efforts. The tax affected nightclub performers who acted, sang, "declaimed," or provided music for dancing; instrumental groups were exempted. Many clubs filled their dance floors with tables, and several of the spots on The Street displayed large signs reading "No Tax." Shaw reasoned that Eckstine would fare better singing in nontaxed theaters with a big band than in taxable clubs, and the group's itinerary was heavily weighted toward theaters like the Regal in Chicago, the Howard in Washington, and the Apollo in New York.

Shaw felt confident enough about the band's future to schedule an April 13, 1944, record date with a small label, Deluxe. The sixteen-piece group included Dizzy, Pettiford, Johnson, Hart, Shadow Wilson, and the talented young saxophonist Wardell Gray. Three sides were cut, and one of them, "I Stay in the Mood for You," as arranged by Dizzy, became a major hit.

Dizzy had to earn a living while waiting for Shaw's first bookings, and in early May he took a job filling in for Charlie Shavers in the John Kirby Sextet at a restaurant called the Aquarium. Bassist Kirby had created "the biggest little band in the world" in 1937 at the Onyx playing a tightly arranged "chamber" swing and rode it to a decade of success behind a three-horn front line featuring Shavers. On broadcast recordings of May 19 and 24, Dizzy is heard adroitly navigating the complicated arrangements and performing a couple of bebop solos in the swing setting. His rendition of "Rose Room" is outstanding.

Before he joined the Eckstine aggregation on June 9, Dizzy appeared with Bird, Vaughan, and the Woody Herman band at the first ever jazz concert at Philadelphia's staid Academy of Music. Downbeat Club owner Nat Segal produced the event, which advanced the bebop cause.

Eckstine, dubbed "the sepia Sinatra," shot to stardom while with Hines with a blues, "Jelly, Jelly," but his specialty was the romantic ballad sung in a rich bass-baritone. Elegant and handsome, he became the first black male singer to win over a white mass audience, paving the way for such artists as Nat King Cole and Johnny Mathis. He was a frustrated horn man who loved to join bebop brass sections to play trumpet or valve trombone, and he took lessons from Dizzy on those instruments. He never excelled, however.

Eckstine wanted a pure bebop big band, and his outstanding lineup during 1944 included Dizzy, Bird, Vaughan, and future stars Art Blakey on drums and Dexter Gordon and Gene Ammons on saxophone. Dizzy's arrangements, which formed the core of the book, were augmented by a generous loan from Count Basie and a swap with white bandleader Boyd Raeburn against future charts from Dizzy.

Because of its uncompromisingly modern stance, the band found only moderate success at the box office. Many listeners found its music too far out, and some were unhappy when they could not dance to the superfast numbers in its repertoire. In spite of this, esprit de corps was sky high. Eighteen young black people were enjoying themselves on what they believed was a historic artistic mission, breaking musical barriers and spreading the be-bop gospel. Sarah Vaughan summed it up when she said, "We tried to educate the people. . . . We just knocked each other out. Yeah, we had lots of fun. . . . We were just trying to play some music for the people, that we knew was together. . . . We didn't care whether anybody really, actually, enjoyed it or not. We *were*, you know."[7]

Starting in June, the band toured both the East and the Midwest, returning to its New York base twice for engagements at the Apollo and other venues: in September, when Bird quit to join Ben Webster at the Onyx, and in late December.

An eighteen-year-old Miles Davis substituted in St. Louis for Dizzy's friend Buddy Anderson, ill with tuberculosis, but he was not retained when the band moved on. Eckstine remembered, "He used to ask to sit in with the band. I'd let him so as not to hurt his feelings, because then Miles was awful. He sounded terrible."[8] Eckstine also recalled Miles's tremendous improvement when he rejoined the band two years later and took over the solo book that was originally Dizzy's.

Dizzy reigned undisputed over the band's musical affairs. He rehearsed the group relentlessly, tutored acolytes such as Blakey, Ammons, and Benny Harris, and was constantly writing and revising arrangements. And he was forced to cope with the drug contagion that was starting to infect his generation of jazz musicians. On one occasion, the entire saxophone section got high and missed the gig. Dizzy occasionally filled in on piano and drums, and, feeding off the energy of Bird, brought off increasingly dazzling solos. He continued his humorous antics from the trumpet section, but Eckstine, unlike Calloway and Hite, enjoyed them and created a crowd-pleasing comedy routine from the horseplay.

In July 1944, a Leonard Feather *Metronome* profile attested to Dizzy's rising stature:

> Dizzy Gillespie, unknown to many musicians and fans outside New York, had crept up in the music scene during the last couple of years to become as powerful an influence among trumpet players as Wilson and Tatum among pianists.
>
> You meet the Dizzy influence everywhere. You will walk into a Childs Restaurant and hear a nine piece band. In the middle of a stock arrangement, some horn man gets up and plays 16 bars of sheer Dizzy trumpet. You talk to him and find Gillespie is his idol. You go to a Monday night jam session and hear a dozen kids playing Dizzy style. You listen to Georgie Auld's band or Boyd Raeburn's band and the jazz trumpet man turns out to be on a Dizzy kick.[9]

Accompanying the article was a photo of Dizzy, laughing and leaning out of the frame toward the reader.

Billy Shaw believed that Dizzy's increasing prominence could soon be translated into commercial success, and during the autumn of 1944, proposed that he organize first a small group and then a big band of his own. Dizzy accepted the proposal and, as he began to recruit personnel, he told Eckstine that he would resign as of December 31. He pleased Eckstine when he recruited the brilliant Fats Navarro to succeed him on trumpet and convinced Budd Johnson to take over as musical director.

Unfortunately, the only recorded legacy of the touring Eckstine band during Dizzy's incumbency is a Deluxe session of December 5 that produced six tracks. He soloed only on "Blowing the Blues Away," producing a short, searing chorus after a smooth Eckstine blues vocal and a rousing tenor sax duel between Gene Ammons and Dexter Gordon.

Before ending his Eckstine sojourn with a New Year's Eve dance in Harlem, Dizzy accompanied Sarah Vaughan that afternoon in a seven-man backup group at a record date produced by

Leonard Feather. Vaughan had left Eckstine to strike out on her own a few weeks previously, and Dizzy had come to her aid by helping her produce a demo disc. He gave the disc to Feather one night on Fifty-second Street, and Feather liked it so much he arranged to produce a session with Continental, a minuscule label willing to take a chance on a young, little-known singer. Feather had no budget for a pianist and performed himself at the keyboard on three of the four cuts. Vaughan received eighty dollars for the session.

Her voice is lush and inviting as she negotiates a blues and three ballads. "A Night in Tunisia" was renamed "Interlude" for the occasion and fitted out with romantic lyrics and a slower-than-usual tempo. Because Feather could not manage the tune's tricky cadences, Dizzy played both piano and solo trumpet on the track. He took another solo on "East of the Moon" and provided obbligatos on the other tunes.

As 1945 began, Dizzy found several signs that the jazz establishment was starting to recognize him. *Esquire* magazine gave him its "New Star" award, Hawkins's recording of his "Woody 'n You" was named a "record of the year" by *Metronome*, and for the first time he made that magazine's list of top trumpeters, placing tenth. In addition, *Metronome* ran an article in its January 1945 issue on the rapid rise of the Eckstine band; it was written by Feather, who was fast becoming a cheerleader for the bebop movement, and it extolled Dizzy's virtues and contained a photo of him in the trumpet section.

As he savored his brightening prospects, Dizzy contracted for an eight-week quintet gig starting in early March 1945 at the Three Deuces on Fifty-second Street opposite the Erroll Garner Trio. He quickly put together a dream group—Bird, Roach, Bud Powell, and a reliable young bassist named Curley Russell.

The Laurinburg Institute Band, circa 1934. Laurinburg provided Dizzy with a wonderfully nurturing environment for musical and personal growth. Dizzy is in the second row at the far left end. *The Laurinburg Institute*

Roy Eldridge, Dizzy's idol, in a 1968 photo. He revolutionized jazz trumpet during the 1930s. *Herman Leonard Photography*

Kenny "Klook" Clarke in a 1956 photo. He began the bebop revolution with Dizzy during the late 1930s and radically transformed the role of the drummer in the jazz ensemble. *Frank Driggs Collection*

Charlie Christian, bebop pioneer and lyrical master of linear improvisation, 1940. *Frank Driggs Collection*

Dizzy (top center) blowing in Cab Calloway's band, 1941. He was fired later that year after he stabbed Calloway in the buttocks. *Frank Driggs Collection*

Clark Monroe (seated, center) partying in 1943. Monroe provided an incubator for bebop at his Uptown House during the early 1940s, and he helped launch Dizzy's great 1946–1950 big band at his Spotlite Club on Fifty-second Street. *Courtesy of Leonard Gaskin*

Members of Billy Eckstine's bebop big band—Dizzy, Charlie Parker, Eckstine—in 1944. Eckstine's group spread the nascent gospel of bebop throughout the United States. *Frank Driggs Collection*

The groundbreaking Onyx Club bebop quintet—Max Roach, Budd Johnson, Oscar Pettiford, George Wallington, and Dizzy—in 1945. As with the Eckstine band, the Onyx group brought bebop out of its Harlem birthplace and into a wider world. *Frank Driggs Collection*

Mary Lou Williams's Harlem salon, 1947: Dizzy, Mary Lou, Tadd Dameron, Hank Jones, two unknowns, and Jack Teagarden. Mary Lou was one of a handful of Swing Era titans who nurtured the young beboppers. *Photograph by William Gottlieb*

Thelonious Monk, Howard McGhee, Roy Eldridge, and Minton's manager, Teddy Hill, in front of the renowned jazz club, 1947. Minton's, along with Monroe's Uptown House, was a seedbed of bebop during the early 1940s. *Photograph by William Gottlieb*

Ella Fitzgerald sitting in with Dizzy's band, 1947. Dizzy's bassist Ray Brown, who would soon become her husband, is behind her on the left. Ella became a bebop convert while touring with Dizzy. *Photograph by William Gottlieb*

Thelonious Monk at Minton's Playhouse, 1948. Dizzy learned much from Monk—the great composer, performer, and bebop icon. *Herman Leonard Photography*

James Moody, Chano Pozo, and Dizzy wailing, 1948. Moody collaborated fruitfully with Dizzy for more than forty years, and Chano was the key participant in Dizzy's Afro-Cuban revolution. *Frank Driggs Collection*

Dizzy with his wife, Lorraine, 1948. Their love endured for more than fifty years, until his death in 1993. *Herman Leonard Photography*

Charlie Parker and Dizzy share a joke at a recording session, 1949. The two men formed one of the most creative partnerships in all of jazz history. *Herman Leonard Photography*

Dizzy's 1950 gift to Charlie Parker. The inscription reads, "To 'Yard,' my better half." *Collection of Theoren and Michelle Demarest*

1945—A GREAT 19
NEW YORK VINTAGE

WHILE REHEARSING THE QUINTET AT HIS HOME AND AT
the Three Deuces, Dizzy remained solvent by working occasional
freelance engagements and by putting his arranging and performing skills to work for small and frequently ephemeral record companies. These recordings, eight in number, provide a pungent taste
of the gumbo of blues, swing, Dixieland, stride, and bebop sim-
mering in New York at the time. Three of the labels—Continental, Manor, and Guild—did not survive 1945.

The first of the record dates, a blues and swing session aimed
at the black (or "race") market by Continental Records, took place
on January 4, 1945. Dizzy joined Don Byas, Bird, and trombonist
Trummy Young in the horn section of a septet organized by
Clyde Hart to back up the singing of Henry "Rubberlegs"
Williams and Young. Hart, ill with tuberculosis, had elected to
soldier on despite his doctor's orders to rest.

This was the first recording session for Williams, a huge man with a gritty voice who had worked carnivals, vaudeville circuits, and minstrel shows for thirty years as a blues singer, female impersonator, and eccentric dancer (hence the nickname Rubberlegs). The session was scheduled for 2:00 a.m. to accommodate musicians with club gigs, and Williams imbibed a large quantity of a powerful whiskey called "Joe Louis" as the men straggled in.

All went well until they took a coffee break following the first two numbers. Benzedrine was one of Bird's favorite stimulants, and to counteract the effects of whatever depressants he had consumed that night, he dropped the contents of a Benzedrine inhaler into a cup of coffee.

No one is sure what happened next. Either Bird deliberately spiked Rubberlegs's coffee as a practical joke (as Dizzy believed) or Rubberlegs inadvertently drank from Bird's cup. In any case, the results were chaotic as the combination of whiskey and Benzedrine drove Rubberlegs increasingly berserk. He lifted Dizzy off the floor with one arm and threatened to thrash him for not being bluesy enough, and after his singing became almost incoherent, he was ushered from the scene making violent gestures at all concerned.

The musicians then backed Trummy Young on four pleasant tunes, creating a musical texture similar to that achieved by the John Kirby Sextet. Both Dizzy and Bird managed sprightly bebop solos over the swing beat of the rhythm section.

Dizzy's next record date, on January 9 for Manor Records, was in two parts: a big band segment led by Oscar Pettiford, and a later sextet session that marked, at age twenty-seven, Dizzy's first recordings as a leader. The date began almost as chaotically as the one five days earlier. Rubberlegs was involved again, but this time the cause of the confusion was Pettiford; he had assembled an eighteen-piece orchestra but had neglected to supply any arrangements. Dizzy came to his rescue, quickly writing charts for "Max Is Making Wax" (renamed "Something for You" for the occasion) and "Empty Bed Blues," a vehicle for Rubberlegs recorded in two parts. Byas and Dizzy contribute stellar solos on "Something for You," and they provide tasty obbligatos for Rubberlegs on the blues.

From the big band, Dizzy selected for his sextet Trummy Young, Byas, Hart, Pettiford, and drummer Shelly Manne, a sailor and a prewar veteran of The Street. The personnel reflected the "swing to bop" evolution then taking place in jazz: Young was an unabashed swing player, Byas and Hart were situated between the two worlds, and Dizzy, Pettiford, and Manne were modernists. They cut four tracks: "I Can't Get Started" (arranged by Tadd Dameron) and "Good Bait" (written by him), "Salt Peanuts," and a new composition by Dizzy, "Bebop." (By naming his tune "Bebop," Dizzy gave formal recognition to the word he inadvertently gave birth to in 1944, and which had gained wide currency by 1945.) Dameron, whose work Bird had admired in Kansas City in 1940, had become an associate of Dizzy's in New York.

In choosing Vernon Duke's ballad "I Can't Get Started" as a vehicle, Dizzy was issuing a dual challenge: he wanted to show that the bebop language could express the tenderest emotions, that it was not limited to complex, up-tempo tunes; and he was inviting direct comparison to a classic swing record, Bunny Berigan's rendition of 1937. The importance of the 1937 version is evidenced by its receipt in 1975 of a Grammy Hall of Fame Award reserved for "early recordings of lasting qualitative or historical significance." Berigan's touching vocal and a stunning Armstrong-style cadenza serve as preludes to Berigan's trumpet solo that builds passionately to a bravura climax.

Dizzy crafted a much subtler, more contemplative version of the song, sacrificing none of its beauty and creating his first masterpiece. Dameron's excellent arrangement had Byas and Young playing lovely countermelodies under Dizzy in both the A and B sections. In his solo, Dizzy modernized the A sections by using four pairs of chromatically linked descending chords in place of the original diatonic ones, and he achieved a subtle climax in the B section with a series of linked chromatic phrases. Authoritative without being melodramatic, Dizzy created, with his modern harmonies, a penetrating lyricism that plumbed even deeper levels of emotion than Berigan had reached. Dizzy finished with a stirring coda that he later refashioned as his introduction to Monk's "'Round Midnight." Vernon Duke was delighted with

Dizzy's interpretation of his song: "This is a musician's joy. It is extraordinary—it has no end of imagination and it is completely unpredictable. The whole performance has a fresh, invigorating quality. . . . One of the most imaginative things I have heard."[1]

"Good Bait," a relaxed swing track that featured Young and Byas, contained a startling, high-velocity improvisation on the B section by Dizzy. He pulled out all the stops on "Salt Peanuts" with a sixty-eight-bar solo and on "Bebop," where he unfurled a profusion of original ideas over ninety-eight bars at a breakneck tempo.

Dizzy's recording debut as a leader was a clear success. He had displayed a full command of the new bebop vocabulary, a rich musical imagination, and virtuosity at a variety of tempos. And he had stamped the performance with a truly personal style; no knowledgeable listener could attribute these tracks to another trumpet player.

Three days after this breakthrough session, Dizzy found himself and another modernist, guitarist Chuck Wayne, recording four tunes for the Black and White label with Dixieland clarinetist Joe Marsala's hybrid New Orleans/swing group. In a congenial melding of genres, Dizzy participated happily in Dixieland polyphonic ensembles but sailed above the insistent beat of the rhythm section as he broke loose with his bebop solos.

Dizzy's tenure with Boyd Raeburn's orchestra during late January and early February 1945 is marked by a successful week at the Apollo and the opportunity to record two excellent solos and one of pure magic (on "A Night in Tunisia"). Raeburn had turned his garden-variety dance band into a modernist aggregation in 1943 and, as we have seen, he made a deal with Eckstine in 1944 for a group of Dizzy's arrangements; "A Night in Tunisia" was one of them. Dizzy recorded again with a big band for Guild on February 7, taking short solos on two tracks with a group led by saxophonist Georgie Auld, a swing convert to bebop who had been a star with Berigan, Goodman, and Artie Shaw.

Lacking the clout of an entertainer with a large popular audience, Dizzy was constantly frustrated by the managers of the small record companies when he tried to recruit compatible musicians for his recordings. A case in point was the lineup for Dizzy's Guild sextet session on February 9, two days after he recorded with Auld. He was happy with Chuck Wayne, former Eckstine saxophonist Dexter Gordon, and Shelly Manne, but disappointed with the choice of Murray Shipinski on bass and Frank Paparelli on piano.

The group recorded two new Dizzy compositions, "Groovin' High," a pleasant medium tempo tune based on the chord structure of "Whispering," written in 1920, and "Blue 'N' Boogie." Dizzy created a complex arrangement for "Groovin' High," which became one of his most enduring hits; it encompasses a six-bar introduction, three key changes, transition passages between solos, and a half-speed coda as it demonstrates his skill in fashioning interesting textures using only six instruments. "Blue 'N' Boogie" is more straightforward, a jump blues. Gordon, Wayne, and Paparelli solo acceptably on both numbers, and Dizzy is impressive on "Groovin' High."

Although Dizzy was not enamored of Paparelli's pianistics, he found another of his skills useful. Paparelli transcribed several of Dizzy's solos and arrangements, and received in return joint composer credit on "A Night in Tunisia" and "Blue 'N' Boogie."

In 1979, Dizzy wrote, "The height of perfection of our music occurred in the Three Deuces with Charlie Parker."[2] That engagement began in early March. Parker was eager to sign on with Dizzy, because he had been barely getting by as a freelancer in New York following his resignation from Eckstine's band in September 1944. He appeared with Ben Webster's group at the Onyx and Cootie Williams's big band at the Apollo and performed occasional gigs on Fifty-second Street at the Three Deuces and the Spotlite leading a trio with Stan Levey on drums and Joe Albany on piano. (The Spotlite had become the second club on The Street operated by a black when Clark Monroe opened it in 1944 after breaking up the band he had been fronting at Kelly's Stable.)

Although Bird had proved easy to recruit, Dizzy failed to hold together the dream band he had begun rehearsing in January as Roach and Powell left for greener pastures. They were replaced by Levey and Al Haig, respectively, as Curley Russell remained on bass. Haig, a gifted twenty-year-old who hailed from the white middle class suburbs of northern New Jersey and who had attended the elite Oberlin College, brought to the group a deep grounding in classical music and a self-taught mastery of the bebop vocabulary; he quickly became a dynamic presence in the quintet.

Including the Rubberlegs Williams session, Dizzy and Bird recorded together seven times in 1945. All of these occasions are important, but three stand out as milestones in jazz history: two Guild dates of February 28 and May 11 led by Dizzy and a Savoy date of November 26 led by Bird. They are great art, and they embody the defining moments when modern jazz was crystallized for the world at large by its two outstanding practitioners.

The Guild dates both emanate from the seminal Three Deuces engagement and therefore form a unity; the May 11 session produced greater music, because the rhythm section was far superior.

The February 28 session took place while the quintet was rehearsing one week before it was to open at the club, but the Three Deuces group was represented only by Dizzy and Bird. Dizzy was again saddled with accompanists who were not beboppers: swing musicians Remo Palmieri on guitar, Slam Stewart on bass, and Cozy Cole on drums, plus the transitional performer Clyde Hart on piano. Hart, ravaged by tuberculosis, would succumb to the disease at age thirty-five less than three weeks later, on March 19. Dizzy served as a pallbearer.

The session produced three tracks that demonstrate the near-telepathic rapport that Dizzy and Bird had achieved during their many hours of jamming: "Dizzy Atmosphere," a new Gillespie tune; "All the Things You Are," a Jerome Kern ballad; and a remake of "Groovin' High." Their work brilliantly transcended the pedestrian output of the rhythm section.

Because "I Got Rhythm" was familiar to every musician of the 1940s, its harmonies, alongside those of the blues, became part of the lingua franca of modern jazz; the song provided performers with a comfort zone as tunes of many varieties were based on its chord changes. For example, on a concert recording of a number unknown to Bud Powell, one hears Coleman Hawkins tell him, "Rhythm changes," and after that, Powell knew just how to accompany him.

"Dizzy Atmosphere," a "Rhythm" artifact, provided the high point of the February 28 date. It is the only track where Dizzy and Bird both improvised full choruses. Bird achieved dramatic effects in his solo by emphasizing the offbeats, and Dizzy's chorus was explosive. The track also featured two thirty-two-bar unison passages where the two men sound uncannily as one, confirming Parker's statement that Dizzy was "the other half of my heartbeat."[3]

Dizzy borrowed, for the introduction and coda of "All the Things You Are," a phrase he created in his arrangement of Eckstine's "Good Jelly Blues"; it has been widely used ever since. The recording was marred by pedestrian solos by Stewart, Hart, and Palmieri, but is redeemed by Bird's masterful eight-bar improvisation on the B section and by Dizzy's lovely statement of the theme and his sparkling out chorus.

The reworking of "Groovin' High" makes one important change in the complex arrangement. Dizzy curtailed his chorus to allow Palmieri a short improvisation. Again, Dizzy and Bird managed a magical unison theme statement, and each performed intricate melodic improvisations over the unvarying swing rhythm.

Dizzy and Bird were finally blessed with a compatible rhythm section when they arrived at Guild for one of the great record dates in jazz history on May 11. They were joined by Sid Catlett on drums and Haig and Russell from their Three Deuces group. Catlett was the best nonbebop drummer of the period, a swing master who possessed both the skill and the intelligence to blend creditably with a group of modernists. He was pressed into action because Stan Levey had just left the quintet for a stint with Woody Herman. Haig set a standard for other bebop pianists to follow as he performed brilliantly on all four tracks, and Russell, who was not asked to solo, was rock solid throughout.

The group recorded, with joyous energy, three instrumentals: Tadd Dameron's "Hot House" and two "I Got Rhythm" derivatives, "Salt Peanuts" and "Shaw 'Nuff." The melodies of "Salt

Peanuts" and "Shaw 'Nuff" (named for booker Billy Shaw) are very different; the former is a basic riff tune while the latter displays a complex line with a vaguely Middle Eastern tonality. The group also backed Sarah Vaughan on the ballad "Lover Man," providing a richly nuanced accompaniment to her poignant portrayal of youthful longing.

Dameron composed "Hot House" specifically for the date. A chromatic melody with unusual leaps between chords, it is based on the harmony of Cole Porter's "What Is This Thing Called Love." Haig's energetic commentary and Russell's powerful bass lines undergird the performance, and Dizzy and Bird respond with hard-driving solos.

Although major scholars such as Dan Morgenstern and Martin Williams consider "Shaw 'Nuff" the masterpiece of the session, I believe that "Salt Peanuts" achieves equality with it because its more complex arrangement allows Dizzy and Bird a wider opportunity to display all the facets of their art. Parker scholar Lawrence O. Koch has analyzed the recording:

"Salt Peanuts" sums up in a nutshell the Gillespie-Parker music. The line, composed by Gillespie, is rifflike and humorous. The piece is based on standard chord changes with subtle variations, and the line must be harmonized differently from the improvisational sections. Then there are the difficult transition sections hard to execute and difficult to remember; the chunking offbeat piano chords; the hard-driving solos, coming together in swinging clockwork; and the hard-punched four-four rhythm, holding its own against solo syncopations and ensemble breaks in the tempo. There is a great balance of simplicity and complexity, of humor and seriousness, of harmony and dissonance, of logic and absurdity, of aloofness and emotion, and perhaps, of love and hate. The scales that measure all art need to be looked at, perhaps, as to their balance from time to time, and bop would measure quite well when judged on this performance.[4]

The reactions of four young men who became outstanding artists illustrate the tremendous impact of the May 11 recordings on an entire generation of jazz musicians. Singer Jon Hendricks was returning from Europe on a troopship:

> I suddenly heard this song over the ship's radio. It was frenetic and exciting and fast and furious and brilliant and beautiful and I almost bumped my head jumping off my cot. I ran up to the control room and said to the guy, "What was that? . . . That last song you just played, the one you just played!" He said, "I don't know." I said. "Where is it?" He said, "It's down there on the floor." I looked down there on the floor, the floor's covered in records. . . . Finally, I found it. . . . It was called "Salt Peanuts." And it was Charlie Parker and Dizzy Gillespie. And I gave him thirty dollars and I said, "Play this for the next hour!"[5]

The great trumpeter, composer, and bandleader Thad Jones remembered the power of "Shaw 'Nuff":

> I was in the army on an island called Guam. . . . There were about six of us listening to the radio, and all of a sudden Dizzy comes on playing "Shaw 'Nuff" with Charlie Parker. . . . I can't describe what went on in that tent. We went out of our minds! . . . It was the newness and the impact of the sound, and the technique. It was something we were probably trying to articulate ourselves and just didn't know how. And Dizzy and Bird came along and did it. They spoke our minds.[6]

In California, bassist Red Callender and saxophonist Art Pepper were similarly impacted. Callender recalled: "We used to play these records—we'd get in a room and live with them all night. It was unbelievable. Something from outer space." And Pepper was viscerally affected: "I said, 'Oh my God,' and I just got sick. I just couldn't believe it. I couldn't listen to any more at the moment."[7]

Not everyone understood the new music, but fans crowded the Three Deuces in such numbers that its owner doubled Dizzy's salary to two hundred dollars per week less than a month after the band opened and raised the other musicians from sixty to one hundred dollars per week. Dizzy satisfied his love of Latin jazz and audience curiosity about it by augmenting the group frequently with the Cuban conga player Diego Iborra. The basic quintet remained intact until early May when Levey left, but his departure actually meant no reduction in quality as Max Roach took his place. The lineup then remained stable until the gig ended on July 5.

The Three Deuces quintet (with Levey and Harold West substituting for Roach and Russell) appeared in May and June in three concerts produced by the pretentiously named New Jazz Foundation (in reality, Monte Kay and Mal Braveman, two producers who possessed little talent for organization). A June 5 event in Philadelphia went smoothly, but May 16 and June 22 concerts at New York's Town Hall were marred by the absence of such scheduled performers as Coleman Hawkins, Hot Lips Page, pianist Teddy Wilson, and Georgie Auld. The quintet received a rave review from Barry Ulanov in *Metronome*:

> Dizzy was in magnificent form [on May 16]. I've never heard him play so well, muff so few notes, and reach such inspired heights. . . . Dizzy and Charlie played their unison passages with fabulous precision. . . . Charlie's solos almost never failed to get a roar from the audience because of his habit of beginning them with four-bar introductions in which the rhythm was suspended . . . then slamming into tempo, giving his listeners a tremendous release.[8]

A writer for the staid *New York Herald Tribune* turned up his nose at the music, although he was impressed by Bird:

> Gillespie himself is gifted technically, but his style is one of transparent showmanship, fantastic rather than musical. The group boasts one player of artist's stature, the alto saxophonist Charlie Parker. . . .
>
> The music presented was hectic but not hot and by no means jazz. As modern music, it attempts a variational development while discarding the melodies to be developed. Since no harmonic evolution is substituted, the net product is a wandering kind of rhapsody.[9]

On May 25, Dizzy and Bird backed Sarah Vaughan on three tracks, and on June 6 they recorded four sides with six swing musicians in a group organized by Benny Goodman's excellent vibraphonist, Red Norvo. Norvo, like Clyde Hart and Don Byas, was a veteran of the swing milieu who admired the beboppers. He remembered, "Bird and Diz were dirty words for musicians of my generation. But jazz had always gone through changes, and in 1945 we were in the middle of another one. Bird and Diz were saying new things in an exciting way. I had a free hand, so I gambled."[10]

Norvo did not attempt to blend bebop and swing; he had the good sense to create a loose format wherein each soloist was free to do his own thing, and the results were excellent. Dizzy, Bird, Norvo, Teddy Wilson, saxophonist Flip Phillips, and bassist Slam Stewart stretched out happily, and the up-tempo "Congo Blues" was the highlight of the session. *Metronome* called it "probably the top date of the year."

Bird's addiction caused him frequently to be late or to miss entire shows at the Three Deuces, and this constantly irritated Dizzy, but he never stayed angry for long. Roach remembered an incident at the Three Deuces that is a case in point:

> Bird arrived one night while we were performing the first set and headed directly to the bathroom to shoot up. Dizzy went in there and observed him in the act and, very angry, charged back to the bandstand saying, "That motherfucker is shooting dope in there." And all the folks in the club heard it, because Dizzy didn't realize he was walking past an open mike.
>
> Bird ran out of the bathroom very bitter, berating Dizzy for hurting him this way. But we pushed both of them into the dressing room and lectured Bird on how he was ruining his life and betraying his people and his art. Dizzy calmed down. He loved Bird so much.[11]

Bird also vexed Dizzy by arriving, from time to time, at his doorstep in the middle of the night. Dizzy recalled one of these visits:

> Three in the morning the doorbell rang, and I opened it as far as the latch chain permitted. There was Bird, horn in hand, and he

says, "Let me in, Diz, I've got it; you must hear this thing I've worked out." I had been putting Bird's solos on paper, which is something Bird never had the patience for himself. "Not now," I said. "Later man, tomorrow." "No," Bird cried. "I won't remember it tomorrow; it's in my head now; let me in please." From the other room, my wife yelled, "Throw him out," and I obediently slammed the door in Bird's face. Parker then took his horn to his mouth and played the tune in the hallway. I grabbed pencil and paper and took it down from the other side of the door.[12]

Miles Davis once said something like, "To be a friend of Bird, you've got to pay your dues." Dizzy paid them time and again and seldom regretted it.

Bird opted out of Dizzy's next venture, the creation of a big band. He and Monk of the surviving bebop pioneers were indifferent to big band music, while Dizzy and Kenny Clarke loved it. Dizzy was overjoyed, therefore, when Billy Shaw and his son Milt offered in May to finance a tour by an eighteen-piece band led by Dizzy. The group would be part of a package called "Hepsations of 1945" ("hep" was the precursor of "hip" in the lexicon), which would be headed by the popular Nicholas Brothers dance team and would include Patterson and Jackson ("600 pounds of comedy, singing and dancing"), bebop vocalist June Eckstine (Billy's wife), shake dancer Lovey Lane, and a chorus line. The tour was aimed exclusively at black audiences and took place primarily in the Deep South.

Dizzy could never have put his band together on short notice without the help of Gil Fuller, his colleague from the 1942 Les Hite aggregation. Fuller, an efficient organizer, worked with Dizzy to create big band arrangements from the small-band bebop repertoire that had been developed in Harlem and on Fifty-second Street, and he drove the group's hastily assembled recruits through rigorous rehearsals. After participating in a few of these sessions, Bird elected to remain in New York and form his own combo; early in August, he went into the Three Deuces with Haig, Levey, Russell, and Don Byas.

"Hepsations of 1945" left New York on July 8, three days after the Three Deuces engagement ended. Dizzy took with him several outstanding musicians, including Max Roach, trumpeters Kenny Dorham and Elmon Wright, and saxophonist Charlie Rouse; before the tour ended he also employed the excellent trumpeter Freddie Webster and Miles Davis, then nineteen.

Lorraine accompanied Dizzy, and she helped her husband nurse Roach through withdrawal from a heavy heroin habit. Roach was deeply affected: "He gave me so much TLC and attention, spent hours nursing me. His caring made me feel like somebody again after I thought I'd blown it all away. With everything that he did for me, I felt inspired to put all the drug crap behind me and build a life again. And I did."[13]

The Nicholas Brothers, the comedians, and the shake dancer were successful, but, due to a basic misconception, Dizzy's band and June Eckstine were not. They had been told that they would play concerts in theaters where listeners could sit back and try to absorb what was a revolutionary new music; instead, they were booked only into dance venues (some of them tobacco warehouses), where the numbers were too complex and fast for audiences who had come to relax with a few drinks and boogie to down-home blues.

The Nicholas Brothers, who were thrilled with Dizzy's music, and the bookers pleaded with him to lace his program with traditional swing tunes and the blues, but Dizzy refused. He realized that, with bebop, jazz had been transformed from pure entertainment into an art form, and he would not compromise. Because he was depressed by his band's failure to connect with its audiences, Dizzy's normal ebullience deserted him as master of ceremonies, and he ceded the task to the Nicholas Brothers.

Audience response improved when the band left the hinterlands and performed in theaters in New York, Chicago, and Detroit during September and early October. Dizzy saw no immediate future for the group, however, and sadly disbanded after closing in Detroit on October 4.

His morale received a boost when he read "Dizzy—21st Century Gabriel," a full-page article by Leonard Feather in the October issue of *Esquire*. For the first time he was being profiled in a wide-circulation, national magazine and not in a trade publication like *Metronome*. A PR man could not have been more laudatory than Feather:

> Dizzy has a phenomenal combination of technique and style, plays incredible cascades of fast notes at breakneck tempos, and makes every note mean something. He has set a new milestone in jazz improvisation. Just as every once in a while a new novelist comes along who is more subtle and oblique than any predecessor, and can give more hidden value and meaning to each word and phrase, so can Dizzy do these things with musical notes and phrases. . . . His musical thinking has left an ineradicable mark on jazz.[14]

When Dizzy returned to New York, he found that Billy Shaw had booked him into Billy Berg's Supper Club in Hollywood for an eight-week quintet engagement starting on December 10, 1945; Berg had stipulated that Bird be a member of the group. Shaw had also found for Dizzy a series of gigs in New York and Washington to tide him over until he was ready to leave for California.

Soon after Dizzy began recruiting for these engagements, he came upon a brilliant nineteen-year-old bass player named Ray Brown. They were introduced at the Spotlite on Brown's first evening in New York by the pianist Hank Jones, a mutual friend who raved about the bassist's skills. Dizzy answered Jones's encomium by telling Brown to show up at the Gillespie apartment the next evening for a tryout.

The teenager was very apprehensive when he found Parker, Roach, and Bud Powell in attendance, but he held his own in their exalted company, and two days later Dizzy hired him. He had quickly endeared himself to Dizzy because he had a firm grounding in harmony based on years of study at the piano, he could improvise with ease at fast tempos, and he projected a big, luminous sound. In short, he possessed the talent to join Pettiford in the first tier of jazz bassists.

A few weeks later, Dizzy hired another young star in the making, Milt Jackson, a twenty-two-year-old vibraphonist from the Detroit area. Dizzy had jammed with him there in 1943 and quickly bonded with him as he heard Jackson's blues tonalities and his rhythms testify to his background in the Sanctified Church. Dizzy encouraged him to come to New York and asked Jackson to look him up when he did. This happened during a whirlwind visit in 1944. Jackson remembered, "I just ran around, stayed up for over forty-eight hours, didn't even get no kind of sleep, and went from club to club. Because all the musicians I'd always heard about and dreamed about seeing, suddenly here they were, right here in the flesh—and I just went completely nuts."[15]

Thus inspired, he decided, in October 1945, to make his move: "I got what little money I could, packed my clothes and came back to New York. And in three weeks . . . I had a job with Dizzy."[16]

Dizzy had added Jackson to the roster for California because of Bird's predilection for missing engagements. Although his salary came out of Dizzy's pocket, Jackson represented a necessary insurance policy against Bird's unreliability. Dizzy worked hard to bring Brown and Jackson up to speed during quintet engagements at the Spotlite and at a club in Washington. As the departure date for California approached, he was forced to make personnel changes; Roach and Powell dropped out and were hastily replaced by Haig and Levey.

Dizzy rehearsed with Bird during November but did not gig with him because Bird was leading a group with Miles Davis on trumpet. Davis had idolized Bird since they had met during Davis's short stay with the Eckstine band in the summer of 1944. Chagrined by his failure to find permanent employment with Eckstine, Davis improved his technique with local bands in the St. Louis area before his prosperous father sent him off in September 1944 to the Juilliard School of Music in New York with a generous fifty dollars per week allowance.

Miles's real aim in coming to New York was to find Bird, and after he tracked him down, he made the always-broke, addicted, vagabond saxophonist an offer he could not refuse: move in and share my digs. Davis became Bird's acolyte, studying and jamming with him until the summer of 1945 when he had acquired sufficient skills to quit Juilliard and join Bird's group.

Dizzy broke his club routine on November 20 to star with Art

Tatum, Coleman Hawkins, Thelonious Monk, and guitarist Mary Osborne in a highly successful concert at Philadelphia's Academy of Music hosted by Leonard Feather. And he was pressed into service six days later at the record date that showed Bird at his best, provided Davis with his first opportunity to record, and produced at least one masterpiece, "Ko Ko."

The occasion was Charlie Parker's debut as a leader at age twenty-five; he had been signed by Savoy Records, a small, aggressive company owned by Herman Lubinsky, a noted cheapskate who worked out of his radio parts and record store in Newark, New Jersey. Dizzy biographer Alyn Shipton has accurately described the dynamic of the session: "Parker's first record date under his own name was a curious reflection of his own personality: random, disorganized, occasionally touching genius, but ultimately reliant on his own spur-of-the-moment instrumental and improvisatory prowess."[17]

Because Bird had lined up Davis, Roach, Bud Powell, and Curley Russell for the date, producer Teddy Reig was taken aback when he went to pick Bird up: "He was walking down the street with Dizzy . . . and I said 'Where are you two nuts going?' Dizzy says, 'I'm your piano player.' I says, 'Where's Bud?' Dizzy says, 'He went to Philadelphia to buy a house with his mother.'"[18]

Dizzy chose the pseudonym Hen Gates for the date, because he was under contract to Guild at the time.

When they arrived at the studio in midtown Manhattan, Reig discovered that Bird had created complications by inviting another piano player, Argonne Thornton (a.k.a. Sadik Hakim), to the session. Thornton was apprehensive about participating because he didn't possess a union card.

Bird's program comprised "Thriving on a Riff" (an "I Got Rhythm" variant by himself and Dizzy that was known later in slightly altered form as "Anthropology"), "Cherokee," one of his favorite vehicles for improvising, plus two blues he had written that morning—"Now's the Time," a simple riff tune, and "Billie's Bounce," a more complicated piece (named for Billy Shaw but misspelled). Thornton, who performed on "Thrivin' on a Riff" and the first run-through of "Cherokee," left the premises hurriedly when the union representative arrived after the latter take. Dizzy played piano on the remaining take of "Cherokee" and all the other numbers; he never took a solo, but his accompaniments were deft and strongly supportive.

Bird's saxophone squeaked loudly as he worked through the first tune, "Billie's Bounce," and he poured a pitcher of water into his horn in an attempt to moisten the key pads. When this didn't work, attention was focused on his reeds, and the proceedings were halted as a gopher was dispatched to buy some. Soon girl-friends, hangers-on, and a miscellany of musicians crowded into the studio, and the recordings were interrupted several more times as they sent out for booze, food, and narcotics.

Lubinsky grew apoplectic as he realized that the session would run far past the three-hour studio rental he had contracted for. He attempted to recoup some of his losses when Bird tested his horn after the third take of "Billie's Bounce" by improvising over "Cherokee" chord changes; Lubinsky screamed to the engineers to record it and later released the track as "Warmin' Up a Riff."

By the fifth take of "Billie's Bounce," a complicated blues line, Bird was in magnificent form as, for the first time on record, he was backed by a full complement of bebop musicians. Roach, in particular, was outstanding on this and every other track recorded that day, and Russell consistently provided solid bass lines. Davis offered intimations of his future greatness in his thoughtful and harmonically advanced improvisations on both of the blues.

Parker took twenty-three choruses on the several takes of the two blues tunes and, never repeating himself, produced a profusion of melody both earthy and sophisticated as he demonstrated his unique ability to get to the marrow of the blues without compromising the most subtle modern harmonies and rhythms. The second and third takes of "Now's the Time" are especially masterful, and the fifth take of "Billie's Bounce" is almost their equal.

Bird sold in the studio that day the exclusive rights to "Now's the Time" for fifty dollars. Renamed "The Hucklebuck," it became a pop hit during the late 1940s. Bird was again inspired on "Thriving on a Riff," an archetype of bebop composition with its jagged lines and offbeat rhythms.

He continued to have trouble with his reeds, and it was decided that he would venture out to purchase new ones. Reig, who accompanied him to make sure he didn't try to score drugs, later asked rhetorically: "You think I'd leave Charlie Parker alone in midtown? What am I, crazy?"[19]

They returned to find Davis asleep on the floor. When they woke him, they discovered that he did not have the skills to perform complex trumpet parts worked out by Bird and Dizzy for the introduction and coda of "Cherokee." Lubinsky threw a tantrum, and Dizzy was prevailed upon to perform on trumpet.

After Bird warmed up with a beautiful improvisation on Gershwin's "Embraceable You," which Lubinsky recorded and released as "Meandering," the band dug into "Cherokee." They aborted—for two reasons—the first take soon after the melody statement. First, Bird would earn a composer's fee of seventy-five dollars for his improvisations if they did not state the melody, and, second, they wished to give him two full solo choruses. "Cherokee" imposes time constraints because, at sixty-four bars, it is double the length of the usual popular song. Reig, who was in trouble with Thornton gone, recalled what happened next:

> We got to figure out how to do this thing with no piano player. So Dizzy plays trumpet on the opening and then goes to the piano and we put in the drum solo so Dizzy would have a chance to get back for the ending. All the time this craziness is going on, Herman [Lubinsky] is yelling at me, "What's the name of this?", so I just yelled back at him, " 'Ko Ko,' K-O-K-O."[20]

After the intense thirty-two-bar introduction that had been worked out at the Three Deuces and that involved both written and improvised passages by Bird and Dizzy, Parker created 128 bars of incandescence at the herculean speed of three hundred beats per minute in one of the greatest improvisations in jazz history. He unleashed, without seeming effort, an irresistible flow of melodic phrases, weaving them seamlessly into a logical and beautiful construct.

The Library of Congress in 2003 chose "Ko Ko" as one of fifty essential American recordings to preserve for posterity.

The great New York vintage of 1945—from "I Can't Get Started" to "Shaw 'Nuff" and "Salt Peanuts" to "Now's the Time" and "Ko Ko"—had consolidated the bebop revolution with an array of masterworks. Dizzy and his cohorts would have to travel a long and difficult road before they found true public acceptance, however.

L.A. SOJOURN 20

DIZZY AND LORRAINE WERE RELIEVED ON DECEMBER 4, 1945, when they were able to get Bird on board their train for Los Angeles without incident. They were accompanied by Ray Brown, Stan Levey, and Milt Jackson; Al Haig was already on the West Coast and would meet them in California.

Things began to go wrong on the second day of the trip during a ten-hour layover in Chicago. Dizzy and Lorraine tried to push his guys out the door of the South Side joint where they had been jamming, but there was one double scotch too many and one good-bye too many, and they missed their speedy Santa Fe Chief going west and were forced to book a substitute that added two days to their journey.

This prolonged an agony for Bird, who had exhausted his heroin supply and was suffering from withdrawal sickness. Levey, who had been introduced to the drug by him, became his unofficial guardian, bringing him numbing shots of booze, forcing him to eat, and cleaning him up when he soiled himself.

Dizzy shook Levey awake after the train had stopped to take on water at a tiny depot in the Nevada desert and asked, "What the hell is that out there?"

Levey looked out the dusty window to see Bird staggering through the sand and the sagebrush with his saxophone case under his arm and said, "I think it's your sax player."

Dazed, hallucinating, and in pain, Bird had wandered off looking for a fix. Levey, fearful that the train would leave without them and physically fit from his second career as a professional boxer, sprinted fifty yards to Bird as he was trying to crawl under a barbed wire fence. The drummer pulled him erect and half carried him, sweating and shivering, back to the train. There Levey and Dizzy strapped him into his berth and sedated him with whiskey for the final twenty hours of the trip.[1]

An admirer took Bird directly from the Los Angeles railway station to a doctor, and Bird conned him into a prescription for a three-day supply of morphine for a nonexistent kidney ailment. He shot up as soon as he checked into his hotel room. Drugs were scarce and expensive in Southern California, but Bird quickly found a reasonably reliable source in Emry Byrd, a.k.a. Moose the Mooche, a cripple who ran a shoe-shine stand as a front. Three months later Bird used the dealer's sobriquet as the name for one of his most famous compositions, and a week after recording the tune for Dial Records, he paid for a consignment of heroin by signing away to Moose half his royalties from his recordings for the company.

The musicians settled into a cheap hotel in downtown Los Angeles, as Lorraine served as their paymaster and as the den mother for the youngsters, Ray Brown and Milt Jackson. The two of them, together with Levey, soon made a transportation deal with the men's room attendant at Billy Berg's; they each paid him one dollar per week to take them to and from the club on Vine Street in Hollywood in the open trunk of his 1939 Plymouth while other passengers rode up front.

Dizzy was elated when Berg's was packed on opening night, December 10, and he felt relief that he had hired Jackson, because

Bird appeared only for the last of three sets. The crowd was swelled by fans of two popular comedian/instrumentalists who shared the bill with Dizzy, Slim Gaillard, and Harry "The Hipster" Gibson.

Gaillard, a swing pianist/guitarist who had invented a surreal jive language that he called "vout," interjected this lingo into a series of novelty tunes that became pop hits. The first of these, "Flat Foot Floogie," swept the country in 1937 and put his career into the fast lane. Two of his hits of the 1940s, "Poppity Pop (Goes the Motor-Sickle)" and "Cement Mixer," also moved into the upper reaches of the pop charts.

Gibson, a white pianist who delivered his iconoclastic patter and songs in a hip black patois, ridiculed the Christian religion and other established institutions and scattered many references to drugs in his routines (his signature song was called "Who Put the Benzedrine in Mrs. Murphy's Ovaltine?").

Berg was a veteran nightclub entrepreneur and a brave one, because his was the only major Southern California venue that welcomed integrated audiences; the region's deep-seated racism had earned it the nickname "Mississippi with Palm Trees" among black entertainers. He had brought a taste of modern jazz to the area in early 1945 when he booked a Coleman Hawkins quintet whose recordings demonstrate that its idiom was advanced swing with bebop touches. The success of that engagement had emboldened him to hire Dizzy's pure bebop band.

Dizzy's opening-night elation was short-lived, because attendance dropped off precipitously during the second week of the engagement. The reaction of the West Coast audience was similar to that of Dizzy's southern Hepsations audience earlier in the year. They were simply not ready for the new music. Dizzy remembered, "They were *so* hostile out there. They thought we were just playing ugly on purpose. They were so very, *very* hostile. . . . Man, they used to stare at us *so* tough."[2]

And Ray Brown recalled that they were reduced to playing for their peers:

> The club was mainly full of musicians who knew how good those guys played. I remember Art Tatum used to come in there every

night, because he knew that Dizzy Gillespie and Charlie Parker were of his ilk.

The newspaper write-up said, "Men from Mars at Billy Berg's." And you don't need to be a space scientist to figure out what that means.[3]

As Ross Russell has written, the musicians were not the best of customers:

> Within a week the band was playing to half-filled houses. . . . Berg's clientele was reduced to a hard core of hipsters and jazz musicians. Bar receipts were unaccountably low. Customers would remain at a table for hours, catching set after set, ordering an occasional bottle of beer or an iced coffee. Between sets they would adjourn to the men's room, there to light up and turn on, remaining pleasantly high for the evening, but not on Berg's poured drinks.[4]

Dizzy was forced to accede to two of Berg's demands in order to salvage his contract: he agreed to add vocal numbers and, because of Bird's repeated absences and tardiness, to pay for the services of an additional saxophonist. Brown recalled what happened next: "Bird wrote a couple of arrangements with us singing, and Dizzy hired Lucky Thompson. He was out of place there. He was a great saxophone player, excellent musician. But, he didn't fit in with these guys."[5]

Dizzy's frustrations surfaced when, backstage one evening, he inveighed against the high number of "Uncle Toms" he had encountered in California. Slim Gaillard's wife overheard him, assumed that Dizzy was referring to her husband, and reported the alleged slight to him. In the ensuing fracas, Dizzy decked Gaillard and had to fight off his wife with a chair when she charged him with a butcher knife.

He and his adversaries were quickly reconciled, however, and Gaillard invited Dizzy and Bird to join him, two other swing musicians, and a Dixieland drummer for a December 29 record date for the tiny Beltone label. During a patter interlude, Gaillard introduced Dizzy as Daz McSciven-vouts-oroony and Bird as

Yardbird-oroony, and the musicians proceed to have a relaxed good time with "Flat Foot Floogie," "Poppity Pop (Goes the Motor-Sickle)," and two blues.

Evidence of the artistry of Dizzy's band is found in four tracks recorded later in the day of the Gaillard session; they have been preserved from the *Jubilee* radio show, broadcast weekly to troops overseas by the Armed Forces Radio Service. Lucky Thompson did not participate.

The full sextet performed on "Dizzy Atmosphere" and "A Night in Tunisia," and Jackson laid out for "Shaw 'Nuff" and "Groovin' High." Freed from the three-minute constraints of the 78 rpm record, the musicians stretched out on tracks that ran for roughly five minutes. They were all in top form as they provided a fitting climax to a year of stellar bebop recordings. Parker specialist Lawrence O. Koch believes that "these tracks should be in every jazz collection."[6]

Early in the new year, Johnny Richards, an outstanding West Coast arranger, enlisted Dizzy in an ambitious recording project with members of the Los Angeles Philharmonic. A tribute to Jerome Kern, the great, recently deceased composer, it involved nine stringed instruments, several flutes and woodwinds, a flügelhorn, a harp, and Dizzy with a rhythm section of Haig, Brown, and local drummer Roy Porter. Dizzy played brilliantly against the rich, imaginative backgrounds as four tracks were cut.

It is a measure of establishment resistance to bebop that the Kern estate forced the withdrawal of the first released track because of "distortion of the original melodies." The estate had no legal standing in the matter but possessed sufficient music industry clout to intimidate the record company, Paramount. During the mid-1970s, the four tracks surfaced on an obscure label.

Norman Granz, a social crusader turned jazz entrepreneur, hired Dizzy and Bird to perform on January 28, 1946, at a concert at L.A.'s Philharmonic Hall. Using a jam session format, the promoter had built a loyal following while presenting more than a dozen concerts (dubbed "Jazz at the Philharmonic" or "JATP") at the venue during the previous eighteen months. Granz had heard bebop in New York in August 1945 and was unimpressed, telling a *Downbeat* correspondent: "Maybe Gilles-pie was great but the 'advanced' group that Charlie Parker is fronting at the Three Deuces doesn't knock me out. It's too rigid and repetitive."[7]

Granz probably invited the beboppers because he wanted to determine how his swing-oriented fans would react to the new music. The response was reasonably positive, and Granz would later play an important role in the careers of both Dizzy and Bird.

The two men were booked for the first half of the concert to allow them to return to Billy Berg's in time for their early set. A recording shows that, after Dizzy opened energetically with saxo-phonists Lester Young, Willie Smith, and Charlie Ventura on "Crazy Rhythm" and "The Man I Love," the group was joined by Bird and trumpeter Al Killian for a hot rendition of "Sweet Georgia Brown."

Dizzy departed, but Bird defied him and remained for the sec-ond half. Dizzy's loss became the jazz lover's gain as Bird unfurled a solo on Gershwin's "Lady Be Good" that has become legendary. Lester Young's 1936 improvisation on the tune had attained the status of a jazz classic, and Bird, who worshipped Young, would often play it at triple tempo when warming up for a gig. Perform-ing in the company of his master, Bird eschewed even a trace of Young's interpretation and produced a masterpiece that was to-tally fresh.

The horn players waiting in the wings were so intimidated that no one wished to follow Parker. Bass player Billy Hadnott, who almost never soloed, came to their rescue as he improvised for almost two minutes while they pulled themselves together. Young finally came forward and played a version filled with lovely melody, but it lacked the searing beauty of Bird's statement. Three other soloists followed with workmanlike renditions.

Ross Russell, the proprietor of a hip Hollywood record store called the Tempo Music Shop, was a regular at Billy Berg's during Dizzy's gig and had been mesmerized by Bird's "Lady Be Good" solo, and he wished to record Dizzy's musicians before their sched-uled departure for New York on February 9. He convinced them and Lester Young to record for his new label, Dial, under the lead-ership of George Handy, Boyd Raeburn's pianist, and he organized a dress rehearsal for February 5, the day after the Billy Berg engagement ended; the recording was scheduled for the following day.

The rehearsal quickly became a nightmare. Young and Milt Jackson didn't show up, Bird was far below par, and a rowdy group of fans overran the studio while the musicians struggled with inferior engineers and faulty equipment. Dizzy and his men left in anger after they made a single subpar track, "Diggin' Diz."

Handy, who was supposed to shadow Bird wherever he went, lost him and called in the next day to cancel the session. But Russell desperately wanted to put bebop on wax, and he prevailed upon Dizzy to bring in his band minus Bird. They recorded six tunes as the Tempo Jazzmen; Dizzy took the pseudonym Gabriel for contractual reasons.

The results were splendid. The group laid down Dizzy's first recorded version of Monk's "'Round Midnight," two variations on "Dizzy Atmosphere" ("Dynamo A" and "Dynamo B"), the first ever waxing of Bird's most beautiful composition, "Confirmation," a revised "Diggin' Diz" (renamed "Diggin' for Diz"), and "When I Grow Too Old to Dream," one of the vocal numbers featured at Billy Berg's.

When Dizzy and Lorraine attempted to distribute tickets to their musicians for the February 9 flight, Bird could not be found. Dizzy gave his ticket and twenty dollars to Levey to hire a cab to look for him. The search was futile, and Dizzy left the ticket at the desk of their hotel. Bird later retrieved it, cashed it in for a drug binge, and remained in California for fourteen more eventful months.

Dizzy and Bird would subsequently team up for concerts and record dates, but they would never again perform together in a working band.

Dizzy found compensation for the problems and frustrations of California in the music he and his men had made there. He later reflected: "There were lots of wonderful moments at Billy Berg's. They washed away the disappointments. We played for ourselves and the hip musicians in the audience. Bird at a peak. The protégés Brown and Jackson coming on like 'Gangbusters.' Those young white guys Haig and Levey playing their asses off every night. Definitely a high point in my career."[8]

CONTROVERSY 21

BEBOP STIRRED UP BITTER CONTROVERSY DURING THE late 1940s, and Dizzy, its poster boy, was usually at the center of it.

In a reception reminiscent of the reactions to the Fauve painters in 1905 and Stravinsky in 1913, an old guard attacked bebop as an alien force. These traditionalists came from two factions, the Dixielanders and the swing musicians; they turned in 1944 from quarreling with each other to fighting bebop, and their principal forum was *Downbeat*.

In contrast to *Downbeat*, which saw itself as the trade paper of the working musician, *Metronome* fostered a self-image as a champion of the arts, and its principal writers—Barry Ulanov, George Simon, and Leonard Feather—backed bebop strongly. As we have seen, Feather wrote laudatory *Metronome* profiles of Pettiford in 1943 and of Dizzy in 1944, and starting in 1945, he wrote pro-bebop pieces for *Esquire* and the British magazine *Melody Maker*.

The mainstream press and, in particular, the Luce publications, almost always sided with *Downbeat*. The conflict began in 1944, as Simon reflected in January of 1945: "In the pages of *Metronome* and elsewhere, vigorous discussion of the merits and limitations of the schools of jazz represented by Condon [a Dixielander] on the one side, and the *Esquire* and *View* musicians on the other, was conducted. Verbal disagreement grew so intense that fists were brandished, blows struck."[1]

While the anti-bebop forces were quiescent during 1945, *Metronome* stayed on the offensive and, in a January 1946 article, anointed Dizzy as "Influence of the Year." Its profile read in part:

This [1945] was the year in which Dizzy Gillespie became the symbol of a revolution in jazz circles. In two years, rising from the status of a semi-obscure sideman with Earl Hines and others, Dizzy has become the central figure in a new movement of harmonic and rhythmic ingenuity, coupled with technical mastery, in jazz improvisation . . .

The Dizzy tide flows on unchecked. . . .

We feel that Dizzy, having become the focal point of this new scene in jazz history and being its most potent and fascinating personality, is a very important figure.[2]

Dizzy placed second on trumpet behind Roy Eldridge in *Metronome*'s annual reader's poll but did not earn a mention in *Downbeat*'s voting, which listed twenty-three trumpeters.

The counterattack came swiftly. In the March 25, 1946, issue of *Downbeat*, a reviewer of Dizzy's "Dynamo B" from his February 6 Tempo Jazzmen session wrote that the recording shows "a higher degree of musicianship and taste than other Gillespie acetates, perhaps because there's less ensemble work, less Gillespie trumpet, and more solo work by others."[3] An April 22 *Downbeat* critique of Charlie Parker's "Billie's Bounce" and "Now's the Time" tracks read:

These two sides are excellent examples of the other side of the Gillespie craze—the bad taste and ill-advised fanaticism to Dizzy's uninhibited style. Only Charlie Parker, who is a better musician and who deserves more credit than Dizzy for the style anyway, saves these from a bad fate. . . . The trumpet man, whoever the misled kid is [Miles Davis], plays Gillespie in the same manner as a majority of the kids who copy their idol do—with most of the faults, lack of order and meaning, the complete adherence to technical acrobatics . . . Good, bad or indifferent, the mass of Gillespie followers will love these sides, for even bad music is great if it is Dizz! This is the sort of stuff that has thrown innumerable impressionable young musicians out of stride, that has harmed many of them irreparably.[4]

Ted Steele, a disc jockey at Radio KMPC in Los Angeles, caused a furor in late March 1946 when, in a publicity stunt, he banned bebop from the station because it "tends to make degenerates out of young listeners." His main targets were Slim Gaillard and Harry "The Hipster" Gibson, but he tarred the entire bebop movement with his brush. His ploy might have met a quick death had not *Time* magazine picked up the story and told the nation that bebop was "hot jazz overheated with overdone lyrics full of bawdiness, references to narcotics, and doubletalk."[5] The wire services followed *Time*'s lead, and the episode received coast-to-coast coverage in major newspapers.

Downbeat decried Steele's attempt at censorship, but *Metronome*, as would be expected, went further and attacked *Time*'s attempt to slander the modernist movement in jazz. The main effect of the controversy, which petered out after several weeks, was to give national currency to the word *bebop* in a context of decadence.

Leonard Feather and editor-in-chief Arnold Gingrich made *Esquire* a major force in jazz beginning in 1943 when it sponsored what they termed All-Star Polls by panels of experts. The men were reacting negatively to the polls of readers conducted by *Metronome* and *Downbeat*, which, they believed, rewarded too many mediocrities.

Each year the magazine published handsome "*Esquire* Jazz Books" containing profiles of its winners as well as scholarly articles, and it produced concerts with the winners (mostly swing greats such as Armstrong, Tatum, Holiday, Goodman, and

Ellington). *Esquire* put a patriotic spin on the 1945 event, which was held at New York's Metropolitan Opera House and raised six hundred thousand dollars for the U.S. war effort. That same year, the magazine initiated a "New Star" category to honor younger, cutting-edge musicians. Dizzy was among the winners in 1945, followed by Bird in 1946, and Miles Davis in 1947.

The publication of *Esquire*'s 1947 jazz book created a firestorm. Primarily because Gingrich had taken a leave from the magazine, editorial control had passed to Ernest Anderson, the manager of Dixieland guitarist and bandleader Eddie Condon. Condon, who characterized bebop as "slop," had told a reporter, "Every time I hear a chorus of 'Whispering' or any other of Gillespie's Ka-Lunk specialties, I have to drown my sorrows. With each Ka-Lunk, I reach for a glass."[6]

Predictably, the book's survey of noteworthy recordings for 1946 listed eighty discs by Dixieland and swing musicians and one by a bebopper (Dizzy). It contained articles by several Condon friends, a single mention of Sarah Vaughan contrasting with a full-page piece about Condon singer Lee Wiley, and a lavish eight-page spread about Condon on tour with his favorite musicians.

Dizzy, who was a panelist in the "New Stars" voting, eagerly signed a musicians' letter of protest on February 14, 1947. It began with a series of grievances and ended with:

> We regard the entire book as an insult to the musical profession and to the jazz musicians who have helped *Esquire* by taking part in its jazz activities.
>
> As long as the present unfair set-up continues, we do not wish to vote in future polls, and we will refuse to accept any future awards.[7]

The thirty-three signatories included Armstrong, Ellington, Hawkins, Eldridge, Vaughan, Fitzgerald, Nat King Cole, Miles Davis, Pettiford, Holiday—the elite of the era.

When twenty of its twenty-two "All Star" panelists resigned in another letter, the protest became totally effective as *Esquire* ended the four-year run for its polls, concerts, and jazz books.

Many bebop fans at the time reacted defensively to the continuing critical assaults by building a cult around Dizzy.

Dizzy, who never met a head covering he didn't like, took to wearing blue berets that—together with his black horn-rimmed glasses, large-bowled meerschaum pipe, high-waisted suits, and goatee—made a distinctive fashion statement. The goatee was grown below his lower lip to cushion the pressure of his metal mouthpiece and was common practice among both trumpeters and trombonists. Because of his reputation for clowning, Dizzy was often accused of wearing the goatee as a fashion eccentricity, and he was forced to make several public statements to set the record straight.

As *Metronome* noted, his devotees wanted to dress like him and move like him:

He [developed] . . . a visual personality, little bowing motions and big, characteristic wearing apparel, such as his beret-caps, characteristic heavy eyeglasses, a characteristic goatee. All over America, young boppers, who had never been able to raise a sufficient hirsute covering to prove their age, struggled with chin fuzz in an attempt to build the Gillespie goatee: young boppers with their own little bands began to lead from the waist and the rump; some, with perfectly good eyesight, affected the heavy spectacles.[8]

Downbeat carried ads that offered bebop berets for two dollars and bebop suits for fifty-nine dollars.

As the Dizzy cult grew in America, the ideological battle crossed the Atlantic to England and France. A new English publication, *Jazz Journal*, sided with the traditionalists, while Feather, working both sides of the ocean, made the established magazine, *Melody Maker*, a bebop outpost. Across the channel, the controversy split the two doyens of French jazz: Charles Delaunay became a bebop stalwart, while Hughes Panassié remained with the old guard. The French debate was enriched by the emergence of André Hodeir, a brilliant new critic who argued persuasively for bebop.

Important economic and social changes in postwar America spelled catastrophe for the big band business, which had dominated pop music since Benny Goodman's Palomar Ballroom explosion in 1935. During the single month of November 1946, Goodman, Harry James, Tommy Dorsey, Benny Carter, and Les Brown announced that they were disbanding. The hundreds of successful touring bands would be reduced, in a few years, to less than twenty.

Many of the swing musicians whose livelihoods were threatened blamed bebop, which was slowly gaining public acceptance, and started in late 1946 to join the Dixieland critics in berating Dizzy and his cohorts.

An exception was Duke Ellington, whose band survived the late 1940s and prospered until his death in 1974. He welcomed bebop: "It's stimulating and original, which is what I, personally, look for in music."[9]

For the other side, Tommy Dorsey said, "Bop stinks. It has set music back twenty years,"[10] and Benny Goodman opined: "I've been listening to some of the Re-bop musicians. They're just faking. They're not real musicians. Bop reminds me of guys who refuse to write a major chord even if it sounds good. A lot of things they do are too pretentious. They're just writing or playing for effect, and a lot of it doesn't swing."[11]

Louis Armstrong added his criticism. He told a *Time* reporter, "Mistakes, that's all bop is . . . and a whole lot of notes, weird notes . . . that don't mean nothing. All them young cats playing their weird chords. And what happens? . . . No one's working."[12]

And he weighed in at *Downbeat*: "The beboppers are full of malice and all they want to do is show you up. . . . It's really no good and you got no melody to remember and no beat to dance to."[13] And at *Metronome:* "They never learned right. It's all just flash. It doesn't come from the heart the way real music should."[14]

Dizzy preferred to spend his energies on music rather than polemics and kept a low profile in the face of the continuing invective. And he was able to draw comfort from two events in September 1947 that signaled that the tide was beginning to turn for bebop.

More than one hundred Mutual Radio Network stations carried "Battles of Jazz" contests on September 13 and 20 that pitted a traditionalist group against a bebop septet featuring Dizzy, Bird, and Max Roach; the results of a listener write-in ballot over-whelmingly favored the modernists, and they were called back to perform alone on November 8. And on September 29, Dizzy, Bird, and Ella Fitzgerald sold out Carnegie Hall for a concert produced by Leonard Feather.

Following a thoughtful and sympathetic July 3, 1948, profile in *The New Yorker*, Dizzy made a major mistake in agreeing to an October *Life* magazine feature. He believed that the publication would be at least neutral about bebop, but it was far from friendly: "Bebop is a new-school of discordant, offbeat jazz. . . . Its devotees ape the eccentric appearance of bebop's inventor, Gillespie: Horn-rims, goatee, and beret. . . . Skeptics insist there is one way to identify bebop: If the tune is unrecognizable, it's bebop."[15]

This passage was in keeping with the tone of its Luce sister magazine, *Time*, which was characterizing bebop as "a frantic, disorganized, musical cult whose high priest was quid-cheeked Dizzy Gillespie"[16] and calling him "a South Carolina boy whose rapid fire, scattershot talk has about the same pace—and content—as his music."[17]

While clowning for the *Life* photographers, Dizzy allowed himself to be pictured prostrate on a Muslim prayer rug, a gag that he deeply regretted later.

None of the other bebop musicians possessed a fraction of Dizzy's talent for public relations, and almost all of them applauded his publicity efforts on behalf of their music. Never one to dwell very long on negatives, he received a friendly boost when his group was named *Metronome*'s band of the year for 1948, and he maintained his equanimity while being attacked, heaping praise in print on swing trumpeters Bobby Hackett, Billy Butterfield, and Shorty Baker and giving conciliatory interviews in which he urged younger musicians to explore the roots of jazz:

> If the kids get so hip that they frown on everything that isn't out-and-out bebop, we're going to end up with a sad bunch of musicians ten years from now. They have to learn all the rudiments just as the rest of us did. When I was growing up, all I wanted to play was swing, but I had to learn the other stuff too. . . . It took a lot more than learning just one style for Dizzy to get anywhere.[18]

And he did not allow the disputes swirling around him to affect his creativity. The years between 1947 and 1949 marked one of the most fruitful periods in his career as he spearheaded the Latin jazz revolution and made powerful and highly original big band music.

A near sellout at Carnegie Hall for Dizzy, Bird, and Sarah Vaughan on the brutally cold Christmas night of 1948 and the favorable reception in March 1949 of Feather's book *Inside Bebop* confirmed that bebop had staying power. Over several years, its musicians had built a sizable audience that had come to love the dissonances and the jagged rhythms that were once considered shocking.

Bebop was too artistically uncompromising to rival the commercial success of Goodman in 1935 or of Elvis Presley and the procession of rock-and-roll stars who followed him, but from the late 1940s to this day, it has enjoyed both artistic and commercial health. The *Downbeat* people boarded bebop's bandwagon during the early 1950s when they realized that it possessed commercial viability, and the controversy petered out a few years later.

The experience of the beboppers paralleled that of the Fauves and Stravinsky, who gradually found acceptance as audiences came to understand the validity of their artistic visions.

BIG BAND SUCCESS 22

The recordings Gillespie made with his band in those years stand up. . . . among the greatest modernist achievements in jazz. —GARY GIDDINS[1]

It was virtuoso ensemble music opposed to the music that came before. That music didn't demand that the sidemen players be virtuosos. That was left up to the soloists. But not so here. With his [Gillespie's] music, you have to be a virtuoso just to play the parts. —JOHN LEWIS[2]

DIZZY HAPPILY PUT THE TRAVAILS OF LOS ANGELES BE-hind him as he jumped back into New York's thriving jazz scene on February 11, 1946. He returned to offers from both the Three Deuces and the Spotlite and, for two reasons, chose the latter: the club seated more patrons than the Three Deuces, and its owner, Clark Monroe, had made him an intriguing proposition.

He suggested that Dizzy begin with an eight-week engagement leading a sextet while organizing a big band that would follow for an additional eight weeks.

Monroe was aware of the sad fate of the 1945 Hepsations big band tour, but he believed that conditions were now sufficiently different to offer a fair chance of success with a large group. He argued that almost a year had passed since the tour and that the public had became considerably more hip to Dizzy's brand of be-bop as they listened to his records and his radio appearances and heard more from him in person. And he emphasized that the Spotlite was located in sophisticated New York City and not the blues-happy rural South.

Three days before his Spotlite debut, Dizzy led his first date for a major record label, RCA Victor. Leonard Feather organized the session, at which septets led by Dizzy and Coleman Hawkins recorded four numbers each. Feather remembered the circumstances:

> [Dizzy] was due to sign soon with Musicraft. Just in time I corralled him for an album I was recording at Victor, to be called "New Fifty Second Street Jazz." (At that time it would have been useless to try to persuade any major record company to title an album "Bebop.") Victor wanted an all-star group featuring some of the Esquire Award winners, so we used J. C. Heard on drums and Don Byas on tenor, along with three of Dizzy's own men—Milt Jackson, Ray Brown, and Al Haig—and the new guitarist from Cleveland, Bill de Arango. Thanks largely to Dizzy's name we outsold every jazz album of the past few years.[3]

I believe that Feather slights here the drawing power of Hawkins, whose own group, featuring excellent performers such as Charlie Shavers and Shelly Manne, created at least two outstanding tracks for the album: "Say It Isn't So" and "Low Flame."

Dizzy's septet began the session with an as-yet-unnamed Monk tune that several Fifty-second Street bands had been using as an end-of-set sign-off. Feather suggested the name "52nd Street Theme," and, when Monk raised no objections, it stuck; the composition became one of Charlie Parker's favorite vehicles.

The septet also recorded the first small group rendition of "A Night in Tunisia," a Feather tune called "Old Man Rebop" (he used the pseudonym Floyd Wilson as composer because he feared hostility engendered by his championship of the new jazz), and "Anthropology" (without Byas, who left early for another engagement). Jackson and Byas performed well, and as the British critic Richard Palmer has noted, Dizzy was in superb form:

> There can be no doubt that by late 1945 Gillespie was a maturely focused artist whose technical virtuosity was matched by an outstanding musical brain. But nobody surely could have been prepared for the music laid down . . . on February 22, 1945. . . .
>
> All the performances remain electrifying, but it is the master take of "Night in Tunisia" that is the most astounding, containing one of the greatest trumpet solos in jazz, fit to rank with Armstrong's "West End Blues," I think. Its glorious assurance, as full of melody as of guts and passion, is all the more notable in view of the engineering; forgivably primitive.[4]

The commercial success of "New Fifty-second Street Jazz" led RCA Victor to sign Dizzy to a contract roughly sixteen months later.

Dizzy drew large and enthusiastic audiences to the Spotlite during the entire sextet engagement, which began on February 25 opposite a Coleman Hawkins quartet. Saxophonist Leo Parker had joined Al Haig, Milt Jackson, Stan Levey, and Ray Brown in the group, but—at Monroe's suggestion—he was soon replaced by a brilliant twenty-two-year-old named Sonny Stitt.

The son of a music professor and composer, Stitt had mastered the language of Charlie Parker while touring with the Tiny Bradshaw and Billy Eckstine big bands from 1943 to 1945. He claimed that he had arrived at his conception independently, but his reputation as a Parker clone dogged him until death; the subhead of his 1982 *New York Times* obituary read, "Style Likened to Charlie Parker's." In 1946, he was a fierce and fluent improviser who relished the intricacy of bebop harmony, and he immediately felt at home in the sextet.

Dizzy was plagued, during the early part of the Spotlite gig, by a painful infection in his upper lip, and he was relieved when a fellow trumpeter arranged for him to see Dr. Irving Goldman, one of New York's premier nose-and-throat specialists. The doctor, whose office was located on Manhattan's high-toned Upper East Side, sequestered Dizzy in a small private room because he did not want him to mix with his white patients in the general waiting area. Dizzy endured this humiliation because the doctor got results; he cured him quickly by reaming out the affected area and packing it with an antibiotic powder.

Dizzy did not begin organizing the big band in earnest until early April when he asked his able Hepsations lieutenant, Gil Fuller, for help. Fuller, who had only three weeks to prepare for an April 24 opening, quickly made himself indispensable.

As we have seen, the spring of 1946 was an inauspicious time to launch a big band as rapid changes in American society were undermining the conditions that had caused the large orchestras to flourish. An abundance of gasoline, federal housing subsidies, and television were the main villains.

The basic World War II gasoline ration of three gallons per week severely restricted travel and caused the public to spend a high proportion of its leisure dollars on activities close to home such as dancing to big bands and watching movies. When rationing ended, the renewed freedom to travel fostered rapid growth in what sociologists call "active leisure" and a concomitant decline in the passive kind. The postwar public shifted large amounts of leisure dollars to such pastimes as beach resort vacations, golfing, trips to national parks, and boating.

The late 1940s saw a major population shift out of the cities and into the suburbs. The GI Bill of Rights, which guaranteed banks against loss on mortgages to millions of veterans and provided generous federal subsidies for low-cost apartments, gave great impetus to this diaspora. It cost you a nickel to travel via subway from Brooklyn to Manhattan's Commodore Hotel to hear Benny Goodman in 1942. If you had moved to suburban New Rochelle in 1946 and still had a yen for Goodman, you were faced with a forty-five-minute drive to Manhattan or with the $1.65 cost of a round-trip train ride. Many decided that it was easier to stay at home and dance to Benny's records.

Although it did not achieve avalanche force until the early

1950s, television was beginning in the late 1940s to present a very attractive, no-cost way to entertain oneself of an evening. Starting with its infatuations with *Kukla, Fran, and Ollie* (a children's show viewed by more adults than children) in 1947, Milton Berle in 1948, and Ed Wynn in 1949, the American public was voting overwhelmingly in favor of free entertainment at home.

Dizzy sailed into this economic maelstrom with the enthusiasm of a true believer. He could have prospered easily with small groups, but he elected to enter the risky big band business because his heart was set on transforming bebop into world-class big band music.

Fuller and Dizzy worked at a breakneck pace, as they recruited musicians, created a "book" of scores, and whipped together a cohesive unit in rehearsal while Dizzy's sextet held down its full-time gig at the Spotlite.

Sextet members Stitt, Brown, and Jackson formed the core of the new big band as Dizzy replaced Levey with Max Roach and brought in Bud Powell for a trial period at the piano. When he proved too erratic, Dizzy hired Thelonious Monk, hardly a paragon of reliability. The other musicians were recruited from all points of the compass. Dizzy ran into Howard Johnson, a friend from the Teddy Hill band and a reliable saxophone section lead player, in a Harlem club and hired him on the spot; Johnson and Stitt were soon joined on saxophone by Ray Abrams, a veteran of the band at Monroe's Uptown House, and Leo Parker. The excellent trumpeter Kenny Dorham was one of several Hepsations veterans who came on board, and Monk recruited a fine trombonist.

The book came from several sources. First, Fuller and Dizzy updated the Hepsations scores. Then they turned to Billy Eckstine, the pioneer of big band bebop, who proved to be a generous helpmate; he provided ten arrangements—about one-third of what was needed. The highlights of the Eckstine cull were three Tadd Dameron charts of his own compositions which became mainstays of Dizzy's repertoire: "Our Delight," "Cool Breeze," and "Stay on It."

Finally, in a furious burst of creativity, Dizzy and Fuller and their crew produced a slew of outstanding arrangements and compositions in a couple of weeks. Fuller took small band bebop numbers such as "Woody 'n You" (renamed "Algo Bueno") and

"Shaw 'Nuff" and adapted them for seventeen instruments, and he and Dizzy composed "Things to Come," "I Waited for You," "Oop Bop Sh'Bam," and "That's Earl Brother." Monk contributed "'Round Midnight," Stitt and Al Haig wrote "A Handfulla Gimme," and Ray Brown collaborated with Fuller on "Ray's Idea," and with Dizzy and Fuller on "One Bass Hit." Fuller turned out twenty-one arrangements in a single week.

Like all of the great big bands, from Fletcher Henderson's to Goodman's and Basie's and Ellington's, Dizzy's had a distinctive sound; its aural signature melded massive power with precise virtuosity. The energy came mostly from Fuller's tightly packed brass where the trumpets played clusters of notes near to each other, and the trombones bracketed them with tones far apart (an interval of ten notes, for example). Fuller reinforced the power of the brass by opting for a hard-edged, almost vibrato-less sound from the saxophone section.

Stan Kenton had previously wielded similar power with his band, but he had not combined it with a virtuoso rendering of the complex, serpentine lines of small band bebop. This was Dizzy's unique contribution to the genre; he transformed big band music by bringing to it bebop's unique phrasing and its harmonic and rhythmic innovations. The critic Gene Seymour has reflected on the originality of Dizzy's concept:

It is still possible to listen to the powerful recordings made by Dizzy Gillespie and his Orchestra in the late 1940's and feel everything around you transformed. What Orson Welles did for movies with "Citizen Kane," Gillespie did for big band jazz. By using the full resources of their respected mediums and adding their particular inventiveness and daring, they redefined their forms. And both were jumped on by audiences too used to the Way Things Were Done to appreciate innovation.[5]

The full band had barely a week to come together, and Fuller was shocked to find that the musicians were not being paid to rehearse. He immediately cadged five hundred dollars from booker and manager Billy Shaw and gave each of the performers ten dollars per day. He also banned Dizzy from the proceedings until the final run-through. Fuller, who drove the band relentlessly through five-hour rehearsals, found Dizzy's constant tinkering and kibitzing a distraction, and he prevailed upon Lorraine to convince her husband to stay away. When Dizzy did appear, he took command and led the band through the charts with great seriousness.

The Spotlite, with a large DIZZY GILLESPIE'S BIG BAND sign draped above the entrance, violated New York's fire ordinance on opening night, April 24, as 150 people crowded into a space limited by law to 120. Fuller remembered how the band took off:

> Man, [Dizzy] hit into that opening. . . . They weren't expecting that noise, the whole band, a little club, and [they] started with the whole band hitting one note. And Dizzy brought his hand up, and everybody jumped. And by the time they landed on their feet, [the crowd] thinking it was over—no, he hit another one—another one—another one! And old Max was going . . . took off with the shit.[6]

After this tumult, Dizzy cooled things down with the two-part theme, the swinging "Shaw 'Nuff" segueing into the sedate ballad "I Waited for You."

Dizzy dedicated the last number of the first set, the up-tempo flag-waver "Things to Come," to Duke Ellington, who was in the audience. Ellington responded by telling the crowd that he loved the music and that, for him, the words *things to come* captured the progressive message of the band.

Roach left for a more lucrative gig in early May, and Dizzy eagerly hired Kenny Clarke to take his place. The drummer had been discharged from the army in late April after almost three years of service, most of it in Europe. Dizzy's warm welcome boosted Klook's sagging morale; he was depressed and considering another line of work, because he had not handled drumsticks in two years and he believed that modern jazz had passed him by:

> When I came home, I knew a great change had taken place. The development of music then was phenomenal. . . . I thought I'd been

away too long and couldn't absorb it fully. I thought I wouldn't be capable enough to play for Diz. But he encouraged me. He said: "I don't care how you play, man. You're gonna join the band. We want your spirit." . . . He was really good to me.[7]

A May 15 record date shows that Klook need not have worried. He performed skillfully as he joined Dizzy, Haig, Stitt, Brown, and Jackson in a relaxed four-tune session for Dizzy's new label, Musicraft. Musicraft management knew Dizzy's work well because they had purchased the assets of the now-defunct Guild, where he was formerly under contract; the new association pleased him, because Musicraft offered stronger distribution than the independent labels for which he had worked previously, and it had major artists such as Duke Ellington and Artie Shaw under contract.

Clarke's recruitment was soon followed by the hiring of James Moody. His arrival began a close and loving relationship with Dizzy that did not end until forty-seven years later, when Moody was at Dizzy's bedside as he died in a New Jersey hospital.

They had met in July 1945 when the Hepsations tour took Dizzy to North Carolina, where Moody was playing saxophone in an air force orchestra. Dizzy was already thinking ahead to a successor to the 1945 band, and he told Moody and his bandmate, trumpeter David Burns, that he would be regrouping in New York and that the two men should look him up when they arrived there. Nine months later, Moody and Burns, freshly discharged from the service, showed up at a Gil Fuller big band audition. Burns made it, but Moody didn't. He remembered:

Fuller said I didn't play loudly enough. I guess I was very nervous, and he started yelling: "Come back when you're ready." But then about a month later I got this telegram from Burns saying, "You start with us tonight at the Spotlite." I guess I got the gig because somebody decided to give me another chance and because they needed someone like right now.[8]

Twenty-four tracks recorded from Spotlite radio broadcasts during June 1946 convey the excitement of the big band in action; they contain more than eighty-one minutes of explosive, imperfect, extravagant music. Milt Jackson recalled the élan that possessed the performers: "We had a bunch of musicians who loved music, and the musicians, they loved each other. Now in the daytime, we're sitting about and everybody's on edge . . . 'cause we couldn't wait to sit down and get to that band and hit that first note. From the first note to the last you could hear . . . that happiness, that togetherness, you can hear it all in that music."[9] As the jazz historian Ira Gitler recalled, the ebullient spirit of the musicians spilled out over the bandstand: "To be in that little club, the Spotlite, with its low ceiling and hear the band play 'Things to Come.' It would take your head off. Incredible. Definitely one of the most exciting experiences you could ever have."[10]

The Spotlite recordings confirm what Ray Brown has long maintained—Klook was Dizzy's ideal percussionist: "Kenny Clarke was the only guy he could find that played drums to fit in with the stuff he wanted to do . . . so it was perfect."[11] And Clarke was overjoyed that he and the pal with whom he had started the modernist revolution in 1938 were reaching new peaks together eight years later. He would say, "The power, the rhythm, the harmonies of that band were like something I've never heard before. . . . It was a wonderful part of my life. Diz was the pivot. We got to a point where there was nothing we couldn't do."[12]

The Spotlite broadcast tracks possess special historical importance, because they contain the only examples of Monk's playing during his short tenure with the band. He provided pungent punctuations behind the horn soloists throughout, performed a highly original duet with Ray Brown on "Algo Bueno" ("Woody 'n You"), and, during a fine arrangement of his own " 'Round Midnight," accompanied Jackson brilliantly and contributed a short, biting solo.

Monk's departure from the band was swift. Clarke had met pianist/arranger/composer John Lewis in France in early 1945 when they both played trombone in an army band. Lewis had come to New York later in 1945 to study at the Manhattan School of Music, but he did not contact Clarke until the following June when he telephoned as the drummer was leaving for a rehearsal. Clarke invited him along and told him to bring his charts for

"Bright Lights," an arrangement that had been a standout with their army orchestra.

Dizzy agreed to hear it and asked Clarke to pass the parts out to the band. He remembered what happened next: "We got through the introduction and to the first chords, and [Dizzy] looked at John. He stopped the band, and he says, 'You want to work with us?' So John, you know, he was timid, and he said, 'Well, yeah, you know.' So Dizzy said, 'You're hired.'"[13] "Bright Lights," which was renamed "Two Bass Hit," immediately became a companion piece to Ray Brown's feature "One Bass Hit."

During the week starting June 28, 1946, the band yo-yoed between 52nd and 125th streets as it fulfilled engagements at both the Spotlite and the Apollo. One afternoon, Klook and Monk lingered too long at a bar near the Apollo and arrived backstage after the opening theme; they found Milt Jackson playing drums and no one at the piano. While Clarke nudged Jackson off his stool, Monk tiptoed onto the stage. He did not progress very far as Dizzy, exasperated by his constant tardiness, pointed a finger at him and shouted, "You're fired." He then turned to Lewis, who was standing in the wings, and beckoned him to the piano chair. Lewis occupied it until March 1948. Monk's firing disappointed Fuller, who had hoped to work with him on incorporating several of his compositions into the band's repertoire.

Lewis's arrival marked the genesis of one of the most celebrated bands in jazz history, the Modern Jazz Quartet. As Milt Jackson remembered, the group got its start because Dizzy's trumpeters and trombone players needed a respite from lip-shredding tempos and intricate, spiraling lines: "The music Gil Fuller wrote was sort of difficult, especially for the brass section. So one night Dizzy suggested, 'Hey, why don't you and John and Ray and Klook play a little bit—give the guys a rest!' Which we did and it immediately became a spontaneous reaction."[14]

Dizzy was so pleased that he responded by bringing the four musicians on for fifteen minute mini-sets every night at the midpoint of his show. Soon the quartet began to develop its own material, and in early 1947 made its independent debut as The Atomics of Modern Music at Small's Paradise in Harlem. After a couple of name changes, the Modern Jazz Quartet jelled in 1952 when bassist Percy Heath joined Jackson, Clarke, and Lewis (who doubled as music director). Brown had other commitments at the time.

Dizzy skipped a Spotlite set on June 17 to perform as a guest for a second time with Norman Granz's touring "Jazz at the Philharmonic" group at a well-attended Carnegie Hall concert. Dizzy interpreted the invitation as an important vote of confidence from the impresario.

Two Musicraft sessions of June 10 and July 9, 1946, showcased the band at its powerful, combustible best. Monk arrived too late to participate in the June recording and was replaced by Jackson, who abandoned his vibraphone for the date.

The band scored a major triumph with the first of two tracks, Dameron's medium-tempo "Our Delight." Brown's bass provided an ultrapowerful underpinning, Clarke complemented his work with subtle percussion commentary, and Dizzy and saxophonist Ray Abrams soloed well, but it is the band itself that is the star of the performance. Playing with a polish and precision not heard in the Spotlite recordings, the brass and reed sections swing flawlessly through sinuous and complex bebop lines as they lay claim to a place among the big band elites.

The second track was "Good Dues Blues," featuring Alice Roberts, a mediocre vocalist whose work was inexplicably favored by Dizzy and detested by Fuller. The only outstanding feature of the recording is a fine closing chorus by Dizzy.

Five tracks were cut at the July 9 session, which marked the recording debut of John Lewis. One of them, "Things to Come," is a masterpiece. Musicians were amazed when Charlie Parker, with the help of Dizzy and Max Roach and Curley Russell, created a fabulous recording at three hundred beats per minute with "Ko Ko" in 1945. That was a quartet performance; "Things to Come," a roaring, shouting tornado of sound, was performed with virtuosity at this mind-boggling tempo by seventeen men.

Brown, Clarke, and John Lewis provided an inexorable, driving beat; the five trumpeters performed intricate lines in unison with Dizzy and launched fierce punctuations behind the three soloists (Dizzy, Jackson, and saxophonist John Brown); the reeds negotiated the twists and turns of the score with the skills of slalom skiers, and everyone participated in a chilling, spiraling glissando to finish things off. "Things to Come" is my favorite big band recording.

Earlier in the day, Fuller's excellent arrangement showcased the band's power behind solos by Dizzy and Ray Brown on "One Bass Hit II," and Moody marked his studio debut with a fluent improvisation on "Ray's Idea." The session ended with two versions (one with Alice Roberts, one with Dizzy) of the tepid novelty vocal, "He Beeped When He Should Have Bopped."

Billy Shaw, working out of the Gale Agency, parlayed the Spotlite success into wide-ranging tours that teamed the band with Ella Fitzgerald.

When the group left New York on July 13, Kenny Clarke took a leave of absence to accept a series of lucrative small-group gigs in the city. Joe Harris, who replaced him, drove the band vigorously, but he lacked the imagination and subtlety that Clarke brought to the job, and he never achieved the rapport with Dizzy that Clarke had.

Ella, accompanied only by her pianist Ray McTooney and her cousin and helpmate Georgianna Henry, joined the group on July 17 in Indianapolis on the way to a successful week at the Regal Theater in Chicago. Ella was billed there as "the first lady of song," and Dizzy was described as the "merry, mad genius of music."

The band toured the Midwest on its own for the remainder of the summer and rejoined Ella for the week of September 27 in Detroit, for the period from October 18 to November 5 in Washington, DC, Baltimore, and Norfolk, and for a dance in Chicago on November 17. They came together again for twenty Deep South one-nighters from December 10 through January 4.

The band always opened the shows and warmed up the audiences for Ella. A hard worker who responded generously to audience enthusiasm, she closed with a package of five numbers followed by two or three encores. Ella had built a strong following during eleven years as a swing star, and her partnership with the band added legitimacy and prestige to Dizzy and the bebop movement in general; it also helped greatly at the box office.

Dizzy was thus in Ella's debt, but he gave her something in

exchange that was probably equally important—a new musical vocabulary, bebop. One of her biographers, Stuart Nicholson, has noted that she was unique among swing stars in making the transition to modernism:

> For the Swing Era players, many of them still young and at the height of their powers, like Benny Goodman, Roy Eldridge and Buck Clayton, it was a bitter pill to discover that almost overnight their style had become old hat. Some, like Coleman Hawkins and Don Byas, almost succeeded in adopting to bop, but only one—Ella Fitzgerald—successfully made the transition.[15]

Ella used bebop to great career advantage as she changed her entire approach to scat singing. Scat involves using the voice as an improvising instrument, substituting wordless sounds for the lyrics of a song. It became a jazz staple after Louis Armstrong began the practice with his recording of "Heebie Jeebies" in 1926. Dizzy could work with Ella as an equal, because, as the critic Barry McRae has noted, he was a master of the scat genre:

> Gillespie's singing style, with its emphasis on wordless scat, changed the rules of jazz vocal for the first time since Louis Armstrong sang with Fletcher Henderson in 1924. . . . Gillespie organized his wordless gibberish with a draughtsman's hand. Inevitably, he phrased his phonetic shorthand in the same style as his trumpet, although . . . the limitations of his voice reduced his options. . . .
>
> He had no alternative but to extricate himself from melodic cul-de-sacs by sleight of vocal creativity. To do so he demonstrated amazing dexterity, disguising the limited number of sounds he used by shaping the solo and by the unpredictable direction of his melodic line.[16]

Ella, who possessed a great harmonic gift and who could reproduce on demand the most intricate phrases, found pleasure in her on-the-job course in bebop, according to a second biographer, Jim Haskins: "Musically, that . . . tour was one of the happiest times of Ella's life. Bebop was a revelation to her, and she felt challenged as she had not been since her [1945] foray into calypso. . . . She later told an interviewer, 'It was the greatest education I ever had.'"[17]

Ella relaxed on the tours as she enjoyed an easy comradery with the band members, and her cousin Georgianna won favor with the musicians as she prepared delicious meals with assistance from Lorraine. Dizzy, who loved Georgianna's cooking, raised one caveat; he would allow only Lorraine to prepare his special-recipe eggs.

Ella was an excellent dancer, and on late night visits to local clubs, she and Dizzy would dazzle everyone with their athletic Lindy Hopping. She would lindy with Dizzy, but she danced the slow numbers with Ray Brown, nine years her junior. A romance between the two blossomed quickly, and Ray moved into Ella's apartment in early 1947.

During respites from touring in the summer and fall of 1946, Dizzy and his musicians participated in two important recording sessions and appeared in a movie, *Jivin' in Bebop*. For the first date on September 26, Dizzy worked as a sideman for Ray Brown in his debut as a leader. Dizzy used the pseudonym Izzy Goldberg, because Brown was recording for Savoy, a rival of Dizzy's label, Musicraft. The bassist had assembled "The Bebop Boys," an octet that included trumpeter David Burns, saxophonists John Brown and James Moody, Milt Jackson, and Joe Harris from the big band, and one outsider—Hank Jones, the pianist who had introduced him to Dizzy.

The eight musicians achieved a rich, dense sound as they romped through four tunes composed by Fuller, Burns, Moody, and their leader—two easy swingers, a blues, and "Moody Speaks," a fast "I Got Rhythm" derivative showcasing the saxophonist. Jones performed forcefully, Burns proved that he was a apt student of Dizzy as he ably jousted with his mentor through competitive choruses on "Smokey Hollow Jump," Brown contributed two robust bass solos, and Moody showed that he was fast mastering the bebop vocabulary.

For the second session on November 10, the big band cut two

tracks; it provided mellow backgrounds for crooner Kenny "Pancho" Hagood's rendition of its theme song, "I Waited for You," and it swung through "Emanon," a relaxed bebop blues. John Lewis's highly enjoyable arrangement of the latter is notable for its bright call-and-response passages, its bristling unison trumpet themes, and a lyrical introduction performed by him. Dizzy and Jackson soloed with verve, and Moody showed why he had quickly emerged as the band's leading saxophone improviser with a beautifully articulated chorus where Lester Young cadences peep through his bebop lines.

Jivin' in Bebop was aimed at black audiences by its white producer, William Alexander, and it found commercial success in both northern and southern black movie circuits. The film, a one-hour variety show brought to life on celluloid, provides fine music, glimpses of vintage black vaudeville, and invaluable images of Dizzy's exuberant body language fronting the band. He leads his musicians through sixteen selections, and during eight of them, the men are placed behind a curtain as they back an assortment of tap dancers, jitterbugs, and "interpretive" dancers in harem costumes. In the vaudeville tradition, Dizzy engages in banter between numbers with comedian Freddie Carter (sample: "How long was Cain mad with his brother?" "As long as he was Abel"). Musical highlights include the band backing the excellent singer Helen Humes on two blues and rousing renditions of "One Bass Hit," "Salt Peanuts," and "Things to Come."

Dizzy returned from the South in January 1947 to find that, despite the boost from Ella Fitzgerald, the tours had barely made expenses. He was not overly discouraged, however, because Billy Shaw informed him that the band's travels had generated sufficient interest and publicity to ensure profitable bookings for the first three months of 1947.

Shortly after the tour ended, Dizzy and Ella performed a bebop scat duet on Gershwin's "Lady Be Good" for a New York radio show. She enjoyed the performance so much that she used the tune for her first bebop recording on March 19, 1947; it became one of her best-selling discs.

Dizzy received a boost when Billy Eckstine, breaking up his

big band to perform as a soloist, gave him all his equipment, including music stands, uniforms, and microphones. Shaw started the band on January 17 with a week opposite Sarah Vaughan at the Apollo and followed with a one-month Midwest tour and a lucrative six-week engagement at the Savoy Ballroom that ended on April 11. Charlie Parker sat in with the band at the Savoy on April 8, one night after he returned to New York following sixteen tumultuous months in California.

After Dizzy's departure from Los Angeles on February 9, 1946, Bird managed, despite heavy drug use, to hold his life together for a couple of months. But his situation began to deteriorate in April due to a lack of work, an acute scarcity of heroin, the jailing of his pusher, Moose the Mooche, and the precarious financial situation of his record company, Dial. His decline culminated in a complete breakdown on July 31, 1946.

Bird arrived that day for a Dial record date in a weak, wobbly, trancelike state. He had consumed a quart of whiskey, and he made his condition worse by ingesting six phenobarbital "downer" pills during the session. His playing was disjointed and terribly labored as he forgot phrases and missed cues, and producer Ross Russell was called upon to hold him from behind to steady him after he spun through 360 degrees during a solo. Bird's flawed choruses possess a terrible, anguished beauty as they shine through the sickness and the chaos of the occasion.[18]

Bird returned to his hotel in a hallucinatory stupor. After he twice came down naked to the lobby to use a pay phone, the owner locked him in his room. A few minutes later, a guest reported smoke coming from under Bird's door, and the manager hurried to let him out. He found that Bird had dropped a lit match on his mattress, setting it and the bedstead on fire. When policemen and firemen arrived at the scene, Bird scuffled with them and was subdued with a blackjack, handcuffed, wrapped in a blanket, and carted off to jail.

Russell needed eight days to locate Bird, because, during the mid-1940s, Los Angeles officialdom was not meticulous in keeping track of black men in the grip of psychosis. He found Bird in a psychiatric ward, confined in a straitjacket and handcuffed to a bed. With the help of a psychiatrist, Russell negotiated both the erasure of criminal charges against Bird and his commitment for six months to Camarillo, a state mental hospital about fifty miles from Los Angeles. Purged of drugs and robustly healthy, Bird was released to Russell's care on February 1, 1947. He was soon using heroin again.

Bird and a girlfriend flew east from Los Angeles in April with tickets purchased from the proceeds of a December 1946 benefit concert organized for him by Russell.

Following their Savoy reunion on April 8, Bird told Dizzy that he needed work while organizing a quintet to go into the Three Deuces, and Dizzy hired him for a weeklong gig at a club in the Bronx. Miles Davis, who was in Dizzy's trumpet section at the time, remembered that Bird didn't last long: "On the night we opened . . . Bird was up on stage nodding out and playing nothing but his own solos. He wouldn't play behind nobody else. Even the people in the audience were making fun of Bird while he was nodding up there on the stage. So Dizzy, who was fed up with Bird anyway, fired him after that first gig."[19]

Shaw, building on the successful Savoy engagement, kept the bookings flowing. After a series of one-nighters and two weeks in Detroit, the band returned to the Apollo with Vaughan on June 10, did a week in Washington, DC, and on July 10, 1947, settled into a seven-week engagement at the Downbeat on Fifty-second Street. By this time Bird was firmly ensconced next door at the Three Deuces, where he employed Roach, Davis, Haig, and bassist Tommy Potter in a stellar quintet, and Billy Eckstine was performing across the street as a single at the Onyx. The singer brought his trumpet to work and sat in with Dizzy's brass section whenever he could.

Dizzy felt content in late July as he signed a lucrative two-year recording contract with RCA Victor, listened to Shaw's talk of a September Carnegie Hall concert (to be produced by Leonard Feather) and a European tour later in the year, and played to full houses at the Downbeat.

With his band consistently profitable and fully booked, Dizzy began to implement a long-held dream: to make Latin rhythms and harmonies an integral element of modern jazz. He kick-started the program in July, when he commissioned the young composer George Russell to write an extended Latin piece for the Carnegie Hall date and when he began a search for an Afro-Cuban percussionist to transform his rhythm section.

Dizzy recorded his first four sides for RCA Victor on August 22, and the band, now fifteen months old, performed with swaggering assurance. The tunes were varied—Dizzy's "Ow," a relaxed "I Got Rhythm" derivative; Tadd Dameron's bright swinger "Stay on It"; "Oop-Pop-A-Da," a scat vocal exercise, and "Two Bass Hit," John Lewis's showcase for Ray Brown.

The session marked the recording debut of the innovative baritone saxophonist, Cecil Payne, four months after he had joined the band. Payne, who pioneered with Serge Chaloff the mastery of bebop lines on the large and cumbersome baritone instrument, provided Dizzy with both a fluent solo voice and an anchoring presence for the sax section. He was featured on "Ow" and "Stay on It" and produced polished improvisations on both.

Dizzy and Pancho Hagood traded nimble scat phrases on "Oop-Pop-A-Da" as the band wailed behind them, and Moody followed with a raucous chorus. Ray Brown's powerful solo on "Two Bass Hit" was his swan song with the band. He and Ella Fitzgerald had fallen deeply in love by the summer of 1947, and they did not want to be separated, especially with Dizzy's European tour in the offing. When she proposed that he quit and join her backup trio, he agreed and departed soon after the RCA Victor date. He was replaced by the talented Al McKibbon.

Brown and Ella were married on December 10, 1947, and he began touring with her early in 1948.

Wishing to pursue freelance opportunities in the New York area, Milt Jackson also left the band in the autumn of 1947.

While he was bringing McKibbon up to speed in early September, Dizzy was delighted by two pieces of news: Feather's Carnegie Hall concert, scheduled for the twenty-ninth, had sold out, and Mario Bauzá had found him an Afro-Cuban percussionist.

THE AFRO-CUBAN 23
JAZZ REVOLUTION

MARIO BAUZÁ, A GIANT OF AMERICAN MUSIC WHO played a vital role in Dizzy's career, was the founding father of Afro-Cuban jazz. For Dizzy and many others the terms *Afro-Cuban* and *Latin* were interchangeable, but in the beginning the music was Afro-Cuban. As the revolution expanded to encompass the music of Brazil, Puerto Rico, the Dominican Republic, and other nations of the Southern Hemisphere, the use of the word *Latin* became more appropriate.

Bauzá brought unique qualifications to his revolutionary task. A black man, he had totally absorbed Cuba's Afro-Spanish musical heritage of rumba, *danzon, son*, and *charanga*, and alone among the outstanding Cuban musicians of his time, he had acquired extensive experience in top-flight American jazz bands. A prodigy who joined the Havana Philharmonic as a clarinetist at age twelve, he became so enamored with jazz that, at age nineteen in

1930, he abruptly quit an excellent job with a Havana dance orchestra and came to New York to try his luck.

He found success quickly and between 1930 and 1941 concentrated on trumpet while doubling on saxophone with the
bands of Noble Sissle, Chick Webb (where he discovered Ella
Fitzgerald and was musical director for four years), Don Redman, Fletcher Henderson, and Cab Calloway. In 1936, he married Estella Grillo, sister of Francisco Grillo (the vocalist better
known as Machito).

Bauzá joined Machito's band, the Afro-Cubans, in 1941, a
year after its formation, and, as its musical director, created the
first true marriage of American jazz and Cuba's native music.
The historian John Storm Roberts has written of his achievement:

> Bauzá's makeover of the original Machito band was epochal. . . .
> Bauzá told me, "Our idea was to bring Latin music up to the
> standard of the American orchestras. So I brought a couple of the
> guys that arranged for Calloway and Chick Webb to write for
> me". . . .
> The formula was simple but enormously powerful: to blend a
> Cuban repertoire and a Cuban rhythm section (with its crucial for-
> mal underpinning, the two-bar offbeat call-and-response rhythmic
> pattern called clave) and a trumpet and sax front line with the
> power of the black swing bands. . . .
> One of Bauzá's innovations was to hire non-Latin horn players,
> because his jazz-inflected sound would come not just from the jazz
> voicings in the arrangements but from the details of the
> phrasing. . . . The Afro-Cubans' essence was not the instrumenta-
> tion—but the embryonic enriching of the black, and thus largely
> African-derived, elements of the highly complex Cuban tradition
> by the use of the *African*-American stream of swing.[1]

As the scholars Bobby Sanabria, Aurora Flores, and Phil
Schaap have pointed out in a recorded conversation, naming the
band the Afro-Cubans in the early 1940s was a brave statement
of ethnic identity:

Sanabria: Not even African Americans had used the term "Afro."

Flores: Anything African was frowned upon. Even by African Americans. It was looked down upon as something tribal, something savage, something from another country that was not them.

Schaap: Mario did that because he knew . . . that it said "black is good."[2]

Of the five bebop pioneers, only Dizzy had a deep passion for Afro-Cuban music. It had burned brightly from the time in 1937 when Bauzá had secured gigs for him in Latino bands in East Harlem and Dizzy had found his "Africa" there, and it had continued through his 1939 engagement with Alberto Socarrás's Cuban orchestra; his attendance at Bauzá's groundbreaking "Tanga" recording session in 1943, his composition of tunes with Latin rhythms, such as "Pickin' the Cabbage," "A Night in Tunisia," and "Woody 'n You" ("Algo Bueno"); his fruitful collaboration with Cuban percussionist Diego Iborra during the 1945 Three Deuces engagement with Bird, and the frequent jams that he enjoyed during 1946 and 1947 with the bands of Machito and his confrere Noro Morales.

Bauzá remembered how he supplied the fuse to Dizzy's Afro-Cuban explosion—the master Cuban conga player, composer, and dancer Luciano Chano Pozo y Gonzalez, better known as Chano Pozo:

Dizzy got hold of me. He got a concert, he wanna do some Afro-Cuban Jazz, something that we talk many, many, many, many times when we was together with Cab Calloway. And I did it myself first for the Latin people, and he wanted to do it to his American audience. So he said the only thing that stop him is he didn't have the rhythm. . . . So I say I got the man for you. I took Dizzy to Chano house. I introduce to Chano. I was interpreter there because Chano didn't speak English. Neither Dizzy Spanish.[3]

Dizzy, who hired Chano on the spot, remembered his comments on language: "Deeksy no peaky Spanni. I no peak English. But both we peak Africa."[4]

Chano exuded Africa. His style of percussion came in a direct line from the Yoruba people of West Africa, the ancestors of Dizzy's maternal great-grandmother, and he practiced the Yoruba's Lucumi religion, which became known in Cuba as Santeria. For two principal reasons, its complex rituals and theology survived almost intact through the 360 years of Cuban slavery that ended in 1886: first, Santeria worshippers deceived the Spanish slave owners by taking the names of Catholic saints for their gods, or orishas (for example, the orisha Shangó became Saint Barbara). And second, they took advantage of the fact that the Spaniards, contrary to their counterparts in the United States, allowed slaves to use drums.

The drums lie at the center of their rituals, which employ both dancing and chanting and use more than two hundred separate rhythms. Chano seemed to know them all, and he frequently incorporated Santeria chants into his performances. Bauzá remembered:

> Chano had so many things. . . . He hear the band play and had a way to play a rhythm for that particular arrangement. The other conga players just had one rhythm, and that rhythm they played for practically everything. But Chano had a million and one rhythms . . . and knew exactly where to apply. He always got to have something to go with the phrase, something that you don't expect.[5]

Chano, born in 1915 to a bootblack and a housewife, grew up in Havana's poorest and most violent black slums and spent his adolescence in a reformatory. He gained local fame during his early twenties as a dancer and drummer in neighborhood rumba festivals but had difficulty breaking into professional Cuban show business because of antiblack prejudice.

He set up his own bootblack stand in 1940 in the lobby of a radio station featuring a leading Latin orchestra and always brought a conga drum to work, entertaining the musicians as they walked in and out. They were sufficiently impressed to invite him to join in broadcasts and recordings, and his career took wing. Within three years, he had achieved stardom playing the conga, writing songs that became highly popular, and dancing.

His composition "Blen, Blen, Blen" became a number one hit in Cuba in 1940, and in 1942 Machito adopted another one, "Nague," as his theme song.

Chano was shot in a dispute over cocaine money in 1945 and carried the bullet, which was near his spine and too difficult to remove, for the rest of his life. He recovered quickly, and his career was back on track by the time he arrived in New York with a dance team in early 1947.

He had no trouble finding work; he recorded once with Machito and Bauzá and three times leading his own groups, accompanied the Katherine Dunham dance troupe at concerts and recitals, and played at weekend rumba matinees and in floor shows at major nightclubs. He was performing solo at the glittery Broadway club, La Conga, when Dizzy hired him.

Bauzá, Machito, Dizzy, and Chano were making a revolutionary cultural statement by incorporating a second pure African element into jazz roughly sixty-five years after the first, the blues, became an essential part of the music. The blues were the profane late-nineteenth-century brother of gospel that had evolved over a century's time from the spirituals born in the 1750–1780 period. Afro-Cuban music had its roots in the same late eighteenth-century era.

Afro-Cuban polyrhythms and harmonies have become an essential part of the jazz canon since the 1940s, changing the music's direction and enriching its content. Outstanding artists such as Tito Puente, Chucho Valdés, Celia Cruz, the Palmieri brothers, Paquito D'Rivera, and Arturo Sandoval have built a formidable body of work on the foundations laid down in the 1940s. And Afro-Cuban traditions lie at the core of the work of highly successful pop artists such as Ricky Martin, Gloria Estefan, and Marc Anthony.

Dizzy, the self-proclaimed "rhythm man," was drawn irresistibly to Afro-Cuban music by its guiding principle, polyrhythm. He recognized that the music of American slaves, who were deprived of drums and cut off from their polyrhythmic traditions, became, like the music of the slave owners, monorhythmic. He spoke of this years later: "Our music in the United States and that of the African concept of rhythm have one difference—the

African is polyrhythmic and we are monorhythmic. It is just recently that we [in the United States] have begun to understand that rhythm is not just 'one' [rhythmic line], but can be as many as six or seven lines of rhythm combined."[6]

The typical Afro-Cuban band has at least three percussionists playing different rhythms that relate contrapuntally. Mike Longo, Dizzy's close collaborator for more than twenty years, has described this practice: "Polyrhythm is a combination of several independent rhythmic melodies that agree vertically as well as horizontally. . . . Even though these are horizontally independent melodies, they also mesh with each other from a vertical point of view, in what would seem like a form of rhythmic harmony."[7]

The music of Bauzá and Machito, though authentically polyrhythmic, was not aimed in the mid-1940s at the mainstream jazz audience; it was performed primarily in Latino clubs like La Conga, which drew dance aficionados enamored of the rumba, the conga, and the mambo.

Dizzy broke important new ground on September 29, 1947, when he pioneered African polyrhythms (in the person of Chano Pozo) before a mainstream American audience in a major venue, Carnegie Hall. The sold-out concert, less then three weeks before his thirtieth birthday, was a landmark event for Dizzy, a double triumph. He was moving jazz in a vital new creative direction, and he was proving that bebop, despite four years of bitter establishment attacks, had significant commercial viability.

The second half of the concert featured Chano's debut as a soloist and sets by guests Charlie Parker and Ella Fitzgerald. Advertising posters made no mention of Bird because his behavior at the time was so unpredictable that Dizzy wasn't sure he would show up. Teddy Reig, who was dispatched to get him, remembered that Bird almost didn't make it: "He was out in the bathtub. We went into his room and broke down the bathroom door. We got him out of the bathtub, dried him, dressed him, got him into a cab, stuck his horn in his hands, and pushed him from the wings onto the stage."[8]

Bird and Dizzy performed in a quintet with three men from the big band: John Lewis, Al McKibbon, and Joe Harris. Bird was in a feisty, competitive mood, and as Dizzy answered his challenges, they produced some of the most exciting music they ever made together. Their brilliant warm-up on "A Night in Tunisia" was a prelude to the pyrotechnics of "Dizzy Atmosphere." Taken at a mind-bending tempo that left Lewis and Harris struggling to keep pace, the thrusting horns assaulted the listeners with torrents of creative energy. The two men reached an even higher artistic peak on the next number, "Groovin' High," as they traded solos packed with lustrous melodic lines.

Dizzy featured Bird for the final tunes of the set, where he fashioned masterful improvisations on his own composition "Confirmation," and his favorite vehicle, "Ko Ko." Bird mellowed later in the evening. During a break between big band numbers, he walked on stage and gave Dizzy a long-stemmed rose and kissed him on the mouth.

Chano was spotlighted on "Cubana Be, Cubana Bop" (sometimes known as "Afro-Cuban Drum Suite"), a well-constructed seven-minute piece that George Russell had put together from his own ideas and those of Dizzy and Chano. It was avant garde for its time in jazz because Russell's harmony was based on a scale rather than a chord progression. Dizzy proved very comfortable with the concept, which did not gain wide acceptance in jazz until more than eleven years later with Miles Davis's LP *Kind of Blue*.

Chano's conga rhythms undergirded all the written portions as he was supported by a percussionist playing bongos (small hand drums held between the knees). After Russell's somber introduction was followed by a sweet melodic line written by Dizzy, Chano transported the Carnegie audience to Africa as he took a one-minute solo and backed up a two-minute improvisation by Dizzy. The initial material was then reprised by the full ensemble, and the piece ended loudly on powerful dissonant chords. *Downbeat* reported that Chano's performance elicited the most enthusiastic audience response of the evening, and the wild cheering gave Dizzy added confidence to push forward with his Afro-Cuban agenda.

Ella and the big band closed out the proceedings with a happy, swinging set. She sang three ballads before launching into scat vocals on "Flyin' Home," "Lady Be Good," and "How High the Moon," and Dizzy provided sensitive accompaniment on "Lover Man" and used his trumpet to trade explosive four-bar improvisations with her on "How High the Moon."

The fans, who paid between $1.00 and $3.60 for their tickets, got their money's worth, as did Dizzy and Feather, who split $2,000 in profits.

As the band toured during the weeks following the concert, Chano created a dramatic setting for his solos. Dan Morgenstern remembered:

> When he came out front for "Afro-Cuban Suite" (or was it "Cubana Be, Cubana Bop"?)—a powerfully built black man stripped to the waist, bathed in purple light—lit up his oil lamp and began to heat up the skins of his congas, it was a tableux [*sic*] that created tremendous anticipation. And when he had finished his beautifully timed, unhurried, stately and dramatic preparations and began to play and chant, he gave everything the prelude had promised, and more.[9]

While they traveled, Dizzy ravenously imbibed Chano's percussion lessons and worked with him every day to indoctrinate the other musicians, who initially had difficulty assimilating his rhythms. The situation improved when Joe Harris quit in a dispute over money and was replaced by Kenny Clarke, who adjusted more readily to Chano's innovations. Clarke can be heard on the band's first pure Afro-Cuban studio recordings, "Cubana Be, Cubana Bop" and "Manteca," which took place on December 22 and December 30, 1947, respectively.

Almost every band in America had rushed into the studios near year-end, because union leader James Petrillo had called for a second strike against the record companies to start on January 1, 1948; it concerned compensation for record sessions, and it ended on December 14, 1948, when the musicians won a 37.5 percent increase.

The studio version of "Cubana Be, Cubana Bop" is more starkly dramatic and offers much more Chano than does the

Carnegie Hall concert version. The bongo player was considered a distraction and eliminated, and at Russell's suggestion, Chano's solo became the centerpiece of the recording and its duration doubled. In addition, he chanted vigorously in call-and-response patterns with the band members.

Gary Giddins is one of the many critics who have acclaimed the "Manteca" track as a jazz milestone, "one of the most important records ever made in the United States . . . an instant classic . . . which doesn't disguise or vitiate its dual patrimony. The jazz and Cuban aspects—plush harmonies, passionate rhythms—exist side by side with equal integrity."[10]

"Manteca" provides a perfect example of the compelling power of layered African polyrhythms. Chano came to Dizzy with a short piece encompassing four separate rhythms introduced in succession by congas, bass, baritone saxophone, and trombones. The composition embodies a hypnotic kaleidoscope of rhythm and song as the congas provide a steady flow of eighth notes while everyone else plays melodies accented in irregular rhythmic groupings.

Dizzy, realizing that Chano's melodies had created the eight-bar A section of a tune, immediately wrote a double-length, sixteen-bar B section in flowing swing rhythm over Chano's incessant beat. They took this AABBA composition to Gil Fuller, and he fashioned an arrangement whose ingenious interludes linked everything together. The polyrhythms dare the listener to keep any limb still as Clarke provides subtle support for Chano, Dizzy contributes two brilliant eight-bar solos, shouts of "Manteca" (which translates to "grease" in Spanish) fuel the excitement, and the ensemble performs with verve. Gary Giddins, in *Visions of Jazz* (Oxford University Press, 1998), and musicologist Barry Kernfeld, in *What to Listen for in Jazz* (Yale University Press, 1995), furnish extensive musical analyses of "Manteca."

Five tunes from the band's standard repertory were also recorded at the late December sessions. The Latin-tinged "Algo Bueno" ("Woody 'n You") became more overtly Afro-Cuban as Chano took the lead percussion role, and on the other four—"Cool Breeze," "Minor Walk," "Ool-Ya-Koo," and "Good Bait"—he blended well with Kenny Clarke to give fresh rhythmic heft to the arrangements.

The California bandleader Stan Kenton also made an important Afro-Cuban jazz recording in December 1947: "The Peanut Vendor." To achieve authenticity, he added to his band Machito on maracas (handheld rhythm instruments made from gourds filled with seeds) and Machito's sidemen—Cuban Carlos Vidal on congas and Jose Mangual, a Puerto Rican, on bongos. Kenton made several recordings with Latin percussionists, but his group never achieved legitimacy in the eyes of knowledgeable musicians. Dizzy heartily agreed with Mario Bauzá's verdict, that Kenton's "band never was a good jazz band and never could be no Afro-Cuban because the band was too clumsy. . . . Nobody could dance by that band. There was no rhythm. The band was so heavy. . . . That band never, never, never, never could swing."[11]

In a gesture one part brotherhood and one part public relations, Kenton and his band serenaded Dizzy, his musicians, Lorraine, and Billy Shaw's son Milt (who was serving as road manager) from a Hudson River pier on January 16, 1948, as they departed on the SS *Drottningholm* for Europe. They were headed for Gothenburg, Sweden, the first stop on a two-month tour that was slated to take them to several Swedish cities and then to Denmark, Holland, Belgium, France, Czechoslovakia, and perhaps England. When they left, the English government was mulling over a request from the local musicians' union to contravene regulations and issue visas for a UK visit.

The trip was a tremendous success artistically but a nightmare logistically.

Dizzy boarded the ship in high spirits, because he had just been given a copy of *Metronome* with his picture on the cover and the news that he and the band, for the first time, had both achieved number one status in the magazine's annual poll. His elation was short-lived; moments later he discovered that his entourage had been allotted third-class cabins when their contracts stipulated that they travel first class. The information sparked a fracas as Kenny Clarke, jumping to the conclusion that the Shaws were skimming the difference in fares, had to be restrained from assaulting Milt. Tempers were later assuaged when it was discovered that the perpetrator was the band's Swedish promoter, Harold Lundquist. For the moment, however, the musicians seethed as they settled into their third-class cabins in the bowels of the ship.

Tensions eased somewhat as the men fell into a lazy shipboard routine, spending lots of time (and money) at the bar and rehearsing during the afternoons. Their idyll ended brutally when, at dinnertime on the second day out, a horrendous North Atlantic storm hit the *Drottningholm*. Dizzy and several others were thrown to the floor, and he suffered a nasty bruise on his head. The ship had to be turned sideways several times to avoid the worst assaults from forty-foot waves, and the storm pounded the vessel for nearly a week. Dizzy and John Lewis were the only members of the group who did not fall ill, and they ate hearty meals and rehearsed with whomever was able.

Dizzy's woes continued as, in midvoyage, he heard from Billy Shaw that Lundquist had absconded with the 50 percent of the band's fees that he had promised to wire to a New York bank. When the band arrived more than a day late on January 26, they were told that a crowd of fourteen thousand was waiting in Gothenburg for their first concert to begin. Milt Shaw, on being informed that strong tides were preventing the *Drottningholm* from docking, commandeered a tugboat to take them ashore. After he and Clarke almost came to blows again on the ride in, Dizzy was able to kick off the proceedings two and a half hours late.

The fans cheered wildly at their entrance and kept it up after every number. A similar success the next night in Stockholm caused the promoters to schedule two more concerts there, and the band broke local attendance records by attracting almost twenty-seven thousand spectators during the three nights. They also set records in Copenhagen, Denmark, where on February 9, they drew more than nine thousand fans to three concerts in one day.

The enthusiastic response to Dizzy's band was rooted in scarcity. His group, the first major jazz aggregation to visit Europe after World War II, was satisfying a tremendous pent-up demand for modern sounds. Europe had been subsisting since 1945 on a diet of swing and Dixieland and, with the exception of a short Swedish tour by Chubby Jackson's sextet, had only known the bebop and Latin jazz revolutions through recordings.

At a time when a decent hotel room rented for three dollars per night, the 1945 Gillespie/Parker Guild masterpieces sold for ten dollars each, and Paris musicians queued up for hours at the Hot Club of France for the opportunity to hear them. The almost total lack of live modern jazz helped polarize European fans; because they did not have a Fifty-second Street or a Billy Berg's to accustom their ears gradually to the new music, the schism between modernists and the adherents of swing and Dixieland was deeper and more bitter than in the United States.

Dizzy saw virtually no money despite his Scandinavian box office success and took to sleeping on the floor outside Lundquist's hotel room to prevent him from pocketing each night's takings. The musicians suffered real privation; Lars Hansen, a Danish seaman, remembered coming upon Cecil Payne and trumpeter Dave Burns sitting forlornly in a Copenhagen railway station with no money for food. He bought them a large meal and began a friendship with Payne that thrives more than fifty years later.

The British Ministry of Labour rejected the band's request for visas on February 6 and, soon after, the chaos surrounding Lundquist's chicanery caused the concerts in Holland and Czechoslovakia to be canceled. Dizzy cut all ties to Lundquist and secured enough money to move the band from Denmark to Belgium on February 11, but he ran out of funds by the fifteenth and jeopardized concerts scheduled for the eighteenth and nineteenth in Antwerp and Brussels.

He was rescued by Charles Delaunay, the leader of the modern jazz partisans in France. When the Frenchman heard about Dizzy's plight and satisfied himself that Lundquist was out of the picture, he dispatched an assistant to pay all Dizzy's Belgian bills and bring the band to Paris. In addition, he hastily booked the Salle Pleyel music hall for a concert on the twentieth, secured a week's engagement at the upscale nightspot, Le Club Champs Elysées, and launched a lightning publicity campaign.

The band, arriving by train at the time the sold out concert was to begin, was delayed by zealous customs agents. Fortunately, Delaunay had hired a decent piano trio who diverted the audience until Dizzy led his men onstage almost two hours later.

The fans were amazed when the band began performing the complex numbers without sheet music. Music stands and scores had been misplaced en route, and after a few moments' hesitation, the musicians decided that they knew the arrangements well enough to wing it from memory. The Paris audience, notoriously hard to please, was so impressed by the band's power and virtuosity that it sat in awed silence following the first number. But as the critic Boris Vian has written, it soon found its voice: "The audience was fiery with enthusiasm. . . . The ambience was beyond belief. . . . We should mention Gillespie's remarkable use of Afro-Cuban rhythms, and his remarkable percussionist Chano Pozo. Bebop, the most recent evolution in the history of jazz, has conquered Paris. Thanks to Dizzy Gillespie."[12]

The music made a particularly serious impact on the jazz professionals in the audience, as critic Claude Carrière has noted: "This was the jazz most young French musicians were destined to adopt, which meant that they were undergoing a sort of initiation ceremony, one that was to condition their whole future."[13] Passions were still running high later that night when the band performed a set at Le Club Champs Elysées, and bebop partisans came to blows with a group of Dixielanders. The next morning Delaunay booked the Salle Pleyel for concerts on February 22 and 28, and they sold out quickly.

The band is powerful, uninhibited, and utterly confident on a CD that preserves more than forty-five minutes of the February 28 performance; the recording evaded Petrillo's ban because it was made privately and released several years later. The percussion was outstanding; Klook's drumming provided both propulsion and nuance, and Chano enriched the mix with great subtlety. He shone for almost four minutes on "Cubana Be, Cubana Bop," starting with a duet with Dizzy and building to a chanting climax that drew wild applause. Dizzy scatted gleefully on "Ool-Ya-Koo" and performed outstanding trumpet solos on "'Round Midnight,"

"I Can't Get Started" (where he couldn't resist inserting a quote from "Jingle Bells"), and "Ool-Ya-Koo." The CD and the concert came to a thundering close with one of the best versions of "Things to Come" on record.

The scholarly and fastidious John Lewis was angry with Dizzy for indulging in japes such as leaping onto the piano for impromptu dance routines and leaning on McKibbon's bass strings as he raised his trumpet in a solo. Lewis, who felt an intense rapport with audiences during the tour, believed that the band was creating crowning spiritual and artistic moments that should not be marred by clowning, but he made no headway with Dizzy.

While the band was ensconced in Paris, Billy Shaw flew from New York to Sweden to confront Lundquist. He spent several hours in jail after he kicked Lundquist in the testicles and hit him in the head with a lamp, but he found satisfaction when he recovered significant monies and the Swede was arrested on a variety of charges. Although the tour ended in the red, the musicians were fairly recompensed and even received the difference between their third- and first-class passages on the *Drottningholm*.

The band headed south for a March 3 engagement in Lyons and one on the fifth in Marseilles, where they shared billing with Mezz Mezzrow, an unreconstructed Dixielander who once said of bebop, "It's a waste of breath to talk about stuff like this."[14] When Mezzrow, who had served time for dealing in New York, shared some dynamite reefer with Dizzy and his men, all past utterances were forgiven.

The group returned to Paris for two evenings at the Les Ambassadeurs cabaret, where Dizzy had performed eleven years earlier with Teddy Hill, and, for a second time on the tour, they precipitated a fistfight between modernists and Dixielanders.

Kenny Clarke, who had fallen in love with Europe during his 1937–38 tour with Edgar Hayes, decided to stay in Paris when a French drum company offered to create a percussion school for him. He would settle there permanently in 1956. John Lewis also opted to remain in Paris to pursue studies in classical piano.

Dizzy, Lorraine, Chano, and Milt Shaw flew back to New York on March 12; the others returned by sea and arrived on the eighteenth after an uneventful voyage. Dizzy led the band in a successful "welcome home" concert on March 20 at Town Hall, a venue about half the size of Carnegie Hall, and then shut down for a month. During this period, Lorraine prevailed on Dizzy to secure new management, and he ended his five-year relationship with the Shaws and signed on with the more powerful Willard Alexander Agency.

After making several personnel changes that included hiring Teddy Stewart on drums and Tadd Dameron on piano, Dizzy began in late April to rehearse prior to a week at the Apollo and two concerts: one at Carnegie Hall on May 8 (where he introduced a Gil Fuller piece called "Swedish Suite" that featured decidedly non-Scandinavian Latin rhythms) and another on the eleventh at Philadelphia's Academy of Music.

He then embarked on a tour of Illinois and Pennsylvania that brought him back to New York on June 16 for a two-week engagement at a nightspot called the Royal Roost. The club, located in a large basement on Broadway and Forty-seventh Street, was born in 1946 as a fried chicken joint called Ralph and Bill's Chicken Roost. It was transformed when the manager, Ralph Watkins, who had become knowledgeable about jazz during the early 1940s when he ran the Famous Door, agreed in April 1948 to host "Tuesday Jazz Nights" run by bebop disc jockey "Symphony Sid" Torin and his partner, promoter Monte Kay.

Aided by Sid's advocacy on radio and talent such as Charlie Parker, Billy Eckstine, Miles Davis, and Dexter Gordon, these sessions were an instant success (police were called to disperse the crowd on the first night), and Watkins switched in May to a six-nights-a-week jazz policy and gave the place a new name, the Royal Roost.

The club's success gave proof that bebop had built a firm commercial base, that Dizzy's September 29, 1947, Carnegie Hall concert was truly the start of a permanent change in jazz taste.

The Royal Roost represented the beginning of a shift in the center of gravity of the New York jazz scene from Fifty-second Street to Broadway. It was larger, more comfortable, and better lit than its rivals on The Street; it provided a milk bar for those under drinking age, and it pioneered an attractive admissions policy by offering, for seventy-five cents, seats but no tables in a "bleachers" section where drinks were optional. It became a model for other large Broadway-area clubs that followed—the Aquarium, Bop City, Birdland, and Basin Street.

Sid, who dubbed himself "the all-night, all-frantic one," always introduced the artists over the strains of "Jumpin' with Symphony Sid," a tune Lester Young had written for him. He possessed a deep Brooklyn baritone and he sprinkled his spiels with Yiddishisms (Dinah Washington was his "verblundet" one and Charlie Parker was his "feigele," and he would threaten an unruly patron with "Watch out, or I'll go Sephardic on you").

After he arranged to have a radio wire installed at the club in June, he broadcast the last set on Friday evening live and said things like, "We're taking our microphone down to 'The House that Bop Built,' the Royal Roost, the Metropolitan Bopera House, where the music is in a real knocked-out groove, and you can relax until 4 a.m. digging the gonest sounds of pure progressive jazz"[15] and "When Fate deals you one from the bottom of the deck, fall by the Sunshine Funeral Parlors. Your loved ones will be handled with dignity and care, and the cats at Sunshine will not lay too heavy a tab on you."[16]

Hundreds were turned away at Dizzy's Roost opening, but hundreds more were squeezed into the club, as Barry Ulanov noted in his *Metronome* review:

> Tables were piled on tables and people upon people so that it was impossible to tell whether you were stepping on your own feet or someone else's. . . . The old and the new [music] was dispatched with Procrustean precision with what Dizzy's recent French audiences would call *élan*, a vivaciousness of performance which very properly engendered a vitality of response. Nearly everybody in the band deserves credit for the superb showing of this disciplined but not dispirited band.[17]

Following the Roost engagement, the band reached peaks of popularity on a three-month tour that began on June 30 and would place them on the West Coast from July 16 to September 9. Two thousand fans were turned away from a July 19, 1948, concert in Pasadena, California. A recording of it shows that the band was attaining artistic peaks as well.

The forty minutes preserved from the California event give the listener a better opportunity to judge the group than does the recording made at Salle Pleyel twenty weeks earlier, because the sound is much cleaner and brighter. As with the Pleyel recording, this disc slipped by the Petrillo ban because it was privately made and released several years after the fact.

One immediately notices that Chano Pozo had assumed a more prominent role in the arrangements, giving the band a new kind of propulsion and putting his stamp on everything from the fast blues "Emanon" to "'Round Midnight," with its slow ballad cadences, to "Manteca," where he was given free rein and elicited frenzied cheering from the crowd during a four-minute improvisation. There are excellent solos from Dizzy, James Moody, and Cecil Payne, but what makes the recording exceptional is the cohesion and power of the band as a whole. It reached new heights of precision as the brass and saxophone sections nailed the most difficult ensemble passages with unstinting verve and discipline, and the rhythm section provided an irresistible pulse.

The highlight of the return trip from the West Coast was a September 26 concert at Chicago's Pershing Ballroom; Bird sat in, and he and Dizzy drove the crowd of three thousand wild with chorus after incandescent chorus.

Dizzy suffered a serious loss in late 1948 when James Moody left him. Moody moved soon after to Europe, in large part because he found the racial climate there more congenial than in the United States. He returned in 1951 and was reunited with Dizzy in 1963.

The band returned in triumph to New York for four sold-out weeks at the Roost and one at the Apollo and then headed south for a series of one-nighters that kept them on the road until December 7.

Dizzy interrupted the tour for an impromptu visit to Laurinburg, where he gave a concert at his alma mater. The McDuffies honored him with a football letter and the diploma he had just missed earning when he left the institute late in his senior year in 1935.

Chano Pozo's congas were stolen in North Carolina on November 22, and he returned to New York to have new ones made to his personal specifications. He decided not to head south again, because he detested the racism he had encountered there, and he hung out in Spanish Harlem romancing women, dancing, drinking rum, and smoking pot. On November 30, he bought twenty-five joints from Eusebio "Cabito" Munoz, a Cuban-born dealer and numbers runner, and was infuriated when he found that their quality was decidedly inferior. Chano suspected that Cabito, to lower costs, had mixed oregano in with the marijuana.

The next day Chano confronted him, threatened him with a knife, and demanded his money back; when Cabito refused, Chano knocked him out with a blow to the face and took fifteen dollars from his pocket as he lay unconscious.

The following afternoon, December 2, Cabito walked into the Rio Café on Lenox Avenue and 111th Street where Chano was dancing with a waitress to a jukebox tune. Cabito called his name and when Chano turned to face him, he killed Chano instantly with a shot to the heart. He then pumped six bullets into the lifeless body and walked away.[18]

The first great chapter of the Afro-Cuban jazz revolution had come to an end. Dizzy was blessed to be a father of this liberating movement and of bebop, and he would spend the rest of his life enriching their legacies and spreading their gospel.

BIG BAND FAILURE 24

DIZZY, THOROUGHLY SHAKEN, FLEW TO NEW YORK FROM Memphis in time to attend the second day of Chano's wake on December 4, 1948, and paid his respects alongside Duke Ellington, Count Basie, Machito, Mario Bauzá, Cab Calloway, and Tito Puente, a rising star at twenty-five. At 4:00 a.m. the following morning, Chano's body was flown to Havana for burial.

Dizzy returned to Memphis to wind up the southern tour and to bring the band back to New York for a breakthrough engagement, the first bebop gig at one of Broadway's grand movie palaces, the Strand. For two weeks ending December 23, they performed opposite *The Decision of Christopher Blake*, a divorce melodrama starring Alexis Smith ("Was she Eve? . . . Was she angel?") and were joined on stage by Maxine Sullivan, the Berry Brothers dance team, the Deep River Boys vocal group, and two other acts. A *Downbeat* reporter was impressed: "Diz and his band came through to panic the house with his bop specialties, broke it up with 'Manteca,' and killed 'em with 'Oopapada.' . . . The Diz lived up to all expectations as a showman, and his band delivered its wares in an amusing and capable manner. Too bad the show, which ran 70 minutes, was so overloaded with other acts."[1]

The Luce press continued its vendetta against bebop: a writer in *Time*'s December 20 issue damned the music while reporting its commercial success at the Strand Theater with Dizzy's band and at the Royal Roost, the Clique, and other clubs. He commented that instrumentalists played "with loud, emotionless precision"; "Sarah Vaughan squeezed her tooth-paste smooth voice out among the customers singing in the style of a kazoo"; Dizzy was "the high cockalorum of bop," and the music was "carefully disorganized." He concluded, "To the naked ear its shrill cacophony seems anarchistic: on repeated hearings it becomes clear that the players planned it that way."[2]

Bebop fans came close to filling Carnegie Hall on a bitterly cold Christmas night to hear the band anchor a sterling all-star concert. The event, produced by Symphony Sid and Leonard Feather, also featured Charlie Parker, Sarah Vaughan, Tadd Dameron, and the small group of saxophonist Charlie Ventura. Dizzy reached down to his gospel roots as he paid tribute to Chano with a stately rendition of "Nobody Knows the Trouble I've Seen," and the band drove the audience into a frenzy with a wild version of "Manteca" featuring Sabu Martinez, a more than adequate successor to Chano. Dizzy used the occasion to welcome his colleague of old, Budd Johnson, to the saxophone section and to introduce the crooner Johnny Hartman, who shared vocal chores with the scat specialist Joe Carroll. Symphony Sid managed three plugs for one of his radio sponsors, Music Hall Crown Jewelers, as he presented plaques to Dizzy, Bird, Vaughan, and Ventura for winning 1948 *Metronome* polls.

Four days later, Dizzy took his men into a studio for their second RCA Victor session fifty-three weeks after their first; Petrillo's fifty-week record ban, which ended on December 14, had intervened. The band cut four varied sides. Three percussionists—Martinez on bongos, Joe Harris on congas, and Teddy Stewart on drums—supplied powerful polyrhythms on "Guarachi Guaro," Dizzy's final collaboration with Chano, and they provided distinctive Latino underpinnings for the other numbers. The high point of the date was Dizzy's exciting solo on "Duff Capers," an up-tempo exercise named for a fan, the actor Howard Duff. The third track was all Dizzy; he achieved dramatic contrasts on the venerable Sigmund Romberg song "Lover Come Back to Me," by sandwiching a fast, explosive improvisation between two elegiac melodic statements over a slow Afro-Cuban beat. For the final track, the novelty number "I'm Be Boppin' Too," he delivered the vocal and shared horn choruses with Budd Johnson.

Nineteen forty-nine was a grueling year for the band as they spent the entire period from January 1 through June 1 on the road and toured for forty-one weeks in all. When in New York, they made their home at a successor to the Royal Roost, a considerably larger place called Bop City located on Broadway two blocks north of the Roost site.

Dizzy started the year in the Midwest but flew back to New York for a January 3 RCA Victor session with twelve other *Metronome* poll winners including Bird, Miles Davis, Fats Navarro, and Charlie Ventura; four tracks were recorded. The date produced moments of high-caliber music, but, to accommodate so many stars, solos were kept short and no one was given the time to develop his ideas adequately. Dizzy was never allotted more than a half chorus.

When he flew to Salt Lake City to rejoin his band, he found that a blizzard had stranded his good friend Woody Herman there and that the same storm had immobilized his own group in Denver. As Woody's saxophonist Zoot Sims remembered, the two leaders worked together to save the day:

Once the band's [Herman's] Pullman car was stranded in Salt Lake City by a snow storm. Meantime, Dizzy Gillespie's band, which was scheduled to play there, was stuck in Denver—which was where the Herman band was supposed to be. We played their gig and they played ours. But Dizzy made it to Salt Lake City by flying, and he sat in with us. That was a ball. He played with the section, and was featured in front of the band on different numbers. You know Dizzy—he's never at a loss for what to do.[3]

Dizzy was elated when the publication in March 1949 of Leonard Feather's excellent book *Inside Bebop* was received favorably by both the critics and the general public; he had helped Feather edit the text and had written the introduction. The book is divided into three parts: "When" (a short history of the movement), "How" (an astute analysis of bebop's harmonic and rhythmic principles), and "Who" (biographical sketches of ninety-two musicians). The publisher, reacting to the continuing pejorative implications of the word *bebop*, convinced Feather in 1951 to change its name to *Inside Jazz*. The book, which has become an essential part of jazz literature, was still in print in 2004.

Dizzy had sailed against the winds of change since 1946, but during the spring of 1949 the economic and social forces inimical to big band success were inexorably gaining strength. The migration to the suburbs was reaching a peak as Levittown, the archetypal bedroom community outside New York City, grew from scratch to thirteen thousand homes between 1947 and 1949; weekly movie attendance fell from ninety million in 1946 to seventy million in 1949 as Americans sought more active types of leisure; and the tidal wave of television rolled forward as Milton Berle in 1949 became the first entertainer to be seen by five million people at once.

The first sign that the band's popularity was waning was a disappointing three-week engagement that began on May 2 at Chicago's Blue Note Club. Dizzy tried to revive his fortunes by introducing arrangements with strong danceable beats and by emphasizing songs with catchy lyrics. To reinforce his new strategy, his advertisements, for the first time, featured the vocalists Johnny Hartman and Joe Carroll.

Dizzy's record sales mirrored his decline at the box office, and RCA Victor told him that they would not renew his contract when it ended in August. To fulfill his obligations to the company, he recorded twelve tunes in sessions in April, May, and July. In an obvious bid for a commercial revival, vocals predominated: Hartman sang four ballads and Joe Carroll and Dizzy performed three novelty numbers. The band maintained a high degree of excellence for the remaining five tracks, particularly on Gil Fuller's

"Swedish Suite" and Budd Johnson's version of "St. Louis Blues"; the latter drew the wrath of composer W. C. Handy for being too modern.

The quality of the band's music did not diminish during Dizzy's commercial slide as he drew to his side such outstanding musicians as John Coltrane, Jimmy Heath, Paul Gonsalves, J. J. Johnson, John Lewis (for a second tour of duty), Melba Liston, and Yusef Lateef and hired first-rate arrangers such as Jimmy Mundy, Mary Lou Williams, Budd Johnson, and Gerald Wilson.

Adding to Dizzy's burdens during his box office slump was a verbal attack from a surprising source—Charlie Parker. In a profile that appeared in the September 9, 1949, issue of *Downbeat*, Bird released long-standing resentments concerning the public's perception of Dizzy as the principal father of bebop. The authors reported:

> The fact that Dizzy Gillespie's extroversion led the commercially minded to his door irks Charlie in more ways than one. As part of Dizzy's build up, he was forced to add his name to several of Charlie's numbers, among them "Anthropology," "Confirmation," and "Shaw 'Nuff." Dizzy had nothing to do with any of them, according to Charlie.[4]

Dizzy's claims to coauthorship of "Anthropolgy" and "Shaw 'Nuff" were entirely legitimate, and he never demanded a composer's credit for "Confirmation."

Bird followed the untenable assertion that "Bop is no love child of jazz" but "something entirely separate and apart" with the statement that the distinctive feature of bop was its strong feeling for the beat. He implied that Dizzy had lost this feeling, and he criticized Dizzy's musicianship: "That big band is a bad thing for Diz. A big band slows anybody down because you don't get a chance to play enough. Diz has an awful lot of ideas when he wants to, but if he stays with the big band he'll forget everything he ever played. He isn't repeating notes yet, but he is repeating patterns."[5]

Parker expert Lawrence O. Koch has commented about the rivalry between Dizzy and Bird:

> Jealousy, of course, was the core, and Parker was a jealous man. . . .
> For Diz, a person with a strong self-image, competitiveness was a
> game, an intellectual duel that was fun. Bird's ego, however, was
> not strong and needed constant feeding; he therefore was envious
> of Gillespie's music success, although respectful of his musical
> abilities. . . . One forms a picture of the relationship that is proba-
> bly close to the truth: Gillespie, a highly competitive, success-
> oriented individual who did not hold grudges, versus Parker, an
> insecure, equally competitive individual with inwardly directed
> drives that resulted in self-destructiveness and an inner confusion
> of motives.[6]

Dizzy ignored Bird's personal criticisms in his response in the
October 7 *Downbeat*. He refuted the claim that bebop had no
roots in jazz and, to publicize his newfound determination to give
the public more danceable music, he concentrated on a discussion
of the beat: "Bop is part of jazz and jazz music is to dance to. The
trouble with bop as it is played today is that people can't dance to
it. They don't hear those four beats. . . . We'll use the same har-
monics but with a beat, so that people can understand where the
beat is. . . . I want to make bop bigger, get it a wider audience."[7]

He began in the autumn of 1949 to understand that this new
stylistic emphasis was unlikely to turn the commercial tide as he
watched Guy Lombardo, the king of smooth dance music, suffering substantial losses, and Count Basie and Cab Calloway reduced
to leading septets. (Calloway would close down completely in
1950.) More seriously, he witnessed the outstanding bands of
Artie Shaw, Woody Herman, Benny Goodman (resurrected after
a 1946 shutdown), and Charlie Barnet—dance-oriented groups
with highly visible singers—collapse before the end of 1949. Still,
he soldiered on.

Willard Alexander obtained a contract for him with Capitol
Records in October, and the band recorded for the new label on
November 11, 1949, and January 9, 1950. These sessions reflected
a desperate attempt to capture an audience and produced little of
aesthetic or commercial value. A low point was reached with a
tune called "You Stole My Wife You Horsethief." The Capitol

contract was terminated during the spring of 1950.

Dizzy was forced to interrupt his touring in March 1950 to attend a jury trial in Reading, Pennsylvania, to answer a charge by a twenty-one-year-old acquaintance, Helen Donaldson, that he fathered her son Reginald, born on March 16, 1949. Her case fell apart when she refused blood tests for herself and the boy and when several of her witnesses had memory lapses. Lorraine cut a conspicuous figure in the courtroom as she told reporters that, after almost nine years of futile efforts within their marriage, she did not believe that Dizzy was capable of fathering a child.

Lorraine saw more clearly than anyone the futility of Dizzy's struggle in the face of the mounting deficits that threatened their hard-earned savings, and when she confronted him in Chicago in late May with the ultimatum "You got a hundred musicians or me. Make up your mind,"[8] he gave up the ghost.

Dizzy would lead many bands in the future, but he would come to know that his 1946–50 group was unique—a truly revolutionary and joyous aggregation that, like no other big band before or after, had turned the jazz world on its head.

25
THE ECLECTIC EARLY FIFTIES

THE BITTER DEPRESSION DIZZY FELT AT THE DEMISE OF the big band did not prevent him from taking decisive action. He brought his musicians back to New York from Chicago in early June, chose five of them—saxophonists John Coltrane and Jimmy Heath, pianist John Lewis, drummer Specs Wright, and bassist Al McKibbon—to join him in a sextet, and sadly dismissed the rest.

Lewis and McKibbon were soon replaced by Milt Jackson and Jimmy Heath's brother Percy, respectively. Jackson performed on the vibraphone only in New York; on the road he played piano, because Dizzy could not afford to move the bulky vibraphone set from gig to gig.

Dizzy faced an anemic economic climate for jazz that would persist throughout the early 1950s; the collapse of the big bands threw hundreds of out-of-work performers into a shrinking market, and outstanding musicians such as Max Roach, Oscar Pettiford, Thelonious Monk, Miles Davis, and Charles Mingus performed only sporadically.

Against this backdrop of economic hardship, Dizzy's search for a viable commercial formula led him to an exploration of several musical genres. During the three years following the collapse of his big band, he tried his hand at pop, rhythm and blues, lush "symphonic" compositions, bebop, and ballads. He got by, but he never truly prospered.

As he hustled, Dizzy worked in a variety of groups, but the sextet was his "bread and butter" unit. Unfortunately, dwindling revenues meant a decline in the quality of his sidemen. Percy Heath, for instance, was forced to leave in 1951, because he could not support his growing family on what he earned with Dizzy, and Dizzy's 1950 sextet earned more and was considerably more talented than the 1953 group that featured saxophonist Bill Graham, pianist Wade Legge, drummer Al Jones, singer Joe Carroll, and bassist Lou Hackney.

Dizzy canceled sextet rehearsals on June 6, 1950, to take part in a Charlie Parker record date. While Dizzy was struggling through agonizing months to keep his big band alive, Bird had reached his highest artistic and commercial peaks leading quintets. Bird's genius had flowered as never before during the three years beginning in the spring of 1947 as he directed small groups anchored by the drummers Max Roach and Roy Haynes and the trumpeters Miles Davis, Kenny Dorham, and Red Rodney.

Bird produced at least two masterpieces among the forty-three magnificent recordings he made for Dial and Savoy between May 1947 and September 1948. They are "Parker's Mood," which stands with Armstrong's "West End Blues" at the zenith of jazz blues recordings, and "Embraceable You," a ravishing stream of romantic invention.

Listeners can also find wonderful music on a number of Bird's live recordings—with Dizzy at both the September 1947 Carnegie Hall concert and the performance at Chicago's Pershing Ballroom in September 1948 and in numerous private recordings from the Hi-De-Ho in Los Angeles and the Three Deuces, the Onyx, and the Royal Roost in New York.

Bird's career gained significant momentum in November 1948 when he came under the aegis of concert producer/record mogul Norman Granz. Dizzy and Bird, in February 1946, had been the first beboppers Granz had added to a roster of swing players, and the promoter thereafter regularly mixed musicians of both genres in his Jazz at the Philharmonic (JATP) concerts.

Because of his big band responsibilities, Dizzy made only sporadic JATP appearances during the late 1940s, but Bird became a regular member of the troupe when he and his quintet joined up for a twenty-six-city tour beginning on April 18, 1948. On November 6, he signed a recording contract with Granz and embarked on another junket that touched down in more than thirty cities. He remained under contract to Granz for the rest of his life.

Granz enjoyed placing Bird in a variety of settings—soloing with Machito's band; fronting a string orchestra; jamming at JATP concerts; leading a quartet, a quintet, and a septet—and he longed to reunite him with Dizzy. He knew in the spring of 1950 that he had a rare opportunity to bring the two men together, because Dizzy was unaffiliated following the conclusion of his contract with Capitol Records. Granz quickly scheduled them for the quintet session on June 6 with Bird as leader.

Bird recruited Thelonious Monk for the date, partly because he valued Monk's abundant talents and partly because he wanted to advance the pianist's career. Monk's fortunes were at an ebb, because in 1950 his quirky style was too "far out" for all but a handful of jazz fans; it would be another decade before the jazz public would absorb and understand what he was doing and give him the acclaim he deserved. Except for this session, Monk, who was at the height of his powers, went unrecorded for more than three years, from July 2, 1948, to July 23, 1951.

Bird wanted to use Roy Haynes, the drummer from his working quintet, but Granz intervened and inserted one of his favorites, the unreconstructed swing percussionist Buddy Rich. Curley Russell, the bassist from Bird's "Ko Ko" session, rounded out the group.

The only recordings bringing together these three bebop pioneers produced excellent music. Bird wrote two blues and three other tunes for the occasion and completed the program with the 1912 song favored by sentimental drunks at 4:00 a.m., "My Melancholy Baby." Dizzy and Bird performed as if they had never been parted, reeling off unison horn lines with panache and spurring each other to robust and intelligent solos.

Rich, ignoring Kenny Clarke and almost everyone who came after him, insisted on beating out the rhythm on the bass drum, but he did not become overly obtrusive, because he played loudly only when he soloed. Monk stimulated the horn players with prodding accompaniments and contributed wonderful solos on "My Melancholy Baby," the two blues, and a tune called "Relaxin' with Lee"; he also crafted several original introductions. He did not solo on the date's most exciting track, "Leap Frog." Based on the chords of "Exactly Like You," it was entirely improvised as no theme was stated, and Dizzy, Bird, and Rich engaged in a highly creative, up-tempo competition.

After a Bop City gig with the sextet, Dizzy began on July 27, 1950, a five-week engagement as a single at Birdland, the Broadway club that was named for Parker as his popularity peaked in 1949; it opened on December 15 of that year. Bigger and fancier than any New York jazz spot before or since, it held four hundred patrons and occupied a cellar between Fifty-second and Fifty-third streets, which now houses an elaborate strip joint. Morris Levy, its principal owner, was partial to Dizzy and became his unofficial banker, and Dizzy made the club his home base for much of the 1950s. During 1951, for example, his engagements there totaled five months.

Levy adopted the successful Royal Roost/Bop City policy of providing a "bleachers" area where drinks were optional and where one could sit and listen all night for one dollar. He covered the walls with striking life-size black-and-white photos of jazz greats such as Bird, Dizzy, Max Roach, and Sarah Vaughan, and on opening night he displayed more than twenty golden finches in cages hanging from the ceiling behind the bar. Tobacco smoke killed them soon after.

At Birdland, Dizzy reencountered Symphony Sid, who, operating from a glass booth at the rear of the club, broadcast six nights a week from midnight to 5:45 a.m. His ABC station, WJZ, possessed enough wattage to bring his show to fans along the eastern seaboard from Maine to North Carolina and as far west as Indiana. He devoted one hour to a live feed from the bandstand and the rest to recordings.

Dizzy quickly came to know the club's emcee, Pee Wee Marquette, a black Alabama midget who had a predilection for all-white tails outfits and green velvet suits with extra-wide lapels. As bassist and author Bill Crow remembered, he wielded a frightening cigarette lighter:

> Pee Wee had one of the first adjustable butane cigarette lighters on the market. He used it to ostentatiously light the large cigars he sometimes smoked, but he carried it mainly as a service to patrons at Birdland. To compensate for his height he would adjust the lighter for maximum flame length. It was an unnerving experience in a dark nightclub to put a cigarette in your mouth and have a two-foot flame suddenly shoot up from waist level with Pee Wee leering hopefully at the other end.[1]

With a voice harsh and shrill, Pee Wee would garble the names of the performers unless they paid him off. Once Lester Young, furious at his constant demands for loot, called him "half a mother-fucker."

Pee Wee earned further enmity from the musicians by leaving the microphone at the three-foot level when he finished his announcements, and Dizzy frequently drew laughs by hobbling out on his knees to introduce his sidemen.

During his first Birdland engagement, Dizzy performed with a house rhythm section opposite an unusual band led by Bird, and the two men sat in with each other's groups almost every night.

Bird was backed by his own rhythm section plus three violins, a viola, a cello, a harp, and an oboe; he loved to be cushioned by the lush symphonic string and woodwind sounds, and he believed that he had reached the peak of his career when he convinced Granz to record him in November 1949 with a similar group. Ironically, Bird, one of the towering figures in twentieth-century music, was so in awe of classical musicians that he quit several of the rehearsals out of fear, and the success of the album convinced him that he had met an important test of musical worth.

Dizzy, in a spasm of sibling rivalry, also became intrigued with the "symphonic" concept, and he commissioned Johnny Richards, the man who wrote and produced his controversial Jerome Kern session in 1946, to organize a classical ensemble for him. Dizzy told reporters that, once this was done, he and Bird could tour successfully together backed by strings and woodwinds; this idea died stillborn.

Dizzy realized his dream of a "symphonic" album when he recorded eight tracks with Richards in Los Angeles for the Discovery label on October 31 and November 1, 1950. Richards brought varied talents to the task; he had mastered several instruments, led his own bands, scored films in Britain and Hollywood, and created arrangements for the Boyd Raeburn Orchestra.

He backed Dizzy with Specs Wright on drums and thirty-one other musicians playing strings, woodwinds, congas, brass instruments, and a harp as he attempted to create a program richer and more varied than the one Bird had recorded.

Aside from a sublime solo on "Just Friends," Bird's strings session did not produce great music. Parker scholar Carl Woideck has noted its shortcomings:

> These ballads with strings do not add any new masterpieces to Parker's discography. A significant factor . . . is the lack of unbroken time for Parker to create. . . . In only one [track] did Parker have a full chorus to himself. . . . The arrangements, while competent, are not very inspiring. [They] resembled common Hollywood movie music more than the twentieth-century concert music Parker admired and longed to emulate.[2]

Richards' writing for Dizzy was more ambitious, as he constructed a program that included a spiritual, songs with themes by Tchaikovsky and Rachmaninoff, three ballads, and two medium-tempo swingers; he did not, however, avoid "Hollywood movie music" clichés, particularly on the slower numbers. Dizzy was in a relaxed mood throughout and excelled on "Swing Low, Sweet Chariot," where Richards effectively alternated an Afro-Cuban clave beat with a swing rhythm, and on the swingers, "On the Alamo" and "I Found a Million Dollar Baby." Dizzy proudly introduced the Richards material to a New York audience several weeks later when he performed with an orchestra directed by Ralph Burns at a Symphony Sid Carnegie Hall concert on Christmas night 1950.

Dizzy fired Jimmy Heath for heroin use soon after the concert, and three months later he dismissed Coltrane for the same reason. Heath had been such an intense Dizzy fan that, as a twenty-year-old in 1946, he followed the big band from city to city wearing a beret and a goatee. The following year, he organized a group modeled on his hero's, recruiting such future Gillespie sidemen as his brother Percy, Coltrane, saxophonist Benny Golson, and Specs Wright; Dizzy hired him and Coltrane in September 1949 to fill two vacancies, and they joined Paul Gonsalves to form the most powerful saxophone section Dizzy ever led. Heath and Coltrane both conquered their drug habits and went on to distinguished careers.

Dizzy knew that the readers' polls of the jazz magazines were highly imperfect gauges of worth. Nevertheless, he believed them important enough to show, in an appendix to his autobiography, how he fared in each of them. He was disappointed in early 1951 when he discovered that he had been supplanted, after four consecutive years as the top trumpeter, by Miles Davis in *Metronome*'s poll.

What propelled Miles into first place was a series of nonet recordings called *Birth of the Cool*. Created with essential help from arranger Gil Evans, the discs helped consolidate the bebop revolution with an aesthetic extension called cool jazz. The new genre incorporated the harmonic and rhythmic innovations of bebop while it emphasized an impressionist tonal palette and lyrical melodies. Miles explained:

> Their [Dizzy's and Bird's] musical sound wasn't sweet, and it didn't have harmonic lines that you could easily hum out on the

street with your girlfriend trying to get over with a kiss. . . . Bird and Diz were great, fantastic, challenging—but they weren't sweet. But "Birth Of The Cool" was different because you could hear everything and hum it also.[3]

The cool writers also placed new weight on the ensemble, paying serious attention to blending the soloist and the group. Drummer Shelly Manne summed up their approach: "What we wanted to do was write some new kind of material . . . where the solos and the improvisation became part of the whole, and you couldn't tell where the writing ended and the improvisation began."[4]

Cool was just a way station for Miles, the most restless of jazz giants, as he returned to bebop from 1951 to 1957 and moved on to spearhead the modal revolution of the late 1950s, to radically reconfigure jazz rhythms with his 1960s quintet, and to fuse jazz and rock with *Bitches Brew* and subsequent albums in the 1970s and 1980s. His "cool" legacy was carried forward by colleagues such as Gerry Mulligan and Lee Konitz, and it found its most enthusiastic audiences on the West Coast. The movement was absorbed into the mainstream of jazz by the end of the 1950s.

Dizzy emerged from the collapse of his big band without serious monetary loss, and, because Lorraine had saved assiduously, they were able in 1951 to move from their Harlem digs to a larger and more commodious apartment in Flushing in semisuburban Queens.

The following year, with the help of Morris Levy, they bought a building in Corona, a contiguous neighborhood. Levy lent Dizzy the money for the down payment, charged him no interest, and recouped by deducting a portion of Dizzy's performance fee every time he worked at Birdland. The men never signed a loan agreement. Levy later made Dizzy a gift of most of the down payment when he invited him to his office one evening and gave him a shoebox filled with money. Dizzy and Lorraine lived on the ground floor while renting two apartments on the second and third, and they built themselves a rec room and a bar in the basement.

Dizzy launched his first business venture in February 1951 when he founded Dee Gee Records with Dave Usher, a native of

Detroit who, at twenty-one, was twelve years his junior. Usher recalled how their partnership worked:

> I put up the capital and ran the business side and did a little pro-
> ducing; Dizzy put up his talent as musician and producer. I made
> about $175 a week driving a truck and selling our services for my
> dad and, living at home, I had maybe $100 a week surplus which
> financed the business.
>
> We had a mission: to expand the jazz market by reaching a pop
> audience, to broaden the appeal of jazz.[5]

Usher had never graduated from high school, and his haphaz-
ard education began at age six on the city's streets when he started
helping his father, a Russian Jewish immigrant, with his truck
route. His dad owned an interest in a bar, but his main business
was filtering and cleansing waste oil gathered from factories, gas
stations, and Great Lakes ships and then reselling it. He also
cleaned out the ships' oil tanks.

In later years, Dave expanded brilliantly on the latter activity
to build a world-class oil-spill cleanup company that has handled
major projects such as the Exxon Valdez disaster and the tar and
oil devastation caused by the 1991 Gulf War. Dizzy served, during the last six years of his life, on Dave's board of directors.

His friendship with Usher was deep and enduring, and it began in November 1944, when Dizzy was performing in Detroit
with the Billy Eckstine band. Usher remembered:

> I had classical training, but I had fallen in love with Dizzy's music,
> and I went back stage, just had the compulsion, you know, and
> said, "I'm here to see Dizzy Gillespie." The guy at the door didn't
> push me away, and Dizzy and Lorraine come out and say, "Hi."
>
> The oil delivery drivers were on strike, but my Dad was able to
> use his trucks for emergencies, and we had gas when no one else
> had it. At fourteen I had a driver's license because so many guys
> had been drafted, and they needed drivers for the war effort. I of-
> fered to take Dizzy and Lorraine home and they said, "Yes." The
> joke was: their hotel was only one block away. We got acquainted
> on a one-block ride.[6]

Dave's father had difficulty dealing with a streak of adolescent unruliness in his son, and for a dose of discipline sent him to Farragut Academy, a naval prep school in New Jersey. Dave renewed his friendship with Dizzy during the spring of 1946 when another boy covered for him as he went AWOL from the school and headed to Fifty-second Street to hear Dizzy's sextet at the Spotlite. Their friendship blossomed quickly, and by 1947 eighteen-year-old Dave was traveling in the band bus and attending recording sessions, including the historic one that produced "Manteca."

As Dizzy explained, he did not intend Dee Gee to be a cutting-edge modern jazz label: "We were reaching out to several audiences—the blues crowd, the people who liked Louis Jordan's early version of rock and roll, the jazz fans, the folks who liked crooners. We wanted to make money appealing to a broad spectrum of the public."[7] Of the twenty-four sides he recorded for the company during 1951 and 1952, none were pure bebop and seventeen featured pop or rhythm and blues vocals. The scholar Dan Morgenstern has countered the arguments of the aesthetic purists who criticized Dizzy at the time for downplaying bebop:

> Why did Gillespie choose to record such material? First of all, because it was popular, especially with urban black audiences. Louis Jordan and his jumping little band had been so successful in this vein that many followed—trumpeter-singers Red Allen, Lips Page and Roy Eldridge among them, and all with a similar instrumentation. Secondly, because Dizzy liked to play such material. And also because at the time there seemed to be hardly any audience for unadulterated jazz, modern or otherwise. The breakthrough of the LP would quickly build that market in the near future, but that still lay ahead.[8]

In addition, Dizzy had become convinced that a major factor in the failure of his big band was the difficulty in dancing to its music, and with Dee Gee he deliberately deviated from the rhythmic complexity of bebop in favor of simplistic dance beats. He told Nat Hentoff in June 1952, "We got too far away from the beat; people couldn't dance to our music—couldn't pat their feet to it. And jazz, after all, must swing. . . . If you play a concert, that may be something else again, but if it can't be danced to, don't call it jazz."[9]

When the occasion demanded, Dizzy could still perform bebop of astonishing quality and vitality. Bill Crow described a night in a Los Angeles club:

> While singing a simple riff tune called "Hey Pete, Let's Eat Mo' Meat," [Dizzy] noticed two hipsters at a front table making disparaging faces about this un-hip tune. After the vocal, Dizzy put his trumpet to his lips and played three of the most brilliant, explosive, difficult choruses ever played by any trumpet player. When he finished, he leaned over to the hipsters, and said pointedly, "Seee?" Then he went right back to singing, "Hey Pete, Let's Eat Mo' Meat."[10]

Proof of Dizzy's continuing bebop credentials is also found in an air-check recording from March 31, 1951, soon after his first Dee Gee date. It captured him, Bird, Bud Powell, drummer Roy Haynes, and bassist Tommy Potter on a 1:00 a.m. Symphony Sid broadcast from Birdland.

It was just another day at the office for the performers, but it is bebop heaven for the listener as the musicians blaze through "Blue 'n' Boogie," "Anthropology," "'Round Midnight," and "A Night in Tunisia" and close with "Jumpin' with Symphony Sid." Bird again pushed Dizzy to heights he seldom reached with other musicians, and Powell was brilliant. This is the first recording that joins Dizzy with Powell, who was his initial choice as pianist for the groundbreaking 1945 Three Deuces quintet and the 1946 big band and whom he never hired due to Powell's unreliability.

Symphony Sid noted the importance of the occasion: "Never in life again probably will it happen where you can get three great gentlemen of modern music . . . together in one group. Don't forget. Make it here at Birdland, the jazz corner of the world, Broadway and Fifty-second Street, dollar admission. How can you go wrong?"[11] They did get together again, one more time, for a historic concert in May 1953.

Dee Gee folded after two and a half years, primarily because it was underfinanced. An investment of five thousand dollars per year couldn't cut it against multimillion-dollar corporations like RCA Victor and Columbia. In the end, Dave and Dizzy paid off all their debts and leased their catalog to Herman Lubinsky at Savoy in return for future royalties. The partners saw virtually no money from this deal.

Dizzy introduced three tunes with Dee Gee that became a permanent part of his repertoire: "Swing Low, Sweet Cadillac" (his humorous take on the revered spiritual, which contains lines like "There's a band of Fleetwoods comin' after me" and "Old Cadillacs never die; the finance company takes them away"), "Birks Works" (a blues in a minor key), and "Tin Tin Deo" (Chano Pozo's last composition). Recordings of the last two tunes, together with a fast blues romp called "The Champ" and a tender rendition of "Stardust," represent the cream of his Dee Gee output.

In addition to his own work, he and Usher produced the first four tracks ever recorded by the Modern Jazz Quartet (named the Milt Jackson Quartet for the occasion) and introduced to the public future stars Kenny Burrell and Wynton Kelly. On his own, Usher produced for Dee Gee sides by soul star Jackie Wilson and by such outstanding jazz musicians as Kenny Clarke, Shelly Manne, Shorty Rogers, Conte Candoli, Jimmy Guiffre, Annie Ross, Bill Russo, Art Pepper, and Blossom Dearie.

On February 24, 1952, Dizzy and Bird appeared on Earl Wilson's television variety show to accept plaques from Leonard Feather marking their victories in the 1951 *Downbeat* polls. Their excellent rendition of "Hot House" on the show has become a historical artifact, because it marks the only time one can hear Bird on tape or film in performance. The clip has been shown hundreds of times at academic gatherings and in documentaries.

A last-minute decision by Dizzy to accept Charles Delaunay's invitation to perform during March and April 1952 as a soloist in an international jazz festival in Paris and at concerts in Holland and Belgium caused him to cancel several weeks of U.S. bookings; in his absence, saxophonist Bill Graham took over his band and manager Willard Alexander booked enough club dates to keep the group intact. Dizzy traveled without Lorraine.

The festival was a stopover on JATP's first European tour, a resounding success that featured Ella Fitzgerald, Roy Eldridge, Lester Young, Flip Phillips, and Oscar Peterson. Dizzy enjoyed sitting in with the JATP musicians at an elegant club called the Ringside and jitterbugging with Ella at several Parisian boîtes.

Delaunay teamed Dizzy up with expatriate saxophonist Don Byas, his 1944 Onyx Club colleague, and a group of excellent French musicians for his concerts on March 29 and 30 at the Théâtre des Champs-Elysées. The Paris audiences gave him a wildly enthusiastic welcome as he performed in a brightly colored tartan beret and mixed sober ballads ("I Can't Get Started," "Yesterdays") with high-speed bebop ("Groovin' High," "Birks Works") and several novelty vocals.

Dizzy went on a recording binge in Paris and, between March 25 and April 11, waxed thirty-two sides for the French labels Blue Star and Vogue. He performed with his French concert associates, with Byas, with a string group culled from the orchestra of the Paris Opéra-Comique, and with American rhythm sections.

Three of the thirty-two tracks were bebop tunes, four were blues, and twenty-five were romantic ballads. For whatever reason, Dizzy used his sojourn in Paris to hark back to "I Can't Get Started" and other past romantic statements for an in-depth exploration of the work of Berlin, Rodgers and Hart, Porter, Gershwin, and the other composers who created what has become known as "the great American songbook."

Several excellent tracks emerged from the small group dates. As with "I Can't Get Started" seven years previous, Dizzy used modern harmonies and subtle rhythmic shifts to imbue his balladry with a poignant lyricism. And during the intervening years, he had added a muscularity of tone and a firmer control of dynamics to create what critic Don Waterhouse has called "a new classicism." This classicism is embodied in his outstanding renditions of "They Can't Take That Away from Me," "Somebody Loves Me," "I Cover the Waterfront," "She's Funny That Way," "I Don't Know Why," and "Everything Happens to Me." Dizzy's solos are the only things that redeem the string recordings, whose ensemble passages are filled with forgettable treacle.

Delaunay and Byas tried to convince Dizzy to stay in Europe for at least a month longer and perhaps even to settle in Paris with Lorraine. Delaunay felt certain that he could line up lucrative bookings for Dizzy all over Western Europe, and Byas argued that the racial climate in France was far superior to that in segregated America. When Dizzy wired Lorraine suggesting an extended stay, she replied that he'd better get his butt home in a hurry. He boarded a plane for New York soon after.

He met with calamity following his return when he seriously injured a jay walker with his automobile during a rainy night in Queens. He stayed until an ambulance arrived, but, afraid that Lorraine would discover what happened, did not report the accident to the police; the truth came out, and he was forced to forfeit his license for a year. In addition, he was required to pay the victim five thousand dollars because his insurance coverage was inadequate.

Dizzy had one of his rare reunions with Bird when they performed together at a midnight concert at Carnegie Hall on November 14, 1952, celebrating the twenty-fifth anniversary of the Ellington band. Dizzy arrived from a gig at the Apollo to join the Ahmad Jamal trio, the Stan Getz quintet, Billie Holiday, and Bird with strings for the festivities, and he and Bird revisited "A Night in Tunisia" and "Anthropology" in thrilling fashion.

During a New York respite from a heavy touring schedule, Dizzy experienced a fortuitous accident on January 6, 1953, at Snookie's, a Manhattan club where he was performing; it occurred during a birthday party for Lorraine attended by Sarah Vaughan, Illinois Jacquet, the comedians Stump 'n Stumpy, and several other show business friends.

While Dizzy repaired to a nearby hotel for a radio interview, Stump 'n Stumpy performed a comedy routine onstage behind a small upright stand where Dizzy had left his trumpet. Stumpy pushed his partner, who fell back on Dizzy's horn and bent the bell at a forty-five-degree angle; the valves were unharmed.

When Dizzy returned and saw the damage, he reined in his

anger because he did not wish to spoil Lorraine's evening. She remembered that he picked up the horn tentatively and played it and smiled when he heard the softened sound that emerged. And he became elated when he perceived the notes reaching his ears very clearly a fraction of a second earlier than they did with a straight trumpet. He told her, "Damn. I've heard myself play for the first time." He soon ordered a custom-made forty-five-degree "bent" trumpet, and he used one until he died. He sang its praises loudly and convinced protégés such as Jon Faddis and Arturo Sandoval to perform with them for a time.

The bent trumpet barely survived his death, however; no prominent musician plays one now. It appears that the main advantage conferred on Dizzy by the bent horn was not improved acoustics but the creation of a logo that became known the world over. With his unerring instinct for publicity, he had created a simple, angled two-line image that was amazingly effective in reinforcing his distinctive persona. The *New Yorker* cartoon of April 28, 1973, illustrates how the image permeated the public consciousness (see figure 3).

Dizzy's new trumpet was not yet ready in February when he took his sextet to Europe for a whirlwind three-week tour of Scandinavia, France, Spain, Italy, Belgium, and West Germany. He busied himself again with recordings in Paris, waxing a Salle Pleyel concert and a sextet date for Vogue and quartet and string sessions for Blue Star.

At the concert, which took place on February 9, he immediately won over the standing-room-only crowd by entering with his tartan beret tilted at a rakish angle and introducing himself as Louis Armstrong. He then provided his fans with what had become his standard 1953 repertoire: a mix of ballads, novelty vocals with Joe Carroll in the forefront, bebop, and blues.

Dizzy created almost all of the evening's excitement as his sidemen produced a series of mediocre solos. In fact, in early releases of the recording of the event, much of their work was electronically eliminated. The second half of the concert was sparked by an appearance by Sarah Vaughan, whom Dizzy coaxed from the audience to sing "Embraceable You." When she finished, the

"Who the hell is Dizzy Gillespie, anyway?"

Figure 3

crowd cheered her for five minutes before allowing her to return to her seat.

The small-group Paris sessions produced lovely renditions of the ballads "My Man," "Moon Nocturne," and "This Is the Way" for Vogue and brisk bebop solos on "Undecided" and "The Way You Look Tonight" for Blue Star; the string recordings were, if anything, worse than those made the previous year.

Dizzy's second and last recording (after "Manteca") to achieve the rarefied status conveyed by a Grammy Hall of Fame Award was *Jazz at Massey Hall*, a fabled concert taped in May 1953 and honored in 1995. What the historian and Dizzy biographer Alyn Shipton has called "one of the most celebrated events in jazz history"[12] had an unlikely genesis.

The New Jazz Society (NJS), a group of Toronto bebop enthusiasts with very little money, decided in late 1952 that they would produce an all-star quintet concert on May 15 of the following year. They chose, ambitiously, a large venue—Massey Hall, which boasted a capacity of 2,765, only 39 seats short of Carnegie Hall.

Four NJS members drove to New York on the weekend of January 25 and signed up Dizzy for $450, Bird for $200 plus a percentage of the profits, and Max Roach for $150.

They were required to wait for the release of their pianist of choice, Bud Powell, from New York's Creedmoor Psychiatric Center on February 4 before they could negotiate a contract with his legal guardian, Oscar Goodstein. Goodstein, the manager of Birdland, obtained five hundred dollars for him. For Powell, whose mental illness had been either caused or exacerbated by a beating about the head administered by police in 1945 when he was twenty-one, his sojourn at Creedmoor came at the end of his fourth stay in a mental institution. Electric shock treatments had been administered to him on several occasions while he was incarcerated.

The NJS corralled the final member of the quintet, the brilliant and volatile bassist/composer Charles Mingus, shortly after he was fired by Duke Ellington in February following a fracas in which he squared off with a fire ax against another musician brandishing a machete. Mingus was signed for $150, bringing the total cost of the quintet to $1,450.

The prospect of the concert excited Dizzy, because, for the first time, he would be able to perform with the musicians who formed the core of the dream group he rehearsed but could not cement together eight years earlier—himself, Bird, Powell, and Roach. In addition, in Mingus, he would be working with a more innovative and powerful bassist than his 1945 colleague, Curley Russell.

Mingus and Roach, who owned the Debut record label, agreed with the president of the NJS, a General Electric parts clerk, to make a commercial recording of the event on equipment borrowed from General Electric. They told Dizzy about their plans, and he asked Dave Usher to travel to Toronto to help him negotiate with them. It is highly unlikely that Bird and Powell knew about the recording before the concert.

The NJS people realized in early May that they were headed for financial disaster but, intoxicated by the prospect of producing a historic event, pushed on. They were in peril because Toronto in 1953 was a bebop backwater and because they did not possess the promotional resources to reach out to wider audiences. To make matters worse, they faced competition on May 15 from the telecast of a heavyweight title fight between Rocky Marciano and Jersey Joe Walcott.

Dizzy volunteered to shepherd Bird to the gig, and he missed the morning flight that took Goodstein, Powell, Roach, Mingus, and Mingus's wife to Toronto, because Bird had gone underground. He found him in Harlem around midday and scrambled to arrive late in the afternoon.

Dizzy was depressed when he saw only seven hundred spectators arrive and scatter themselves around the cavernous hall, and, since the dream quintet followed a Roach drum solo and sets by a local big band and a Powell/Roach/Mingus trio, he repaired to a nearby saloon to watch the boxing telecast with Usher. Marciano knocked Walcott out in the first round, and Dizzy announced the result, with mock sadness, when he stepped to the microphone for his set.

The quintet's program was decided upon spontaneously as the musicians set up; it comprised five numbers from the standard bebop repertoire—"Salt Peanuts," "A Night in Tunisia," "All the Things You Are," "Wee" a.k.a. "Allen's Alley," and "Hot House"— plus Juan Tizol's swinger, "Perdido."

Powell, who was led to the piano bench by the hand by Goodstein, emerged from a state of withdrawal only when he touched the piano keys. He had shown that he was in top form during his trio set, and his articulation, which at this stage of his career sometimes became sloppy, was flawless even at the ultrafast tempos of "Wee" and "Salt Peanuts." Dizzy, who was still waiting for his bent horn, performed on his straight trumpet, Bird used a rare white plastic saxophone, and a colleague of Mingus operated the tape recorder from a sound booth.

The quintet's first chorus brought the audience to a high state of excitement; its enthusiasm never abated, and it continually inspired the musicians. Apart from roughness in the ensemble passages occasioned by the absence of rehearsal, they produced music of a very high order.

Bird gave no quarter as he sustained a high level of creativity through almost twenty choruses, and as usual, he spurred Dizzy to a prime effort. He created tension when he called Dizzy "his worthy constituent" during his introduction of "Salt Peanuts," and Dizzy countered by angrily yelling the tune's name several times during the first sixteen bars of Bird's solo. According to Roach, they relaxed after this contretemps and enjoyed themselves for the balance of the concert.

Roach, for his part, drove the performance with infectious energy, and Powell, who accomplished a harmonic tour de force by introducing a new chord on every beat during his accompaniments on "All the Things You Are," created exciting solos as he imbued his sophisticated melodic inventions with transparent passion.

Mingus became furious when he listened to the tapes after the concert and discovered that his bass parts were almost inaudible. He skillfully overdubbed them when he returned to New York, and during a couple of passages on the CD, one can hear him accompanying himself.

Dizzy and Usher negotiated a decent royalty formula for Dizzy, but, due to the vagaries of the small-label record business, he received no compensation until the 1970s and then it was meager. The record company listed Bird as "Charlie Chan" on the album, because of his contractual obligation to Norman Granz.

Dizzy came away empty-handed from "one of the most celebrated events in jazz history." He should have followed the examples of Bird and Mingus and forced the Canadians to pay him cash, because when Lorraine went to deposit his check, it bounced.

Dizzy suffered another financial setback when he was hit with a paternity suit in June 1953 by Ruth Agee, a Pittsburgh woman who had him arrested every time he entered the city; Dizzy denied paternity and settled the case in October 1954 for $3,000 (worth roughly $17,500 in 2004).

Dizzy's eclectic period ended soon after the financial fiasco of Massey Hall when Lorraine convinced him to stop scuffling and accept an attractive offer from Norman Granz to record for his labels and to tour for roughly three months a year with the all-star

JATP troupes. Dizzy's future, for the first time in more than three years, was no longer deeply dependent on the fortunes of his sextet. In fact, he would earn as much during one month on the road with Granz as he would touring for three months with his own group.

Granz was both a bleeding-heart liberal and a ruthlessly effective capitalist. His prime career motive, as he told *Downbeat* in December 1951, was to achieve racial justice: "My aims should be listed in this order—first, sociological. To promote tolerance and the elimination of racial discrimination; second, pure business, or to put it as plainly as possible, to make money; and third—and last, mind you—to sell jazz."[13] He never deviated from this credo and never permitted his musicians to perform before segregated audiences.

Granz began his jazz career in 1942 at age twenty-three while idling as a civilian between two stints in the army. Indignant that Los Angeles jazz spots only admitted white patrons, he began renting the clubs on off-nights (usually Mondays) to stage jam sessions with integrated bands before integrated audiences.

His confidence received a major boost when, on July 2, 1944, he organized a successful benefit concert at the Los Angeles Philharmonic Auditorium to provide legal aid for the Sleepy Lagoon Boys, twenty-two Mexican Americans who were languishing in San Quentin Prison and other jails after being convicted of an August 1942 gang-related murder.

The concert drew two thousand people and featured Swing Era musicians: saxophonist Illinois Jacquet, guitarist Les Paul, clarinetist Barney Bigard, and pianists Joe Sullivan, Nat King Cole, and Meade Lux Lewis. Jacquet drew the most attention; according to *Downbeat*, he "had the kids wild with the screaming high notes of his tenor sax."[14]

The music critic of the *Los Angeles Times*, who was wedded to classical music, declined a personal invitation with the statement that it would be "beneath her dignity" to cover such an event. Granz would not be cowed by such comments: "We were battling not only anti-black discrimination, but discrimination against all jazz musicians. I insisted that my players were given the same respect as Leonard Bernstein or Heifetz, because they were just as good—both as men and as musicians."[15] The money raised by

Granz helped set the Sleepy Lagoon Boys free when their convictions were unanimously overturned on appeal in October 1944.

The success of the Sleepy Lagoon benefit emboldened Granz four weeks later to organize a commercial event at the Philharmonic venue. It starred Cole, Paul, and Sullivan and earned a tidy profit. Soon Granz was staging concerts every few weeks and dubbing them Jazz at the Philharmonic, or JATP. He convinced himself early on that he could make extra money by selling recordings of his concerts, but he was continually rebuffed by big distributors who believed that discs containing audience applause and shouts would alienate listeners.

Granz persevered until he found, through the New York City Yellow Pages, a decidedly minor distributor who was willing to take a chance with him; his name was Moe Asch and he specialized in folk genres from around the world—Malaysian dream songs, Appalachian ballads, Ethiopian ritual chants, and the like.

To everyone's surprise, the first JATP record sold more than 150,000 copies, and subsequent ones were even more successful; Asch suffered a bankruptcy due to bad decisions unrelated to JATP, but Granz's fortunes took off. The widespread popularity of the recordings encouraged him to book his artists for national tours. After a false start in 1945, the junkets met with mounting success beginning in 1946. A tepid emcee but a dynamo backstage, Granz micromanaged every one of his concerts.

He preferred musicians who played in a directly emotional, visceral manner. He told Leonard Feather, "My concerts are primarily emotional music. . . . I could put on as cerebral a concert as you like, but I'd rather go the emotional route. And do you know, the public's taste reflects mine—the biggest flop I've ever had in my life was the tour I put on with some of the cerebral musicians like Dave Brubeck and Gerry Mulligan."[16]

And he later commented to Nat Hentoff:

Jazz is so alive that it makes *you* feel alive. . . . I think that music should make you happy. It should have energy, a lot of energy. When I hear Oscar Peterson, Roy Eldridge, Dizzy, or Benny Carter, I'm swept up in a marvelous burst of energy and good feeling . . .

Roy [Eldridge] is so intense about *everything* that it's far more
important for him to dare, to try to achieve a particular peak—even
if he fails in the attempt—than it is to play it safe. That *is* jazz.[17]

Granz almost always delivered a product with a high degree of
artistic integrity, but at times his preference for the emotional
caused his musicians to push artistic considerations aside as they
unleashed barrages of honks and squeals to whip an audience into
a frenzy.

As a prelude to a formal contract with Granz, Dizzy participated on September 2, 1953, in "Norman Granz Jam Session #8."
A few honks and squeals can be heard as Dizzy joined Roy Eldridge, Lionel Hampton, and heavyweight saxophonists Johnny
Hodges, Flip Phillips, Ben Webster, and Illinois Jacquet in a fierce
studio blowing session. Oscar Peterson, Ray Brown, and Buddy
Rich made up the rhythm section.

26

TEAMING UP WITH NORMAN, BIDDING BIRD GOOD-BYE

DIZZY HAPPILY FULFILLED A PRIOR COMMITMENT WHILE easing into the Granz organization. He participated in a two-part tour over the course of four months as a featured soloist with the Stan Kenton band, and his first major Granz project took place between the tour segments. The Kenton show was billed as "The Festival of Modern American Jazz."

The initial junket also starred singer June Christy, the Erroll Garner Trio, saxophonists Lee Konitz and Stan Getz, Cuban conga drummer Candido, and Slim Gaillard. It stretched from November 1, 1953, into early December.

Kenton's orchestra was one of four major aggregations that had survived the big band debacle of the late 1940s to prosper in the 1950s and beyond; the others were led by Ellington, Herman, and Basie. Kenton's group prevailed mainly because of the total dedication of its leader, who was described by a biographer as "a lifetime product and prisoner of the Puritan ethic."

His aesthetic, based on masses of sound, was quite a distance from Dizzy's. Kenton's orchestra was to the average big band what the heavy metal pioneers of the 1970s were to the average rock band of their era—loud, bruising, and powerful.

Kenton was wise enough, however, to accommodate the stars he had assembled for his shows. He adopted, for Dizzy's numbers, charts by Gil Fuller, Johnny Richards, and Budd Johnson that Dizzy had brought with him.

Dizzy relaxed and enjoyed himself on tour. He didn't have to worry about a booking that just fell through, a piano player with a drug problem, a plane to a gig grounded in a snowstorm, a club owner who shortchanged him. He would perform his three numbers every evening, share a joint in the back of the bus with the young Kenton musicians who adored him, schmooze with friends in the towns along the way, and collect his paycheck.

Granz's first significant recording session with Dizzy involved a pairing with tenor saxophonist Stan Getz after the two men had completed the first leg of their Kenton tour; it occurred on December 9, 1953. Granz had recorded Getz several times with his own groups, but he had never paired him with an artist of Dizzy's stature, and Getz felt especially challenged.

Originally a disciple of Lester Young, Getz was more than nine years younger than Dizzy and had absorbed the lessons of bebop as he forged his own style during his late teens. His hauntingly romantic solo on "Early Autumn" with Woody Herman's band in 1948 catapulted him to stardom at age twenty-one, and he was so talented that he never again joined anyone else's band, performing as a featured soloist or with his own groups for the balance of a long career. He took it as a high compliment when Granz began recording him in December 1952.

The JATP house rhythm section of pianist Oscar Peterson, bassist Ray Brown, and guitarist Herb Ellis, a headline act in its own right, had become by 1953 eerily adept at accompanying soloists of many styles and persuasions. For the Getz-Gillespie date, Granz added Max Roach to this sterling group.

After they led off with "Girl of My Dreams," a ballad, they tore into "It Don't Mean a Thing (If It Ain't Got That Swing)" at the kind of blazing tempo that Dizzy loved, and, although Getz made a creditable effort to keep pace, Dizzy took the honors with a daring flow of melody. Nonetheless, Getz prized the track enough to include it in an anthology of his best work issued twenty-seven years later.

The rest of the album bristled with "mano a mano" energy as Getz held his own at both slow and medium tempos. He peaked on the ballad "The Talk of the Town," where he achieved a poignant lyricism that reached deeper layers of emotion than Dizzy's interpretation. Getz later expressed his empathy for his cohort: "Diz has always been close to my heart musically and personally. We two seem to go together. We think alike, and yet we are entirely our own men with our own way of expressing ourselves—traveling different yet parallel paths."[1]

Dizzy took time off after the Getz session to undergo eye surgery for cataracts. Today the procedure is quite routine, but in 1953 it involved significant risk. Lorraine remembered that Dizzy became severely depressed during the recovery period when he feared that his vision might be permanently impaired. The operation was a success, however, and he was able to return to the Kenton tour when it reconvened on January 28, 1954, in Wichita Falls, Kansas.

Getz was scheduled to rejoin Kenton as well, but his arrest for heroin possession on December 18, nine days after the session with Dizzy, precluded this. Ironically, Charlie Parker, still in thrall to the drug, was hired in his place. Kenton presented him and Dizzy in separate segments of the program, and the two men did not perform together.

To reduce his intake of heroin, Bird was drinking a quart of whiskey a day. Dizzy was deeply disturbed both by his friend's self-destructive behavior and by the related deterioration in his playing. In a drunken stupor every night, Bird was performing pitiably and was consistently bested by Konitz, the other featured saxophonist. Dizzy, appealing to Bird's pride, convinced him to stop boozing, and his performances immediately returned to a high level.

A Portland, Oregon, concert recording of February 28, 1954, provides evidence of this. Bird soloed vigorously and with considerable originality on "Night and Day," "My Funny Valentine," and his old favorite, "Cherokee." The arrangements were obviously constructed as backgrounds to Bird's improvisations, and his interactions with the band were minimal.

Dizzy, on the other hand, was using charts written for his own big bands but performed by Kenton musicians, and his improvisations were woven deeply into the arrangements. At Portland, his solos on "On the Alamo," "Oo-shoo-be-do-be," and "Manteca" provide a joyous assault on the eardrums as they soar over Kenton's massed brass, and he is greatly aided by his former protégé Stan Levey, now Kenton's drummer, and by Candido. The high point of his performance was a blistering duet with Candido on "Manteca"—Dizzy at his best.

When he returned to New York in March after the Kenton tour, Dizzy formed a quintet featuring Hank Mobley, his best saxophonist since Coltrane and Heath. Mobley, a protégé of Max Roach, possessed at age twenty-three a distinctive, gritty sound and a penchant for creating and solving rhythmic puzzles. Dizzy also hired Charli Persip, an excellent drummer who became the mainstay of his units for four and a half years.

As he began to record in earnest for Granz after the Kenton interlude, Dizzy realized that he had joined the impresario at a very opportune time, the period when the 33 rpm record emerged as a dominant consumer product. Columbia Records had introduced the 33 in 1948 after copyrighting the "LP" name for it. RCA countered with the 45 rpm disc in 1949, and the two companies battled for supremacy through 1951. In early 1952, the LP emerged with the lion's share of the market, and the 45 found a niche as a medium for four-minute "singles."

LP sales lagged, however, until consumers had purchased a critical mass of new record players; this did not happen until 1953. Dizzy's Dee Gee, which marketed both LPs and 45s, did not survive long enough to take advantage of this development, but Granz had positioned himself to do so, and he exploited the new technology brilliantly.

The LPs possessed overwhelming advantages over the 78s that they supplanted. They were virtually indestructible while the fragile 78s would chip easily and would shatter if dropped on a hard surface. LP sound quality was far better, and, most important, the LP side provided seven times the music of a 78—twenty-one minutes versus three. For the first time, symphonies and other extended works could be recorded on one disc.

As Granz explained in *Downbeat*, the LP was a bonanza for the jazz improviser:

> In jazz . . . the question of time is all important, because the spirit and excitement of jazz is a cumulative one, and the jazz man must have time to pace himself and to build. Nowhere on records, until the LP record came into existence, was that possible. . . . Just imagine how the great Benny Goodman trio could have built and built and built had they but had enough time. . . . Here is the opportunity for the first time of really getting at the core of jazz in much the same fashion as with a personal appearance.[2]

The LP was sometimes the handmaiden of verbosity, but on the whole, it was a great boon to jazz creativity. It also allowed the producer to build forty-two minutes of music around a single concept, and Granz proved to be a master of such construction. Ella Fitzgerald's career reached new heights when he conceived of her "songbook" LPs featuring the works of great popular composers. The series began in February 1956 with *The Cole Porter Songbook* and went on to encompass the compositions of Gershwin, Rodgers and Hart, Berlin, Arlen, Mercer, Kern, and Ellington.

By the mid-1950s, Granz was so prosperous that he could indulge himself with recording projects that satisfied his personal tastes but had minimal profit potential. Among them were a fifteen-LP series of Art Tatum solos and albums by excellent but little-known jazzmen such as guitarist Billy Bauer and pianist George Wallington. He could also offer Dizzy unprecedented opportunities to record.

The struggles of the previous three years receded into memory as Granz delighted Dizzy with sixteen record sessions during

1954 and 1955. He fulfilled Dizzy's wish list with an Afro-Cuban date, three small-group outings, five JATP jam sessions, a reunion with Benny Carter, four big band sets that included a strings album arranged by Johnny Richards, and two sessions with Roy Eldridge. Three recordings stand out: a Latin jazz LP called *Afro*, the Benny Carter date, and a seventy-four-minute duel with Roy Eldridge that was spread over two LPs.

The first side of *Afro* was given over to a work impossible to record in the 78 era, the seventeen-minute "Manteca Suite" in four parts created by the Cuban writer and arranger Chico O'Farrill; the other side paired Dizzy with a Cuban sextet.

Using themes from the original Gil Fuller "Manteca" arrangement, O'Farrill made powerful use of a twenty-piece orchestra that included Dizzy's quintet, percussion by Machito's rhythm section and Candido, and the saxophone soloist Lucky Thompson. The authentic Afro-Cuban rhythms and O'Farrill's varied backgrounds inspired Dizzy to energetic and soulful improvisations throughout the suite.

He was truly galvanized on the small-group side; he unleashed torrid solos on "Caravan" and "A Night in Tunisia" as Candido and Machito's men created a controlled rhythmic frenzy behind him, and he recorded for the first time one of his most beautiful compositions, "Con Alma," providing a beautifully balanced and pensive interpretation.

Dizzy dropped into a studio where Carter, trombonist Bill Harris, Peterson's trio, and Buddy Rich were recording an album called *New Jazz Sounds*, and he was so captivated by what they were doing that he asked if he could participate. Carter agreed and delayed the start of the last two numbers as Dizzy fought his way through New York traffic for two hours to retrieve his trumpet from his home.

Carter was happy that he had waited; the tracks with Dizzy, "Just One of Those Things" and "Marriage Blues," are the best of the session. He solos zestfully, and he energizes Carter and Harris with strong leads in the ensemble passages and booting background riffs. Dizzy had not recorded with Carter since the historic Lionel Hampton "Hot Mallets" session fifteen years earlier.

Dizzy participated on July 17 and 18, 1954, in a landmark event, the first American jazz festival. Elaine Lorrilard, the wife of socialite tobacco heir Louis Lorrilard, wished to spice up the summer social season at the upper-crust resort town of Newport, Rhode Island, and she talked George Wein, a Boston club operator, into staging the event at the Casino, an elite tennis club.

The combined attendance approximated eleven thousand, and the enthusiastic crowds feasted on Dixieland, swing, and bebop served up by Dizzy and an array of stars that included Eddie Condon and his gang, Ella Fitzgerald, Milt Jackson, Kenny Clarke, Lee Konitz, John Lewis, Gerry Mulligan, Oscar Peterson with Ray Brown and Herb Ellis, Percy Heath, Gene Krupa, Milt Hinton, Jo Jones, Lester Young, and Billie Holiday.

Dizzy appeared on both nights with Mobley in his working quintet, and, according to the historian Burt Goldblatt, he ignited a jam session that closed out the first evening:

> The final number was a jamming of "I Got Rhythm" performed by one of the most mixed bags of musicians ever assembled on a stage. . . . When Dizzy wasn't soloing or playing ensemble, he walked around the stage photographing the other performers. Clowning or not, his biting, driving horn sparked the other musicians and gave a cohesiveness to a rather disjointed assemblage.[3]

Wein, who had hoped to emulate the success of the classical music festival at Tanglewood in western Massachusetts, had been wary and nervous as he approached his pioneering task. He need not have worried. He had taken no salary, and the festival had cleared only $142.50, but he had achieved his artistic goals splendidly, and he had made the Lorrilards happy enough to insist upon a second festival the following year.

From such relatively modest beginnings, festivals have become a significant jazz phenomenon and an important source of income for performers. *JazzTimes* magazine in May 2002 listed more than 250 festivals on six continents, and roughly 50 of them (including Newport, which survives) attract major artists.

Responding to critics who disparaged Dizzy's comedy, Wein talked him into throttling his onstage antics. He came to regret it:

"Later I realized the foolishness of what I had done. I had advised an artist—a man whose comic genius was comparable to that of Charlie Chaplin—to stifle his natural performance."[4]

Many in the jazz community argued that Dizzy's jesting was diluting his art. But he couldn't help it. Comedy had entered his blood when, as a child, he watched his grandfather regale the neighbors on Huger Street, and it never left. He was a master of timing and of body language—the raised eyebrow, the swiveled hip, the sagging shoulder, the sudden smile.

Dizzy relished his role as the daring but nonthreatening enemy of convention, and he delighted in comedic wordplay when introducing numbers. For example: "Here is a tune that has withstood the vicissitudes of the contingent world and has moved into the realm of the metaphysical—'A Night in Tunisia.'" Or, "I would like to give y'all a version of a tune that has been closely associated with me over many decades. Mainly because I wrote it." And when he finished a set one night on the 1954 Kenton tour, he said: "Ladies and gentlemen, you're so wonderful I'd really like to do two or three hundred more numbers for you, but I don't want to take up the time of any of the other superb artists on the bill, and I'm not taking up any of their money either. But I think I do have time for just one more short one."[5] He and the Kenton band then hit a single thundering chord, and the audience exploded in laughter and applause.

Dizzy loved to make audiences laugh, but when, to use a favorite expression of his, he "put the metal to his lips," he was entirely serious. Lalo Schifrin remembered an incident at a JATP concert:

I will tell you how strict he was about harmony. Dizzy was so generous, and so warm to everybody, but he was ruthless when it came to music, because he had an ear. He could hear anything going on. We were playing something very fast, and he turned in front of the audience. This is not a rehearsal. He said to a famous bass player, "Man, how can you play an E natural in an A minor seven with a flat fifth? It should be an E flat." And we were going at lightning speed.

Remember the conductor Pierre Boulez? The members of the New York Philharmonic called him "the French Correction" because of his incredible ear. Dizzy was the "South Carolina Correction."[6]

Boo Frazier, a nephew of Dizzy's, became a boarder at the Corona house soon after the Newport event and remained for the better part of eleven years. Dizzy employed him as a road manager until 1957, when he departed for a career in the record industry. His tenure overlapped with that of a successor, Jimmy Atchison, with whom he worked frequently during vacations in the late 1950s. Boo developed a deep and loving relationship with Dizzy and Lorraine and became a charter member of their inner circle.

Dizzy was reunited with Charlie Parker on August 26 when he began a three-week engagement at Birdland opposite both Dinah Washington and Bird with his string ensemble. Bird had deteriorated seriously both physically and mentally since the Kenton tour had ended six months before, and Dizzy was shocked by his appearance, his indifferent performances, and his nonstop drinking and doping.

The gig ended disastrously for Bird on its fourth night. He fired his string group in midperformance after a senseless altercation and was in turn fired by Birdland's manager, Oscar Goodstein. He binged at a nearby bar, headed home, argued with his companion Chan, and attempted suicide in the bathroom by washing down a handful of aspirin with a bottle of iodine. Chan rushed him to Bellevue Hospital where, after the doctors saved him by pumping out his stomach, they placed him in the psychiatric ward. He was discharged on September 10 but voluntarily recommitted himself on September 28 and remained until October 15, when he became an outpatient. Dizzy visited his friend several times at Bellevue and helped Chan out financially before he had to leave for Hartford, Connecticut, to begin his first JATP tour on September 15.

He had studied the roster and understood that it included three sets of paired soloists for the musical "battles" Granz enjoyed so much: himself and the most competitive of jazz soloists, Roy Eldridge, drummers Louis Bellson and Buddy Rich, and saxophonists Flip Phillips and Ben Webster. Oscar Peterson and his trio, Ella and her pianist Don Abney, trombonist Bill Harris, and clarinetist Buddy De Franco completed the group. They would perform in forty-two cities before closing down in Los Angeles on November 8. Dizzy later reflected on the instrumental jousting: "Norman loved to set his guys up for those musical duels; I didn't see that they had much artistic value, but he got his rocks off on them and the fans did too. Roy and I surprised him when we embraced and laughed after cutting each other up on stage. Norman expected us to be glaring at each other in anger."[7]

Granz was impatient to record the rivalry, and he took Dizzy and Eldridge into a studio in midtour on October 29. After battling for six weeks, they knew each other's every gambit, but recording for posterity had them keyed up like Ali and Frazier awaiting the first bell.

Eldridge, at age forty-three, was only six years older than his disciple. He was full of fire, and Dizzy was forced to use every weapon in his arsenal to counter his passionate thrusts. He also had to supply his own bebop rhythms, because the accompaniment (the Peterson trio plus Louis Bellson on drums) settled into the kind of swing groove that Eldridge loved.

The result is a hugely entertaining and exciting two-LP album. The two men blast through chorus after incendiary chorus on "Trumpet Blues," "Blue Moon," and "Limehouse Blues"; they scat humorously on "Pretty-Eyed Baby"; and they keep the temperature high on the ballads.

Eldridge's raspy, very human vibrato provides a clear contrast to Dizzy's clean, classical sound on the slower numbers such as "Sometimes I'm Happy" and Dizzy's old standby, "I Can't Get Started." On the latter, Dizzy fashions one of the most moving and harmonically fascinating of his many renditions of the song; Eldridge sticks close to the melody in his version.

The tour swung into the South in late September at a time of rising racial tension in the United States. Four months before, in *Brown v. Board of Education*, the Supreme Court had ruled 9–0 that segregated schools were illegal. It was the first great victory for the civil rights movement, and it elicited defiant reactions from segregationists throughout the South.

Granz created a storm in Charleston, South Carolina, on Sep-

tember 27 when, by threatening to cancel his show, he forced a local promoter to adopt integrated seating and forgo his policy of
segregating blacks in the balcony. As the concert neared its end,
the stage manager informed Granz that roughly thirty white men
were milling around the stage door threatening mayhem on the
performers. Granz told the pilots of the chartered JATP plane to
leave quickly for the airport, and he instructed the drivers of three
limousines to wait on the opposite side of the hall from the stage
door. Dizzy remembered:

> The drummer broke down his gear before Ella finished her final
> number, her assistant Georgianna stuffed the night's receipts into
> her bra, and we all scrambled out of there and into the cars. The pi-
> lots had fired up their engines before we climbed into the plane,
> and as we went down the runway, I saw the headlights of at least
> twenty cars barreling into the airport. Thank God the rest of the
> tour was peaceful. I didn't want to live through any more nights
> like that.[8]

Dizzy embarked on his second Granz junket, a whirlwind cir-
cuit of Sweden, Denmark, Germany, Switzerland, and France, on
February 7, 1955. His colleagues were the usual JATP suspects—
Eldridge, Phillips, De Franco, Peterson's trio, Harris, Bellson, and
Ella Fitzgerald—and they sold out everywhere. The tour ended
with four wildly successful Paris concerts on February 19 and 20.

A few days after his return from Europe, Dizzy ran into Charlie Parker, looking bloated and unhealthy, at a midtown jazz club.
Bird had led a vagabond existence since his stay at Bellevue,
prowling southern Manhattan, riding the subways for hours,
drinking prodigiously, and dossing down in a friend's ramshackle
Greenwich Village apartment. He had performed erratically on
occasional gigs and suffered from ulcers and varied respiratory ail-
ments. When they encountered each other, Bird begged Dizzy to
save him. Dizzy felt sad but helpless, because he knew that Bird
had to free himself from his addictions before anyone could even
attempt to save him.

Soon after, Bird charmed Goodstein into giving him a chance

at a comeback, a weekend Birdland gig on March 4 and 5 with Bud Powell, Charles Mingus, Art Blakey, and Kenny Dorham. When Powell arrived on the second evening too drunk to play, Bird cursed him out, and Bud left. Instead of trying to continue without him, Bird stood at the microphone calling, "Bud Powell! Bud Powell!" a dozen times, and his comeback ended in chaos.

Four days later, on the way to an engagement in Boston, Bird paid an impromptu visit to Baroness Nica Rothschild de Koenigswarter, a wealthy helpmate to many jazz musicians, at her Fifth Avenue apartment in the posh Stanhope Hotel. When he began vomiting blood, she summoned a doctor. He examined Bird and concluded that he was suffering from ulcers, a respiratory infection, and advanced cirrhosis of the liver and, because his condition was critical, should be admitted to a hospital immediately; when Bird refused, the doctor reluctantly agreed to treat him at the apartment.

While Nica and her daughter provided around-the-clock nursing help, the doctor ministered to Bird thrice daily with penicillin and other medicines. Three days after his arrival, on the evening of March 12, Bird experienced a sudden seizure while watching a television show and died. The coroner's report stated that the cause of death was visceral congestion associated with lobar pneumonia.

Nica immediately telephoned Dizzy, who was home alone. Once he digested the news, he went down to his basement and cried. Lorraine found him there sobbing when she returned to the house soon after. It was the first time in their years together, she later reflected, when he did not don a mask to disguise his pain.

Chaos dogged Bird in death as in life. Nica wanted Chan to know of his death before the media did, but she could not locate her until forty-eight hours later, on March 14. The next day the headline of the staid *New York Times*—"Charlie Parker, Jazz Master, Dies"—was balanced by that of the tabloid *New York Mirror*: "Bop King Dies in Heiress Flat."

Bird died broke, and Dizzy joined Mary Lou Williams, Charles Mingus, entertainer Hazel Scott, author Maely Dufty, and Bird's lawyer in an ad hoc committee whose aims were to give

Bird a decent burial and to secure royalty income for his family. Their task became complicated when Chan, who wished to bury Bird in a cemetery close to New York, lost control of the corpse. Bird had never married her and had never bothered to divorce his previous companion, Doris Sydnor. Doris took possession of the coffin and decided that Bird should be buried in Kansas City.

When Dizzy realized that there was no money for this, he telephoned Norman Granz, and Granz told him to get the coffin on a plane and he would pick up all expenses. Then Dizzy and the committee turned to organizing benefit concerts at Carnegie Hall and in Philadelphia.

The funeral took place at the Abyssinian Baptist Church, Harlem's largest, on a wet, chilly day, March 21. Hazel Scott's husband, Congressman Adam Clayton Powell Jr., was the pastor there, and he appointed an assistant to preside at the ceremony. Dizzy joined Leonard Feather, Sonny Stitt, pianist Lennie Tristano, Teddy Reig, Louis Bellson, and Charlie Shavers as pallbearers.

The Carnegie Hall concert, which ran from midnight to 4:00 a.m. on April 2 and drew 2,760 people, netted $5,740. More than sixty outstanding jazz musicians donated their services; among them were the three surviving bebop pioneers—Dizzy, Monk, and Kenny Clarke. The Philadelphia benefit raised more than a thousand dollars; Dizzy left the committee after he heard that a significant portion of the money had been stolen.

Dizzy found a week in his schedule during August 1955 to join John Lewis, Milt Jackson, Max Roach, and George Russell on the faculty of the Lenox School of Jazz during its inaugural year. The participants stayed in the idyllic, 136-acre Tanglewood complex in the Berkshire mountains of Massachusetts where, every summer, the Boston Symphony performed and taught. The Lenox School's numerous backers included Norman Granz, United Artists Films, Atlantic Records, a beer company, a wealthy philanthropic couple, the Newport Jazz Festival, and Sol Hurok, the classical music impresario.

It drew students from every state and from Africa, Europe, South America, and Asia. The faculty taught basic techniques while trying to help each student find his or her unique voice.

Teachers were required to perform in concert, and Dizzy and his group played to a full house on August 15. The ambience and the mission of the school provided a therapeutic contrast to Dizzy's normal regime of smoky saloons, and the knowledge that jazz was at last being taught in a dignified and beautiful setting left him spiritually refreshed.

After Lenox, Dizzy squeezed in a two-week gig at Birdland before heading to Hartford, Connecticut, on September 16 for the kickoff of his second JATP U.S. tour. It would end forty-two cities later in San Diego on November 8.

Because racial tensions had been escalating during 1955, Granz knew that he would create controversy when he produced the first ever integrated event in Houston, Texas—two back-to-back concerts on October 7. Blacks, who were outraged by the Mississippi lynching in August of fourteen-year-old Emmett Till for allegedly whistling at a white woman, were testing the power of *Brown v. Board of Education* by attempting to enroll students at previously segregated schools ranging from kindergartens to colleges, and many southern whites were girding to fight the Supreme Court decision with violence if necessary. Granz remembered, "Houston, far and away, is the toughest town in the south and the reason is simple: it's the richest. And so the people that run things, the rich whites, they could come on as strong as they wanted, and the police department would, of course, agree with that."[9]

To ensure freedom of operation, Granz bypassed local promoters and hired the previously segregated hall himself. He then removed the "Blacks Only" and "Whites Only" signs from the toilets and water fountains, and installed his own ticket sellers. When a patron requested a change of venue because a black was seated nearby, the seller would say, "We can't do that, but we can refund your money." Most of the objectors took the money.

Granz violated one of his primary rules when he allowed two strangers, white plainclothes policemen, to stand backstage; they told him that they were sincere jazz fans and would be unobtrusive, and he believed them.

Both shows sold out, and as the first one was nearing an end,

Dizzy and Illinois Jacquet were shooting craps on the floor of Ella Fitzgerald's dressing room as Ella and Georgianna ate pie, drank coffee, and watched. Suddenly, the police "spectators" pushed in the door with guns drawn and told everyone they were under arrest for gambling. When Granz rushed over to find out what was going on, they arrested him for running a gambling house.

Granz followed one of the policemen into a toilet, because he feared that he would employ an oft-used police tactic and plant drugs there. He remembered what happened next: "He said, 'What are you doing here?' and I said, 'I'm just watching you. I want to be sure you're not gonna plant anything.' He got furious and said, 'I ought to kill you,' and stuck a gun in my stomach. . . . Then they said, 'We're taking you all down to the station house.'"[10]

Granz warned that he would announce the cancellation of the second show to three thousand waiting fans if the policemen didn't accomplish the booking quickly, and they complied. Dizzy told the clerk that his name was Louis Armstrong, Granz posted ten dollars bail for each of the five persons arrested, and everyone hustled back for the concert, which started a half hour late and went off without a hitch.

The authorities expected that Granz would put the incident behind him and forfeit the token bail, but he spent two thousand dollars on the best lawyer available and won a dismissal of the charges. He was convinced that the arrests were the Houston establishment's retaliation against him for breaching, for the first time, the city's unwritten law of segregation.

The troupe went on to perform before capacity crowds everywhere, and it set a record for a one-night stand, twenty-three thousand dollars, on its penultimate night, October 30, 1955, in Los Angeles.

In later years, Dizzy expressed his deep appreciation for the many things Norman Granz had done for him: "I admire him. He fought racism tooth and nail, and he always hired top-flight musicians and saw to it that they traveled first class. He paid me excellent money and gave me many opportunities to record things that were dear to my heart. And he loved to surprise you with presents."[11] Dizzy told Nat Hentoff that Granz "gave Oscar Peterson a Mercedes-Benz and he gave me a chronograph, a collector's item so rare it's like the Rolls Royce of watches. And in my home, there's a marvelous tapestry that came from him. Just like that. Norman doesn't waste time giving little presents."[12]

In mid-November, Congressman Adam Clayton Powell Jr. summoned Dizzy, who was performing at a Washington club with his own group, to his congressional offices and told him to bring his trumpet. He then conducted a press conference with Dizzy at his side and announced that he had obtained a commitment from the Eisenhower State Department to finance foreign goodwill tours by big bands led by Dizzy, Louis Armstrong, Count Basie, and Tito Puente. Dizzy's band would lead off.

The pioneer civil rights activist had been a congressman since 1945, and his seniority and his flamboyant energies had earned him considerable clout in the halls of government. He expounded on his initiative to a *Downbeat* reporter:

> I have been working on this plan since last July. The State Department has allotted $5,000,000 for an international cultural exchange. I have convinced them that instead of emphasizing ballet dancers and classical music, they can get real value out of spending the vast majority of the money on jazz and other Americana such as folk music, mambos, spirituals, American Indian dancers, Hawaiian music, and so forth.[13]

The media followed Dizzy across the street to the steps of the Capitol, where the celebratory cadenza he blew made it to the CBS-TV national news roundup that night.

The moment he returned to New York, Dizzy began planning for his new role as a goodwill ambassador.

GOODWILL AMBASSADOR ²⁷

DIZZY'S JUNKET HAD TWO STRONG COLD WAR SUBTEXTS: first, the U.S. government wanted to demonstrate that it celebrated the cultural achievements of its people of color during a period of increasing racial turmoil. And it also wished to show that American artists of color could work harmoniously with whites. Accordingly, the band that Dizzy put together comprised black and white Christians and a Jew; it also included two women, trombonist/arranger Melba Liston and singer Dottie Saulter. In addition to political correctness, Dizzy sought musical excellence; he later judged the 1956 group as the finest big band he had ever led.

The jazz musician was a Johnny-come-lately to the cold war; Congressman Powell was boosting him onto a bandwagon that already included classical orchestras, a professional basketball team, opera companies, and literary lions such as William

Faulkner. The cultural historian Carol Polsgrove has commented on Faulkner's role: "Winning the Nobel Prize in 1950 had made him a public figure, internationally known and traveling abroad as a representative of his country. Like the jazz bands that the State Department sent around to show that Negroes did have a place in American culture, Faulkner was sent around to show that all white southerners were not bigoted; some could even write."[1] On his own State Department tour in September 1955, Faulkner commented on the Emmett Till lynching and put it squarely in a cold war context: "The white man can no longer afford, he simply does not dare, to commit acts which the other three-fourths of the human race can challenge him for."[2]

Dizzy was not as sanguine as Faulkner about what the white man might dare to do.

The State Department decided in January that, between late March and mid-May, Dizzy's band would perform in India and, in succession, five Muslim countries (Iran, Pakistan, Lebanon, Syria, and Turkey), a rogue Communist state (Tito's Yugoslavia), and Greece. Bookings were handled by a private organization, and the U.S. government agreed to absorb any losses generated by the performances (in this case, they amounted to $92,500—roughly $520,000 in 2004 dollars).

The State Department schedule presented Dizzy with a serious problem; he was committed to a JATP European tour from February 18 to March 15, a crucial organizing period for his band. His solution: hire the precocious twenty-two-year-old arranger/trumpeter Quincy Jones to whip the unit into shape. Jones had impressed Dizzy when he assisted him with the production of a couple of Granz big band albums in 1954 and 1955. The young man was intelligent, a master of bebop and swing arranging, and, above all, dependable.

Dizzy knew that big band economics dictated that he would have few other opportunities to organize an orchestra at someone else's expense, and he was determined on this occasion to create a world-class aggregation. By the time he departed for Europe on February 15, he knew that he and Jones had done so. Everyone could swing with power in the ensembles, and saxophonists Billy

Mitchell and Phil Woods, trumpeter Joe Gordon, drummer Charli Persip, pianist Walter Davis Jr., and trombonists Melba Liston and Frank Rehak could improvise with both skill and imagination. As a visual flourish, Dizzy ordered forty-five-degree upswept horns for the four-man trumpet section.

After Dizzy left, Jones rehearsed the group relentlessly and spruced up Dizzy's book of arrangements. He reworked several older charts, wrote three himself, and commissioned new ones from Liston and another band member, saxophonist Ernie Wilkins.

The visit to India was canceled when that country decided not to align itself with either cold war bloc, and the first concert was rescheduled for Abadan in Iran with the shah and his sister in attendance.

Dizzy left it to Lorraine to fend off State Department bureaucrats who wanted him to return to the United States for a "briefing." He knew that they would lay out for him the official line on U.S. racism, and he was sure that he knew more about that subject than an entire cadre of government functionaries.

Lorraine had felt a spiritual disquiet during the mid-1950s and had turned, with Dizzy's support, toward the Roman Catholic Church for solace. A source of strength to her during this period was Ada Beatrice Queen Victoria Louise Smith (known as Bricktop because of her red hair), who had become a staunch member of the faith after her conversion to Catholicism in 1943.

A black, light-skinned native of West Virginia who had become a singer and a protégé of Cole Porter, Bricktop ran the most celebrated café in Paris from 1926 to 1939. The Prince of Wales took private Charleston lessons from her, Josephine Baker benefitted from her largesse, T. S. Eliot wrote a couplet to celebrate her birthday, Porter composed the song "Miss Otis Regrets" for her, and F. Scott Fitzgerald boasted, "My greatest claim to fame is that I discovered Bricktop before Cole Porter." She became friendly with the Gillespies during World War II when she landed in New York after fleeing the Nazis.

Bricktop was running a successful club in Rome in 1956, and, after the JATP tour ended, Dizzy visited her there as he waited to meet the plane that would carry the State Department band to the Middle East. She pressed him to encourage Lorraine's exploration of Catholicism, and she gave him a rosary blessed by the pope for her.

Lorraine and the band arrived in Rome on March 24 to be greeted by Dizzy performing the old love song "Sweet Lorraine" on the airport tarmac. They soon took off for Abadan and arrived, in the prejet age, twenty-nine hours after their departure from New York.

Dizzy and the other musicians at first resented the presence of Marshall Stearns, an English professor and jazz scholar hired ostensibly to supplement the concerts with lectures on jazz history. They believed that, as Quincy Jones has written, "the State Department had sent him along as the great white father to make sure the brothers didn't get out of control."[3] They relaxed when they discovered that Stearns liked to party, would undertake onerous chores such as tracing lost luggage, and possessed a sophisticated knowledge of jazz. The Institute of Jazz Studies, which Stearns founded in 1952, is now the world's premier jazz research center; it is run by Rutgers University in Newark, New Jersey.

The band members experienced dysentery, bigotry from State Department employees, a menagerie of insects, forty-eight-hour stretches in hundred-degree heat without showers, and jolting treks over primitive terrain, but their morale never wavered. The musicians felt proud about their historic mission for jazz, and their spirits were constantly elevated by the terrific music they were producing.

The group presented a gospel/Dixieland/swing/bebop history of jazz in the first half of its program and performed its own repertoire during the second. Audiences almost always followed an arc from confused ignorance to foot-tapping enthusiasm. A *Pittsburgh Courier* writer, reporting from Abadan, described this process:

> Most of the Moslem audience had never heard this strange music before . . . then a miracle began to unfold. These Arabs, who were completely ignorant of what jazz was and how to act at a jazz concert, started to catch the beat, awkwardly clapping in time to the music. Soon whistles and screams reached the stage. By intermission . . . the theater was as hot as any American spot where Dizzy performed for long-standing fans.[4]

Dizzy proved to be a near-perfect ambassador of goodwill. Never diluting the quality of his music, he was, by turns, enthusiastic about teaching jazz, hostile to pretension, encouraging to local musicians (including a snake charmer), comedic, and eager to mix with his hosts at every social level. The egalitarian instincts bred into the boy from Cheraw always drew him to the people in the streets and the hovels, and the international media portrayed him as the virtuoso who hobnobbed with shahs, presidents, ambassadors, and emirs and, at the same time, was the champion of the common man. He surprised and pleased the State Department when he drew favorable headlines worldwide for his populist actions in Pakistan, Turkey, Syria, and Greece.

When he realized in Karachi, Pakistan, that a concert was not sold out because the tickets were priced too high, he grabbed hundreds of them from the box office and gave them away in a nearby park. He was furious in Ankara, Turkey, when he realized that the audience for a concert on the spacious U.S. embassy grounds was limited to the well-to-do while a raffish crowd pressed eagerly against the gates. He told the ambassador that he would not perform until the crowd was allowed to enter, arguing vociferously that America already had the support of the elites and that it should be trying to win over the poorer people. He won the day, and the crowd poured in and ate all the refreshments before they loudly cheered the performance.

Arif Mardin, a Turkish composer and arranger, has called his encounter with Dizzy in Istanbul "the biggest event of my life." Mardin never intended to pursue a musical career until he impressed Dizzy with a composition, and Dizzy had the band perform it in concert. Soon after, Mardin became the first recipient of a Quincy Jones scholarship at the Berklee School of Music in Boston. From there, Mardin went on to an outstanding career as a producer and composer for Aretha Franklin, Barbra Streisand, Whitney Houston, Diana Ross, Willie Nelson, the Bee Gees, and others; he has garnered six Grammy Awards in the process.

Dizzy was performing at a late afternoon concert in Damascus, Syria, during the season of Ramadan, a time when religious Muslims fast until sundown every day. The moment he saw the sun dip below the horizon, he yelled "food" and stopped the music, and the audience headed for a buffet where they supped until he called them back for the completion of the performance.

Dizzy's most spectacular goodwill triumph occurred in Greece. Many Greeks were angry with America for its lukewarm attitude toward their struggle against Turkey for control of Cyprus, and as the band flew into Athens, Dizzy received word that rioting students had just stoned the offices of the U.S. Information Service.

Officials considered canceling the band's first concert, which was for students only, but Dizzy told them he wanted to proceed. The government people need not have worried. The audience went wild over Dizzy and his music. They drowned out the band with their cheers, danced in the aisles with the policemen who were there to ensure order, and chanted Dizzy's name as they carried him home on their shoulders and blocked traffic for almost an hour.

The publicity generated by the tour's triumphs led to nine weeks of solid bookings for what Dizzy called the "State Department" band starting with a Birdland gig three days after the group returned to New York on May 15, 1956. It also led the musicians into a studio on June 6, where they recorded seventeen numbers for Norman Granz.

After Edward R. Murrow discussed the tour with Dizzy on his prime-time *Person to Person* TV show and members of the American establishment press, such as the *New York Times*, the *Saturday Review*, and the *New York Herald Tribune*, trumpeted Dizzy's diplomatic successes, the State Department and President Eisenhower took notice. The president invited the band to perform at the annual White House Correspondents Dinner, and he honored Dizzy there with a plaque. More important, he authorized another goodwill tour, this time to South America, during July and August. Dizzy made only one change in his lineup as he headed south; Benny Golson replaced Ernie Wilkins on tenor saxophone.

Dizzy was eager to break in a new Ampex 600 tape recorder, and he asked Dave Usher to assume the role of engineer and make live recordings of the band during the tour. Dave, who braved the wrath of his wife and father to leave work for the four-week trip, was issued credentials by the State Department as a public information officer and lugged the bulky equipment from country to country in two pieces of Samsonite luggage.

Dizzy couldn't release the recordings on his own because he was under contract to Norman Granz, but he hoped to sell them to Granz when he returned. After forty-four years of indifference, Granz approved their release by Usher in the year 2000.

The result is two hours and forty minutes of music on three CDs that, together with the seventeen Granz tracks recorded in June 1956, define the output of the big band that Dizzy considered his best. The Usher CDs also offer a fascinating musical bonus—Dizzy sitting in with a tango orchestra in Argentina and a samba group in Brazil. The band also visited Ecuador and Uruguay on the tour, which ran from July 25 to August 17 and duplicated the artistic and diplomatic successes of the Middle Eastern trip.

On the flight southward, Dizzy held his own in a chess game with fellow cold warrior Secretary of State John Foster Dulles, while Father Theodore Hesburgh, the president of Notre Dame University, kibitzed.

The only casualty of the trip was trumpeter Joe Gordon, who was forced to head home from Ecuador because he could not find enough heroin to feed his habit.

One incident blemished the atmosphere of good feeling surrounding the musicians. Because the Savoy Hotel in Buenos Aires refused accommodation to the band's black members, the entire group was forced to find lodgings elsewhere. The story received worldwide exposure and caused the Argentine president to issue a formal apology and to punish the hotel with a fine. The visit to Buenos Aires marked the beginning of Dizzy's friendship with one of his leading collaborators, Lalo Schifrin.

The son of the concertmaster of the Buenos Aires Philharmonic, Schifrin is a musical polymath. He routinely dashes off scores to major movies such as *Cool Hand Luke*, *Bullitt*, *Dirty Harry*, *The Amityville Horror*, *Mission Impossible*, and *Rush Hour*; he conducts the London Philharmonic in classical pieces he has written; and, as a pianist, he leads jazz groups at important clubs such as New York's Blue Note. He has won four Grammys.

Schifrin remembered his first encounter with Dizzy when he was the twenty-four-year-old leader of a radio jazz band:

> When I heard for the first time Dizzy and Bird, I was knocked out. It was like a religious conversion. . . . For Dizzy's week in Buenos Aires, I cancel everything. When the stage opened, it was almost like destiny for me. . . .
>
> We played at a reception they gave for Dizzy in a nightclub, and Dizzy came to me and asked, "Did you write this chart?" When I answered "Yes," he replied, "Would you like to come to the States and write for me?" I thought he was joking, but I said, "Of course."
>
> Many things intervened. But four years later I answered his invitation and came to him in Corona, New York.[5]

As Dave Usher remembered, a man who became an important religious adviser to Lorraine turned up one afternoon in a hotel corridor in Buenos Aires:

> The corridor is like a rush hour subway car because everybody is trying to get a piece of Dizzy. Along comes this tall, redheaded priest with an Adam's apple, Father John Crowley. He's from a mission church outside of Boston.
>
> He says, "I'm a Redemptionist stationed in Paraguay. I heard on the radio about you people playing here, and I came over to hear Dizzy. I used to play jazz saxophone." I brought him in to meet Dizzy and Lorraine, and she really perked up when she met him.
>
> Before, she mostly stayed in her room; now she started going out with Crowley and us. He wrangled a leave of absence to travel with us up to Brazil, and they had many discussions; he became a kind of spiritual guide.[6]

Crowley urged Lorraine to move boldly toward becoming a Catholic and recommended that she take formal training for entry into the church. She took his advice when she returned to New York and began catechism study with a brilliant Jesuit, Anthony Woods.

Dizzy was delighted to explore tango music in Argentina and the samba in Brazil, because he recognized that they shared the same foundation as America's jazz and Cuba's rumba—the African rhythms brought by slaves. Before recording with an Argentine tango orchestra, he told an interviewer: "In jazz, we try to exploit the whole harmonic range of European music, but we must remember that the basis of the music is the rhythm. If we lose sight of the rhythm, the foundation of what we're doing, then the building topples. . . . Jazz and tango music are a perfect combination because they come from the same source. Tango music can progress as long as they don't lose the basic spirit of the rhythm."[7]

On the four tunes recorded by Usher with the Argentinians, Dizzy sounds as if he had been performing tangos all his life. In addition to falling unerringly into the proper rhythmic groove, he creates brooding improvised melodies that embody an Argentine definition of the tango as "a sad feeling that can be danced."

The high point of the trip for Dizzy was a night of percussion and dance at a samba "school" in the hills behind the wretched favelas, the slums of Rio de Janeiro. The "schools" were neighborhood organizations that were judged on dancing, music, and costumes in fierce competitions at Mardi Gras time, Carnevale.

The rollicking samba beat and the stately tango rhythm, worlds apart, illustrated for Dizzy the richness of the African rhythmic heritage. He remembered:

This was my first visit to the Latin countries. I knew Cuban music, but I'd never been to Cuba. And I'd just learned the tango in Argentina.

This night of samba was the real thing, a ritual straight out of Africa. Almost everyone was black. They set me and Lorraine up in sedan chairs like royalty, and they roasted a goat on a spit, and about a dozen percussionists played different instruments as the people danced. No horns. The rhythms created the melodies.

Wooee! It never stopped. Sometimes they dance for ten hours straight. It was like a revival meeting down in South Carolina. Singing and shouting. Bodies twisted around by the rhythms.

It was deeply spiritual for me to dance and perform with them. It showed me the unity in diversity of our music, how the music of different cultures can meld and still remain unique.[8]

A couple of days later, Dizzy and Usher heard a samba band rehearsing as they walked through the garden of their Rio hotel. Without saying a word, they smiled at each other, and Dizzy headed to his room for his trumpet as Usher retrieved the Ampex recorder. Dizzy had never met the musicians before, but they knew who he was, and they enthusiastically welcomed him to jam with them. The session produced two outstanding recordings. Dizzy again negotiated a new idiom as if he were native to it, roaring through a harmonically sophisticated samba tune and performing a delicate ballad duet with a flautist.

Riches abound among the thirty-nine big band tracks recorded for Granz and Usher: Melba Liston's swinging, sensuous chart for "Annie's Dance" and her lusty solo over her own arrangement of "My Reverie"; Charli Persip's magnificent drumming throughout; Phil Woods's haunting bebop interpretation of Jerome Kern's "Yesterdays" and his jaunty ride on "Groovin' High"; the roaring strength of the brass and reed sections rolling through "Cool Breeze," "Dizzy's Blues," "Annie's Dance," and "Tin Tin Deo"; Billy Mitchell brawny and boppish on "Groovin' for Nat"; Quincy Jones' skillful reworking for big band of Tadd Dameron's small-group arrangement of "I Can't Get Started"; Benny Golson soulful on "A Night in Tunisia."

Dizzy played inspired trumpet on almost every chorus, and he was on fire during two South American renditions of "A Night in Tunisia" (a comparison of these solos and Joe Gordon's on the Granz studio version illustrates the difference between genius and great talent) and on "Groovin' High," "Cool Breeze," and "Tour de Force."

Dizzy was in high spirits when he returned from South America in late August. His artistic and diplomatic success at age thirty-eight reinforced his confidence in his public persona—part surpassing artist, part comedian, part intuitive politician. After the great burst of creativity that gave birth to two musical revolutions between 1938 and 1949, he had experienced the lean years, 1950 to 1953, when his artistic opportunities were constricted by economic circumstance and his confidence was buffeted.

His fortunes revived when he took vigorous advantage of the

opportunities provided by Norman Granz and Adam Clayton Powell Jr. They enabled him to cease burning precious energies scuffling for gigs and to use them again in high artistic endeavor. Granz provided financial security, a near carte blanche in the recording studio, and the chance to work consistently with world-class musicians. Powell gave Dizzy a magnificent band and a chance to star under a bright spotlight on a world stage. He would perform comfortably on that stage for the remaining thirty-five years of his career.

Dizzy put the band on hold from September 15 to late October as he joined JATP on a junket that marked the tour debut of both Stan Getz and the Modern Jazz Quartet. Granz made Dizzy part of a concert team with Getz and Sonny Stitt, and he was so excited by the nightly high-energy jousting of the horn men that he brought them into a Los Angeles studio on October 16, 1956—immediately after the tour ended—to create the album *For Musicians Only*. An excellent bebop rhythm section—John Lewis, Herb Ellis, Ray Brown, and Stan Levey—provided powerful support to the horn players, who took all the solos.

As with Getz's first recorded encounter with Dizzy three years before, a feeling of intense competition pervaded the session. Stitt contributed strongly to the tension; he prided himself on being the fastest saxophone player in the world, and he pushed Getz hard as three of the four numbers were taken at Mach 2 tempos. Getz had learned a lot about high speed improvising since his previous recording with Dizzy, and, according to Levey, he surprised everyone when he matched Stitt and Dizzy with agile improvisations. The end result was a very satisfying all-out "blowing" session.

When the "State Department" band reconvened on November 1 for a gig at Birdland, Quincy Jones was no longer with it. He had accepted a lucrative arranging job, and the brilliant Lee Morgan had replaced him. Jones coveted a unique souvenir:

> When I left the band, I was dying to hold on to that special Dizzy trumpet with the upright bell that they'd given to the trumpet players, but Dizzy told me, "Naw, we need it for Lee." I thought he was pissed at me for leaving the band. We let it go and I moved on.

Not long after . . . there was a ring at the front door of my New York apartment on 92nd Street. I opened the door and there was no one there. Just next to the door there was a little plaid tote bag. . . . Inside was Dizzy Gillespie's original Martin trumpet in two separate pieces with "Diz" engraved on the bell bent to the sky, and a tiny note that said, "Q, one lick from the back, love, Birks." That was our running joke from the tour. We'd meet so many fine women that all you wanted to do was to dream about giving them one lick on the back of the neck because sometimes in the Middle East, that's as close as you could ever get.

I ran down into the street to thank that crazy, talented, soulful Geechie sapsucker, but just like a leprechaun, he was gone.[9]

28
SMALL GROUPS AGAIN

Dizzy took a limited risk in November 1956 and kept the big band together without government subsidy, because the momentum created by the State Department tours had resulted in six months of decent bookings. He also improved the group by adding three excellent soloists: Lee Morgan, the pungent trombonist Al Grey, and Wynton Kelly, an imaginative pianist with whom he had performed briefly in 1952. (Kelly was a close friend of the Marsalis family, and Wynton Marsalis is named for him.)

The sound of the "State Department" band is defined by Granz recording sessions in April and July 1957 that produced fourteen tracks; most of them were released on an album entitled *Birks Works*. The tune "That's All" introduced Morgan while he was polishing his abundant natural talents under Dizzy's tutelage. In his solo, he used a virtuoso command of the horn, a crisp but soulful tone, and a deep blues sensibility to create a statement of electric urgency. The album is also notable for a rendition of "Over the Rainbow" that became a jukebox hit, three excellent improvisations by Kelly, the precision and power of the ensembles behind solos by Dizzy and Benny Golson, and two beautiful Golson tunes that have become part of the jazz canon, "Whisper Not" and "I Remember Clifford."

When they returned from South America, Dizzy and Lorraine were deeply disturbed to find Mary Lou Williams, their close friend of fifteen years, despondent and broke. Born in 1910, Mary Lou was one of the few members of the swing old guard to welcome bebop, and during the early 1940s she became a den mother to Dizzy, Monk, Bud Powell, Sarah Vaughan, Tadd Dameron, and other aspiring modernists.

Putting singers such as Holiday, Fitzgerald, and Vaughan to one side in a unique category, Mary Lou was undoubtedly the premiere jazz woman of the twentieth century. No one else has come close to equaling the body of work she left as a pianist, a composer of both popular songs and extended works, and an arranger.

A debilitating anguish, a frightening emptiness of the spirit, had gripped her for two years and left her an emotional and financial basket case by early 1957. She had stopped performing and spent her days either praying at a local Catholic church or helping the strung-out and the destitute who had turned her apartment into a homeless shelter; sometimes she and her charges subsisted on apples and water. The Gillespies, Baroness de Koenigswarter, and a few other friends gave her money, and Lorraine would drop by every few days with a basket of food.

Dizzy and Lorraine helped in other ways. He coaxed her into returning to music and joining him for an April gig in Atlantic City, and to everyone's delight, she performed with undiminished skill. He also hired her to join his big band at the Newport Jazz Festival in July, where they would perform three movements of her *Zodiac Suite* and be recorded by Norman Granz. The suite, introduced in 1945, fused jazz and classical elements, and Dizzy commissioned Melba Liston to refashion the three pieces for a large jazz ensemble.

Lorraine provided spiritual support by introducing Mary Lou to Father John Crowley when he came through New York on his way from Paraguay to a new assignment in Boston. Mary Lou's biographer has commented on his influence:

> [The] meeting was highly significant. At last Mary had met some-
> one she would listen to: a priest who loved jazz. Crowley was able
> to temper her extremism. Concerned for her safety, he warned her
> not to take in any more people addled by narcotics or alcohol. . . .
> "Crowley told me to get back to my work and offer this up as a
> prayer for others," Mary remembered.[1]

Soon after, former *Metronome* editor Barry Ulanov, a convert from Judaism to Catholicism, introduced Mary Lou to Father Anthony Woods, Lorraine's catechism instructor. At Ulanov's urging and Lorraine's, she joined his classes. The two women progressed rapidly, and on May 9, 1957, they were baptized as Catholics. Father Woods and Bricktop, who flew in from Rome for the occasion, served as Lorraine's godfather and godmother, and Ulanov and his wife performed these roles for Mary Lou.

Bookings for the big band began to shrink during the spring of 1957, and as Dizzy compared the tepid American reaction to his music with his triumphant reception overseas, he became angry. He found an outlet for his displeasure by writing an article titled "Jazz Is Too Good for Americans" that appeared in the June *Esquire*. Passing over the fact that his overseas tours would have been serious commercial failures if it were not for U.S. government subsidy, he vented:

> Jazz has never really been accepted as an art form by the people of
> my own country. The great mass of the American people still con-
> sider jazz a lowbrow music. . . .
>   When my band toured Asia, the Middle East, the Balkans, and
> South America last year, I became more and more concerned with
> the problem. In far-off countries . . . the people have a healthier
> attitude toward jazz than we do. They are interested in jazz for jazz
> sake. They listen to it for its musical message, not its sociological

implications. And their response to the jazz they have heard in recent years is tremendous. . . .

The folk music of America today is a mongrel made up of
strains of Presley, Liberace, Tennessee Ernie [Ford], [Guy] Lombardo, and Sh Boom.[2]

His anger carried over to Louis Armstrong, whom he criticized for remaining silent during America's intensifying civil
rights struggle. Referring to him as "Louis Armstrong with
whom I violently disagree because of his Uncle Tom–like sub-
servience," Dizzy admonished, "Nowadays no cat should be a
Tom."[3]

Armstrong finally spoke out a few months later when he attacked President Eisenhower for not protecting the black children
attempting to integrate a school in Little Rock, Arkansas. He and
Dizzy became reconciled soon after, and frequently partied at
each other's homes, which were only a block apart in Corona.

Dizzy and Lorraine wanted Mary Lou to look elegant for her
Newport Jazz Festival appearance, and, as July approached, they
gave her a mink stole, a gown, and a fancy watch for the occasion.
Father Crowley telephoned every day, exhorting her to practice,
and she rehearsed diligently with the band.

The 1957 Newport events drew fifty thousand spectators, up
from eleven thousand in 1954, the inaugural year—a prime indi-
cator of the burgeoning success of the festival movement. Dizzy
and Mary Lou appeared before an enthusiastic, standing-room-
only Saturday-night crowd, and she gave an excellent performance. *Downbeat* reported that she was "inspired," and Gary
Giddins praised her use of "dissonances, dynamics, wit, subtle
quotations, liveliness of ideas and clarity of articulation."[4]

The concert was also remembered for Lee Morgan's scorching
solo on a "A Night in Tunisia" and Melba Liston's most celebrated
improvisation, a vibrant interpretation of "Cool Breeze," which
was mentioned in her *New York Times* obituary in 1999.

The "State Department" big band stumbled through the balance of 1957. After a triumphant appearance before twenty-four
thousand people at the New York Jazz Festival in August, revenues

dwindled dramatically, and at one point, Dizzy could pay his musicians only thirty dollars per week. He disbanded after a New Year's Eve gig. Meeting a payroll for seventeen musicians was far more difficult than meeting one for five, and he returned in 1958 to a small-group format.

The core of his quintet for the next eighteen months was the rhythm section—bluesy pianist Junior Mance, bebop drummer Lex Humphries, and rock-solid interchangeable bassists Sam Jones and Art Davis. The second horn chair was occupied first by Sonny Stitt and then by flautist/guitarist Les Spann.

Dizzy closed out 1957 with one of the greatest albums of his career, a Granz recording that brought him and Stitt together with tenor saxophone giant Sonny Rollins. This album marked for Dizzy the start of an extremely fertile artistic period that ran well into the 1960s.

Rollins, born in 1930, had been a major presence since the early 1950s when he recorded with Miles Davis, Charlie Parker, the Modern Jazz Quartet, and Thelonious Monk; by the time he teamed up with Dizzy, he had already created a masterpiece, "Blue 7," in a quartet with Max Roach. Rollins has exhibited remarkable staying power, and after five decades, he stands as the outstanding jazz performer of the early twenty-first century.

On *The Sonny Rollins/Sonny Stitt Sessions*, Dizzy performed two tunes with Rollins, two with Stitt, and four with both saxophonists. The atmosphere was intensely competitive, and Dizzy brought all his skills and passions to bear as he responded to the challenges posed by his colleagues. The recordings are greatly strengthened by the presence of an excellent bebop rhythm section—drummer Charli Persip and pianist Ray Bryant from Dizzy's big band and Bryant's brother Tommy on bass.

Four of the tracks rank at the highest level of the Gillespie canon. Two of them pair him with Rollins: "Wheatleigh Hall," named by Dizzy for the vast, ornate mansion that served as a dormitory at the Lenox School of Jazz, and "Sumphin'," a blues. The others involve Dizzy with both saxophone players: "The Eternal Triangle," an "I Got Rhythm" derivative written by Stitt, and "I Know That You Know," a bouncy 1926 love song.

Stitt was a great bebop player, but for Rollins bebop was only one strand in a distinctive style based on muscular melodic invention, transparent passion, and a remarkable rhythmic acuity. All three characteristics are on display in his "Wheatleigh Hall" solo, a powerful construct of laid back phrases, knifelike thrusts, and robust asides. Dizzy answers with an improvisation where raw emotion and technical acumen are partners in the creation of a breathtaking melodic statement. Rollins gets "down in the alley" in his sensual chorus on "Sumphin'," and Dizzy responds with one of his greatest blues solos on record.

The energy generated by "The Eternal Triangle" threatens to burn holes in the speakers of CD players as all three horn men unfurl ferocious solos. Rollins opens "I Know That You Know" with a stark, slashing chorus accompanied only by Ray Bryant hitting a chord on every fourth beat. The critic Richard Palmer believes that this solo "remains arguably the most exciting 80 seconds of tenor [saxophone] on record." Energetic responses by Stitt and Dizzy come close to Rollins's brilliance but cannot match it.

As Dizzy gigged with his quintet in early 1958, he was disappointed to hear that an anemic 1957 season had caused Norman Granz to close down his JATP tours in the United States. Granz cited three reasons for his decision: the rise of Elvis Presley and rock and roll, the staggering growth of television, and the proliferation of jazz festivals.

The advent of Presley in 1956 began a dark fifteen-year period during which rock and roll took from jazz much of the youthful audience that had sustained it during the post–World War II era. Young people did not return until the early 1970s when they finally sought a sophisticated antidote to rock and roll's simpler rhetoric.

The 1950s were the years when television ascended to its dominant position in American entertainment as the percentage of households with sets rocketed from 22 percent in 1951 to 56 percent in 1954 and 83 percent in 1958.[5] To Granz's chagrin, the U.S. public in great numbers was seduced away from concert halls by _I Love Lucy, The Friday Night Fights, Gunsmoke_, and other no-cost fare.

The festivals, two to four days in length, provided a much richer experience than Granz could offer. They usually took place outdoors in attractive settings such as Montreux in the shadow of the Alps on Lake Geneva and in seacoast resort towns like Newport and Monterey; many fans, relishing the relaxed holiday ambience, would build mini-vacations around them.

In contrast to a Granz concert, which usually spotlighted ten or twelve musicians, Newport in 1957 provided a four-day aural feast featuring more than two hundred performers. The festival showcased everything from Dixieland to avant-garde pianist Cecil Taylor, and an array of stars shone in between. Among them were Louis Armstrong; the stylistically varied big bands of Basie, Dizzy (with Mary Lou Williams), and Kenton; four great jazz singers—Ella Fitzgerald, Billie Holiday, Sarah Vaughan, and Carmen McRae; the gospel queen Mahalia Jackson; JATP veterans Lester Young, Roy Eldridge, Coleman Hawkins, Jo Jones, and the Oscar Peterson Trio; master trombonist Jack Teagarden; rising stars Cannonball Adderley, Gerry Mulligan, Gigi Gryce, and Donald Byrd; and the outstanding pianists Dave Brubeck, Erroll Garner, Horace Silver, and George Shearing and their groups.

The market forces that closed down JATP in America were not nearly as strong in Europe, and Granz continued with his tours there through 1967.

Dizzy easily made up for his lost Granz touring income by becoming a mainstay of the festival circuit, where he was delighted to find that the relaxed atmosphere and the loose format allowed his uninhibited spirit to thrive. *Metronome*'s correspondent took note of this at Monterey's inaugural festival in September 1958: "Contributing especially to the general good humor was Dizzy Gillespie. Diz, with his little hat, was everywhere, all the time. He gagged on stage, took photographs in the audience, played trumpet and maraccas with other groups, until folks laughingly exclaimed: 'It's Dizzy's festival.'"[6] *Downbeat*'s writer corroborated these observations:

The event truly was A Dizzy Weekend. Dizzy just took over—lock, stock, and barrel. More importantly the funnyman-trumpeter endeared himself to most of the 25,000 persons who came to listen and watch. . . . There are two incidents which telescope the event: Max Roach and composer Peter Phillips emotionally embracing after performance of Phillips' work for the drummer, and the sight of Dizzy Gillespie playing trumpet for a child-in-arms to stop her crying. A Dizzy Weekend? You Betcha![7]

Dizzy had begun to explore the television medium in earnest during the late 1950s, and, on January 7, 1959, he made his first appearance on a major program, *The Timex All-Star Jazz Show* hosted by Jackie Gleason on CBS. It marked his only performance with Louis Armstrong, and the two showmen enjoyed themselves as they played sterling trumpet and mugged through the novelty number "Umbrella Man."

During February, Dizzy and his quintet (with the help of a conga player on three numbers) recorded sixteen laid-back tracks that Granz released in two albums, *Have Trumpet, Will Excite* and *The Ebullient Mr. Gillespie*. Dizzy created a series of beautifully crafted ruminations and Junior Mance contributed a couple of memorable solos, but the albums were emotionally flat. A principal reason was the presence of Les Spann; he could spin out well-constructed bebop lines, but he lacked the energy to ignite a performance. He was replaced by the saxophonist/flautist Leo Wright six months later.

Whitney Balliett, in an article that dealt with *Have Trumpet, Will Excite* and two other recordings, found Dizzy at a peak:

Gillespie, at forty-two, an age at which a good many jazz musicians begin falling back on a card file of phrases—their own and others'—built up through the years, is playing with far more subtlety and invention than [at] any time in his past. . . .

His tone has softened, taking on a kind of middle-age spread; his baroque flow of notes has been judiciously edited; his tailless phrase endings seem less abrupt; and he now cunningly employs a masterly, restless sense of dynamics that mixes out-and-out blasts with whispers, upper-register shrieks with soft, plaintive asides. However, his remarkable intensity, together with his built-in rhythmic governor, which still sets the basic course of his solos, remains unchanged.[8]

During 1959, revolutionary ideas that had long been simmer-
ing in the jazz community exploded with great force. Fifteen
years after the triumph of the sophisticated chordal aesthetic of
bebop, a small but influential group of artists was finding that the
use of chords as the basis for improvisation no longer provided
sufficient stimulus for their imaginations.

For them, the chords had become overly familiar signposts on
roads that had been traveled too often. A veteran like Miles Davis
might easily by 1959 have performed "All the Things You Are"
three hundred times, and on each occasion, he would have found
the tune's harmonic movement unvarying. When encountered for
the three-hundredth time, such a chord sequence had, for some,
become restrictive and boring.

The most important improvisers who grappled with this problem of imaginative stimulus were Davis, Ornette Coleman, John
Coltrane, Charles Mingus, Gil Evans, Cecil Taylor, and Lennie
Tristano. Coleman and Coltrane had the greatest immediate impact, and Coleman's approach, which came to be called "free jazz,"
was the most radical.

Coleman simply did away with all harmonic structures; his improvisations grew from motif to motif without any harmonic ref-
erence points. The critic Ekkehard Jost has described the process:

Coleman invents, as he goes along, [motifs] independent of the
theme and continues to develop them. In this way—independently
of the chord progressions, let it be noted—an inner cohesion is
created that is comparable to the stream of consciousness in Joyce
or the "automatic writing" of the surrealists; one idea grows from
another, is reformulated, and leads to yet another new idea.[9]

Coleman's concepts challenged the improviser as had no jazz
aesthetic before or since. In his music, the improviser has nothing
to fall back on but his own ability to create—continuously—new
melodies out of thin air. Coleman, a prodigious maker of song,
was up to the task, but few others have been able to match his
imaginative flights. He came to prominence during a November
1959 quartet engagement at a New York club called the Five Spot,

and during 1959 and 1960 made four groundbreaking albums cul-
minating in *Free Jazz*, which gave his aesthetic a name.

During the same period, Miles Davis and John Coltrane pioneered an approach to improvisation that was considerably less
radical than Coleman's. They staked out a middle ground by using
modes as the basis of their system. A mode is a scale, a set of
notes played in sequence—for example, the five black notes on
the piano keyboard. Modes, which have been used for centuries in
Western music and provide the structure for forms such as the
Gregorian chant, were suggested as a basis for jazz improvisation
by George Russell, Dizzy's former colleague, as early as 1953.

The key to Russell's concept was that the notes of the mode or
scale would dictate the harmony for extended periods—sixteen
bars, for example. If the improviser were to choose the five black
keys as his mode, he would then be free to create any melodies he
wanted from the mode notes throughout the sixteen-bar segment.
Instead of eight or sixteen or even more chords in sequence defining his choices, he would base his improvisation on what was essentially one large chord made up of the five black notes.

Miles Davis, who became the first major jazz musician to be
influenced by Russell's ideas, said this about his fascination with
scales (or modes):

> When Gil Evans wrote the arrangement of "I Love You, Porgy," he
> only wrote a scale for me to play, no chords. . . . When you go this
> way, you can go on forever. You don't have to worry about chord
> changes and you can do more with the line. It becomes a challenge
> to see how melodically inventive you are.
>
> When you're based on chords, you know at the end of 32 bars
> that the chords have run out and there's nothing to do but repeat
> what you've just done—with variations. I think a movement in jazz
> is beginning away from the conventional string of chords and a re-
> turn to emphasis on melodic rather than harmonic variations.[10]

Davis created five selections for the first all-modal jazz album,
Kind of Blue, recorded in March and April 1959. The title tune
consists of five modes, each played as long as the soloist wishes;

the second employs one mode in ten-bar sequences, a third uses two of them over thirty-two bars, and the fourth and fifth use modes based on blues scales.

For *Kind of Blue,* Davis recruited a sextet comprising saxophonists Cannonball Adderley and John Coltrane, bassist Paul Chambers, drummer Jimmy Cobb, and Bill Evans on piano for four tunes and Wynton Kelly for one. Adderley and Kelly were not entirely comfortable with the modal approach, but it inspired Davis, Coltrane, and Evans to a series of stunning, melodic statements.

The freshness and beauty of *Kind of Blue* hit the jazz world with great force, and soon many of the brightest young musicians were demanding to learn about the new creative approach; it attracted many more adherents than did Coleman's free jazz, because most of the younger artists felt a need for some degree of structure to undergird their improvising. *Kind of Blue* has become the all-time top-selling jazz album.

Davis was the most intellectually impatient of the jazz innovators, and for him modality was a step on a journey to further changes in harmony, form, and instrumentation during the 1960s and the 1970s. For Coltrane, however, modality released unprecedented creative forces and in a few short years made him a figure of historic importance. After making his first recorded modal statement with *Naima* in December 1959, Coltrane embarked on a thorough exploration of modal harmony that culminated in the epochal albums *My Favorite Things* in 1960 and *A Love Supreme* in 1964.

When the dust had settled, the end result of the aesthetic battles of the late 1950s and early 1960s was to broaden the resources available to the improviser. Since then, jazz musicians have been able to choose among the chordal, the modal, and the free as their imaginations dictate; some will even use all three approaches during a single set in a nightclub.

A decidedly unscientific survey of six top New York jazz clubs (including the Knitting Factory, a haven for free and modal performers) during 2004 showed that roughly 55 percent of the groups played bebop. More than four decades after *Kind of Blue* and *Free Jazz,* bebop was the contemporary mainstream, and the modal and free variants were important tributaries. In other

words, most early twenty-first-century jazz musicians find sufficient stimulus and nourishment in the structures pioneered by
Dizzy and the bebop innovators in the 1940s.

While aesthetic conflict boiled in the jazz community, racial
conflict continued to rage in the American polity. Mayor Russell
Bennett of Cheraw, however, was a member of a new breed of
southern politician who foresaw the eventual triumph of the civil
rights movement, and he cautiously pushed the racial envelope
with initiatives that would have been anathema a decade earlier.
One of them was to celebrate Dizzy's achievements with a "Dizzy
Gillespie Day" in early 1959 marked by two Cheraw firsts: an integrated parade and an integrated concert.

Dizzy initially believed that, in light of the fierce national civil
rights struggle, such a celebration might seem trivial, but the opportunity to bring a measure of integration to his hometown made
him change his mind. He scheduled his visit for March 7, 1959,
between quintet engagements in Florida and North Carolina.

The most important event of the day for Dizzy was not the
parade or the concert, but Dizzy's highly emotional meeting with
old James Powe at which Powe revealed to Dizzy that his great-
grandmother Nora, bought in Charleston to be a nanny to the
Powe children, was the daughter of a Yoruba chieftain. James's
narrative then led Dizzy to the profound and startling conclusion
that James and Dizzy's mother, Lottie, were cousins who shared a
grandfather, Dr. Thomas Powe, Cheraw's leading antebellum
slave owner.

Soon after, Dizzy bought a magnificent Yoruba robe and often
wore it in performance.

An atmosphere of calm prevailed as Dizzy enjoyed the parade
from an open convertible and gave a rousing concert at a local
high school. The facts that the only adult whites in the parade
were the mayor and his entourage and that several whites at the
concert covered their faces when a reporter from *Ebony* magazine
took photographs gave evidence that Cheraw still had a long way
to travel on the road to racial amity.

Lottie, who was living with a daughter in Springfield, Massachusetts, was diagnosed with throat cancer about the time of
"Dizzy Gillespie Day," and she weakened considerably while

Dizzy participated in a two-month Newport Jazz Festival tour of Europe during the autumn of 1959. He made it to her bedside a day before she died in mid-November and was convinced that she had held on until he got there. She was seventy-four.

No one could console Dizzy for several weeks as the pain of loss overwhelmed him. When his wounds began to heal, he emerged with a deeper understanding of the shortness of life and a determination to make the best of the time left to him: "When my mama passed away, I truly understood how short our time on earth is. I regretted the chunks of my life I had frittered away, and I committed myself to making what was the rest of my days count—both as a human being and as a musician. Achieving this has been difficult. You know human nature. You can't always live up to your ideals. But there are times when you do."[11]

Norman Granz, civil rights activist, record producer, and concert impresario, with Dizzy in 1955. Granz gave Dizzy's career a significant lift during the 1950s and again in the 1970s. *Metronome/Getty Images*

The 1956 "State Department" big band trumpet section—Joe Gordon, E. V. Perry, Dizzy, Bama Warwick, and Quincy Jones. Dizzy believed that this 1956 group, which toured the Middle East, Greece, and South America as goodwill ambassadors from the United States, was the greatest big band he ever led. *Herman Leonard Photography*

Mario Bauzá and Machito, giants of Afro-Cuban music, circa 1959. Among Bauzá's many contributions to Dizzy's success was providing the introduction to Chano Pozo. *Popsie Randolph/Frank Driggs Collection*

The great singer Sarah Vaughan in 1960. She loved Dizzy's music and performed with him many times. *Photograph by Chuck Stewart*

Lalo Schifrin, Dizzy's brilliant collaborator for three decades, in 2002. "The Gillespiana Suite," which Lalo wrote for Dizzy, is a jazz classic. *Lawrence Lucier/Getty Images*

Mike Longo, Dizzy's dear friend, who worked with him for twenty-seven years, in 1989. *Collection of Mike Longo*

President Carter, Dizzy, and Max Roach performing "Salt Peanuts" at the White House, 1978. *Courtesy of the Jimmy Carter Library and Museum*

Dizzy with Dave Usher, his friend and associate of four decades, strolling on the French Riviera, 1981. *Courtesy of Dave Usher*

Dizzy displays his renowned cheeks in 1981. *Charles "Whale" Lake*

Dizzy shares a happy moment with his protégé Jon Faddis in 1982. *Photograph by Carol Friedman*

Dizzy with old pals Bill Cosby and Whale Lake on the French Riviera in 1984.
Charles "Whale" Lake

Dizzy with Fidel
Castro in 1985.
Dizzy enjoyed ex-
ploring his African
heritage in Cuba.
*Frank Driggs Col-
lection*

Dizzy with Charlie Fishman, his business manager, during a 1989 trip to Nigeria. Fishman guided Dizzy's career from 1988 to 1992, a highly creative period. *Courtesy of Charles Fishman*

Arturo Sandoval, whom Dizzy helped defect from Cuba, blowing with his mentor in 1990. *Michael Wilderman/Jazz Visions*

Dizzy with Paquito D'Riviera, the brilliant Cuban reedman, in 1991. Paquito made outstanding contributions to Dizzy's bands for well over a decade. *Photograph by Dany Gignoux*

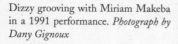

Dizzy grooving with Miriam Makeba in a 1991 performance. *Photograph by Dany Gignoux*

Jeanie Bryson, Dizzy's daughter, in 2004. *Courtesy of the author*

ENTER LALO **29**

Despite the advent of valid post-bebop jazz styles and the unimpeded growth of rock and roll, Dizzy managed to thrive during the early 1960s. He worked the festival circuit in the summer, toured Europe with JATP in the fall, and played a variety of lucrative club gigs and concerts during the rest of the year. A healthy cash flow enabled him to people his quintets with excellent musicians, and a fortuitous collaboration led him into fresh creative territory.

Dizzy received an important boost when Norman Granz singled him out for a promotion blitz with full-page ads in the trade publications and a giveaway campaign featuring five thousand copies of *A Portrait of Duke Ellington*, his February 1960 LP. When the offer was wildly oversubscribed, Granz changed course and sold the albums for a nominal charge of one dollar each.

Lalo Schifrin found it difficult to connect with Dizzy in New York during 1960:

I was calling him and he was out of town all the time. I thought Dizzy was trying to avoid me. I was shy and afraid that he would turn back on his word from Buenos Aires that he would work with me.

Finally I went to hear him at a club in the Village. He says, "Why didn't you call me?" I answer, "I called, but you were never home." Then, "Why don't you write something for me?" I said "OK," and in a few days I wrote the *Gillespiana Suite*.

It just exploded in my mind. Which is what people call inspiration. I had studied Dizzy's music and Dizzy's style, so the inspiration—which was instantaneous—came from Dizzy's idiom.

I sketched out all the themes, and I went to his house and played them for him. He asked, "How are you going to orchestrate this?" I said, "I hear a brass band plus the old jazz quintet with a saxophone, double the flute, and you yourself with a rhythm section. I surround the quintet with trumpets, trombones, and French horns and one tuba and Latin percussion. No saxophones except Leo Wright in the quintet."

So immediately, in front of me, he called Norman Granz and covered the phone and asked, "How long will it take you to orchestrate this?" "Three weeks." So he tells Norman, "One month from now, book two sessions. We are going to record this thing. It's a classic."

And as a bonus, he hired me for the quintet. Junior Mance was about to launch his own trio, and I replaced him at the piano. If Dizzy hadn't hired me, I might have gone back to Argentina, because I was becoming discouraged with my prospects in New York.[1]

Lalo's studio in Beverly Hills contains one major artifact, a large photo of Dizzy that sits on the piano. When I interviewed him, he pointed to the picture and said:

I have had many mentors but only one master—Dizzy. I had an almost religious conversion when as a youngster I heard his discs with Charlie Parker and working with him exposed me to a tremendous musical mind and spirit. What a thrill it was for me, twenty-eight years old, to walk into that studio for *Gillespiana* and to play my music with him and that superb band he had assembled.

People like Clark Terry, Gunther Schuller, Candido, Urbie Green. I felt like a pilgrim arrived in Mecca.[2]

The Gillespiana Suite, in five parts ("Prelude," "Blues," "Panamericana," "Africana," and "Toccata") was recorded on November 14 and 15, 1960. Gunther Schuller, who participated in the recording on French horn, has described Schifrin's goals for the work:

Schifrin wished to pay homage to the many facets of Dizzy's enormous musical talent. Lalo felt that it was not possible to do this in terms of some kind of "synthesis." He therefore resolved to write a work in which each movement would reflect a different aspect of Dizzy's personality, ranging from the melancholy "Blues" to the vigorous "Toccata," from allusions to Dizzy's African forebears to his interest in Latin American music.[3]

Schifrin chose to cast the suite as a *concerto grosso*, an eighteenth-century form in which a small group takes the role of concert soloist and interacts with a full orchestra that surrounds it. In this case, the small group—Dizzy, Lalo, Leo Wright, bassist Art Davis, drummer Chuck Lampkin—interacted with thirteen brass instruments and Candido and two other Latin percussionists.

Lalo fashioned a bold piece filled with memorable song and vivid colorations and rhythms. He used the brass masterfully, giving them intriguing melodies and countermelodies, playing their tonal textures skillfully against blizzards of Latin percussion, and using their deep sonorities for chordal punctuations. He even coaxed elephant shrieks from them in the "Africana" section.

And he invariably created dramatic settings for improvisations by himself and the other four members of the quintet. Dizzy soloed with both subtlety and passion and was particularly inspired during the last three sections in which Lalo undergirded him with Latin rhythms. His steamy improvisation drove the suite to a rousing climax over the roiling cadences of "Toccata."

Gillespiana received its public premiere in Paris in December during a JATP tour, and it was introduced to American audiences on March 3, 1961, first at Wesleyan University in northern Connecticut and then at Carnegie Hall at midnight.

Dizzy was resplendent in a raspberry tuxedo for the New York event, which ran for three hours. The concert featured Schifrin's treatments of Gillespie standards such as "Manteca," "Ool-Ya-Koo," "Con Alma," and "Things to Come" and showcased—in addition to the suite—two new compositions: "Kush," Dizzy's tone poem about an ancient black civilization that had flourished south of Egypt, and "Tunisian Fantasy," Lalo's brilliant variations on "A Night in Tunisia." Inspired by the freshness of Lalo's writing on "Tunisian Fantasy," Dizzy unfurled one of the most stirring and inventive solos of his career.

The *Gillespiana* LP, released two months later to favorable reviews, was Dizzy's worthy and highly individual answer to two successful orchestral Miles Davis albums written and produced by Gil Evans—*Porgy and Bess* and *Sketches of Spain*. Following Miles's victories in the *Downbeat* polls in 1958 and 1959, Dizzy had tied him in 1960 and bested him in 1961. In addition, Dizzy was elected to *Downbeat*'s prestigious Hall of Fame at the end of 1960. Schifrin's suite certainly helped Dizzy mount his comeback. More than forty years later, *Gillespiana* was performed by such major aggregations as the Lincoln Center Jazz Orchestra.

The suite also attests to the vitality and skill brought to Dizzy's quintet by Leo Wright, who had replaced Les Spann in August 1959. A powerful, slashing master of bebop and the blues, he harked back to Sonny Stitt as a fitting small-group saxophone partner for Dizzy, and his mastery of the flute provided Dizzy with an additional asset.

Further proof of Wright's talents can be found on *An Electrifying Evening with the Dizzy Gillespie Quintet*, recorded in concert on February 9, 1961, at New York's Museum of Modern Art.

Wright sparkles during a program comprising "Kush," Duke Ellington's "The Mooche," and two of Dizzy's standbys: "Salt Peanuts" and "A Night in Tunisia."

Soon after Lalo joined Dizzy, Tulane University in New Orleans invoked their policy barring integrated ensembles and canceled a concert by the quintet when they discovered that Lalo was white. Dizzy kept his thousand-dollar deposit, to the chagrin of university officials.

Norman Granz shocked Dizzy and the rest of the jazz community in February 1961 when, at age forty-two, he sold his record labels (consolidated under the Verve name) to MGM for $2.5 million (roughly $12.7 million in today's currency). He agreed to remain with the company to direct its European operations and to supervise selected recording sessions; in addition, he consented to refrain from reentering the record business on his own until 1967. The agreement dealt with record operations only; Granz retained unrestricted rights to promote tours and to manage artists such as Oscar Peterson and Ella Fitzgerald.

Buoyed by the success of *Gillespiana*, Dizzy commissioned trombonist J. J. Johnson to write another orchestral work for him. Entitled *Perceptions*, it is a dense and intriguing suite that draws more from the classical idiom than from jazz. Dizzy, the only soloist, responded with skill and passion to its challenges in a May 1961 Verve recording; he later said that it was the most difficult composition he had ever performed.

By the time he had recorded *Perceptions*, Dizzy had become uncomfortable with Granz's successors in the Verve studios, and soon after he switched to Philips, where he remained until April 1964.

During the last three weeks of July 1961, Dizzy took the quintet to Argentina and Brazil. The short tour was significant, because it immersed Dizzy in an important new form of Latin music whose harmonies he had strongly influenced—bossa nova. Antonio Carlos Jobim, João Gilberto, Luis Bonfa, and other pioneering Brazilians had created the new genre during the late 1950s by taking the samba, a powerful, street dance music, and transforming it in two ways: they recast its hard-driving, symmetrical rhythm

into a subtle, asymmetrical one that flowed hypnotically, and they
added sophisticated bebop harmonies flavored with the tonal palette
of bebop's tributary, cool jazz.

Lalo remembered the visit to Brazil:

> In Rio and São Paulo, there were streets similar to what Fifty-second
> Street used to be for jazz. One club next to the other. The only differ-
> ence was that these were elegant clubs, because the bossa nova
> was not really a mass popular movement but more elitist.
>
> Dizzy became fascinated with the bossa nova, and we went
> every night to the clubs so he could learn the tunes and work out
> the chord structures. Jobim and those guys were delighted that he
> had taken such a deep interest in their creations, but Dizzy didn't
> talk to them much, because he was so keen on learning. After we
> got the tunes down correctly, I arranged them for him.[4]

Thus, Dizzy continued his love affair with Latin music by becoming the first major American musician to add bossa nova tunes
such as "Desafinado" (where a bebop flatted fifth plays a key role
in the melody), "Morning of the Carnival," and "Chega de
Suadade" to his repertoire.

A bad strategic decision prevented him, however, from releas-
ing the first American bossa nova album and thereby reaping
great rewards from what was to become a blockbuster entertainment phenomenon. Schifrin remembered the circumstances:

> Dizzy respected Artie Shaw, the bandleader, as a shrewd business-
> man, and Shaw told him that he was not going to have his skills all
> his life, and that his best insurance was to record all of the things
> that he was doing, and put them away. Then, when he was older
> and couldn't play anymore, release the material which would be
> very valuable.
>
> After that, Dizzy taped our concert at Monterey in September
> 1961, and paid us an extra fee for the recording. We played the hell
> out of those tunes we had learned in Brazil.
>
> I said to Dizzy, "When are you going to release it?" He said,
> "I'm not. Artie Shaw said to keep it as insurance, remember?"

"Wait a second. You can keep as insurance 'Manteca,' 'Night in Tunisia,' all your classics, but this is a novelty. This is going to be a hit. You have to release it right away." "Oh no, I'm doing what Artie Shaw said." A few months later Stan Getz came with his huge bossa nova hit.[5]

Guitarist Charlie Byrd fell in love with bossa nova during a 1960 State Department tour of South America. He featured some of the Brazilian tunes in his performances when he returned home and became frustrated when he could not convince his record company to commit any of the material to wax. He turned to his friend Stan Getz for help, because he believed that bossa nova was ideally suited to Stan's melodic style and because he knew that Stan possessed more clout with record companies than he did. When Byrd played tapes for Stan in December 1961, the saxophonist also fell in love with the music, and he conveyed his enthusiasm to Creed Taylor, his producer at Verve.

Taylor, who saw only modest commercial possibilities in the Brazilian genre, agreed to produce an album, and he and Getz flew the shuttle from New York to Washington on February 10, 1962, to make what they thought was a routine recording with Byrd, two bassists, and two percussionists. The session was completed in four hours, and Getz and Taylor arrived back in New York in time for dinner. Getz, who had never visited Brazil and had never studied its music, possessed a deep affinity for bossa nova. He performed brilliantly on seven varied tracks as he projected both a joyous, compelling lyricism and a sultry melancholy.

Taylor, knowing the term *bossa nova* was unfamiliar to the American public and believing that the music was a marriage of jazz and samba, called the album *Jazz Samba*. The LP was released in June and began selling furiously in August. Like other unexplainable American pop phenomena, such as Davy Crockett coonskin hats and the hula hoop, bossa nova quickly became a national craze, and Getz was in the vanguard.

Jazz recordings rarely sell well enough to make it to *Billboard* magazine's pop charts, but *Jazz Samba* and "Desafinado," its hit single, arrived there in September. By March 1963, *Jazz Samba* had reached number one pop status, the only jazz album ever to do so. It made Getz a rich man.

The moment to release Dizzy's Monterey recording had passed; he kept it in the can until 1974, when he gave it to his nephew Boo Frazier; Boo, who was starting a new label, called the LP *A Musical Safari*.

Dizzy made a studio bossa nova LP, *New Wave*, in May and July 1962, but it flopped on release in early 1963. A first-rate album produced by Quincy Jones, it was swamped in a flood of recordings by the hordes who had jumped on the Getz-driven bandwagon. Elvis Presley recorded "Bossa Nova Baby," Eydie Gorme waxed "Blame It on the Bossa Nova," and during October 1962 alone, two dozen leaders of jazz groups, including such luminaries as Sonny Rollins and Coleman Hawkins, hit the market with bossa nova albums.

Deeply impressed by *Gillespiana* in 1961, the directors of the Monterey Jazz Festival commissioned Schifrin to write an extended work featuring Dizzy for the 1962 festival. Lalo responded with a six-part tone poem called *The New Continent*. He and Dizzy performed it on opening night, September 21, with an orchestra of top-flight Los Angeles musicians, and a few days later, recorded the piece with many of the same performers; Benny Carter conducted, and Quincy Jones produced the album.

The New Continent—rich, powerful, and varied—achieves artistic eminence both as a vehicle for Dizzy and on its own merits. Lalo has described its genesis: "[Dizzy] is always hungry for new musical foods. Calypso today, bossa nova yesterday—tomorrow, who knows? So I wanted to write a piece for Dizzy using many such elements . . . and I wanted to create my own kind of format spontaneously as I went along . . . improvise with a pencil. . . . I call it 'open' form."[6] "Open" form meant providing Dizzy with a shifting kaleidoscope of themes, moods, rhythms, and textures to work against, and he responded with several solos so appropriate that they weave seamlessly into the tapestry of the piece.

Leo Wright elected to move on soon after Monterey, and Dizzy replaced him with a former star of his big band, James Moody. Moody had trod a varied path since he left Dizzy's group in late

1948 and took off for Europe. He scored a big hit there in 1950 with "Moody's Mood for Love" (his classic variation on "I'm in the Mood for Love"), returned to the United States in 1951, and led his own stateside groups until he rejoined Dizzy. He became addicted to alcohol during the late 1950s, and following a traumatic 1958 fire that destroyed his band's instruments, uniforms, and arrangements, he checked into a New Jersey mental institution called Overbrook for nine months.

Dave Usher, who was working for the Argo label in Chicago, visited him at the sanatorium and encouraged him to record again. When Moody emerged clean, sober, and broke, Argo rented for him alto and tenor saxophones and a flute, and Usher produced for him the triumphant album *Last Train from Overbrook*.

By late 1962, Moody was worn out by the pressures of leadership, and when Dizzy asked him to replace Wright, he jumped at the chance; he remained, a pillar of strength, for six years. Thus, starting with Wright's arrival in 1959, Dizzy benefited for almost a decade from superb talent at the all-important second horn position.

Fortunately for Dizzy, Moody performed at a level a notch or two above Wright. His improvisations displayed greater harmonic sophistication, he had mastered a broader range of sounds and colorings to express his emotions, and he projected more passion. In addition, Moody possessed comedic talents and became an apt foil in several of Dizzy's humorous routines.

Moody performed on saxophone when *The New Continent* received its eastern premiere on November 11, 1962, in the first jazz concert presented at the newly completed Philharmonic Hall in New York's Lincoln Center. Dizzy was attired in white tie and tails, and Lalo conducted from the piano; it would be his last gig for Dizzy.

He left with the blessings of his boss to take on lucrative writing and arranging assignments for Count Basie, Sarah Vaughan, Stan Getz, and Verve Records. The executives of MGM, Verve's new parent, quickly recognized his talents and in 1964 lured him to Hollywood to write the film and TV scores that were to take him to new levels of fame and fortune. *The New Continent* remains a fitting valedictory to his wonderfully fruitful partnership

30
FILM STAR/ PRESIDENTIAL CANDIDATE

THE SUCCESS OF DIZZY'S COLLABORATION WITH LALO Schifrin found confirmation when *Downbeat* named Dizzy, Stan Getz, and Sonny Rollins "Jazzmen of the Year" for 1962.

Dizzy did not have to look far to find a successor to his Argentine confrere. Pianist Kenny Barron had exhibited outstanding talent in James Moody's last band, and, at Moody's urging, Dizzy hired him following the Lincoln Center concert. Dizzy voiced pleasure with his new recruit, a nineteen-year-old prodigy who had launched his career two years earlier with Jimmy Heath's band: "This teenager had totally mastered the bebop vocabulary, rhythmic and harmonic. He didn't have the native feel for the Latin stuff which Lalo had, but he handled it beautifully in his own way. He had a sense of adventure, and he could swing his ass off."[1] And Dizzy was happy with a couple of other new hires:

"Before Kenny and Moody joined us, I had a friendly parting with my bass player and my drummer, and I replaced them with two excellent musicians, Chris White and Rudy Collins. So, with Kenny on board, I had a whole new band, and it was as bitchin' as the last one."[2] The unit stayed together for three and a half years.

The excellence of this new quintet, which Gary Giddins rates as second only to Dizzy's 1940s quintet with Bird,[3] is validated by *Something Old, Something New*, an album made for Philips in April 1963. The "old" portion consisted of five tunes associated with Dizzy since the 1940s, while the "new" segment featured three pieces composed by Tom McIntosh, who had been Moody's trombonist, and a bossa nova cowritten by Dizzy's former Turkish protégé, Arif Mardin.

Dizzy and Moody burned fiercely on two up-tempo bebop anthems, "Dizzy Atmosphere" and "Bebop," and Moody unfurled a magnificent, passionate solo on "'Round Midnight." McIntosh challenged the group with a fifty-six-bar modal piece with gospel flavorings, a jaunty fifty-four-bar tune in five sections, and a brooding ballad. He forced them to use all their musical muscles as they worked through the structures with agility, intelligence, and spirit.

During July 1963, Dizzy traveled to Paris with Schifrin arrangements in hand to undertake *Dizzy and the Double Six of Paris*, a complex recording project that came off successfully. The Double Six was actually a seven-person vocal group led by Mimi Perrin, a sister of the composer Michel Legrand. With backup help from French bassist Pierre Michelot and Dizzy's old pals, the expatriates Kenny Clarke and Bud Powell, they essayed with Dizzy both small-group and big band arrangements of ten bebop classics (the Double Six overdubbed their voices to provide as many as fourteen parts for the "big band" tracks). Dizzy was in top form, the singers performed with precision and verve, and Perrin excelled in vocal renditions of Moody's 1946 "Emanon" solo and Bird's classic improvisations on "Hot House" and "Groovin' High." Powell, in precarious physical and mental health, was below par, but Clarke and Michelot performed well. Two more tracks, recorded in Chicago ten weeks later with Dizzy's working quintet, were less successful than the ones made in Paris.

Dizzy was a major participant in two important 1963 films—
The Hole, an animated short that won an Oscar, and *The Cool
World*, Shirley Clarke's searing feature that the *New York Times*
called "sensational" and *Newsweek* described as "a work of art informed by knowing compassion." (*The Cool World* was Clarke's
second triumph of 1963; she won an Oscar that year for her documentary *Robert Frost: A Lover's Quarrel with the World*.)

John and Faith Hubley, who created *The Hole*, loved jazz, and
featured Dizzy, Benny Carter, and Quincy Jones extensively in
their productions, which used highly imaginative animation to es-
pouse causes such as disarmament, saving the environment, and
the preservation of native cultures. Dizzy contributed music to
seven of the ten Hubley movies he made between 1956 and 1990,
but *The Hole* isn't one of them.

The fifteen-minute film is carried by brilliantly improvised dialogue from Dizzy and actor George Matthews, who play workers
moving dirt in an excavation beneath Third Avenue in New York.
Dizzy's character on screen looks more like a generic black man
than he does like Dizzy, and his partner is squat, bald, and white.
The two men maintain an idiosyncratic freshness as they move
their conversation smoothly from mundane matters to the possi-
bility of human error in the U.S. missile defense system; as the
film ends, they survive an accidental nuclear catastrophe because
they are tunneling in their hole.

Dizzy helped create music for *The Cool World*, a fictional portrait of a Harlem teenager trapped in the gang life. His improvisations carry the viewer deeply into the action as he led an all-star
quartet in pianist Mal Waldron's evocative jazz portion of the
film's jazz/rock sound track; Dizzy was joined by Yusef Lateef on
saxophone, Art Taylor on drums, and Aaron Bell on bass.

Dizzy reprised the Waldron score in a peak effort by his own
quintet in a 1964 album. As with the work of Tom McIntosh, Waldron's compositions inspired the group to performances of singular
power. Barron, maturing rapidly, played with fluent authority,
Dizzy and Moody tore into the material like hungry carnivores,
and Collins and White laid down a brawny rhythmic foundation as
they communicated almost telepathically with the soloists.

Dizzy's only foray into politics began as a lark in 1963 when his booking agency had some "Dizzy for President" buttons made up as a publicity gimmick, but the stunt quickly acquired an aura of seriousness when Dizzy began to speak out on issues about which he felt passionate. Martin Luther King's March on Washington, which culminated in his "I Have a Dream" speech on August 28, 1963, had strongly inspired Dizzy, and he was angry and disappointed when President Kennedy, fearing the wrath of powerful southern senators, rejected King's request for a White House meeting. His anger increased exponentially with the racist murder of four black Birmingham, Alabama, schoolgirls on September 15. Five days later, his campaign for the presidency moved into high gear at the Monterey Jazz Festival.

Ralph Gleason was a columnist for the *San Francisco Chronicle*, the host of a jazz TV program, and a Monterey organizer, and he and his wife Jean had for several months been pushing, in a lighthearted manner, a Gillespie candidacy as a beacon of common sense, humor, and decency in an increasingly depressing political environment. Galvanized by recent events, they went into action at the festival; they organized a noisy demonstration, unfurled a large "Dizzy for President" banner, and passed out hundreds of buttons and balloons. Ross Firestone remembered the atmosphere at Monterey:

John Lewis's announcement that he was dedicating the Modern Jazz Quartet's performance of "The Sheriff" to Martin Luther King was greeted with a round of applause. When Jon Hendricks asked for a moment to honor the dead children of Birmingham, the crowd fell into a reverential silence. . . . The spirit-rousing sounds and unrelenting good feeling that flowed from both sides of the bandstand over the course of the long weekend did, in their own way, echo the vision of community that Dr. King's impassioned oration had called for.[4]

After Dizzy announced the second number of his set, he and Moody engaged in the following dialogue:

Dizzy: We would like to play one of the tunes now from the motion picture "Black Orpheus"—excuse the expression.

Moody: Dizzy, you can say black. It's all right.

Dizzy: All right.

Moody (shouting): Yeah. Don't be ashamed to say "BLACK Orpheus." Say "BLACK Orpheus" . . . Yeah, Malcolm told me.

Dizzy: Everything must be cool if Malcolm say so baby. . . . .Here's "Morning of the Carnival" from "Black Orpheus," and I mean it too.

Moody: Yeah. That's right. If they don't like it, we can lay down here and demonstrate.[5]

Dizzy's candidacy took on heft later in his set when Jon Hendricks led the crowd in a rousing rendition of his campaign lyric, "Vote Dizzy," written to the music of "Salt Peanuts." Dizzy's deeper emotions surfaced when he ended his scat chorus on the piece with: "Nobody knows the trouble I've seen. Nobody knows my sorrow. FREEDOM NOW!"[6]

Jean Gleason became Dizzy's campaign manager following the festival. Brandishing the slogan "Dizzy for President: Because We Need One," she raised money, distributed bumper stickers, buttons, and other paraphernalia, and organized a write-in campaign in twenty-five states. A week after Monterey, Dizzy angrily told a heckler at a midwestern jazz club: "I was just about ready to move down to Mexico, but not now, not after Birmingham. We're on the march now, and before we're through we might change the color of the White House."[7]

The murders of President Kennedy and three civil rights workers in Mississippi and the surprise victory of Barry Goldwater, an opponent of civil rights legislation, over Nelson Rockefeller for the Republican presidential nomination energized Dizzy to call for the appointment of Malcolm X to head the Department of Justice and for mass boycotts in favor of civil rights. He opposed U.S. involvement in Vietnam, and he favored the creation of a strong world government, the replacement of the income tax with a national lottery, and diplomatic recognition of China. He chose a Native American woman, Ramona Crowell, as his running mate.

Of course, any campaign mounted by Dizzy would involve humor. He wanted to change the name of the White House to the

Blues House, and he proposed that Max Roach run the Defense Department, that Miles Davis lead the CIA, and that Mississippi's segregationist governor, Ross Barnett, be appointed U.S. Information Officer in the Congo. And he wanted a law requiring job applicants to cover themselves with colored sheets so prospective employers could not discern their ethnicity in advance.

The write-in votes Dizzy earned failed to scare either of the major candidates, but he looked back on his joust for the presidency with satisfaction; it enabled him to influence the national debate as he spoke out on issues dear to his heart, and it garnered him reams of publicity.

A NEW FAITH IN DIFFICULT TIMES

31

THE NIGHT OF FEBRUARY 9, 1964, WHEN SEVENTY-THREE million people watched the Beatles on the *Ed Sullivan Show*, marked the beginning of the worst economic period jazz has experienced to date; the slump would last into the early 1970s. This second rock-and-roll juggernaut was much more potent commercially than the first one launched by Elvis Presley in 1956; it reshaped American culture as it helped fuel the social revolution of the 1960s.

The Beatles were in the vanguard, but rock and roll was erupting everywhere: with the Rolling Stones, the Who, the Kinks, Jimi Hendrix, and Eric Clapton following the Fab Four in England; the Supremes, the Temptations, Stevie Wonder, Marvin Gaye, and other Motown stars blazing trails in Detroit; Aretha Franklin and James Brown exploding out of studios in the Deep South; Bob Dylan, Paul Simon, and Joan Baez turning heads in New York; and Janis Joplin, the Grateful Dead, the Jefferson Airplane, the Beach

Boys, the Doors, and Frank Zappa creating fresh sounds on the West Coast.

During the ten years ending in 1973, U.S. record sales almost tripled to more than two billion dollars,[1] and analogous gains were made in major foreign markets. Producers devoted great amounts of time and money to rock and roll, where million-selling albums were not uncommon, and spent few resources on jazz, where sales of fifteen thousand traditionally spelled success.

The jazz mainstream, which by this time had come to include Dizzy's bebop, had more to contend with than the external forces of rock and roll. It was beset within the jazz community by competition from two sides. On one flank stood the avant-garde of Ornette Coleman and John Coltrane, and on the other loomed Miles Davis and his cohorts in the "fusion" movement attempting to marry jazz and rock and roll.

Sarah Vaughan and Roy Eldridge both went five years without making records during the drought, Oscar Peterson recorded sporadically with no contract from 1966 until 1972, Duke Ellington and Theloniuos Monk were dropped by Columbia Records in 1970, and Dizzy made only two albums, both with small groups, between 1967 and 1971.

As he fought for economic survival, trouble descended on Dizzy from another quarter. He was arrested at Birdland on December 11, 1964, on a family court warrant issued in favor of Connie Bryson, a twenty-seven-year-old white woman. Bryson claimed that Dizzy was the father of her daughter Jeanie, born May 10, 1958, and she described an affair that had lasted from 1955, when she was a student at Sarah Lawrence College, until the early 1960s; she alleged that Dizzy's financial support of the child had been both sporadic and inadequate, and she asked that the court enforce a regular payment schedule. Dizzy agreed to submit to a blood test at his arraignment and was released on bail. His lawyer, Charlie Roisman, handled the case with such discretion that the media never reported Dizzy's arrest or his subsequent court appearances relating to the case. Lorraine had no knowledge of the Brysons until Dizzy's arrest.

The blood test proved to be inconclusive; it did not rule out paternity, and it did not provide hard proof that Dizzy was the father.

Dizzy signed an agreement on May 29, 1965, that stated he "does hereby acknowledge paternity of the said child and his legal liability for the support thereof." The document also stipulated that he would pay $125 per month toward Jeanie's well-being until she turned twenty-one (he in fact continued the payments until her twenty-second birthday). After initial confusion about lost money orders, Lorraine stepped in and insisted that Dizzy's agent issue the support checks and keep scrupulous records. The payments went smoothly thereafter.

Dizzy was sexually promiscuous for decades and Lorraine dealt with it in her own way:

> Somebody says something about your husband fruiting with a chick. I don't even think about that. I feel as though if she's allowing him to make a fool of her, he's perfectly right, until he gets caught. . . . I really didn't care because most parents, I think, teach their girls that if your husband takes care of you and gives you respect when he's with you and has a decent place for you to stay, and you don't have any trouble, you don't have to worry about it. Because your husband can be anybody's husband after he leaves home. He doesn't have to just be yours. He can be anybody's husband out in that street. All that foolishness never worried me. "How do you do it?" people asked. I say, "By not thinking about it, and if I think about it, I just say to heck with it. If he doesn't get caught, good."[2]

During the summer of 1965, Dizzy and Lorraine sold their house in Corona and bought one in suburban Englewood, New Jersey, five miles from the George Washington Bridge. Their new home, a commodious split level on a well-manicured half-acre plot, was located in an integrated, upper-middle-class neighborhood; a black man lived next door, and Sarah Vaughan owned a house nearby. Dizzy soon outfitted the basement with recording equipment, a piano, and a pool table, and Lorraine created a Roman Catholic chapel in one of the rooms on the upper level.

Rudy Collins and Chris White broke up the quintet that had stayed together for three and a half years when they left Dizzy during March 1966 to form a cooperative called Rhythm Associates. They were replaced by drummer Candy Finch and by Frank Schifano, who became Dizzy's first electric bass player. Dizzy had two reasons for adopting the electric bass, and both were economic. First, the electric instrument could be stowed with the luggage on airplanes while the acoustic bass required a first-class seat; second, Dizzy was attempting to reach out to the young rock-and-roll audience, and the electric bass conveyed a rock-and-roll sonority.

After Schifano quit suddenly, Dizzy went quickly through three bassists before settling on Paul West, who remained with him for fifteen months. One of the short-term incumbents enjoyed partying and performing with Dizzy so much that he drove four hours each way to a San Francisco gig from his home south of the city. His tenure came to an abrupt end when, after a routine traffic stop, police found marijuana in his car and arrested him.

Kenny Barron, who had two small children and had grown tired of the grind of the road, opted out in November 1966 after four years with Dizzy. He was replaced by Mike Longo, a twenty-seven-year-old who had studied with Oscar Peterson and had performed with Nancy Wilson, Roy Eldridge, and Coleman Hawkins. Mike had impressed Dizzy while performing at a couple of New York clubs; of Italian descent, he became the only white member in the quintet.

Dizzy received a phone call in his Milwaukee hotel room on Mike's first day on the job, December 11, 1966, from a woman who has requested that she not be named in this book. She remembered the circumstances:

I had read a book about Charlie Parker, and I was very moved when he said, "Dizzy Gillespie is the other half of my heartbeat."

Only a couple of months later, I saw that Dizzy was coming to perform in Milwaukee, where I was living. I telephoned him and told him about myself: that I was a Baha'i and that I lived in a nearby suburb with my husband, a doctor, and two children.

I told him that I had read this book about Charlie Parker. As a member of the Baha'i faith, I thought it was such a pity that Charlie

Parker died the way he did, because I felt he was just searching for meaning, searching for a way to get warm in the world. Drugs just won't do it. I regretted that he hadn't met a Baha'i, because a Baha'i really believes that this is a special time, a regeneration time for the whole planet, and all things are possible.

And because Charlie Parker said that you, Dizzy, are the other half of his heartbeat, I had hoped, just once, to be able to tell you something about this Baha'i faith. Then I invited him to our house to dinner. The whole thing was sort of blurted out and not too coherent.

After a certain silence, he said, "You know I've learned out on the road not to trust man, woman, child, or beast." Then I asked whether my husband and I could come to his club and send up a card. Dizzy could look at us, and if he didn't want to meet us, we certainly wouldn't take offense. So he said, "OK. That's fine."[3]

She and her husband and another couple attended the performance that night, and Dizzy joined them following the last set. His natural loquaciousness was abetted by three double crème de menthes, and the conversation quickly moved to serious topics such as mortality and threats to world peace. They did not discuss Baha'i that night, but Dizzy struck a chord with the Baha'i woman when he told her of his strong support for the World Federalists, an organization campaigning for a more effective world government. Baha'is are also dedicated to this political goal, because one of the primary tenets of their faith is the unity, the oneness, of mankind.

Before parting, Dizzy and the woman agreed to lunch together the next day. Over Chinese food, she explained that Baha'is believe in one God, one human race, and one evolving religion revealed progressively by God to mankind. Baha'is hold that, as humanity developed, God sent to mankind messengers who have helped humans gradually to understand the world around them—prophets like Abraham, Krishna, Moses, Zoroaster, Buddha, Christ, and Muhammad. And they were followed during the nineteenth century by the Persian founders of Baha'i—the Báb and Bahá'u'lláh. She emphasized that Baha'is believe that this spiritual evolution continues to this day and into the future.

Baha'is look to the Báb, who declared his prophetic mission in

Persia (most of which is now contemporary Iran) in 1844 and was executed for heresy by Muslims in 1850, and to Bahá'u'lláh, "the Messenger of God for this age," who was imprisoned by them in Tehran in 1852 and tortured and then exiled successively to Iraq, Turkey, and Acre in what is now Israel. He died in 1892, and was followed by his son and great-grandson who guided the faithful to the current Baha'i self-governing structure. Baha'is have no clergy; each congregation is headed by a council of nine elected for one year, and this is repeated at the national level. At the international level, Baha'is elect a council of nine for five years. Communicants number roughly six million living in 235 countries and territories, and the center of the faith is in Israel at Haifa.

Dizzy, a nominal Christian as an adult, was particularly impressed by the Baha'i teachings on race at time when frustrated blacks were rioting in several major American cities. Based on the doctrine that all people are equal in the sight of God, Baha'is believe unequivocally in racial and gender equality. Despite the racism that he had endured from the cradle, Dizzy was not tainted by it, and the Baha'i teachings gave him hope for ultimate racial reconciliation.

Baha'is adhere to a strict family-oriented moral code, pray daily, fast from dawn till sunset during a nineteen-day period in March, and attempt to free themselves from dependence on alcohol, drugs, and tobacco.

Dizzy's Milwaukee caller was traveling for the faith during the late 1960s; she and other Baha'is would meet with Dizzy as he was touring, and they would discuss spiritual concerns for hours. Among the pamphlets and books they gave him, he was deeply affected by *Thief in the Night*, a treatise by a Baha'i leader named Bill Sears.

By the time Dizzy met with the Milwaukee woman and a colleague, Nancy Jordan, for lunch in San Francisco in January 1968, he had written out a declaration of faith and was ready to convert. The ladies called Sears, who was in Los Angeles, and he suggested that Dizzy make his declaration there, because Jenabe Samandari, one of the surviving disciples who actually knew Bahá'u'lláh, was visiting the city. Both Sears and Samandari were

called "Hands of the Cause," leaders who were so designated by
Bahá'u'lláh's great-grandson before he died in 1957. Dizzy and
the two women took the shuttle to Los Angeles, Dizzy made his
declaration to Samandari and met Sears, and they flew back to
San Francisco that evening.

Dizzy later reflected on his new faith:

> Baha'i gave me a new spiritual dimension, a new understanding of
> God's plan for mankind, of how people should relate to each other.
> The number one principle of the Baha'i faith is the unity of
> mankind. This is the main lesson coming down from all of God's
> prophets and messengers. All your efforts should be directed to
> that end. You should never forget it. The unity of mankind.
>
> My faith transformed me. I pray every day and my readings in-
> tensify my spiritual awareness. As I make a serious effort to fill
> my life with healthy things, I find I have less and less time for the
> negative.[4]

Lorraine, staunch in her Catholicism, never took Baha'i theology
seriously; she and Dizzy adopted a policy of mutual toleration of
their divergent religious beliefs.

Dizzy believed that there were strong parallels between the
development of jazz and the development of mankind's spirituality. As Buddha, Jesus, Muhammad, Bahá'u'lláh, and other messengers carried the spirituality of mankind to higher levels, he saw
himself as part of a chain of messengers who similarly elevated
the art of jazz. For Dizzy, the evolution ran through Armstrong,
Ellington, Hawkins, Teagarden, Young, and Eldridge to him and
contemporaries such as Kenny Clarke, Bird, and Mario Bauzá and
from them to younger musicians such as Lee Morgan, Jon Faddis,
Paquito D'Rivera, and Arturo Sandoval. He felt the tradition
surging within himself as he advanced it, and he meant it when he
said, "No Armstrong, no me."

Dizzy was always eager to carry the evolution forward by
teaching what he called "our music" to anyone who was interested.
He hoarded no secrets, and he poured out his knowledge in
countless seminars and workshops and in on-the-job training for

members of his bands. During the 1970s, he added a telephone line at his home for callers who wanted his guidance on harmony, technique, and other musical matters. Saxophonist Paquito D'Rivera, an associate who benefited from his teaching, has reflected on Dizzy's feelings about his place in the tradition:

> When people would tell him that he invented bebop he would say, "I didn't invent shit. Everybody was trying to do something good and valuable but I didn't invent anything. We did it all together." He was that way in every corner of his life. He was always very humble and very honest in acknowledging the merits of all the people. . . . It was wonderful working with him, and you learned a lot in all orders of life. He was a blessing.[5]

Dizzy was a blessing to almost everyone who worked with him or for him, but to Lorraine and to an inner circle of friends he was more than that; he was beloved. Mike Longo, James Moody, Dave Usher, Boo Frazier, Lalo Schifrin, John Motley, and Jon Faddis provided Dizzy with a level of devotion that is given to very few adults in our society. He elicited their love with a generosity of spirit leavened by a streak of zaniness and by an emphatic, infectious, democratic openness.

Encounters with Dizzy often turned into adventures when he combined generosity with a thirst for new experience and a lack of inhibition about seeking it. His associate Charles "Whale" Lake recalled:

> Dizzy was the type, if a kid asked him a question, that was the beginning of an interview. Many times people would be in line waiting for an autograph and some kid would say, "Can you tell me something about this instrument?" He'd end up giving the kid his mouthpiece, his mute, giving his trumpet. And he'd start talking, "What's your name? How do you pronounce that? What's your father's name? What's your mother's name?" He was totally inquisitive.[6]

Dizzy's brash zaniness was often used to good effect. Bill Crow remembered a 1958 incident when it defused a tense racial situation. Musicians who had come to French Lick, Indiana, to perform at a festival were housed in a previously segregated resort, and two black members of Gerry Mulligan's quartet were squeamish about using the swimming pool before Dizzy arrived. Crow wrote:

Dizzy Gillespie stepped out of the elevator. He was wearing bathing trunks from the French Riviera, an embroidered skull-cap from Greece and embroidered slippers with curled-up toes that he'd picked up in Turkey. A Sheraton bath towel draped over his shoulders like a cape was fastened at the neck with a jade scarab pin from Egypt. With a Chinese ivory cigarette holder in his left hand and a powerful German multiband portable radio in his right, he beamed cheerfully through a pair of Italian sunglasses.

"I've come to integrate the pool!" he announced. He led the way to the beach chairs at poolside, enthroning himself in one with plenipotentiary panache. After he had the attention of everyone at the poolside, he grabbed Jimmy McPartland [a white man], who had also come down for a swim. Arm in arm, the two trumpet players marched to the diving board and jumped in together, and the last barrier to integration at French Lick was down.[7]

Author Nat Hentoff has summed it up:

Dizzy reached an inner strength and discipline that total pacifists call "soul force." He was always a presence. Like they used to say of Fats Waller, whenever Dizzy came into a room, he filled it. He made people feel good, and he was the sound of surprise, even when his horn was in its case. But in later years, there was a peaceableness in Dizzy. There was nothing passive about it. It was his "soul force" that resolved tensions. . . .

Seeing Dizzy, however casually, was like coming into sunlight. By the warmth of his greeting, his natural considerateness, and the keenness of his intelligence—which made his wit so sharp— he was a delight to be with.[8]

DANGEROUS APPETITES

32

Two events, more than three years apart, demonstrate that Dizzy's transition to a purer Baha'i lifestyle was a gradual process. He was fifty at the time of his conversion, and his partiality toward tobacco, alcohol, and other stimulants was not easily curbed. The first incident occurred on April 4, 1968, less than ninety days after he became a Baha'i.

The quintet had a free day after a concert honoring Dizzy at the Laurinburg Institute, and he decided to use it to take Mike Longo for a visit to Cheraw; although Dizzy was notorious for losing his way when driving, he made the trip without mishap in a station wagon borrowed from the institute.

They visited relatives and friends and Dizzy's former teacher Alice Wilson, and almost every encounter was lubricated with homemade wine. Dizzy and Longo were so busy socializing that radio announcements about the murder that evening of Martin Luther King Jr. hardly registered with them.

Around 2:00 a.m., Dizzy, feeling pretty mellow, decided that he wanted some "creek," moonshine corn whiskey made by a man who lived in the woods outside of Cheraw. Longo remembered what happened next:

The house is dark. The guy's in bed with his wife, sleeping, and Dizzy goes into his bedroom and grabs him by his big toe and pulls him out of bed.

The moonshiner is in his sixties, the wife in her twenties. We went out on the porch to drink from these jugs of "creek," and I'm using a little paper cup, but Dizzy is drinking out of a water glass. All of a sudden, I can see his face drooping like a basset hound—a sure sign that he's getting really drunk. I knew it well; it happened about once a month.

The guy told Dizzy: "Don't give my wife any. She's mentally disturbed. A psychiatrist is taking care of her. She can't drink that stuff."

Dizzy doesn't pay any attention and pours some for the woman. Now the old man gets out a pistol and starts cleaning it. Dizzy reacts by getting his briefcase and calling me into the bathroom. In the briefcase he had a pistol he had bought because he expected trouble in the south with a mixed-race band. He gives me this .38 and says, "Take this in case the guy gets ugly. I'm too shaky to handle it."

We go back in, and now the woman's drunk and angry. She starts shouting at Dizzy: "You think 'cause you're a big star, you're better than us? You really ain't shit." So Dizzy reaches over, and he grabs her hair and it's a wig. He pulls it off, and she's bald. The next thing I know, tables and dishes are flying, and the woman rips Dizzy's shirt off and bites him on the shoulder, and blood's squirting all over.

The only thing I could think of to do is to put Dizzy in a headlock. I pulled his gun out, used his head as a battering ram, and busted the screen door. I'm shooting this gun off, so the guy knows I've got a weapon. And I throw Dizzy into the Laurinburg station wagon and cut out. Then he throws up and passes out. Police cars are now all over the place because of King's assassination.[1]

By the time Longo returned to Laurinburg, and he and Moody had cleaned out the station wagon and sobered Dizzy up, they had missed a plane to their next gig in Atlanta. The McDuffies stepped in and lent them a school bus and a driver, and they arrived three hours late on a Friday for the engagement at the black-owned Paschal's Motor Inn; the inn was so famed as a meeting place for civil rights leaders that Martin Luther King Jr.'s widow would later say, "Paschal's is as important a historical site for the American civil rights movement as Boston's Faneuil Hall is to the American Revolution."[2]

Every American black community was burning with rage that weekend, and the streets around Paschal's were filled with angry people. Some of them spotted Longo in the bus and began rocking it and shouting antiwhite epithets, but the driver kept moving and made it to the entrance without further incident. From the moment Longo was taken to his room until the end of the gig ten days later, he was told to leave it only to perform; on those occasions he was escorted by bodyguards to and from the downstairs nightclub. He sneaked out once, witnessed a stabbing, and was rushed back inside by Moody.

The King family asked Dizzy to participate in the regular Sunday service at their church, Ebenezer Baptist, and he performed the spiritual "My Lord, What a Morning When the Stars Begin to Fall" surrounded by the choir. King was buried two days later, on April 9, 1968.

The quintet's next engagements were in Miami and Fort Lauderdale near the home of Longo's parents, Mike senior and Elvira, in Plantation. Longo, who had cemented a friendship with Moody that remains extremely close to the present, asked them if he and Moody could be their houseguests, and they answered by inviting the entire quintet to stay with them.

Mike senior, a businessman who moonlighted as the bass-playing leader of a local jazz quintet, was a fervent integrationist living in a segregationist community. The Longos' four black guests became the talk of the neighborhood, and cars would screech to a halt when their occupants spotted a black man diving into the swimming pool or playing horseshoes in the backyard.

Elvira became for ten days a den mother to the group—fielding their phone calls, picking up after them, greeting them with snacks at 3:00 or 4:00 a.m., and preparing delicious Italian dinners. Before the quintet left, Dizzy gave Mike's parents a silver tray engraved with the message, "To Mom and Pop Longo, from your five sons: Diz, Moody, Candy, Paul, and—oops—Mike."

Dizzy fell in love with Mike senior and Elvira and adopted them as surrogate parents. Often, when he needed a rest, he would take a week off and relax alone by their pool, accepting few phone calls and allowing Elvira to pamper him and to spoil him with her cooking.

In September of 1968, five months after adopting his surrogate parents, Dizzy found a surrogate son, Jon Faddis. Faddis began studying music at his parents' urging when he was seven in 1960, and he chose the trumpet after admiring a Louis Armstrong performance on TV. Dizzy became his idol three years later when a teacher introduced him to Dizzy's music. Jon studied it intensely, absorbing bebop harmony and phrasing and painstakingly learning difficult Gillespie solos. Sometimes he would spend an hour mastering a single bar.

He met Dizzy when he was twelve but was too shy to say anything to his hero. At age fifteen, however, he mustered up enough courage to lug fifty of Dizzy's albums from his home near San Francisco to the 1968 Monterey Festival and to ask Dizzy to autograph each of them. As Dizzy sat on the grass and complied, Faddis impressed him by humming accurately complex phrases from several of his solos.

He instructed the teenager to appear with his horn two weeks later at the Jazz Workshop in San Francisco, and when he arrived, Dizzy invited him to the bandstand. Jon remembered, "I was fifteen years old with a big afro hairstyle, wearing a sweatshirt which read 'Gillespie for President.' He got me up on the stage and we played [two tunes]. I almost fainted. I was so nervous. I started shaking and the room started spinning, but I was playing with Dizzy!"[3]

After the performance, Jon knew where his career path lay. He tried to stay in touch with Dizzy after that evening but was unable to obtain a valid address and did not make contact again until January 1972, more than three years later.

Mike Longo had steadily taken on more arranging and composing duties for Dizzy, and during the Jazz Workshop engagement, Dizzy made him his musical director.

Drummer Candy Finch was an angry man, and he often vented his hostilities on Longo and Moody. After Dizzy fired him in late 1969 for mocking Longo on stage, Mike suffered an emotional meltdown:

> I started crying when Candy left. There was sort of a love-hate thing with him and so the first night playing without him, I just had a breakdown on the gig—after all those months of tension and everything. I woke up in the middle of the night in a panic attack, and called Nancy Jordan. She came the next morning. . . . and stayed with me all day, talking to me about the Baha'i faith.
>
> She brought me this pamphlet, written by her husband, about becoming your true self. Like a snake sheds its skin, and a new person comes out. In the process you go through an anxiety attack. It's almost like you're dying.
>
> I felt healed and enlightened and began studying the Baha'i faith in earnest. My meeting with Nancy was my first step on the path to my Baha'i conversion two years later.[4]

New Orleans drummer David Lee took Finch's place. When Moody quit soon after, Dizzy took a radical turn and replaced him with a guitarist, George Davis, rather than a horn man. Dizzy's primary reason for the change was his desire for a new quintet sound after a dozen years of saxophone and flute players. A secondary reason was economic; Davis, a virtual unknown, was paid considerably less than Moody, a star. The hiring of Davis, therefore, was a symptom of the commercial malaise that still gripped jazz six years after the Beatles appeared on *The Ed Sullivan Show*. The slump had intensified during the late 1960s and early 1970s, and it drove Dizzy and his producers to search frantically for a formula that would provide a commercial spark and sell records.

As Earl May, Dizzy's bassist of the early 1970s, recalled, they gravitated mainly to the genre where Miles Davis had found success, funk:

> We played funk things. . . . Dizzy was really trying to reach his audience, and his audience was mainly college people. And in those days, college people wore jeans and raggedy hair and that's what we did. . . . Dizzy would go on stage in jeans and try to get his music across and to reach these people.
>
> He really wanted to go into a funk thing, to go in that direction. He's listening to Miles Davis and Miles is listening to Sly & The Family Stone. . . . It made sense in a way because look! . . . All Miles did was change everything underneath him and he just played everything he normally played. Dizzy wanted to do the same thing, to keep your style and instead of playing 4/4 [time] to get the funk [rhythm and backbeat].
>
> It was a real funny thing. We'd beg Dizzy to do some of those great bebop tunes that he used to do. And he would say, "Yeah, yeah!, OK!" We'd rehearse like a son-of-a-gun and get that thing down pat, then we'd go and play the same old repertoire.[5]

Dizzy's love affair with funk led to the worst recordings of his entire career, a trio of LPs from 1969 and 1970 called *It's My Way, Cornucopia,* and *Sweet Soul (Souled Out).* The funk content was mediocre, the jazz was awful, and the LPs sold badly.

When he wasn't diluting his art to appeal to a rock-and-roll audience, Dizzy continued to perform brilliantly. A concert I produced in April 1971 provides proof of this.

I met Dizzy when I asked him to help raise money for Manhattanville Community Centers, which provided day care and Head Start services in Harlem. I served on the board of Manhattanville, whose favorite fund-raising tactic was to buy a block of seats to a Broadway show and sell them to its wealthy patrons at double the price; that year they chose a play starring Katharine Hepburn as fashionista Coco Chanel.

I told my fellow directors that I thought it would be more appropriate to recruit black entertainers to perform in Harlem for our solidly black constituency, and they gave me a green light. First, I secured the Apollo Theater for a nominal fee but on difficult terms; we had to begin at 1:00 a.m., after the regular show had ended. Then I looked for talent.

Dizzy's nephew Boo Frazier, a friend, arranged for me to meet Dizzy at his home in Englewood. On arrival, I received only a glimpse of the main floor that Lorraine had decreed off-limits to all but the closest friends and family, and Dizzy guided me to his lair in the basement. He went to his piano, played some pretty chord sequences by way of introduction, and turned to hear my pitch about the Apollo benefit for black children. He quickly agreed to participate, but he imposed an important condition: the fund-raiser should honor Coleman Hawkins, who had died in May 1969 and who had championed Dizzy and other young beboppers against a doubting jazz establishment during the 1940s. I immediately assented, and he promised to recruit an all-star group for the event.

Dizzy reported a week later that he had signed up Max Roach, Thelonious Monk, James Moody, and Sam Jones. Max, in turn, recruited the gospel choir from his Brooklyn church, and I filled out the bill with Roberta Flack, the Delfonics singing group, and the distinguished actress Diana Sands. The Delfonics were the Apollo headliners that week, and they approached me as I was doing a preperformance sound check and volunteered. Sands agreed to read a eulogy to Hawkins written by John S. Wilson, the *New York Times* jazz critic. Our emcee was Honi Coles, the elegant tap dancer, and he was aided by Duke Ellington, who joined us after a concert performance downtown. Illness forced Monk to withdraw at the last minute, and Mike Longo took his place. Each artist received a hundred-dollar honorarium.

Dizzy took out his horn on arrival at midnight, plunked in his mute, and started to warm up. When he turned to launch blistering choruses into Flack's spectacular Afro, her face registered intense annoyance. Honi Coles averted a crisis by racing over and gently moving Dizzy to another part of the dressing room.

We were thrilled when the box office reported that thirteen hundred people had lined up along 125th Street and around onto Seventh Avenue as we sold every seat in the house.

Dizzy and the group were highly energized as they blazed through "Woody 'n You," "Disorder at the Border," and "Yesterdays" from their days with Hawkins, and struck an elegiac note with " 'Round Midnight." The audience went wild over Roach's spectacular solo using only his hi-hat cymbal set, and they stomped their approval of Dizzy's passionate choruses on "Woody 'n You" and " 'Round Midnight." This was music delivered from the heart, not music fashioned for targeted record buyers, and it showed.

The Apollo concert was not an isolated event. When Dizzy found himself in appropriate settings away from the funk-driven studios, he continued to perform jazz at the highest level. Among the recordings that attest to the excellence of his playing in fitting circumstances during a difficult period are the LPs *Jazz for a Sunday Afternoon*, *Dizzy's Reunion Big Band*, and *Giants*.

Jazz for a Sunday Afternoon, recorded at New York's Village Vanguard in October 1967, caught Dizzy and several of his peers in peak performances at a freewheeling jam session. Dizzy usually reached deeper into himself in the competitive atmosphere of such events, and on this occasion he took over as first among equals, soloing freshly and vigorously and providing inspiration to Ray Nance on violin, Pepper Adams on saxophone, and Garnett Brown on trombone. The all-star rhythm section of pianist Chick Corea, drummer Mel Lewis (spelled by Elvin Jones on one of six numbers), and bassist Richard Davis interacted superbly with the other musicians.

Dizzy organized a "reunion" big band for a seven-week, autumn 1968 European tour sponsored by Newport's George Wein, and the group made an outstanding recording before an ecstatic audience in Berlin on the tour's last evening. The band, which included four veterans of the groundbreaking 1948 aggregation, performed with the verve and power of its 1940s and 1950s predecessors. The repertoire combined updated versions of early classics such as "Things to Come" and "One Bass Hit" with sprightly new numbers by Dizzy and Mike Longo. The recording captures sparkling solos by Dizzy, Longo, James Moody, Cecil Payne, and the young trumpeter Jimmy Owens.

Dizzy and swing trumpeter Bobby Hackett, his good friend

and his longtime neighbor in Queens, talked for years about recording together, but did not find the opportunity until January 1971, when they were invited to perform at the Overseas Press Club in New York. They were joined by Mary Lou Williams on piano, George Duvivier on bass, and Grady Tate on drums. Unlike Dizzy's competitive trumpet jousts with Roy Eldridge, this encounter was a deep and sensitive conversation, a mutual exploration of musical materials spiced by the contrasting styles of the two men. Mary Lou Williams kept pace with the horn players as she weighed in with several imaginative and swinging statements. The recording mightily impressed Dan Morgenstern, who wrote: "[Dizzy] does things here that stagger the mind . . . ideas, speed, power, execution, and harmonic and rhythmic imagination beyond compare. . . . Hackett rises to the occasion; his conception is the essence of musicality. . . . The music on this wonderful record affirms the permanent value of truth and beauty. Run out and get it. Don't wait."[6]

Six months after the Hackett session, when Dizzy was scuffling for dates, George Wein offered him an Asian/European tour in a group with four other bandleaders who also faced sparse bookings: Thelonious Monk, Sonny Stitt, drummer Art Blakey, and trombonist Kai Winding. Bassist Al McKibbon, to be lured from the Los Angeles recording studios, would complete the group. If the musicians were willing to make sacrifices (for example, flying tourist class), Wein believed the venture would succeed. They all agreed, and the band, which was christened "The Giants of Jazz," became a congress of equals with no designated leader. The musicians traveled from early September until mid-November as they pushed themselves through forty-two concerts in New Zealand, Australia, Japan, Israel, and all the major countries of Eastern and Western Europe. They drew large audiences everywhere.

Monk became increasingly withdrawn as the tour wore on, and at the end of the junket he was hardly speaking to anyone. Soon after his return to New York, he was admitted to a psychiatric ward. Sporadically prey to mental illness for the rest of his life, he died in 1982.

The Giants provided many exhilarating moments, but they

broke no new ground, playing only ballads from the 1940s and 1950s and bebop standards. And as George Wein recalled, their work suffered because they were leaderless:

> I'm not sure that the Giants ever really cohered as a unit. The band generally played well; but they weren't carrying out the motivation of a single musical mind. I can't help but feel as if I did Thelonious Monk a particular disservice by asking him to join this group. . . . Neither Sonny nor Kai were accustomed to playing with Monk; they veered closer to Dizzy's musical universe. Only Blakey, and, to some extent, McKibbon really understood Monk's music. So it was as if the Giants were governed by two very distinct personalities. . . . It wasn't the glorious musical success that I'd hoped it would be.[7]

Dan Morgenstern echoed Wein's sentiments in a review of a recording of a Giants' concert: "By all means pick up this bebop banquet, but don't let anyone tell you it's the best these great men can do."[8]

Dizzy ended a two-year search for a top-flight drummer to fill Candy Finch's shoes when he hired Mickey Roker after returning from the Giants tour. Roker's impressive résumé included stints with former Gillespie associates Mary Lou Williams, Ray Bryant, Junior Mance, and Lee Morgan, and he proved a pillar of strength for Dizzy for nine years. Extremely versatile, he took quickly to Dizzy's tutelage: "Dizzy is a new experience for me. He helps me a lot rhythmically 'cause he has so much *knowledge*. Dizzy loves rhythm; that's good for me. [Lee Morgan's] band was much freer, you could play whatever you like playing. I liked that too, but I like the discipline Dizzy instills in the cats."[9] Within Dizzy's tight framework, Roker was soon powering both the small groups and the big bands with verve, intelligence, and a keen sensitivity to his colleagues' rhythmic needs.

During December 1971, Dizzy heard from Jon Faddis for the first time since meeting him in 1968. Jon, now nineteen years old, had become a professional and was touring with Lionel Hampton's band as it was heading for New York. He had heard that

Dizzy would be starting a two-week gig in early January at the Village Vanguard, and he requested permission to sit in during the engagement. When Dizzy agreed, Jon asked Hampton for two weeks off. He was so eager to work with Dizzy that he quit the band when Hampton refused. As he stepped happily onto the Vanguard bandstand for the first time, he had no inkling that he would be witness there to a near tragedy ten nights later.

Mike Longo remembered clearly what happened during the early hours of January 16, 1972:

> This particular night there must have been eighteen coke dealers in the club, and Dizzy let one of them, a guy called Dog, sit in on congas during the first set. Dizzy went off with Dog, and when we go up to play the second set, Dizzy is wobbling. He starts the first tune and collapses face forward, busting his horn. I jumped up from the piano and turned him over, and he says, "It's beautiful," and passes out.[10]

Dog had given Dizzy pure heroin and told him it was coke. This was the first and only time in his life that Dizzy had touched heroin, and his system couldn't take it. His friends didn't know what he had ingested; their first priority was to get him back to Lorraine, and they found in the audience a trustworthy acquaintance who lived near Dizzy in Englewood. The man agreed to take Dizzy home, and they told him to make sure that Lorraine saw the condition that her husband was in.

Mike recalled that Boo Frasier called the next morning:

> He wakes me at eight. He says Lorraine looked in on Dizzy during the night, and he was foaming at the mouth. She called an ambulance, and Dizzy's heart stopped beating on the way to the hospital. They brought him back with machines, but he was in awful shape, in critical condition.[11]

Dizzy's brush with death caused Longo to make a commitment: "I promised myself that if he came through, I would become a Baha'i. It took him six weeks to where he could play again. It was the Playboy Club in St. Louis. We ran into the Baha'i lady from Milwaukee there, and I made my declaration as a Baha'i to her at the club."[12]

Dizzy later talked to me about the Vanguard incident: "After it happened, I was terrified and ashamed. Mostly ashamed, because a Supreme Being put me here with a talent, a gift which I was meant to share with everyone. And I almost threw it away with one foolish act. I resolved to follow my Baha'i faith more deeply, and since 1972 I've made a lot of progress in banishing foolish things from my life."[13]

33
RENEWAL IN
THE SEVENTIES

Following Louis Armstrong's death on July 6, 1971, the mantle of jazz elder statesman moved from his shoulders to those of Dizzy, fifty-three at the time. In contrast to other prospective heirs to the mantle such as the prickly and frequently taciturn Miles Davis, Dizzy was favored by common consent because he possessed both a beloved, ebullient personality and a record as an untiring proselytizer for jazz.

The status of elder statesman brought many accolades; the process went into high gear during the summer of 1972 as Dizzy, following the Vanguard debacle, was subjecting himself with new seriousness to Baha'i disciplines.

Rutgers University conferred on him in June what was to become the first of his eighteen honorary degrees and honored his achievements with the Paul Robeson Award, named for its most prominent alumnus. Dizzy was particularly pleased with the latter, because Robeson ranked first in his pantheon of heroes.

The Handel Medallion, the highest cultural honor that New York City can bestow, followed soon after, on July 5, 1972. Dizzy proved an advocate in advance of his time when, at the award ceremony, he called on Mayor John Lindsay to build a permanent home for jazz in New York; this vision wasn't realized until fifteen years later, when Jazz at Lincoln Center was created in 1987.

Dizzy's childhood friend John Motley had won a Handel Medallion two years earlier for his work in molding New York's one-hundred-voice All-City High School Choir into a first-class ensemble, and the day following Dizzy's colloquy with Lindsay, he joined Motley and the choir in a "sacred" concert at Carnegie Hall.

Alice Wilson, Dizzy's grade-school teacher, had traveled north with a Cheraw delegation to celebrate the town's native sons, and during a quiet moment, Dizzy coaxed her onto the stage. He introduced her as "the cause of my being in music," and she told the audience, "I'm so pleased with everything that has been done by my little bad boy over here."

After Dizzy and his quintet augmented by the conga player Big Black performed a set, they joined the choir for a segment featuring several sacred numbers. Among them were Dizzy's tribute to Martin Luther King Jr., "Brother K," and the spirituals "Precious Lord, Take My Hand," "Sometime I Feel Like a Motherless Child" (sung soulfully by Dizzy), and "Somebody Bigger Than You and I" (with a luminous solo by Angela Bofill, who became a major pop star in subsequent decades). The performers drove the audience into a frenzy as they closed the concert with a wild version of "Manteca" that showcased the power of the massed voices and the percussion pyrotechnics of Big Black.

The Handel Medallion presaged an artistic and commercial renaissance for Dizzy.

After almost ten lean years, the audience for jazz began to grow again during 1973 and 1974 as a sizable public tired of the simpler melodies and rhythms of rock and turned to the more sophisticated aesthetic of jazz. Dizzy benefited greatly from this shift in taste, and his career received an added boost from Norman Granz.

The impresario had not been idle since he sold Verve Records in 1961. From his home in Switzerland, Granz had managed Ella Fitzgerald, Oscar Peterson, Count Basie, and Duke Ellington and promoted tours by them, Dizzy, Ray Charles, and other stars. He enjoyed becoming a gourmet chef, and he found additional pleasure buying and selling Picassos, Klees, Légers, and other modern masters.

Granz returned to the record business in late 1972, because the kind of jazz he adored was being ignored by the major record labels. He had suggested to Columbia's Goddard Lieberson (who had issued a series of pro bono albums of contemporary classical music) that Columbia undertake to record "everything Duke wants to put down for posterity" and argued, "You'd do it for Beethoven if he were alive. And the cost for a year . . . would be peanuts after a tax writeoff."[1] Lieberson turned him down flat.

Granz, who named his new label Pablo for his friend Pablo Picasso, the designer of the company logo, understood clearly why he was drawn back into the business:

> I started Pablo not to make any money. I've got a lot of money so I didn't have to go back in the record business. But I love jazz, and I get my kicks listening to certain kinds of people play. . . . Someone's got to record Benny Carter. For ten years he goes without getting an album. Why? Because these assholes won't record him, because he isn't payable. . . . Yesterday I saw an itinerary for Basie you wouldn't believe. High schools in Tennessee and one place called the Porgy and Bess Nightclub somewhere else. . . . Dizzy is bitter; he's seen the success that has come to people like Miles for instance, who can't wipe his ass playing trumpet, and to Mangione. . . . And here's Dizzy working these terrible night clubs.[2]

Granz was soon turning out 45 records per year, a far cry from the 150 in the heyday of Verve, but a significant number nonetheless.

As Dizzy's fortunes were rising in October 1973, I produced a concert for him and was witness both to his excellence as a teacher and to his anger. The concert grew out of my response to friends at New York University who had asked me to write a proposal to the

National Endowment for the Arts, which had offered to subsidize jazz events with specific educational content. We won a grant of $12,500 for a series of five concerts; we featured Eubie Blake, Roland Hanna, and Danny Mixon exploring seventy-five years of jazz piano, Les McCann describing jazz rhythms, the Thad Jones–Mel Lewis Orchestra illustrating a spectrum of big band styles, Max Roach and the J. C. White Singers demonstrating the connections between gospel and jazz, and Dizzy, Roach, Sonny Stitt, Sam Jones, and Hank Jones explaining how bebop was born.

Excellent versions of bebop classics were interspersed with lecture segments by Dizzy and Roach. Dizzy spoke humorously and eloquently about Kenny Clarke and the new rhythms at Minton's, the importance of Monk, the migration of bebop to Fifty-second Street from its incubator in Harlem, and his conflicts with Cab Calloway over the "new" music. Roach talked about the encouragement Coleman Hawkins had given to the young pioneers and about the immense influence of Charlie Parker. During a middle segment, Dizzy illustrated how bebop tunes were written to the chords of pop standards by playing the melodies of "How High the Moon" and "What Is This Thing Called Love" while Stitt performed their bebop countermelodies, "Ornithology" and "Hot House."

The sound system, which was run by students, faltered several times during the concert, and Dizzy grew increasingly angry with each malfunction. He would not accept his check as he strode out of the hall at concert's end, and we were forced to dispatch a student to look for him at his favorite uptown haunts. Her search took her to three clubs before she found him at 1:00 a.m. By this time, he had mellowed enough to buy her a drink and accept the check with grace.

Dizzy's honors took on an international flavor when, several weeks later, the government of Kenya invited him to perform and speak in Nairobi at the December 12, 1973, celebration of the country's tenth anniversary of independence from Great Britain. He won wide praise when he had his speech translated into Swahili and read it in that language.

Following his return from Africa, he was faced with the departure of Mike Longo after more than seven years of employment. Dizzy encouraged him to make the change, because Mike, at age thirty-four, had just won his first recording contract and had found himself in strong demand for club gigs. Their relationship did not end with Mike's resignation; they would remain the closest of friends and would collaborate on many projects in the years ahead. Dizzy elected not to replace him, but to shrink his unit to a quartet with Earl May on bass, Al Gafa on guitar, and Mickey Roker on drums.

The passing of Louis Armstrong and the fatal illness of Duke Ellington, who would die in May 1974, caused George Wein to fear for the preservation of the heritage of jazz, and he created the New York City Jazz Repertory Orchestra to help safeguard its legacy. He recruited more than one hundred musicians to participate in fifteen concerts at Carnegie Hall between January 26 and June 28, 1974. Classic arrangements were copied, but improvisations were created afresh. Tradition was embodied in the music of Ellington, Basie, Tatum, Monk, Coltrane, Henderson, Webb, Lunceford, and Puente, and the contemporary scene was represented by new works from Cecil Taylor, Gil Evans, and George Russell.

Dizzy received his due; he performed his classic big band arrangements on February 3 with an all-star orchestra that included Jon Faddis, and he played a key role in a June 28 Charlie Parker tribute that also enlisted the talents of Jay McShann, Billy Eckstine, Earl Hines, and Sonny Stitt.

His first album for Pablo, *Dizzy's Big 4*, recorded on September 19, 1974, was a masterpiece. The peak effort of his last two decades, it ranked with the finest work of his career as it brought him together with Ray Brown on bass, Mickey Roker on drums, and Joe Pass on guitar in a particularly emphatic unit. Brown supplied bass lines that were both ingenious and powerful, and Roker, who in almost three years with Dizzy had absorbed every nuance of his style, performed passionately and with total assurance. Pass, originally recommended to Granz by Oscar Peterson, was a deep student of bebop harmony and a master of his instrument; he improvised intriguing melodies at all tempos, and his ultrafast statement of the theme of "Bebop" with Dizzy is reminiscent, in its lightning facility, of Dizzy's unison passages with Bird during the 1940s.

Dizzy, at age fifty-six, had lost none of his exuberance and technical mastery, and here he put them at the service of a wise, mature sensibility. His tone was fuller than in his salad days, and his ideas possessed a more nuanced richness. Dizzy's highlights included exciting solos at two different tempos on Fats Waller's "Jitterbug Waltz," a searing interpretation of Irving Berlin's "Russian Lullaby," and a haunting improvisation on the ballad "September Song."

Dizzy's next recording for Pablo, a duet session with Oscar Peterson that took place on November 28 and 29, 1974, was another dazzling achievement. It came close to the peaks reached by the *Big 4* album, and it won him major kudos for 1975, the year of the LP's release: "record of the year" in *Downbeat*'s critics poll and his first Grammy, awarded for "best jazz performance by a soloist." (Dizzy later won two Grammys for performances recorded before 1974; he was honored in 1979 for "Manteca," created in 1947, and posthumously in 1995 for *Jazz at Massey Hall*, made in 1953.) Peterson remembered that the album was the first in a series conceived by Norman Granz:

> The series that came to be known as *Oscar Peterson Meets The Trumpet Kings* was a very special event for me. This was the latest of Norman's "musical visions," and it was daringly innovative. Usually, sessions of this type would, to all intents and purposes, be jam sessions, with the rhythm section feeding the trumpet soloists and providing helpful ideas and suggestions along the way. But Norman wanted something fresher and more adventurous—something that might help plumb the true soul of all the players concerned. Accordingly, he envisaged this series of recordings as one-on-one sessions, and made it known to all the participants that he would not accept any musical fairgrounding: he wanted only the truth.
>
> The field was as heavy as it was broad: Norman had chosen Dizzy Gillespie, Roy Eldridge, Clark Terry, Harry Edison, and Jon Faddis.[3]

Dizzy and Peterson provided the truth, virtuosically, and they both swung the pulse so strongly that they made a drum and a bass superfluous. They turned "Caravan" into a joyous conversation; "Blues for Bird" became an exploration of elegiac emotion, "Dizzy Atmosphere" a breakneck tour de force, and "Autumn Leaves" an intricate harmonic feast. Dan Morgenstern was moved to comment: "This is music for the ages."[4]

Following the triumph with Peterson, Granz continued to devise challenging studio pairings for Dizzy. In a series of mid-1970s LPs, he teamed him with Machito, Benny Carter, Count Basie, Lalo Schifrin, Roy Eldridge, and a hot Brazilian ensemble. The most successful of these collaborations were *Dizzy Gillespie y Machito: Afro-Cuban Jazz Moods* and *Carter, Gillespie, Inc.*

The former brought Dizzy together with Machito's Afro-Cubans under Mario Bauzá performing two splendid suites by Chico O'Farrill; Dizzy was the lone soloist. The band, its own rhythm section augmented by Mickey Roker, delivered joyous, full-throated backgrounds, and O'Farrill's mastery of orchestral color, rhythmic power, and harmonic contrast inspired Dizzy to a series of solos that conveyed a kaleidoscope of moods. Dizzy and Carter were appropriate foils for each other on *Carter, Gillespie, Inc.* Carter's sinuous lines provided a delicious balance to Dizzy's explosive flights, and their dueling, incendiary rendition of "Broadway" ranked with the best small-group tracks of Dizzy's career.

In addition to pairing Dizzy with stimulating partners, Granz featured him on jam session LPs. The best of these were recorded on the same evening at the 1975 Montreux Jazz Festival: *The Dizzy Gillespie Big Seven* and *The Trumpet Kings*. Dizzy jousted creatively with Milt Jackson and tenor saxophone titans Lockjaw Davis and Johnny Griffin on the *Big Seven* album, and he joined Roy Eldridge, Clark Terry, and Oscar Peterson for a happy romp on *Trumpet Kings*. Granz allowed Dizzy only one lapse into formulaic funk, a disappointing 1976 recording called *Dizzy's Party*.

Dizzy's psyche, buoyed by renewed artistic and commercial success, found new energy during a three-day August 1975 retreat at the holiest Baha'i shrines near Haifa in Israel.

His schedule had become so full and complex since the early 1970s that, upon his return to the United States, he hired Charles "Whale" Lake to assist him as booker and road manager. Lake,

who would remain with him until the end of his career, had
worked previously for Woody Herman, Count Basie, and Buddy
Rich. He was doing PR for a club near Boston when Dizzy hired
him, and he remembered the circumstances:

> One morning I went to pick him up at his hotel, and I knocked on
> the door and got no reply. I got a key from the management,
> opened the door, and Dizzy's laying in bed sound asleep with the
> telephone next to his ear. I picked up the phone, and a French-
> man's going, "Monsieur Gillespie, Monsieur Gillespie, what hap-
> pened to you?" Evidently he had gone to the bathroom, told the
> guy to hold on for a second, came back, and fell asleep.
>
> So I said, "Okay, Birks. That's it. From now on I'll start taking
> care of your phone calls." He was doing everything on his own,
> booking the dates, the planes, and the hotels. He had recently
> blown a gig in Spokane when he went to Seattle instead. He real-
> ized he needed help.[5]

Whale's first assignment involved a three-hour "tribute" concert
to Dizzy at Lincoln Center on September 13, 1975, a musical feast.
After announcing, "I'm the elder statesman. Know it and ain't
scared to show it," Dizzy revved up a big band studded with alumni
such as James Moody, Jimmy Heath, Cecil Payne, Charli Persip,
and Billy Mitchell and launched a torrid four-tune set that featured
a percussion conversation among Mickey Roker, guest star Buddy
Rich, and conga player Azzadin Weston. Dizzy's working quartet
brought the temperature down as they closed the first half of the
concert with a mellow bossa nova and his stately "Olinga."

The high points of the evening occurred during the second
half with outstanding work by two glittering quintets—Dizzy
joined Stan Getz, Max Roach, Percy Heath, and John Lewis in
one, and he brought forward Lalo Schifrin and Moody to reprise
their 1960s collaborations in the other. The concert ended with a
wild version of "Things to Come" by the big band. The event
was marked by a rare appearance backstage by Lorraine, whose
forays out of her home in Englewood had become increasingly
infrequent.

The South Carolina Arts Commission honored Dizzy in March 1976 with a one-week tour of the state that culminated in a reception by the governor and his wife and a ceremony on the floor of the state legislature in Columbia. The packed capitol galleries gave Dizzy standing ovations as he received a plaque from the Arts Commission, performed "Billie's Bounce" with a quintet that included Jimmy Heath, and gave a speech that was a Baha'i sermon. To be paid homage in the chamber once dominated by the minions of Pitchfork Ben Tillman was "the fruition of my wildest dreams" for the black man from Cheraw.

His sermon quoted freely from "200 Years of Imperishable Hope," an article from a Baha'i journal, and it called upon America to put behind it the horrors of racism and lead the way toward the Baha'i ideal of mankind unified in brotherhood. His emotional and carefully reasoned homily was in keeping with a deepening seriousness about his faith. Whale Lake remembered that he was praying every morning, studying Baha'i literature on planes and buses, and fasting during the holy period in March. Although he never totally weaned himself from alcohol, cigars, or marijuana, he had moderated his appetites considerably by the mid-1970s.

Dizzy's quartet was booked for a May 1977 jazz cruise to Jamaica and the Bahamas with the bands of Earl Hines, Stan Getz, Lionel Hampton, Roberta Flack, and Joe Williams when President Jimmy Carter eased restrictions on travel to Cuba, and the tour promoter substituted Havana for Montego Bay as a port of call. Hampton, Flack, and Williams pulled out because they believed that an association with Cuba would hurt their careers, and multi-instrumentalist David Amram and his group were recruited as substitutes.

During the 1970s, Fidel Castro professed to see little worth in jazz, which he deemed a decadent product of American capitalist society. Accordingly, he neither disseminated publicity about the arriving tour musicians, nor did he did send any officials to greet them. (He changed his tune after the collapse of the Soviet Union when he realized that jazz could earn for Cuba considerable amounts of hard currency.)

Arturo Sandoval, a twenty-seven-year-old Cuban jazz trumpeter, had somehow heard about the touring Americans, and he came down to the dockside to introduce himself to them. He recalled:

At that time I couldn't speak any English, nothing, and I felt so restrained. Suddenly Amram's percussionist Ray Mantilla, who is walking behind Dizzy, says in Spanish, "Can I help you?" This is my salvation. I said, "Oh, yea. I wanna tell this guy that I love his music and I'm here for whatever he wants." I never told them I was a musician; I was embarrassed to say that. Or to tell them that I served three months in prison for being caught listening to Willis Conover's jazz program on Voice of America radio.

I was happy when Dizzy asked if I had a car and could I take him right away to where people played those Afro-Cuban rhythms. It was a '51 Plymouth, falling apart, which I had just painted with tar and gasoline.[6]

Mantilla remembered Sandoval's next move:

We drove to a little barrio where all the drummers live and entered the home of the Valdez brothers, a famous percussion family. After about twenty minutes, they returned with the most famous conga players in all Cuba, in fact the most famous black drummers in all the world, the Los Papines quartet of four brothers. Dizzy and I flipped out playing with them. Can you imagine seven or eight people in a tiny little room jamming for hours?[7]

After Sandoval followed the Valdez/Los Papines session with a visit to a bass player's house where musicians performed Santeria rituals with authentic African rhythms and chants, Dizzy and Mantilla returned to the ship in a state of euphoria.

A formal concert by Cuban dance bands on the first night in port was anticlimactic, but Dizzy was inspired the following afternoon by what a *New York Times* correspondent called a "jam session to end all jam sessions" with local musicians. Irakere, Sandoval's group, participated and was a revelation to him; it featured three world-class jazzmen who were, at the time, little known outside of Cuba: Sandoval (who surprised Dizzy when he turned up with his trumpet), saxophonist Paquito D'Rivera, and Chucho Valdés, the leader and pianist. They went on to achieve world renown within a decade, and they now stand at the top of their profession.

Dizzy waved a white towel in mock surrender after a brilliant solo by Sandoval, but he, Getz, Amram, Mantilla, and Mickey Roker soon joined the fray and, carried aloft by Los Papines and other Afro-Cuban percussionists, gave at least as good as they got. Roker was particularly moved by the occasion: "I heard and I wanted to cry. No kidding, I just wanted to cry. It was beautiful man, strong, very religious, from the heart."[8]

The afternoon session marked the beginning for Dizzy of long personal and professional associations with Sandoval and D'Rivera. That evening, Amram led off a formal concert accompanied by Los Papines and Irakere in a piece dedicated to Chano Pozo. Its infectious rhythms put the audience in a raucous mood for the sets by Getz, Hines, and Dizzy that followed. And Dizzy had everyone dancing, stomping, and clapping when he brought all the musicians, nine percussionists included, out for the finale, "Manteca"; he left the stage shouting, "Let's bring Charlie Parker out again. How about a great big hand for Mao Tse-tung?" At 3:00 a.m., he and the other Americans returned to their ship for its journey to Nassau.

Upon returning to the United States, Dizzy and Getz sang Irakere's praises to Bruce Lundvall, president of CBS Records, who traveled to Cuba to hear them and signed them to his label. They made two albums for CBS in New York, and one of them, *Irakere*, won a Grammy for best Latin recording of 1979.

Granz moved quickly in July 1977 when Dizzy arrived in Montreux without his rhythm section; it had been routed erroneously to Holland. The impresario hurriedly recruited Ray Brown, Milt Jackson, pianist Monty Alexander, and drummer Jimmie Smith to lend support to Dizzy and Jon Faddis for a live recording to be called *Dizzy Gillespie Jam*, and the musicians harked back to 1945 with a hot bebop session. A stunning Brown duet with Dizzy attested to more than thirty years of intuitive interaction, and Faddis showed that he had achieved musical maturity at age twenty-four as he traded blistering choruses with his mentor.

Dizzy began attending White House events in 1956, but he never entertained there until November 15, 1977, when President Carter invited him and Sarah Vaughan to perform at a state dinner for the shah and the empress of Iran. Dizzy could not foresee, when he accepted the invitation, that the gig would involve a degree of danger. Violent anti-shah demonstrations had rocked the area around the White House as the artists rehearsed in the East Room, and President and Mrs. Carter and several reporters suffered the effects of tear gas as they awaited the Iranians on the South Lawn. To avoid trouble, the Secret Service used a long, circuitous route to transport Vaughan and Dizzy and their groups between the White House and their hotel, which were only two blocks apart.

Carter was a true jazz enthusiast who would order hours of the music pretaped to listen to during the days when he worked in his small study adjacent to the Oval Office. He thoroughly enjoyed the concert and leapt up to lead the applause after every number. Both Dizzy and Vaughan were in top form as they reprised their first recording together, "Lover Man," and shone in a program that included "'Round Midnight," a wordless blues, "Salt Peanuts," "Ornithology," and "I Got It Bad and That Ain't Good." Vaughan earned the biggest ovation of the night when she sang "Summertime" accompanied by her own trio.

Carter spied Earl Hines seated among the A-list businessmen and politicos invited to such events, and he asked Dizzy if he should invite him to sit in. When Dizzy replied, "It's your house," Carter called Hines to the stage, and the pianist responded with sterling solos on "Memories of You" and "Perdido."

The shah was deposed less than fifteen months later, on January 16, 1979.

Dizzy next performed at the White House on the sweltering Sunday afternoon of June 17, 1978, when Carter brought together the greatest array of jazz musicians ever assembled in one place. They came to celebrate the twenty-fifth anniversary of the Newport Jazz Festival with New Orleans food and a concert on the South Lawn. I was a member of Carter's Political Affairs Staff at the time and attended as a White House employee.

When George Wein approached the White House with his twenty-fifth anniversary proposal, he believed that he would need to sell hard, because he was relying entirely on a single letter of introduction from a Rhode Island congressman. But he didn't reckon with Carter's love of jazz; when he arrived in April for his first meeting with the White House social secretary, Wein found that the project had already been approved.

Spectators feasted on jambalaya, pecan pie, and jazz as they sat at wooden tables or spread out comfortably on the grass. Dizzy gave the president a book of Baha'i sacred texts and took part in a lively set with Dexter Gordon, George Benson, Herbie Hancock, Ron Carter, and Tony Williams. Among the others who performed that day were Sonny Rollins, Stan Getz, Max Roach, Roy Eldridge, Ray Brown, Mary Lou Williams, Eubie Blake, Lionel Hampton, Benny Carter, Ornette Coleman, Pearl Bailey, Chick Corea, Zoot Sims, Louis Bellson, Lionel Hampton, Jo Jones, Teddy Wilson, Clark Terry, Illinois Jacquet, and Cecil Taylor.

After a solo set by Taylor, one of the most avant-garde musicians in jazz history, Carter pulled him aside and engaged him in fifteen minutes of intense conversation about piano technique and theory. Following this encounter, the president, who was enjoying himself thoroughly, told Wein to ignore a preset, two-hour time limit and let the musicians jam on.

When the president joined Dave Usher, myself, Dizzy, Benny Carter, and Max Roach in conversation as the party was winding down, he asked Dizzy and Roach to play one more number. Dizzy agreed on the condition that Carter, the ex–peanut farmer, join them in a performance of "Salt Peanuts," and the president agreed. After a spirited rendition by the trio, Dizzy asked Carter if he wanted to join him and Max on tour, and the president replied, "After that performance, I may have to." Several TV cameramen had crowded around the bandstand, and the trio performance appeared on every major news show that night.

Evidence of Dizzy's late 1970s artistic renaissance can be

found in a two-volume LP set, *Dizzy Gillespie: The Development of an American Artist, 1940–1946*, issued by the Smithsonian in late 1976, and a *New York Times* article by Gary Giddins published one week after the White House Newport bash.

The Smithsonian's Martin Williams reinforced Dizzy's position in the jazz firmament as he presided over a scholarly audio survey of a historic period in Dizzy's career and wrote in his liner notes, "Gillespie is a great figure in American music, in world music, and perhaps the greatest living musical innovator we have."[9]

And Giddins in his article, "It's Dizzy Again," noted:

Much to his surprise, Dizzy Gillespie—who has been called the greatest trumpet virtuoso in or out of jazz—finds himself, at 60, spearheading a bebop revival. . . . Gillespie has been able to observe his reputation grow steadily from the stormy days of the bebop movement . . . to the present when he is cherished as an elder statesman not just of bebop but of jazz itself. . . . He continues to evince signs of musical growth. His tone has mellowed into an increasingly attractive and personal sound and . . . he has become a splendidly authoritative bluesman.[10]

Dizzy continued to grow musically, because he tried always to remain open to new ideas. The self-styled "rhythm man" pulled off a daring percussion experiment when, on June 22, 1979, he performed in concert with Max Roach, Art Blakey, Jo Jones, Tito Puente, Patato Valdes, Roy Haynes, and four other outstanding drummers at Carnegie Hall. He joined them frequently on congas and maintained audience interest by bringing them together in intriguing combinations. As all ten men were producing a symphony of rhythm for the finale, he left the stage and danced down an aisle and out of the hall joyously wiggling his rear end. The audience loved it.

Soon after this celebration with ten percussionists, Dizzy was faced with the loss of a single drummer who had become very dear to him. After nine years, Mickey Roker was worn down: "I learned so much while I was with Dizzy. I stayed with him until I was just wrung out because he put such demands on a drummer. . . . He expected a lot from everybody, but he just loved the drums so much. He expected us to do whatever was possible to make the music more exciting. He would want you to play the rhythm in as many ways as possible. It was exhausting."[11] Roker was replaced by Tommy Campbell.

August 3, 1979, marked the publication by Doubleday of *To Be, or not . . . to Bop*, Dizzy's autobiography created with Al Fraser. The book, five years in the making, is an oral history constructed from interviews with Dizzy and Lorraine and more than one hundred relatives, teachers, musicians, producers, promoters, and friends. Dizzy's commentaries are placed in a continuing counterpoint among the others, and they account for roughly 40 percent of the book's content.

Fraser had known Dizzy since the early 1950s. A professor of African American Studies during the 1970s at Cheney State College in Pennsylvania, he had built an impressive record as an editor, a historian, a journalist, and a poet by the time he signed on in 1973. Fraser helped create a work rich in insight and anecdote as he edited the material to provide a clear narrative, a cogent description of Dizzy's artistic achievements, and an accurate rendering of his religious and aesthetic beliefs.

The book received favorable reviews, with scattered exceptions, such as in *The New Yorker*. Claude Brown, in the *New York Times*, called it "a joyous, boisterous chronicle [and] . . . a desperately needed history." The reviewer for the *Christian Science Monitor* described it as "a verbal jam session of many voices . . . a remarkable addition to the library of modern jazz," and *Downbeat* applauded it as "a marvelous document." Following a profitable run in hard cover, the book proved a successful paperback for Da Capo Press and remained in print well into the 1990s.

The success of *To Be, or Not . . . to Bop* put a fitting close to the 1970s for Dizzy. Following the near-disaster in January 1972 at the Village Vanguard, the decade had been marked by triumph and renewal—artistic, spiritual, and monetary. He took advantage of the opportunities presented by Norman Granz to make recordings of the highest order, and he saw a healthy increase in his bookings and his fees. He won two Grammys and was honored in places as diverse as New York City, the Smithsonian Institution, Nairobi, Kenya, the White House, and Columbia, South Carolina. He returned joyously to his African roots in Cuba, and, most important, as evidenced by his increasing observance of ritual and his speech to the South Carolina legislature, he experienced a deepening of his Baha'i faith.

SUMMING UP AND 34
LOOKING FORWARD

WHALE LAKE REMEMBERED THAT DIZZY WAS BECOMING
increasingly prosperous as the 1980s began:

> The money was pretty small when I joined him in 1975. He just
> wanted to work. He'd never say to me, "How much does it pay?"
> He'd say, "Is there enough to pay the guys in the band?" I would
> say, "John, we shouldn't take this job." He'd say, "The guys got to
> get paid. Take it. Don't worry about me."
>
> When I started with him, I'll never forget it, his contract was
> $3,000 for that week. Well, it got to $4,000, $5,000, and so forth.
> Then maybe $2,000 for one night, $1,750 for one night.
>
> The better money didn't mean he slowed down. He loved the
> road, and he loved to perform, and that meant we were in perpet-
> ual motion.
>
> We were always paid in cash, and he was very loose with it. If

Dizzy went from here to there, you would find a trail of socks, underwear, hundred-dollar bills, passports, pictures from last night,
flowers. So, every time we got into the limo to leave the hotel, I'd
say, "Excuse me, John, I forgot something." I always had an extra
key to his room and I'd run up there, grab a pillow-case and dump
things in it. What things I used to find—clothes, cash, rolls of film,
contracts, his passport. Many times his passport.

And he was a soft touch with his money. All night long, hangers-
on and panhandlers from years ago would knock and say, "Hey,
John, how you doin', man?" He'd open the door, give somebody
twenty, close the door. Sometimes he would ask them in, and they
would tell all the old stories and laugh. He loved those old stories.

All night long. Everywhere we were at. Nobody ever walked
away empty.[1]

Dizzy could not resist a trumpet challenge, and when Norman
Granz asked him in March 1980 to interrupt a busy schedule and
fly from South Carolina to Los Angeles to record with two outstanding horn men, Clark Terry and Freddie Hubbard, and the
rhythm section of Oscar Peterson, Ray Brown, Joe Pass, and
drummer Bobby Durham, he jumped on the first available plane.
Dizzy went directly to the studio, worked from 9:00 p.m. to 3:00
a.m., and took the next flight to New York for a gig that night.
His performance on the two LPs that resulted, *The Trumpet Summit* and *Alternate Blues*, showed evidence of fatigue and the hurried nature of the date; he was brilliant in spots but lacked focus
overall. Terry and Hubbard fared no better.

Dizzy's routine of festivals, nightclub gigs, and workshops was
occasionally interrupted by a special event like the ambitious *Jazz
in America* TV series, a bebop anthology created by KCET-TV of
Los Angeles, Lincoln Center, the Public Broadcasting System,
and National Public Radio with financial assistance from the Atlantic Richfield Corporation and the National Endowment for
the Arts. The project was budgeted at $7.9 million.

Dizzy participated in two of the four broadcasts; he led an
eighteen-piece "Dream Band" and an all-star sextet in a Lincoln
Center concert on February 16, 1981, and he fronted an octet in a

February 25 session filmed at the Concerts-at-the-Sea Club in Redondo Beach, California. The other two events featured quartets led by Gerry Mulligan and Max Roach.

Producer Barry Keys created excellent visuals throughout his four and a half hours on air, and he paced the shows well, inserting short but relevant interviews and including the entire three-minute video of the only performance of Charlie Parker caught on tape or film, his 1952 television rendition of "Hot House" with Dizzy.

The series aired in September 1983 and was packaged for VHS sale soon after; tapes are still available commercially in 2005. No CDs of the concerts were ever issued, however. The sponsors had hoped that the four-part bebop package would be the first of several segments illustrating the history of jazz, but funding shortfalls doomed the project after the initial series.

The Dream Band concert joined such Gillespie alumni as Melba Liston, Jon Faddis, Candido, Jon Hendricks, Jimmy Heath, Milt Jackson, Paul West, John Lewis, and Max Roach with stars like Gerry Mulligan, Slide Hampton, Roland Hanna, Marvin Stamm, Joe Wilder, Basie veterans Frank Foster and Frank Wess, and Paquito D'Rivera, who had recently defected from Cuba.

On May 6, 1980, while touring with Irakere, D'Rivera checked a valise full of bricks, boots, and other detritus for a flight from Madrid to Stockholm but never boarded the plane. He found refuge with a Spanish friend and on October 24 made his way from Spain to New Jersey; there he was reunited with his parents, who had emigrated legally twelve years earlier. His talents were recognized quickly; within weeks, he found numerous gigs and signed a contract with CBS Records, Irakere's label.

Television viewers were happy with what they heard but the Lincoln Center audience was not. The placement of special television audio equipment caused the sound in the hall to be badly muddied.

The program featured Dizzy's eighteen-piece big band, a solo spot for Roach, and a spectacular sextet where Dizzy was joined by Roach, Lewis, Mulligan, Jackson, and West. Highlights included Jackson's solo on "Lover Man," Roach's percussion improvisations, Foster's romp through "Manteca," and Dizzy's entire performance, which caused Gary Giddins to write, "Dizzy Gillespie is the most adventurous and satisfying trumpet player in jazz today. . . . [He is] undergoing an unprecedented personal renaissance. . . . His technique is riveting, his sound compellingly bittersweet."[2]

Dizzy, indifferent to the reactions of a national television audience, began the Redondo Beach broadcast by asking the club crowd, "Who took the joint out of my pocket? It was sinsemilla." (Sinsemilla is a prized species of marijuana.)

Dizzy's octet that evening included his regular backup musicians (Ed Cherry on guitar, Tommy Campbell on drums, and Michael Howell on electric bass) plus Ray Brown, Paquito D'Rivera, trombonist Tom McIntosh (who had composed three numbers for Dizzy's great 1963 album *Something Old, Something New*), and pianist Valerie Capers. The duet segments by Dizzy and Brown are alone worth the price of a videotape; a passionate solo by D'Rivera on "Kush," powerful pianistics by Capers, and soulful blues interpretations by Cherry and McIntosh provide added value.

Dizzy was shaken by the death of Mary Lou Williams from cancer on May 28, 1981. He had last seen her three months earlier on his trip east from Redondo Beach, when he cheered her in a North Carolina hospital room and left her with a final memento, a packet of high-grade marijuana. He performed "Con Alma" unaccompanied at her New York funeral on June 2 as Lorraine, racked with sobs, made a rare public appearance.

Dizzy's involvement with Cuban musicians continued into 1982. He performed frequently with D'Rivera, and he began to use the Cuban drummer, Ignacio Berroa, who had arrived in America via the Mariel boatlift in 1980. On September 9, 1982, he recorded *To a Finland Station* with Arturo Sandoval, while both were touring in Europe. When Norman Granz heard that the two men would be visiting Helsinki at the same time, he hastily arranged a recording date using a Finnish rhythm section. Given the competitive propensities of the two principals, the resulting album, cut in an all-night session, provides enjoyment in a surprisingly low-key manner; it is short on pyrotechnics and surprisingly mellow. The Finns acquitted themselves well, particularly on two Latin numbers. The album title was Granz's homage to Edmund Wilson's great work of political analysis, *To the Finland Station*.

Upon returning from Europe, Dizzy was asked to participate in a concert that was part of a series called "Young Artists in Performance at the White House." He and Stan Getz were asked to introduce, on December 4, 1982, protégés who deserved wider recognition, and the performance was slotted for a nationwide broadcast by PBS on December 21. This was the first time jazz artists were featured in the series, which had previously been the province of classical musicians. Dizzy brought Jon Faddis and Getz invited Diane Schuur, a powerful, blind singer and pianist whom Dizzy had introduced to Getz at the 1979 Monterey Festival.

After Nancy Reagan began the proceedings in the absence of the president, who was traveling in South America, she sat down next to George and Barbara Bush, and turned the evening over to the master of ceremonies, Itzhak Perlman, the classical violin virtuoso.

Perlman began by stating his love for jazz and then introduced Getz and Dizzy. After they performed a spirited version of "Groovin' High" backed by the world-class rhythm section of Chick Corea, Roy Haynes, and Miroslav Vitous, Dizzy seethed as Perlman entered a colloquy with Getz about the origins and meaning of bebop, and Getz never mentioned Dizzy or invited him to enter the conversation. Dizzy, who always held Getz in affection, bore no grudge following the incident.

Getz introduced Schuur, who sang two ballads soulfully while accompanying herself at the piano. Next Dizzy brought out Faddis, who proved his mettle as he traded nuanced solos with his mentor on Dizzy's tune "And Then She Stopped." Perlman returned to demonstrate an acute lack of swing as he joined all the jazz musicians for the finale, "Summertime."

The concert boosted the careers of Schuur and Faddis, both twenty-nine at the time. A top executive of GRP Records reached Schuur soon after watching the December 21 television show and signed her to a record contract that put her career in high gear. Faddis had, during the previous five years, been performing jazz with Dizzy, the Jones-Lewis Orchestra, Charlie Mingus, and others, but most of his income had come from studio work creating advertising jingles and backing up artists like Frank Sinatra, Billy Joel, and the Rolling Stones. The prestige and the publicity surrounding the White House concert gave him the courage to organize a band and venture out on his own. He has never turned back.

Dizzy's next encounter with Getz occurred during the summer of 1984, and it had a dramatic effect on the saxophonist's life. Stanford University, where Getz had informally become an artist in residence, invited Dizzy to join him and other musicians for an intensive two-week workshop with selected students. The planned climax of the fortnight was a gala fund-raising concert on August 5 by Dizzy and Getz to be attended by the university president and other dignitaries; commitments were made to record the event. Getz at the time was in the midst of a struggle to free himself from a thirty-year addiction to alcohol.

Dizzy and he were scheduled to give formal lectures on August 2 and August 4, respectively. Getz, who was notoriously inarticulate, attended Dizzy's talk and became racked with anxiety as Dizzy fascinated the audience with an informative and humorous discussion of jazz rhythms. Feeling sure that his lecture two days later would pale beside Dizzy's, Getz left the hall in a panic after half an hour and launched himself into a three-week binge that caused him to miss the fund-raising concert and took him to San Francisco and Newport, Rhode Island.

A tenth-grade dropout who held intellectuals in awe, Getz believed that he would be ostracized by the Stanford academic community after this damaging fiasco, but they forgave him and rallied behind him on his return. They worked with his girlfriend, Jane Walsh, to provide crucial emotional support, and they enrolled him in an effective rehab program that led him finally to renounce alcohol thirteen months later; he remained clean and sober during the five and a half years left to him. Dizzy's lecture, therefore, had unwittingly become a transforming event in Getz's life.

During 1984, Dizzy failed again to find success in the pop/funk world with *Closer to the Source* for Atlantic Records.

This LP, an inconsistent hodgepodge with six separate lineups for six tunes, stands with *Sweet Soul (Souled Out)* of 1970 at the nadir of Dizzy's recorded output. Branford Marsalis and Stevie Wonder performed on one track each, and the fine young pianist Kenny Kirkland participated on two, but neither they nor Dizzy could salvage much from this effort.

Dizzy fared somewhat better on a second 1984 album with Marsalis and Kirkland, *New Faces*, a mixed outing for GRP Records. The "Birks Works" and "Ballad" tracks, which receive straight jazz treatments, are excellent, but the remaining six offer only pleasant, accessible music with little fire.

Dizzy began to suffer from adult-onset diabetes during 1985. Though the disease can be controlled by medication and by vigilant monitoring of one's sugar intake and other aspects of one's diet, Dizzy was an indifferent patient. Marijuana strongly stimulated his appetite, and he frequently committed excesses like consuming a good-sized cake at one sitting.

Dizzy found that racism was alive and well in South Carolina in January 1985, when he stopped in Cheraw on his way to Myrtle Beach for induction into the state's Hall of Fame. He recalled the incident: "I needed a haircut. Both colored barber shops were full, so I walked into the white barber shop. The barber tells me, 'Sorry, sir, we don't cut colored hair.' Then he recognized me: 'Oh, Mr. Gillespie, the last time I seen you—.' I cut him off: 'I only want a haircut.' I figured I'd better get out of there because he has razors and I've only got a knife."[3]

A few weeks later, Dizzy made a second visit to Cuba, a country with more harmonious race relations than the United States, to perform at a jazz festival and to be the subject of *A Night in Havana*, an affectionate eighty-five-minute documentary produced by Cubana Bop Partners, an American company. His band comprised Walter Davis Jr. on piano, Big Black on percussion, John Lee on bass, and the recently hired father-and-son team of Sayyd Abdul al-Khabyyr and Nasyr Abdul al-Khabyyr on reed instruments and drums, respectively.

Dizzy was filmed chatting with Fidel Castro, making a pilgrimage to Chano Pozo's sister at her home, dancing with children and with a folkloric ensemble, and performing informally and in concert with a sensational twenty-one-year-old pianist, Gonzalo Rubalcaba, and with Arturo Sandoval and his band. In interviews replete with humorous anecdotes and outrageous puns, he struck a serious note when he reflected on the poverty of his childhood and declared, with deep emotion, his identification with Cuba's poor.

While exchanging choruses with Sandoval, he did not follow his confrere into the top range of the trumpet. Dizzy had recently been fitted with dental implants, and they served to weaken his embouchure, the complex of lip and facial muscles that controlled the flow of air into his trumpet mouthpiece. During the balance of his career, he experienced difficulty reaching into the highest octave.

Funding shortages delayed postproduction operations, and *A Night in Havana* was not released in movie theaters until May 1989. It received uniformly favorable reviews, was shown on the Bravo television network during the 1990s, and is currently available on videocassette.

Whale remembered a post-Cuba visit to Melba Liston in 1985 soon after she suffered a stoke that rendered her incapable of performing or arranging.

> Dizzy hadn't known how bad she was. Couldn't use her arm. We ate watermelon with her, her mother, and her niece, and left them five hundred dollars. We were in the car and he says, "What are we going to do?" And I said, "Birks, let's call the union." They sent her a unique computer for handicapped people for writing music. The whole enchilada, special discs and everything. Then Dizzy arranged for her to get checks from the union—money she didn't know she was entitled to. He always found out about things like that.[4]

Liston pursued a successful arranging career until her death at seventy-three in 1999.

One of the most satisfying events of 1985 for Dizzy was a concert in Jerusalem produced by a Brooklyn native named Charlie Fishman. Fishman, a sometime composer and pianist, lived in the city from 1971 to 1973, where he ran a jazz club/cultural center, and from 1976 to 1986, he was a cultural adviser to the Israeli government while residing in the United States. He met Dizzy during 1972 and in 1978 won his approval to present him in concert with the Israel Philharmonic Orchestra. It took seven years to bring this concept to fruition, however; the concert, which was a critical and commercial success, took place in June 1985 with Lalo Schifrin conducting.

The organizational skills, deep understanding of jazz, and quiet persistence Fishman demonstrated in creating the event impressed Dizzy at a time when his schedule was becoming increasingly crowded and complex. Dizzy realized that Whale could no longer handle it alone, and he put Fishman in charge of his business affairs while retaining Whale as road manager.

Mrs. Catherine Filene Shouse, a department store heiress and arts patron, gave Wolf Trap, her hundred-acre farm in the Virginia suburbs of Washington, DC, to the U. S. government in 1966, in an arrangement that created the country's first national park for the performing arts. She provided funds for a 6,800-seat indoor/outdoor theater and for smaller performance and teaching buildings on the site. Her Filene Foundation managed all the artistic activities while the National Park Service maintained the grounds and facilities.

Mrs. Shouse, both a friend and a fan of Dizzy's who long wished to host a Wolf Trap concert in his honor, decided with him and Fishman that his impending seventieth birthday in October 1987 would provide an excellent opportunity to do so, and she signaled approval in October 1986 for a concert on June 6, 1987; Dizzy was so pleased with Fishman's work on the 1985 Jerusalem concert that he asked him to produce the Wolf Trap event. Fishman had strengthened his team when he brought on Ms. Dierdre Henry as his prime assistant in 1986, and she contributed greatly to the success of Wolf Trap and many subsequent projects.

It was a measure of the musicians' love for Dizzy that headliners such as Oscar Peterson and Sonny Rollins, who normally commanded in excess of ten thousand dollars for a performance, accepted fifteen hundred dollars at Wolf Trap. Less celebrated musicians also took reduced fees and were paid either one thousand or five hundred dollars.

I was invited to the event that began at the Penta (now the Pennsylvania) Hotel in New York opposite Penn Station. The hotel presented him with a gigantic cake, and we stopped traffic as we accompanied it across Seventh Avenue and into one of two "American Zephyr" parlor cars for our trip to Washington. Dizzy wanted to provide transportation for musicians and friends and their families, and the Zephyrs, donated by their parent company and affectionately reconstructed in 1940s high style, provided a commodious setting for more than one hundred of us; Wolf Trap contributed food and drink for the journey.

The Wolf Trap event stands with the September 1947 concert with Bird, Ella, and Chano Pozo as a defining milestone in Dizzy's career. The 1947 concert affirmed the victory of the bebop and Afro-Cuban jazz revolutions, while Wolf Trap provided a triumphant summing up of a protean career.

Fishman conceived the five-hour event in twelve segments, each of which illuminated a facet of Dizzy's life in music. Dizzy participated in all twelve and was joined by forty-six established musicians and a twenty-three-piece youth orchestra. Seven of the segments were thematic: Schifrin and *The Gillespiana Suite*, early bebop (with a cross-generational horn section comprising Wynton Marsalis, Benny Carter, and J.J. Johnson), the years with Moody, Dizzy's trumpet progeny (Faddis, Marsalis, Freddie Hubbard, and Jimmy Owens), Cuba and the Carribean (featuring conga masters Candido and Mongo Santamaria), the big bands, and Brazilian influences (spotlighting the husband-and-wife team of Airto Moreira and Flora Purim).

The other five segments involved a set with Carmen McRae, Dizzy reprising two of his greatest recording sessions in collaborations with Sonny Rollins and Oscar Peterson, excerpts from archival films, and one number with the youth band.

Dizzy's inspiration and energy never flagged, despite having rehearsed Friday night and most of Saturday. The seven thousand spectators who spilled out of the auditorium onto the surrounding lawns enjoyed world class music all evening from both brilliant younger players such as Marsalis, Owens, and trombonist Steve

Turre and from veteran Dizzy alumni Faddis, Hank Jones, Mike Longo, Charli Persip, Mickey Roker, Chris White, Rufus Reid, Jon Hendricks, David Amram, and Cecil Payne.

The peak moments for me occurred during Dizzy's blistering encounters with Rollins on "Wheatleigh Hall" and "Dizzy Atmosphere." Other high points involved exhilarating scat vocals by Dizzy, Moody, and Hendricks on "Oop-Pop-A-Da," the twenty-three-member big band's joyous renditions of "A Night in Tunisia" and "Emanon," Dizzy's tender obbligatos behind McRae on "A Beautiful Friendship," and his richly romantic treatment of "All the Things You Are" with Peterson.

While we were partying backstage at 3:00 a.m., I asked Dizzy if he was thrilled by the night's celebration of his achievements, and he replied: "I'll let the critics evaluate my achievements. I'm just happy being out here at my age still putting the metal to my lips and doing it with great musicians. It was a gas tonight—particularly that youth band. Those kids were great; they're the future."[5]

The Maryland PBS television station produced a disappointing ninety-minute documentary about the concert that contained thirty-two minutes of talking heads and archival footage and only fifty-eight minutes of music. It aired nationally on February 26, 1988. Dizzy welcomed this program despite its mediocrity, because its viewers roughly equaled the number of people who would attend three years of his nightclub gigs. Fishman later cut a two-hour version filled with music for Pioneer Laser Disc, but it is no longer available.

During 1987 and early 1988, Dizzy toured with both his own quintet (which featured former avant-garde icon Sam Rivers on saxophone and a rhythm section of Ignacio Berroa on drums, John Lee on bass, and Ed Cherry on guitar) and an all-star big band led by Jon Faddis. The all-stars included the members of the quintet and featured as soloists Dizzy, Faddis, trombonist Turre, and saxophonist Jerry Dodgion. As Lee remembered, Dizzy drove his guys at a frantic pace: "This was early '88—the small group. Went to Europe for thirteen straight concerts. No day off. Then back into Kennedy and to New Jersey for a gig. Next morning to Florida for an afternoon festival, returned at one a.m. Next night to Europe for four straight concerts. Flew to Los Angeles on the fifth day for three more concerts and ended up doing a week at Yoshi's in Oakland—twenty-three gigs in twenty-five days."[6]

When Faddis decided in early 1988 to leave by the end of the year, Fishman began working with Dizzy on an idea conceived during 1987: a big band that would begin to embody Dizzy's Baha'i dream of bringing together diverse musical cultures to create a world music. If, as the Baha'is believe, mankind is a single family, then it followed that this family could create a single music of the greatest richness and variety. Lalo Schifrin gave the band its name, the United Nation Orchestra (UNO), and its inaugural concert took place at Wolf Trap in June 1988. Dizzy, who had performed with indigenous musicians in places like Pakistan, Turkey, and Kenya, realized that all of the UNO's original members would be from the Americas, but he envisioned that the band would broaden its ethnic reach as it matured. Several musicians, including Faddis, performed in both the all-star band and the UNO, as Dizzy toured with each of them during the summer of 1988.

By the time it was fully constituted in early 1989, the fifteen-piece UNO comprised a Panamanian (pianist Danilo Perez), three Brazilians (multipercussionist Airto Moreira, vocalist Flora Purim, and trumpeter Claudio Roditi), a Dominican (saxophonist Mario Rivera), a Puerto Rican (conga player Giovanni Hidalgo), three Cubans (Paquito D'Rivera, Ignacio Berroa, and, on occasion, Arturo Sandoval), and six Americans (Dizzy, trombonists Steve Turre and Slide Hampton, James Moody, John Lee, and Ed Cherry). Perez, Hidalgo, Rivera, and Roditi were little-known but brilliant performers recruited by D'Rivera, while the other newcomers (Moreira, Purim, and Hampton) were stars in their own right. All of the musicians were outstanding soloists, and nine of them had led their own bands. Dizzy made D'Rivera and Hampton his musical directors. Hampton was an excellent arranger, and fresh arrangements of the entire repertoire were ordered from him and several others.

With the UNO in place, Dizzy was poised at age seventy-one for a period of extraordinary creativity that would continue for more than three years.

A CREATIVE RENAISSANCE

THESE CREATIVE YEARS STARTED WHEN DIZZY, JAMES Moody, Giovanni Hidalgo, Ignacio Berroa, John Lee, and Ed Cherry arrived in Cairo on January 1, 1989, for a one-month goodwill tour of Africa sponsored by the United States Information Agency. It would take them from Egypt to Morocco, Senegal, Nigeria, and Zaire. The high point of the trip for Dizzy occurred in Nigeria, when he was installed as a tribal chief, or Baashere of Iperu, in a formal ceremony. Dave Usher recalled the event:

> He knew that his great-grandmother was the daughter of a Yoruba tribal chief from where Nigeria is now, and he felt a close kinship with these people. He said that they all looked like his relatives. He was very serious during the ceremony, where he wore this gorgeous, forty-pound traditional robe in green, beige,

and white. The ritual involved sacred drumming and chanting, and he took off his shoes and danced with the others in the red dirt. The whole observance touched something deep inside him. Truly.[1]

Dizzy's return to the United States was marked by two events, one happy and one sad. On February 20, he traveled to Los Angeles to receive a Lifetime Achievement Grammy along with Sarah Vaughan, Lena Horne, Leontyne Price, and, posthumously, Bessie Smith and Art Tatum. Eight days later at St. Peter's, the Manhattan church to which jazz people flocked, he played a solo rendition of "'Round Midnight" and spoke at the funeral of Roy Eldridge, who had died on February 26 at age seventy-eight.

The spring of 1989 was a golden one for Dizzy. He made four important recordings; two of them were nominated for Grammys, and one triumphed. The first session occurred on March 23, when he interrupted a European tour with his small group to join Max Roach for a duet concert in Paris. Roach remembered talking Dizzy into adopting a new approach to improvisation: "I had made 'free' recordings with avant garde musicians like Cecil Taylor and Anthony Braxton—no chord structure, no modes. Just wing it. Ornette Coleman territory. Dizzy and I had not rehearsed, and on the way to the concert, I suggested that we play 'free.' He said, 'O.K.' It was a first for him, and he more than met the challenge."[2]

The old friends created a ninety-minute musical continuum in which new melodies emerged from the heat of their dialogue and old ones popped up now and again. Roach, the most melodic of drummers, cued and prodded Dizzy, and he responded with daunting skill and creativity. Gary Giddins was amazed by Dizzy's performance:

How did he do it? How did he sustain a ninety minute duet with a prodigiously athletic drummer without the remotest lapse in technique or conception? . . . It's his tone that grabs you, an inimitable purring, refined and genial and austere—the quintessence of the Gillespie sound preserved in spite of the abuses of time, as though

he'd finally tempered the trumpet and made of it a compliant ap-
pendage to mind and body. A lifetime resides in that sound and
the savvy in which he parses his phrases for maximum impact. . . .

His music has never been more deeply beautiful. This is one of
the essential works in his fifty-three-year discography.[3]

The music was released in a double-CD set together with a
flavorful half-hour Gillespie/Roach conversation recorded in a
Paris hotel room. It was called *Max + Dizzy, Paris 1989*, and it
made every jazz critic's top-ten list for the year. It was nominated
for a Grammy in 1990 but did not win.

Dizzy made his next recording on June 10 in London with the
UNO during a three-week European tour that involved eighteen
concerts in eleven countries. It was called *Live at the Royal Festival
Hall*, and it won him his fourth Grammy in 1992. (A fifth was
awarded posthumously in 1995 for *Jazz at Massey Hall*, recorded
in 1953.)

Airto Moreira, Hidalgo, Berroa, Cherry, and Lee provided a
powerful rhythmic foundation for this happy, brawling CD, and
they brought a contagious freshness to old Gillespie classics such
as "A Night in Tunisia," "Tin Tin Deo," and "Kush." Every member of the UNO was an outstanding soloist, and the CD over-
flows with excellent improvisations. The concert elicited a
ten-minute standing ovation.

Dizzy left the UNO at tour's end to journey to Paris to celebrate—at the same time—the bebop revolution in the person of
Charlie Parker and the French Revolution on the occasion of its
two-hundredth anniversary. The French government hosted a
five-day tribute to Bird in the midst of its glittering bicentennial
festivities, and Dizzy played in "Homage to Charlie Parker" concerts on June 14 and 15 as the leader of a bebop all-star septet.

Before they performed, the musicians—Dizzy, Max Roach,
Stan Getz, Milt Jackson, Jackie McLean, Percy Heath, and Hank
Jones—were honored by first lady Danielle Mitterand and Minis-
ter of Culture Jack Lang with induction into the prestigious Order of Arts and Letters. Dizzy was made a Commander, while the
others were appointed as Officers, a lower rank.

Roach praised Dizzy as he reflected on the spirit of the occasion:

> It was the height of Paris tribute. Great moments of togetherness and the chance to thank Parker for all he contributed. . . . Total rapport. Each of us seemed to be putting out a little bit extra. Warmth.
>
> It was also a time for all of us to bow to Diz. He was the catalyst that helped launch it all . . . the scout who inspired players around the country and talked about them when he got back to New York . . . the focal point around whom they gathered when they got to the big town.[4]

Madame Mitterand served as mistress of ceremonies at the concerts, which drew wildly enthusiastic crowds.

An album of the second performance on June 15, with a cover featuring a photograph of the medal of the Order of Arts and Letters, is marked by precise ensemble work, passionate solos, and roars from the audience. Dizzy is featured on three tracks; he is pensive on "Con Alma" and exuberant on "A Night in Tunisia" and "Oop-Pop-A-Da."

Rhythmstick, the final CD of his golden springtime, was recorded on June 19 in New Jersey. The concept album created by producer Creed Taylor used Afro-Cuban, Brazilian, and African idioms to illustrate Dizzy's tremendous contribution to the rhythmic vocabulary of jazz. Taylor's stellar cast included Tito Puente, Phil Woods, Jon Faddis, Benny Golson, bassist Charlie Haden, and trumpeter Art Farmer.

The album's title refers to an instrument Dizzy invented, a broomstick with Coca-Cola tops mounted loosely on nails throughout its length. By banging it against the floor, shaking it, and kicking it, Dizzy was able to raise a polyrhythmic storm. He was in excellent form on the two numbers allotted to him, an African piece on which he performed a rollicking rhythmstick/timbale duet with Puente and played two sizzling trumpet solos flawlessly, and a hot mambo. Gene Lees, in his perceptive essay about the session, "Waiting for Dizzy," and in his liner notes conveys the respect the other musicians felt for Dizzy:

When Dizzy arrived . . . there was an aura about him. It wasn't exactly a matter of people lining up to pay tribute: jazz musicians are too democratic, the music itself is too democratic, for obeisance. But it certainly was an "homage," in the way the French use the word. The young revolutionary of long ago, with the horn-rimmed glasses and the beret and the goatee and the impish smile, had lived to be the elder statesman, the master, the sage of this music, and gathered about him were all these gifted players who were, directly or indirectly, his musical descendants.[5]

On August 25, at the age of seventy-one, Dizzy made *The Symphony Sessions*, his first recording with a traditional symphony orchestra, the Philharmonic of Rochester, New York. Three years in the making, the album nestled Dizzy, his rhythm section, and saxophonist Ron Holloway, a new hire, within burnished arrangements that provided settings for biting solos by the two horn men.

Dizzy toured extensively with the UNO in Europe and the United States during the summer and autumn of 1989, and on Labor Day weekend at the Chicago Jazz Festival, he and the band performed before 120,000 people, the largest crowd of his career.

On October 19, Dizzy and Billy Eckstine embarked on a seven-week tour of forty-four cities with the Count Basie Orchestra called "Dizzy and Mr. B. Salute the Count." Basie had died in 1984, but the orchestra survived and prospered under the leadership of saxophonist Frank Foster, a musician highly respected by Dizzy.

Dizzy enjoyed himself thoroughly. As with the Stan Kenton tour in 1954, he was happy to shed the responsibilities of leadership for a while and perform two or three numbers every night with young musicians who adored him. He loved Basie's music and the comradery of the road and working with Eckstine for the first time in fifty-five years. Frank Foster remembered the experience:

Dizzy and "B" left us with more X-rated road stories from the old days with B's, Dizzy's, and Fatha Hines' band than we can ever recall . . . I have so many Dizzy moments. . . . [including] his sitting down next to me at an airline baggage claim area at La Guardia

Airport, lighting up a pipe full of good reefer and handing it to me
in front of dozens of people. I could never refuse Dizzy anything so
I took it, and with great embarrassment, took a puff and said a
prayer. It didn't matter, it was not meant for us to get busted that
day. "Birks" lived a charmed life right until the end.[6]

Dizzy left the tour on November 17 to receive a National
Medal of the Arts from President George H. W. Bush at a private
reception and lunch at the White House. Although the National
Endowment for the Arts can make recommendations to the president, he alone has the power to choose the medalists. Among the
twelve recipients were writers John Updike and Czeslaw Milosz,
painter Robert Motherwell, photographer Alfred Eisenstat, and
(posthumously) pianist Vladimir Horowitz. Leonard Bernstein
drew headlines when he refused to accept his medal because he
objected to an attempt by the National Endowment for the Arts
to censor an art show catalog.

Late in 1989, Fishman secured a film role for Dizzy in a European production, *The Winter in Lisbon*. Dizzy earned one hundred
thousand dollars for his acting and thirty-five thousand dollars
for creating the score; he paid Slide Hampton ten thousand dollars to arrange the music and conduct the sound-track recording.
During breaks from his European tours, he hopped over to San
Sebastián, Spain, and to Lisbon for four shoots between February
and November 1990. Dizzy portrayed Bill Swann, a bandleader
and mentor to a young pianist played by Christian Vadim, son of
the movie star Catherine Deneuve and the noted director Roger
Vadim. *The Winter in Lisbon* is a standard romantic adventure in
which the Vadim character falls in love with a beautiful, menda-
cious blonde who is involved in a murderous arms smuggling conspiracy. Due to static directing and a lack of empathy between the
leads, the film fails to excite. Dizzy acquitted himself well, particularly in a speech where he denounces racism.

The film is redeemed in part by the score composed by Dizzy
with help from Fishman and Danilo Perez. Dizzy recorded a fine
sound-track album in August in New York with an orchestra that
included Perez, Mario Rivera, bassist George Mraz, drummer

Grady Tate, vocalist Leola Jiles, a string quartet, and four French horns.

Tadia Rice, an American Baha'i whom Dizzy had met in 1968, invited him to be the principal performer at the March 21, 1990, independence day gala of the new southwest African nation of Namibia. An actress and a producer, Rice had befriended Namibian freedom fighters in exile in the United States and Zambia, and they had asked her to help produce their independence celebration. Namibia had achieved nationhood after a bloody, twenty-three-year guerrilla struggle to free itself from neighboring, racist South Africa, which had ruled it under League of Nations and United Nations mandates since 1919 and had imposed the strictest form of apartheid. The country adopted a democratic constitution and elected Sam Nujoma, leader of the SWAPO guerrilla group, to its presidency.

Dizzy was poised to send his regrets, because he had a conflicting commitment in Montreal, but, after protracted negotiations, Fishman saved the day by securing Dave Brubeck's group as a substitute for the Canadian engagement. Rice and Namibian officials prevailed upon the U.S. State Department to make room for Dizzy and Fishman on Air Force Two, which was taking Secretary of State James Baker and his entourage to the ceremonies. Dizzy's musicians and Dave Usher traveled by commercial jet.

Dizzy was thrilled to mingle with Nujoma and world leaders such as Baker, Nobel Peace Prize laureate Bishop Desmond Tutu, the secretary general of the United Nations, President Mubarek of Egypt, the foreign ministers of England, Soviet Russia, and West Germany, and, above all, Nelson Mandela. Mandela, who received a hero's welcome, had been released from jail only six weeks before, after twenty-seven years of imprisonment. He would struggle for four more years before he was elected to the South African presidency in a free, multiracial election on April 27, 1994. Dizzy was deeply moved when Mandela and the other statesmen cheered wildly as he performed, wearing his forty-pound Nigerian robe, with drummer Chuck Redd (the son of his friend saxophonist Vi Redd), Holloway, Hidalgo, Lee, and Cherry.

A month later, when Dizzy participated in the Havana Jazz

Festival with Hidalgo and Moreira, Arturo Sandoval took Fishman aside in an open field away from recording devices and told him that he wished to defect with his wife and young son. When Fishman informed Dizzy of this, he pledged Sandoval his total support.

Sandoval's escape plan had two parts. Part one involved creating a long European tour so that he could obtain permission to base his wife and son in London for a couple of months. This was accomplished in part by adding gigs with the UNO to Sandoval's original schedule. Part two was the defection itself. Here a contact that Fishman had made on Air Force Two proved essential. He remembered that, on the way to Namibia, he had struck up a conversation with David Miller, an important member of President Bush's National Security Council, and that Miller had proffered his card and said, "If there is anything we can ever do for you, please call me." Fishman recalled getting in touch with him:

> After I called Miller and told him what the deal was with Sandoval and the UNO tour, he asked, "Where will you and Sandoval be for more than a day so that you can go into a U.S. embassy or a consulate?" I look at the UNO schedule, and the only place that works is Athens over the July 4th holiday. Miller asked that, in advance of our arrival, I make an appointment with the Immigration Service cat over there. And I did.[7]

Before the UNO tour began, Dizzy made a whirlwind visit in early May to East Berlin, Moscow, and Prague for a series of concerts sponsored by the Baha'is and the United States Information Agency. Dizzy's varied activities were, at this time, generating so much interest that it had become imperative that he hire a publicist. He chose Virginia Wicks, who had handled him from 1947 to 1951 and had also worked with him during the late 1950s when she was employed by Norman Granz. Wicks, who became a highly valuable member of Dizzy's team, began her tenure with him by advancing public relations for the East European tour.

Dizzy was surprised that he was so well known in the East bloc. He drew hundreds of journalists to his press conferences, attracted a block-long line of Moscow autograph seekers, and found that several leading politicians, including President Vaclav Havel of Czechoslovakia, were jazz fans. Audiences at his standing-room-only concerts reacted enthusiastically to the mostly Latin-flavored music provided by him, D'Rivera, Hidalgo, Berroa, Halloway, Lee, and Cherry.

The UNO tour with Sandoval began on June 24, 1990, and Fishman set up the meeting at the American embassy in Athens for July 5. He remembered the adventure that followed:

The American Cultural Attaché hears that we are coming and gets very hyped and invites us to dinner. So we had dinner with him, and the next day Sandoval, me, and Dizzy go to the embassy. Dizzy was so excited that he trips running up the stairs, and cuts open his finger and requires several stitches.

We do all the paperwork and the guy says, "OK, we're gonna start working on this, and we'll let you know what to do," and we leave. We play the concerts and go to the next place.

But we had made a major blunder—taking Sandoval to dinner with the Cultural Attaché. Because he had a photo taken with Sandoval, and it appeared in a local newspaper the next day, and the Cuban Secret Service begins to get suspicious.

Sandoval starts getting very nervous, because his government instructs him to cut short his trip and bring his wife and kid home. Ten days later, we were in Varese, Italy, and at two o'clock in the morning, there is a knock at my door and it's Sandoval, Berroa, and D'Rivera. Things have gotten worse, and Sandoval is really worried; the Cubans are after him threatening mayhem. He's afraid that they will take his wife and kid and pick him up too, and he's gotta get his asylum.

So I called the White House, and said, "I need David Miller; it's an emergency." And they got me to him, and he says, "You're gonna get a call from Ben Ferro from Rome. He's the regional director for the Immigration and Naturalization Service there." So I talk to Ben on one phone and Miller on another, and I'm instructed to fly to Rome with Sandoval the following day while Dizzy and the band move on to the next gig.

When we land, we hear this announcement, "Will Messieurs Fishman and Sandoval please remain on board." The next thing I

know, four armed Italian policemen come up and take us to the
tarmac where we get into an American Embassy car with Mr. Ferro
and security staff. A police escort took us straight to the embassy.

We called England, and they decided that Pete King should
pick up Sandoval's wife and son and drive them to the London embassy. They put her on a plane to New York, and we bought a ticket
for Sandoval, and sent him there too. That's how the defection
came about. It was July 22.[8]

The actor Andy Garcia produced in 2000 an appealing version
of Sandoval's story for HBO in which he played Sandoval and
Charles Dutton portrayed Dizzy; the two-hour film was called
For Love or Country: The Arturo Sandoval Story, and it cost several
million dollars to make. Although a few incidents are altered for
dramatic effect—for example, Dizzy, not Fishman, is shown making the call to Miller from Varese—the movie adheres closely to
the realities of Sandoval's life.

Garcia, a percussionist and record producer whose family fled
Cuba when he was five, exhibited a deep understanding of Afro-
Cuban jazz, and the end credits contain the following statement:
"This film is dedicated to the memory and continuing inspiration
of Dizzy Gillespie with gratitude from Arturo Sandoval." San-
doval has carved out a highly successful career in the United
States since 1990, winning four Grammys along the way.

The UNO toured South America and Western Europe during
the autumn of 1990, returning home in time for Dizzy to be honored by the Kennedy Center in early December. Dizzy was to be
among the five honorees at its thirteenth celebration of the performing arts; the others were Katharine Hepburn, film director
Billy Wilder, composer Jule Styne, and opera singer Rise Stevens.

The weekend of the Kennedy Center Honors is the occasion
for the biggest social/political/show-business event of the Washington season; in 1990, it drew the likes of James Baker, Catherine Shouse, Cicely Tyson, Ted Kennedy, Debbie Allen, Dan
Rather, Dick Cheney, Lynn Redgrave, and Claudette Colbert.

Dizzy warmed up for the big bash by accepting the James
Smithson Medal at the Smithsonian on Friday evening; he per-

formed there before an overflow crowd with fellow medalists Hank Jones and Benny Carter as Sandoval and D'Rivera made cameo appearances.

The weekend began with a lunch at the Kennedy Center and a glittering dinner at the State Department on Saturday, moved on to a White House reception late Sunday afternoon, and climaxed with a gala tribute performance and a late supper at the Kennedy Center on Sunday evening, December 2.

The performance was taped for a two-hour commercial broadcast by CBS on December 28, and the Honors, symbolized by medals hanging from rainbow-colored ribbons, were presented Saturday at the State Department dinner. Dizzy and Hepburn, as excited as teenagers to be meeting each other, were introduced there and had a laughter-filled conversation at her table.

They reprised their tête-à-tête the next afternoon when President Bush gave praise to the five honorees in a short ceremony at the White House. United there by their extraordinary talents, these two had begun their journeys from vastly different starting points. Hepburn, the privileged social register, Bryn Mawr WASP, was raised on a Connecticut estate, and Dizzy, the black boy from the bottom rung of the American social and political ladder, had grown up in a rudimentary wooden structure with no indoor plumbing.

With Walter Cronkite presiding at the Kennedy Center, a three-part format was used to honor the winners: a friend would praise the honoree in a talk sprinkled with anecdotes, film clips would illustrate the artist's career, and live entertainment would follow. Bill Cosby regaled the audience with funny stories about Dizzy, the film clips followed, and the UNO provided the live entertainment by performing "A Night in Tunisia." Slide Hampton overcame time restraints with a skilled arrangement that allowed all the musicians to solo. Dizzy sat in the presidential box between Hepburn and Mrs. Bush (the president had departed on a trip following the White House reception), and he was allowed to seat one guest; Lorraine had decided to stay home, so he chose Norman Powe, his cousin and Laurinburg classmate. Dizzy had the largest entourage among the honorees, and the rules were bent to accommodate fifty-one of his guests at the party following the performance. His sister Genia and his brother Wesley and Wesley's three children were among them.

Dizzy was on the road for 280 days in 1990 and 310 days in 1991. He took 38 days off following eye surgery on January 9, 1991, which meant that he spent only 17 days at home during the balance of that year. As Whale Lake remembered, Dizzy loved the road and was restless when he returned to Englewood:

> When he was home, he wasn't home. He made sure that he had something to do every night. No matter who invited him. I said, "Diz, somebody wants you to go over and say, 'Hello.'" "Yeah, take it, take it. I want to get out of the house." Or else he'd go down to the corner and have a cheeseburger with the guys in the poolroom. I never once recall him sitting down having dinner at home with Lorraine. I'd call him at dinnertime. "Where's Dizzy?" "Oh, he's down at the corner. He's down with the guys." That's what she would say.[9]

Dany Gignoux, who traveled extensively with Dizzy in 1990 and 1991 as she created a beautiful photo book about him, wrote: "Dizzy used to call his wife every day—but he did not last longer than three days at home,"[10] and he told a *Downbeat* reporter in August 1990, "I'd be bored to death [if I quit]. I would die soon if I spent a year doing nothing. . . . I go home too long, my wife says, 'When are you leaving? What are you around here so long for?' Then she shakes her fist at me. I've got to work."[11]

He continued touring with his quintet and the UNO during 1991, but in keeping with his Baha'i world-music ideals, Dizzy added to his schedule the singer Miriam Makeba, an African partner performing African music.

Makeba became the first African entertainer to achieve stardom in the West when she won a Grammy in 1959, and she stayed in the spotlight during the 1960s when she was stripped of her South African citizenship for speaking out against apartheid. During the ensuing decades, she lived in the United States and the West African nation Guinea, and for several years she was a friend and neighbor of the Gillespies in Englewood; Lorraine occasionally babysat her daughter.

Makeba and Dizzy got along famously as they toured Europe and the United States for almost three months during 1991. As Dizzy explained, their musics meshed naturally: "Miriam's music is like my backyard. I don't have to practice it or nothing. One time, I got it. Me and her are a natural combination. . . . Remember, most of my guys are Latinos. They're right where they're supposed to be between her music and mine. They go both directions."[12] Their groups would perform together at the beginning and the end of a typical set and play separately during the middle portion. When they merged, sixteen strong, they would create a joyful vocal and rhythmic pandemonium. Dizzy brought three horn men (Roditi, Turre, and the sensational young Puerto Rican saxophonist David Sanchez), plus a five-man rhythm section (Perez, Hidalgo, Berroa, Lee, and Cherry), and Makeba contributed a guitar player, a bassist, a percussionist, and three female backup singers. Makeba also provided a pianist when Perez could not participate in the American tour.

As Dizzy complemented Makeba's lyrics with mercurial countermelodies, her dynamic voice projected easily over the rhythms of the percussionists, the riffing of the horn section, and the punctuations of the shimmying backups. The two stars drove audiences into hand-clapping frenzies as they danced all over the stage to the infectious beats.

During May 1991, Dizzy recorded in the Bay Area with Bebop and Beyond, a San Francisco band whose devotion to the bebop legacy had won them three National Endowment for the Arts grants. Fishman had dug out of Dizzy's files arrangements from his 1940s big bands, and they inspired a very satisfying LP with a series of excellent solos by him.

While Dizzy was circling the globe during 1991, Fishman was making big plans for his seventy-fifth birthday year, 1992. His proposal to the Alvin Ailey Dance Company to create a ballet set to Dizzy's music was quickly accepted and scheduled for a December premiere. In addition to the usual European, South American, Far Eastern, and American tours by the UNO and the quintet, Fishman scheduled three major special events: a four-week engagement at New York's Blue Note club bringing Dizzy together with forty-nine jazz stars in a variety of bands that

would be recorded by Telarc, a series of Gillespie/Makeba performances in South Africa to which Nelson Mandela would lend his
name as a patron, and an October birthday cruise to the Caribbe-
an with twenty musicians from the Blue Note gig plus twenty-five
others. Dizzy could also look forward in 1992 to a thirteen-part
National Public Radio retrospective of his career hosted by the
scholar and pianist Billy Taylor, and tribute concerts in Carnegie
Hall and at the Hollywood Bowl.

Fishman believed, when he came on board in 1986, that Dizzy
was severely underpricing himself, and he worked hard to increase
his fees. During the next four years, he succeeded in more than
doubling his client's annual income as Dizzy grossed more than
one million dollars in both 1990 and 1991.

During the last months of 1991, there were danger signs that
Dizzy might not be up to the rigors of the 1992 schedule. Mike
Longo's mom became alarmed in October at Dizzy's extreme fatigue during a stay in Fort Lauderdale, and at an early December
engagement with Mike in Detroit, when Dizzy became ill with
what was diagnosed as a virus, he looked so worn out that Mike
tried to dissuade from an imminent trip to Japan. Dizzy replied,
"I'd rather be tired than bored," and moved on.

In Japan, Fishman noticed changes in his routine:

No matter what time he went to bed, he'd wake up real early. He'd
have breakfast, get a paper, take a little walk. Then he'd go back,
start reading the paper, and fall asleep. In Japan he was sleeping
late. And Dizzy used to take a swim or go to the health club, get a
steam bath. He just wasn't doing any of it, and I got concerned.

When we got back, I tried to talk him out of a three-night gig in
Houston, but he insisted on it. Again he was sleeping late, out of
his rhythm. With the Blue Note gig coming up, I said something
about taking it easy, but he brushed it aside angrily.[13]

Fishman had fashioned an engagement for Dizzy at the Blue
Note that would have taxed a man half his age. Starting on January 7, 1992, he would be challenged by outstanding musicians
every night for four weeks, and he could never coast.

The first week, entitled "Bebop Jamboree," brought him together with alumni James Moody, Jimmy Heath, Slide Hampton,
and Kenny Barron, plus John Coltrane's renowned drummer,
Elvin Jones, and Sonny Rollins's bassist, Bob Cranshaw. The second week, featuring the UNO, was followed by "To Bird with
Love" (two saxophonists per night for six nights) and "To Diz
with Love" (two trumpeters per night for six nights).

Among the saxophonists were veteran stars Jackie McLean,
Benny Golson, Clifford Jordan, "Fathead" Newman, Hank Craw-
ford, Junior Cook, and Paquito D'Rivera and hot newcomers
David Sanchez and Antonio Hart, and the trumpeters included
young lions Wynton Marsalis, Jon Faddis, Roy Hargrove, Terence
Blanchard, and Wallace Roney, and the veterans Doc Cheatham,
Jimmy Owens, and Red Rodney. The singer Bobby McFerrin
performed a wonderful impromptu set when Dizzy coaxed him
from the audience the night McLean and D'Rivera were on stage.

Dizzy was tired and sometimes grumpy, but he paced himself
judiciously, stayed away from the higher octaves, and won nearly
unanimous plaudits from the critics. Two CDs from the saxophone week, *To Bird with Love* and *Bird Songs*, and one from the
trumpet week, *To Diz with Love*, have been issued. They represent
the ninth, tenth, and eleventh CDs that Dizzy recorded during
his prolific eighth decade.

Dizzy became extremely angry and upset when he received by
messenger at the Blue Note on January 13 a letter from a lawyer
stating he had "been retained by Ms. Connie Bryson regarding
the matter of Jeanie Bryson." This was the start of a legal
marathon concerning royalty monies and Jeanie's identity that,
more than a decade later, is still winding its way through the
courts. If Jeanie convinces a judge that she is indeed Dizzy's
daughter, she is entitled under federal law to split Dizzy's stream
of royalties fifty-fifty with Lorraine.

Dizzy's signed admission of paternity, statements by several
people who have said that he told them that Jeanie was his daughter, and the idiosyncratic, gritty, realistic flavor of the depositions
given by Jeanie and Connie Bryson in the lawsuit have convinced
me that Dizzy was Jeanie's father.

He was willing to see her from time to time and to help her, but under the condition that such contacts be kept secret from Lorraine and limited to the few who needed to know. Lorraine wanted Dizzy to limit his dealings with Jeanie to the dispatch of monthly support checks, and she would become very upset when news of Jeanie filtered back to her.

Jeanie married early in 1979 and gave birth to a son, Radji Birks Bryson-Barrett, on December 15. Jeanie brought Radji to meet Dizzy soon after an anonymous call to Englewood about his birth caused great consternation there. She graduated from Rutgers University in 1980 and worked odd jobs as she pursued a career as a jazz singer.

The most important thing that Dizzy ever said to Jeanie was: if there is ever a conflict between you and my marriage, you lose. Lorraine might nag him and rag him, but she was his Rock of Gibraltar, the love of his life, his compass, and his best friend. In addition, he was convinced that she had saved him from an early death like Charlie Parker's. He would not tolerate anything that might threaten the foundations of their relationship. If Jeanie dropped her cloak of anonymity and thereby made Lorraine unhappy, all bets were off, and all help would cease.

When Dizzy heard, during 1988, that Jeanie had blossomed as a singer, he called her for the first time in five years and insisted that she bring in Elliott Hoffman, his lawyer, to represent her. Hoffman advanced her career by arranging for her to perform before important record executives and by helping her win a vocal scholarship. He could not participate as a lawyer in the current litigation, because his past roles as coexecutor of Dizzy's estate and as Jeanie's representative created a clear conflict of interest.

Jeanie went public as Dizzy's daughter in 1989, and as Whale Lake remembers, Dizzy's first reaction was to shield Lorraine from the news: "No matter where we were playing the last couple of years, there'd be an article in the paper about her being his daughter. I said, 'Dizzy, that happened last week in L.A. Now we're in Frisco. What is this, a coincidence?' . . . And I'd say, 'I'll call the paper. We know the people. We'll retract what [they're] saying.' He'd say, 'No, no, no. Lorraine will find out. Lorraine will find out.'"[14]

Lorraine did find out as Jeanie's career moved forward. The young woman landed a record contract with Telarc without Hoffman's help, and made the first of her three CDs, *I Love Being Here with You*, for them in 1993. She used Gillespie veteran Kenny Barron on piano and thanked Dizzy's biographer Al Fraser and his alumni Mike Longo and Flora Purim in her liner notes.

Lorraine's legal brief claims that Jeanie is not Dizzy's daughter and, further, that 1965 racial attitudes concerning black/white liaisons created a climate of duress that caused him to sign falsely his admission of paternity. Lorraine in 1999 paid Jeanie fifty thousand dollars to settle all claims through that year. The ongoing litigation concerns post-1999 royalties and, of course, Jeanie's identity as Dizzy's daughter.

FINALE 36

TWO DAYS AFTER HE FINISHED AT THE BLUE NOTE, DIZZY headed out with the quintet for a three-week trip across America that would end with gigs in Emeryville, California, across the bay from San Francisco, and in Seattle. Whale Lake, who caught up with him in Arizona, remembered the last days of the tour:

> On February 16, 1992, we were in Phoenix. Dizzy and I had an adjoining suite, and when I went to the bathroom in the morning, the sink was full of vomit. I said, "What the hell is this? I saw this ten days ago. When the toilet bowl was loaded with puke." He answered, "Nothing, nothing, nothing." I said, "Go see a doctor. For Christ sake, this is not normal." He didn't like to hear that. Did nothing.
>
> Two days later, we are at Kimball's East in Emeryville and Virginia Wicks and his old pal Jimmy Atchison are there. The place is

sold out, and we're ready for the second show, and there's four steps to go up to the stage. He says, "Whale, I can't make it." I said, "Cut the shit, John. They're introducing you out there." Then he gives me this look which means no bullshit.

So I announced, "Can we get medical assistance?" I couldn't bring myself to say, "Is there a doctor in the house?" A nurse comes up and checks him out and right away calls an ambulance. At the hospital, they find his sugar level is five times normal! He's been on pills for his diabetes, but we never had anything like this. Now he needs insulin shots to bring the sugar down.

Next day, he's yelling, "Get me out of here. I've got to go to work." We keep him in for a couple of days, but he breaks out to do the weekend. No trumpet. Just singing and the rhythmstick.

Fishman has canceled Seattle, but Dizzy gets really angry with him and reinstates it. We had bought him a ticket home, and doctors were planning to meet him at Newark Airport.

This guy, he can't fill a fountain pen, never mind giving himself a needle. So we get a nurse to do the injections, and then Atchison helps. We go up to Seattle with Atchison, and Fishman comes out to relieve me, and I go home.[1]

Dizzy had stopped vomiting, but he was very tired in Seattle, and he alarmed Fishman and Atchison when his urine turned orange.

Lorraine insisted that he undergo a thorough checkup when he returned home. His doctors suspected something more serious than diabetes and ordered exploratory surgery for March 12 at Englewood Hospital. They found a cancerous growth in his pancreas gland and were able to remove almost all of it during a six-hour operation. Chemotherapy was ordered to attack the cancer cells that could not be excised.

Among the several important bodily functions that the pancreas performs is the creation of insulin, and pancreatic malfunction explained Dizzy's diabetic symptoms in California. Pancreatic cancers are almost always fatal; they are resistant to both chemo and radiation therapy, and they are difficult to remove because they spread tentacle-like throughout the organ and because the pancreas sits awkwardly between the stomach and the spine.

There are no clear and obvious exterior causes such as occurs with smoking and lung cancer. The disease occurs when a group of cells mutate, for whatever reason, to a cancerous state.

The victim suffers in two ways; the cancer progressively deprives the pancreas of its normal functions, and it spreads and destroys surrounding organs. Dizzy's chemotherapy did not stem the cancerous growth, and his condition progressively worsened. Often, patients die within ninety days of diagnosis; Dizzy's care extended his life for almost ten months.

Mike Longo remembered when Dizzy came out of the anaesthetic:

> Dizzy's close friend Harris Stratyner pulled me over and said: "You deserve to know; he has cancer." I said, "Shit."
>
> Then I was standing at Dizzy's window, and Lorraine called. And Dizzy got on the phone and says: "Yeah, sugar. How are you, honey? I love you too." They were like very tender. Nobody had seen that side of them. It always was Lorraine was yelling at Dizzy. She used to say, half joking: "The most happiest sight in life is Dizzy's black ass goin' out the driveway."
>
> And then she asked to talk to me, and she said, "See, Mike, I told you he was alright, didn't I." She was in denial. I broke down, and my parents had to get me out of there. They didn't want Dizzy to see me.[2]

Elliott Hoffman, Dizzy's lawyer, called Fishman soon after the operation and told him that Lorraine wanted him to continue working for Dizzy but that she did not want Fishman to see him again. Fishman says that he has never received an adequate explanation for this action, and Lorraine and Hoffman have refused to be interviewed about it; her motivation remains a mystery.

In the period following his operation, Dizzy was possessed by an against-all-odds hope that he would recover, and he soldiered on as a stream of visitors kept him company in Englewood. Bill Cosby came by in his Rolls-Royce with hampers of food from New York's best restaurants; John Motley moved in and drove Dizzy around to his favorite local hangouts; Dave Usher and Vir-

ginia Wicks flew in from out of town for extended stays, and Boo
Frazier was there every day. Mike Longo recalled that he and Milt
Jackson played duets with Dizzy in the basement: "It was therapy
for him. He would tire easily, and he had intonation problems, but
his musical concepts were brilliant. Great solos. We recorded my
sessions, so I have a final testament to his incredible musical
mind."[3]

Dizzy was too ill to appear at the JVC Festival concerts honoring him in New York on June 19 and June 21, but he pulled
himself together for a Hollywood Bowl tribute on August 26.
Unable to perform and looking wan, he spoke briefly, thanking
those who turned out and promising them that he would soon be
playing his trumpet again. He enjoyed the highly energized
thirty-person event that was dominated by trumpeters (Clark
Terry, Freddie Hubbard, Claudio Roditi, Basie legend Sweets
Edison, and youngsters Roy Hargrove and Byron Stripling) and
singers (Terry, Dianne Reeves, Dee Dee Bridgewater, and another
Basie legend, Joe Williams). Fishman, who produced the concert,
managed a few words with him backstage; they never spoke
again.

Soon after returning from Hollywood, Dizzy reentered Englewood Hospital for a second surgery to remove cancerous tissue
and make him more comfortable. At this point he recognized that
his days were numbered, and he accepted his fate with equanimity.

He recorded an audiotape that was broadcast at his highly successful late-October birthday cruise, and he made his last public
appearance at a Longo/Moody concert in Tarrytown, a northern
suburb of New York City, on November 14. The audience was
shocked at his appearance, as his once robust frame had been reduced to 120 pounds.

Dizzy's chemotherapy and other forms of care were super-
vised by Dr. Frank Forte, Englewood Hospital's chief of oncology
and a lover of music who performs jazz guitar as an avocation. Before Dizzy's second surgery in September, Forte asked him if the
hospital could do something to honor him, and Dizzy requested
that they organize a program of free medical care for indigent jazz
musicians. Dizzy recognized that the average jazz musician, not

nearly as successful as he, was essentially a freelancer who usually had little or no medical coverage.

Forte promised Dizzy that he, his fellow doctors, and the hospital leadership would meet his wishes, and they launched the Dizzy Gillespie Memorial Fund to carry out his mission. With the essential backing of the hospital, which provides free beds and a panoply of services, Forte has recruited roughly fifty doctors who work for nothing. Most of the patient referrals and some money come from the New York–based Jazz Foundation of America, a social agency that provides assistance with such basic needs as food, rent, and home nursing care. Dizzy's fund is a vibrant, living legacy to him, as the combined value of the services provided by the doctors and the hospital amounts to roughly three hundred thousand dollars yearly. To further honor Dizzy, the hospital named its oncology wing the Dizzy Gillespie Cancer Institute.

Billy Taylor's National Public Radio series of thirteen one-hour broadcasts, *Dizzy's Diamond*, aired from September 29 to December 22, 1992. A brilliantly organized cornucopia of Gillespiana, it featured dozens of outstanding recordings, musical demonstrations by Taylor, Jon Faddis, Max Roach, Mike Longo, Candido, and Nigerian percussionist Olatunji, and interviews with, among others, Quincy Jones, Mario Bauzá, Arturo Sandoval, Paquito D'Rivera, Wynton Marsalis, Kenny Barron, and Lalo Schifrin.

During the same week in which Taylor's series began, a Verve three-CD set called *Dizzy's Diamonds* was issued. Divided into three sections—"Big Band," "Small Groups and Guests," and "In an Afro-Cuban, Bossa Nova, Calypso Groove"—it covered Dizzy's work with Verve from "Leap Frog" with Bird and Monk from 1950 to "Fiesta Mojo" from *Jambo Caribe* in 1964. The liner notes are enriched by a perceptive interview with Jon Faddis. Dizzy listened to the Verve music on cassette and to Taylor's broadcasts during his last hospital stay and carried on a running critique of his work for his guests; he found much that could have been improved.

Thirty-seven thousand Baha'is from two hundred countries attended their Second World Congress at New York's Jacob Javits

Center from November 23 through November 26, and, on the twenty-fifth, Mike Longo directed a sold-out Carnegie Hall concert "Celebrating the Baha'i Vision of World Peace and Presenting a 75th Birthday Tribute to Dizzy Gillespie." Longo recruited Mike Morganelli to produce the event, which featured James Moody, Jon Faddis, Paquito D'Rivera, Slide Hampton, trumpeters Roy Hargrove and Lou Soloff, and saxophonist Doc Holladay. Dizzy was too ill to attend. Peter Watrous of the *New York Times* was impressed:

> They all played well. Tributes like this can often be measured by a good solo or two, but all the musicians had a good night, and the show had obviously been rehearsed. . . . The second half featured a three-trumpet blowout, with Lou Soloff, Mr. Faddis and the young trumpeter Roy Hargrove all ferociously attacking the tune "Bebop." Trading solo spots with bruising competitiveness, the three put on a show that was musically uncompromised and thrilling for the audience, an idea Mr. Gillespie would appreciate.[4]

As Judith Jamison, the director of the Alvin Ailey Dance Company, explained to an opening night audience on December 10, "The Gillespie people approached me about doing a ballet to his music, and I said I have the perfect choreographer." He was Billy Wilson, known for his cheeky exuberance and his mastery of the jazz dance vocabulary. During a protean career, he had been an international ballet star, an Emmy winner, a college professor, and the choreographer of the Broadway hit *Bubbling Brown Sugar*.

Wilson began by asking for a wide-ranging selection of Dizzy's recordings, and he surprised Dizzy and Fishman by choosing only one Gillespie classic, "Manteca," and by featuring a three-song suite from *The Winter in Lisbon*. Wilson choreographed the first song, "Opening Theme (Magic Summer)," composed by Fishman, as a high-stepping party piece, and followed with Dizzy's "San Sebastian," staged as an athletic challenge dance among three street hoofers. He built to a climax with Dizzy's "Lisbon," a sultry love duet that is the romantic heart of the suite. "Manteca" ends *The Winter in Lisbon* in a very different mood. Eight couples, colorfully clad, gyrate sassily to the driving Afro-Cuban rhythms and reach a rousing rumba climax as a huge photo of Dizzy is unfurled across the back of the stage.

The Winter in Lisbon has become very popular in the repertory; it was performed ten times during Ailey's 2003 New York season, second only to the Ailey classic *Revelations*.

The end came less than a month after the premier of the ballet. Mike Longo remembered:

> Moody was staying with me, and we went over on January 5th, the night before Dizzy died. He was awake, but he couldn't talk. He put his finger to his lips and blew out his cheeks, and I said, "John, aren't you carrying this shit a little too far?" and he smiled and grabbed my hand and held it tight. I think he was telling me he loved me. Then he went to sleep, and he didn't wake up.
>
> I had to teach the next day, and Moody, Faddis, Motley, and Jacques Muyal, a Swiss friend of Dizzy's, and Muyal's son were there. Dizzy was sitting up and sleeping, and Moody embraced him as he breathed his last breath, a big sigh. Moody telephoned me and said, "It's over."[5]

Virginia Wicks immediately flew to New York from California to handle the deluge of requests from media all over the world.

Dizzy's funeral, a private event, took place on January 9, 1993, at New York's jazz church, Saint Peter's, with the Reverend John Gensel presiding. Elliott Hoffman organized the service and gave the principal eulogy. Lalo Schifrin, Bill Cosby (via audiotape), Boo Frazier, a Baha'i leader, Milt Jackson, Mike Longo, and Tony Bennett also spoke, and Wynton Marsalis performed an unaccompanied hymn as mourners filed past the open casket. Jon Faddis was too upset to perform, but Dizzy alumni Longo, James Moody, Paquito D'Rivera, Slide Hampton, Steve Turre, Mickey Roker, Hank Jones, and Jimmy Heath were able to honor Dizzy musically. Lorraine sat quietly throughout the service. The funeral cortege visited Fifty-second Street and the Apollo Theater before heading to Flushing Cemetery in Queens for interment.

Jeanie Bryson was barred from the service at Saint Peter's, but a musician close to Dizzy told her where he was to be buried, and she made it to the cemetery. She wore a veil and stood apart from the other mourners. Three days later she attended Dizzy's public memorial service at New York's Episcopal Cathedral of Saint John the Divine with her mother and her son.

Saint John, longer than a football field, is the largest cathedral in the world and a center of artistic and spiritual leadership in New York City. It has been home to the Dalai Lama, Elie Wiesel, and Bishop Tutu preaching, and Leonard Bernstein, Max Roach, and the New York Philharmonic in performance; Duke Ellington, Jim Henson, Alvin Ailey, and James Baldwin were buried from there. In other words, it was the appropriate location for a memorial service for Dizzy. Charlie Fishman and musical director Slide Hampton worked nonstop to organize the event under Hoffman's direction.

On the afternoon of January 12, six thousand people filled every corner of the massive structure to honor Dizzy in spite of rain and sleet and gusts coming in over the Hudson that drove the wind chill down into the twenties. Lorraine did not attend.

Fittingly, Dizzy's music reigned during more than two hours of the three-hour service. Wynton Marsalis and his musicians marched in playing the saddest of dirges, the Episcopalian ministers in their white and gold robes prayed and read scripture, Roberta Flack performed "Amazing Grace" a capella, the choir sang hymns, and Elliott Hoffman presided as Judge James Nelson of the Baha'i faith, Mayor David Dinkins of New York, Ray Brown, Milt and Mona Hinton, Milt Jackson, Jimmy Owens, Chuck Mangione, and Jon Faddis delivered short eulogies. But for the rest of it, Dizzy's musicians—twenty-five strong—rocked the spectators in a raucous, bopping and swinging, Afro-Cuban, bluesy celebration of his life. Jon Faddis, Ray Brown, Milt Jackson, Paquito D'Rivera, Clark Terry, Jimmy Heath, Al Grey, and Roy Hargrove delivered the most memorable solos as the ensembles swirled powerfully around them. As it ended, the spectators eased their way down the cathedral steps nodding their heads to the Latin beat of Dizzy's "Con Alma" crackling behind them.

Dizzy had about ten days to live when he was visited by Alexandra Stratyner, the four-year-old daughter of his friend Harris. When she asked, "You're dying, aren't you, Uncle Dizzy?" he replied, "Yeah, but it's been a great gig."[6]

It was.

NOTES

INTRODUCTION

1. Dizzy Gillespie, interview by Ralph Gleason, *San Francisco Chronicle*, September 30, 1958.

2. Gene Seymour, "The Greatness of Gillespie," *Newsday*, December 14, 1990.

3. Nat Hentoff, "Conversations with Dizzy Gillespie," *Village Voice*, February 9, 1993; Nat Hentoff, "Dizzy in the Sunlight," *Village Voice*, February 16, 1993.

4. Langston Hughes "Trumpet Player," in *The Collected Poems of Langston Hughes* (New York: Alfred A. Knopf, 1998), p. 338.

1: BATHED IN MUSIC

1. Dizzy Gillespie, interview by author, December 13, 1990.

2. John Motley, interview by author, February 19, 1999.

3. Lucile McIver, interview by author, June 9, 1999.

4. Albert J. Raboteau, *A Fire in the Bones: Reflections on African-American Religious History* (Boston: Beacon Press, 1995), pp. 25, 232.

5. Horace Clarence Boyer, *How Sweet the Sound: The Golden Age of Gospel* (Washington, DC: Elliott and Clark Publishing, 1995), p. 12.

6. Dizzy Gillespie with Al Fraser, *To Be, or Not . . . to Bop: Memoirs* (Garden City, NY: Doubleday, 1979), p. 31.

7. Mike Longo, interview by author, December 22, 2001.

2: BLACK AND WHITE IN SOUTH CAROLINA

1. Charles Johnson and Patricia Smith, *Africans in America: America's Journey through Slavery* (New York: Harcourt Brace, 1968), pp. 230, 258; Arthur Zilversmit, *The First Emancipation: The Abolition of Slavery in the North* (Chicago: University of Chicago Press, 1967), p. 222.

2. Stephen Kantrowitz, *Ben Tillman and the Reconstruction of White Supremacy* (Chapel Hill: University of North Carolina Press, 2000), p. 258.

3. Ibid., p. 259.

4. Ibid., p. 156.

5. Ibid., p. 210.

6. Stanley Crouch, "Dizzy Gillespie—A Player's Interview," *Player's Magazine*, January 1976, pp. 19–20.

7. Gillespie with Fraser, *To Be, or Not . . . to Bop*, p. 443.

8. *Cheraw Chronicle*, March 6, 1962.

9. Crouch, "Dizzy Gillespie—A Player's Interview," p. 20.

3: EARLY DAYS

1. Raboteau, *Fire in the Bones*, pp. 142–143.

2. Gillespie with Fraser, *To Be, or Not . . . to Bop*, pp. 1–2.

3. John Motley, interview by author, February 16, 1999.

4. Gillespie with Fraser, *To Be, or Not . . . to Bop*, p. 22.

5. Crouch, "Dizzy Gillespie—A Player's Interview," p. 20.

4: BECOMING A MUSICIAN

1. Gillespie with Fraser, *To Be, or Not . . . to Bop*, p. 23.

2. Kantrowitz, *Ben Tillman*, p. 259.

3. Dizzy Gillespie, interview by author, December 13, 1990.

4. Ibid.

5: LAURINBURG

1. Kantrowitz, *Ben Tillman*, pp. 267–268.

2. Dizzy Gillespie, interview by author, December 13, 1990.

3. Norman Powe, interview by author, June 10, 1999.

4. Ibid.

5. Dizzy Gillespie, interview by author, December 13, 1990.

6. Gillespie with Fraser, *To Be, or Not . . . to Bop*, pp. 38–39.

7. *Cheraw for Dizzy*, South Carolina Educational TV documentary, January 9, 1975.

6: BECOMING DIZZY

1. Dizzy Gillespie, interview by author, December 13, 1990.

7: DIZZY'S SWING INHERITANCE

1. Gunther Schuller, *The Swing Era: The Development of Jazz, 1930–1945* (New York: Oxford University Press, 1989), pp. 5–6.

2. Ibid., p. 199.

3. Ibid., p. 7.

4. Ross Firestone, *Swing, Swing, Swing: The Life and Times of Benny Goodman* (New York: W. W. Norton, 1933), p. 108.

5. Ibid., p. 107.

6. Ibid., p. 115.

7. Ibid., p. 117.

8. Ibid., p. 149.

9. John Chilton, liner notes to the two-LP set *Roy Eldridge—the Early Years*, Roy Eldridge with various orchestras, Columbia C2 38033, 1982.

10. Schuller, *Swing Era*, p. 453.

11. John Wilson, "Roy Eldridge: Jazz Trumpeter for All Decades," *New York Times*, October 17, 1982.

8: MAKING IT

1. Crouch, "Dizzy Gillespie—A Player's Interview," pp. 20–21.

2. W. O. Smith, *Sideman—the Long Gig of W. O. Smith: A Memoir* (Nashville: Rutledge Hill Press, 1991), pp. 47–48.

3. Dizzy Gillespie, interview by author, December 13, 1990. pp. 53–54.

4. Smith, *Sideman*, pp. 38–39.

5. Ibid., pp. 40–41.

6. Crouch, "Dizzy Gillespie—A Player's Interview," pp. 20–21.

7. Firestone, *Swing, Swing, Swing*, pp. 197–201.

8. Smith, *Sideman*, p. 40.

9. Alain Tercinet, liner notes to *Dizzy Gillespie: Volume 1, 1937–1940*, quoting Laurent Godder, "Dizzy Atmosphere," *Jazz Hot*, no. 283, June 1976.

9: SEEDS OF REBELLION

1. Arthur Chandler, "Confrontation: The Exposition Internationale des Arts et Techniques dans la Vie Moderne, 1937," available at http://charon.sfsu.edu/publications/PARISEXPOSITIONS/1937EXPO.html.

2. Leonard Feather, review, *Melody Maker*, July 10, 1937.

3. Hughes Panassié, "Teddy Hill's Orchestra," *Jazz Hot*, no. 18, June–July 1937, p. 3.

4. Ibid.

5. Laurent Clarke and Franck Verdun, *Dizzy Atmosphere: Conversations avec Dizzy Gillespie* (Arles, France: Acts Sud, 1990), p. 36.

6. Leonard Feather, "Feather Forecast and News," *Melody Maker*, December 4, 1937.

7. Dizzy Gillespie, interview by author, December 13, 1990.

10: DIZZY AND KLOOK: THE BIRTH OF BEBOP

1. Albert Murray, *Stomping the Blues* (New York: McGraw-Hill, 1976), p. 106.

2. "Savoy Band Battle," *Amsterdam News*, January 19, 1938.

3. "Basie's Brilliant Band Conquers Chick's," *Metronome*, February 1938, pp. 15, 20.

4. Burt Korall, "View from the Seine," interview with Kenny Clarke, *Downbeat*, December 5, 1963, p. 17.

5. Kenny Clarke, interview by Helen Oakley Dance, September 30, 1977, Jazz Oral History Project, Smithsonian Institution, Washington, DC, tape 1, pp. 80, 90.

6. Nat Shapiro and Nat Hentoff, *Hear Me Talkin' to Ya* (New York: Dover, 1955), pp. 347–48.

7. Schuller, *Swing Era*, p. 421.

8. Teddy Hill, interview by Leonard Feather, *Metronome*, April 1947, p. 44.

9. Gillespie with Fraser, *To Be, or Not . . . to Bop*, p. 99.

10. Ibid., p. 98.

11. Clyde E. B. Bernhardt, *I Remember* (Philadelphia: University of Pennsylvania Press, 1986), pp. 138–39.

12. Gillespie with Fraser, *To Be, or Not . . . to Bop*, pp. 310–11.

13. Ibid., p. 87

14. Kenny Clarke, interview by Helen Oakley Dance, pp. 88–93.

15. Ross Russell, *Bird Lives: The High Life and Hard Times of Charlie (Yardbird) Parker* (New York: Charterhouse, 1973), p. 133.

16. Dizzy Gillespie, interview by Stanley Dance, *Jazz Magazine*, October 1962, p. 9.

11: BEBOP RHYTHM/BEBOP HARMONY

1. Dizzy Gillespie, interview by Ralph Gleason, *San Francisco Chronicle*, September 30, 1958.

2. Lewis Porter, *A Lester Young Reader* (Washington, DC: Smithsonian Institution Press, 1991), p. 36.

3. Gillespie with Fraser, *To Be, or Not . . . to Bop*, p. 92.

4. Shapiro and Hentoff, *Hear Me Talkin' to Ya*, pp. 354–55.

12: NEW DIRECTIONS

1. Gordon Wright, review, *Metronome*, November 1939, p. 22.

2. Scott DeVeaux, *The Birth of Bebop* (Berkeley: University of California Press, 1997), pp. 220.

3. John Hammond with Irving Townsend, *John Hammond on Record* (New York: Ridge Press/Summit Books, 1977), p. 224.

4. DeVeaux, *Birth of Bebop*, p. 230.

5. Cab Calloway and Bryant Rollins, *Of Minnie the Moocher and Me* (New York: Thomas Y. Crowell, 1976), pp. 85–88, 109–11; A. H. Lawrence, *Duke Ellington and His World—a Biography* (New York: Routledge, 2001), p. 157.

6. Schuller, *Swing Era*, p. 330.

7. Shapiro and Hentoff, *Hear Me Talkin' to Ya*, pp. 343–44.

8. Gillespie with Fraser, *To Be, or Not . . . to Bop*, p. 167.

9. Barrelhouse Dan, "No Place for Drum Solos in Jazz, Critic Claims," *Downbeat*, June 1, 1940, p. 120.

13: ENTER BIRD

1. Dizzy Gillespie, interview by author, December 13, 1990.

2. Gillespie with Fraser, *To Be, or Not . . . to Bop*, p. 117.

3. Nathan W. Pearson Jr., *Goin' to Kansas City* (Urbana and Chicago: University of Illinois Press, 1987), p. 106.

4. Russell, *Bird Lives*, p. 56.

5. Ibid., p. 93.

6. Letter of June 19, 2001, to author's researcher, Jill McManus, from Paula Sweeney, Records Manager, U.S. Selective Service System.

14: MINTON, MONK, AND MONROE

1. Ira Gitler, *Swing to Bop* (New York: Oxford University Press, 1985), pp. 81–82.

2. Ann Douglass, "Feel the City's Pulse? It's Be-bop, Man!" *New York Times*, Sec. E, August 28, 1998.

3. Nat Hentoff, "Just Call Him Thelonious," *Downbeat*, July 25, 1956, p. 15.

4. Ralph Ellison, *Shadow and Act* (New York: Vintage, 1972), pp. 199–201.

5. Shapiro and Hentoff, *Hear Me Talkin' to Ya*, p. 335.

6. DeVeaux, *Birth of Bebop*, p. 226.

7. Ibid., pp. 223–24.

8. Shapiro and Hentoff, *Hear Me Talkin' to Ya*, p. 342.

9. Ibid., pp. 341–42.

10. Ibid., pp. 337–38.

11. Mike Hennessey, *Klook: The Story of Kenny Clarke* (Pittsburgh: University of Pittsburgh Press, 1990), p. 47.

15: "CAB CALLOWAY 'CARVED' BY OWN TRUMPET MAN!!"

1. Eric Townley, "Muted Jazz: An Interview with Jonah Jones," *Storyville Magazine*, no. 85, October/November 1979, p. 7.

2. Dizzy Gillespie, quoted in Helen Oakley Dance, interview of Jonah Jones, October 26, 1978, Jazz Oral History Project, Smithsonian Institution, Washington, DC, tapes 7–8, p. 31.

3. Jonah Jones, quoted in ibid., pp. 37–39.

16: JAMMING WITH BIRD

1. Shorty Rogers, interview by author, September 26, 1993.

2. Arnold Shaw, *52nd Street, The Street of Jazz* (New York: Da Capo Press, 1977), pp. x–xi. First published as *The Street That Never Slept* (New York: Coward, McCann and Geoghegan, 1971).

3. Gillespie with Fraser, *To Be, or Not . . . to Bop*, p. 171.

4. Barry Ulanov, "Benny Carter," *Metronome*, January 1942, pp. 11, 47.

5. Morroe Berger, Edward Berger, and James Patrick, *Benny Carter: A Life in American Music*, vol. 1 (Metuchen, NJ: Scarecrow Press and the Institute of Jazz Studies, Rutgers University, 1982), p. 196.

6. Ibid., pp. 194–95.

7. Pearson, *Goin' to Kansas City*, p. 105.

8. Barry Ulanov, "McIntyre, McShann Lead Fine Bands," *Metronome*, March 1942, pp. 12, 22.

9. Russell, *Bird Lives*, p. 127.

10. Firestone, *Swing, Swing, Swing*, p. 297.

11. Jack Kerouac, *Escapade*, April 1959, pp. 5, 52.

12. Joe Wilder, interview by author, January 30, 2001.

17: THE HINES BAND

1. James Patrick, "Al Tinney, Monroe's Uptown House, and the Emergence of Modern Jazz in Harlem," *Annual Review of Jazz Studies* 2 (1983): 163.

2. Dizzy Gillespie, interview by Jon Hendricks, 1974.

3. Schuller, *Swing Era*, pp. 277–78.

4. Ken Vail, *Dizzy Gillespie: The Bebop Years, 1937–1952* (Cambridge, England: Vail Publishing, 2000), p. 21.

5. DeVeaux, *Birth of Bebop*, pp. 260–62.

6. Eileen Southern, "Conversation with . . . William Clarence 'Billy' Eckstine," *The Black Perspective in Music* 7, no. 2 Fall 1979: 197–98.

7. Max Salazar, liner notes to the CD *Tanga*, Mario Bauzá and his Afro-Cuban Jazz Orchestra, Messidor Records 15819-2, 1992.

18: DIZZY LEADS THE CHARGE

1. Stanley Crouch, "He Copped the Bop," introduction to *The Masters of Bebop: A Listener's Guide*, 2nd ed., by Ira Gitler (New York, Da Capo Press, 2001), p. v.

2. Leonard Feather, *From Satchmo to Miles* (New York: Stein and Day, 1972), p. 147.

3. Stuart Troup, "Dizzy Gillespie Gets His Due," *Newsday*, August 31, 1990.

4. Schuller, *Swing Era*, p. 449.

5. Bernie Savodnick, letter to the editor, *Downbeat*, July 1, 1944, p. 10.

6. Budd Johnson, interview by Milt Hinton, March 1975, Jazz Oral History Project, Smithsonian Institution, Washington, DC, tape 4, p. 23.

7. Gillespie with Fraser, *To Be, or Not . . . to Bop*, pp. 192–93.

8. Shapiro and Hentoff, *Hear Me Talkin' to Ya*, pp. 369–70.

9. Leonard Feather, "Dizzy Is Crazy Like a Fox," *Metronome*, July 1944, p. 16.

19: 1945—A GREAT NEW YORK VINTAGE

1. Leonard Feather, "Blindfold Test," interview with Vernon Duke, *Downbeat*, February 24, 1966, p. 35.

2. Gillespie with Fraser, *To Be, or Not . . . to Bop*, p. 231.

3. Leonard Feather, "A Bird's-Ear View of Music," *Metronome*, August 1948, p. 14.

4. Lawrence O. Koch, *Yardbird Suite: A Compendium of the Music and Life of Charlie Parker* (Boston: Northeastern University Press, 1988), p. 61.

5. Geoffrey C. Ward and Ken Burns, *Jazz: A History of America's Music* (New York: Alfred A. Knopf, 2000), pp. 333–34.

6. Gary Giddins, *Celebrating Bird: The Triumph of Charlie Parker* (New York: Beech Tree Books/William Morrow, 1987), pp. 12–13.

7. Tony Gentry, *Dizzy Gillespie* (New York: Chelsea House, 1991), p. 69.

8. Barry Ulanov, "Dizzy Dazzles for an Hour; Rest of Concert Drags," *Metronome*, June 1945, p. 22.

9. "Gillespie and Jazz Quintet in Concert at Town Hall," *New York Herald Tribune*, May 17, 1945.

10. Firestone, *Swing, Swing, Swing*, p. 330.

11. Max Roach, interview by author, November 10, 2001.

12. Robert George Reisner, *Bird: The Legend of Charlie Parker* (New York, Citadel Press, 1962), p. 94.

13. Max Roach, interview by author, March 22, 1999.

14. Leonard Feather, "Dizzy—21st Century Gabriel," *Esquire*, October 1945, p. 91.

15. Milt Jackson, interview by Charles Fox, BBC Radio 3, May 6, 1976; broadcast May 31, 1976.

16. Ibid.

17. Alyn Shipton, *Groovin' High: The Life of Dizzy Gillespie* (New York: Oxford University Press, 1999), p. 175.

18. Teddy Reig, interview by Charles Porter, liner notes to *Charlie Parker: The Complete Savoy Studio Sessions*, S5J5500, 1978.

19. Ibid.

20. Ibid.

20: L.A. SOJOURN

1. Stan Levey, interview by author, March 12, 2000.

2. Richard O. Boyer, "Bop," *The New Yorker*, July 3, 1948, p. 29.

3. Ray Brown, interview by author, November 4, 1999.

4. Russell, *Bird Lives*, p. 201.

5. Ray Brown, interview by author, November 4, 1999.

6. Koch, *Yardbird Suite*, p. 78.

7. "New York Jazz Stinks, Claims Coast Promoter," *Downbeat*, August 15, 1945, p. 2.

8. Dizzy Gillespie, interview by author, December 13, 1990.

21: CONTROVERSY

1. George Simon, "1944," *Metronome*, January 1945, p. 4.

2. "Influence of the Year," *Metronome*, January 1946, p. 24.

3. "Record Reviews," *Downbeat*, March 25, 1946, p. 8.

4. "Record Reviews," *Downbeat*, April 22, 1946, p. 15.

5. "Be-Bop Be-Bopped," *Time*, March 25, 1946, p. 52.

6. Bill Gottlieb, "Condon Raps Tough for 'Re-Bop Slop,'" *Downbeat*, October 7, 1946, p. 4.

7. Leonard Feather, *The Jazz Years: Earwitness to an Era*, (New York: Da Capo Press, 1987), p. 91.

8. "Band of the Year: Dizzy Gillespie," *Metronome*, January 1948, p. 17.

9. Leonard Feather, "Duke Okays 'Be-Bop,' Red Hot News from New York Rushed," *Melody Maker*, June 22, 1946, p. 3.

10. Ralph Gleason, "TD Told to Open Ears to Bop," *Downbeat*, September 23, 1949, pp. 1, 12.

11. George Simon, "B.G. Explains," *Metronome*, October 1946, p. 18.

12. "Satchmo Comes Back," *Time*, September 1, 1947, p. 32.

13. "Bop Will Kill Business Unless It Kills Itself First," *Downbeat*, April 7, 1948. p. 2.

14. George Simon, "Bebop's the Easy Way Out, Claims Louis," *Metronome*, March, 1948, pp. 14–15.

15. "Bebop, New Jazz School Is Led By Trumpeter Who Is Hot Cool and Gone," *Life*, October, 11, 1948, pp. 138–142.

16. "National Affairs," *Time*, January 3, 1949, p. 10.

17. "How Deaf Can You Get?," *Time*, May 17, 1948, p. 74.

18. Jack Egan, "'Learn Everything—Rudiments On Up,' Dizzy Warns Kids," *Downbeat*, November 17, 1948, p. 1.

22: BIG BAND SUCCESS

1. Seymour, "Greatness of Gillespie."

2. Ibid.

3. Feather, *From Satchmo to Miles*, pp. 161–62.

4. Richard Palmer, "The Greatest Jazzman Of Them All? The Recorded Work of Dizzy Gillespie: An Appraisal," *Jazz Journal*, January, 2001, p. 8.

5. Seymour, "Greatness of Gillespie."

6. Gillespie with Fraser, *To Be, or Not . . . to Bop*, p. 255.

7. John Shaw, "Kenny Clarke," *Jazz Journal*, October 1969, p. 5.

8. Howard Reich, "Dizzy's Legacy: James Moody Carries on the Tradition of His Mentor," *Chicago Tribune*, March 28, 1993.

9. Milt Jackson, interview by Charles Fox, BBC Radio 3, May 6, 1976; broadcast May 31, 1976.

10. Bret Primack, "Dizzy!!!, a Diamond Jubilee Salute," interview of Ira Gitler, *Jazz-Times*, October 1992, p. 27.

11. Shipton, *Groovin' High*, p. 183.

12. Shaw, "Kenny Clarke," p. 5.

13. Kenny Clarke, interview by Helen Oakley Dance, p. 6.

14. Milt Jackson, interview by Charles Fox, BBC Radio 3, May 6, 1976; broadcast May 31, 1976.

15. Stuart Nicholson, *Ella Fitzgerald* (London: Villiers House, 1993), p. 96.

16. Barry McRae, *Dizzy Gillespie* (New York: Universe Books, 1988), pp. 44–45.

17. Jim Haskins, *Ella Fitzgerald—a Life through Jazz* (London: New English Library, 1991), p. 87.

18. Koch, *Yardbird Suite*, pp. 94–97.

19. Miles Davis with Quincy Troupe, *Miles—The Autobiography* (New York: Simon and Schuster, 1989), p. 100.

23: THE AFRO-CUBAN JAZZ REVOLUTION

1. John Storm Roberts, *Latin Jazz* (New York: Schirmer Books, 1999), pp. 66–67.

2. Bobby Sanabria, Aurora Flores, and Phil Schaap, in *The Palladium: Where Mambo Was King* (Kaufman Film and Television, Inc., in association with Bravo, 2002).

3. Mario Bauzá, interview by Billy Taylor, on track 1 of the third CD of the three-CD set, *Chano Pozo: El tambor de Cuba*, Almendra Music TCD 308, Barcelona, Spain, 2001.

4. Harry Belafonte, *Routes Of Rhythm—Part 3*, KCET–Los Angeles, 1989.

5. Mario Bauzá, interview by John Storm Roberts, December 13, 1978, Jazz Oral History Project, Smithsonian Institution, Washington, DC, tape 2, p. 7.

6. Dizzy Gillespie, interview by Mike Longo, September 1974.

7. Mike Longo, from his interview of Dizzy Gillespie, May 13, 1974.

8. Reisner, *Bird*, pp. 191–92.

9. Dan Morgenstern, liner notes to the LP *The Dizzy Gillespie Orchestra at Salle Pleyel; Paris France*, Prestige Records 7818, September 1970.

10. Gary Giddins, *Visions of Jazz* (New York: Oxford University Press, 1998), pp. 288–89.

11. Mario Bauzá, interview by John Storm Roberts, pp. 66, 67.

12. Boris Vian, *Round About Close to Midnight* (London: Quartet Books, 1988), p. 31.

13. Claude Carrière, liner notes to the CD *Dizzy Gillespie Pleyel Jazz Concert 1948; Max Roach Quintet 1949*, Vogue Records (BMG) 74321409412, 1997.

14. Leonard Feather, "The Mezz Mezzrow Blindfold Test," *Metronome*, October 1946, p. 25.

15. Symphony Sid Torin, monologue from the 4-CD set *Charlie Parker: The Complete Live Performances on Savoy*, Savoy Jazz SVY-17021-24, 1998.

16. Reisner, *Bird*, pp. 217–18.

17. Barry Ulanov, "Dizzy Atmosphere," *Metronome*, August 1948, pp. 13, 18.

18. Jordi Pujol, liner notes to the 3-CD set, *Chano Pozo, El tambor de Cuba*, Almendra Music, JCD 308, Barcelona, 2001 p. 119.

24: BIG BAND FAILURE

1. "Diz Strong at Strand," *Time*, December 29, 1948, p. 9.

2. "Bopper On Broadway," *Time*, December 20, 1948, pp. 63–64.

3. Gitler, *Masters of Bebop*, p. 108.

4. Michael Levin and John S. Wilson, "No Bop Roots In Jazz: Parker," *Downbeat*, September 9, 1949, p. 12.

5. Ibid.

6. Lawrence O. Koch, *Yardbird Suite: A Compendium of the Music and Life of Charlie Parker*, rev. ed. (Boston: Northeastern University Press, 1999), pp. 120–21.

7. Dizzy Gillespie, "Bird Wrong; Bop Must Get A Beat: Diz," *Downbeat*, October 7, 1949, pp. 1, 12.

8. Dizzy Gillespie, interview by Charles Fox, BBC Radio 3, August 31, 1976.

25: THE ECLECTIC EARLY FIFTIES

1. Bill Crow, *Birdland to Broadway* (New York: Oxford University Press, 1992), p. 88.

2. Carl Woideck, *Charlie Parker, His Music and Life* (Ann Arbor: Michigan University Press, 1996), pp. 180–81.

3. Davis with Troupe, *Miles*, p. 119.

4. Ward and Burns, *Jazz*, p. 376.

5. Dave Usher, interview by author, July 14, 2002.

6. Dave Usher, interview by author, August 14, 1999.

7. Dizzy Gillespie, interview by author, December 13, 1990.

8. Dan Morgenstern, liner notes to the 3-CD set *Dizzy Gillespie Odyssey, 1945–1952*, Denon Records–Savoy Jazz SVY17109, 2002, p. 19.

9. Nat Hentoff, "Crazy Like a Fox," *Downbeat*, June 18, 1952, p. 15.

10. Bill Crow, *Jazz Anecdotes* (New York: Oxford University Press, 1990), pp. 309–10.

11. Symphony Sid Torin, from the recording *Summit Meeting at Birdland*, Columbia Records LP #34831, 1977.

12. Shipton, *Groovin' High*, p. 252.

13. "Critics Still Irritate Granz as Another Season Ends," *Downbeat*, December 28, 1951.

14. "LA Session Heps Kids; Granz to Do Second One," *Downbeat*, August 1, 1944, p. 12.

15. Nat Hentoff, "Uncompromising Impresario," *Quest*, February/March 1980, p. 79.

16. Leonard Feather, "Jazz Millionaire," *Esquire*, January 1957, p. 47.

17. Hentoff, "Uncompromising Impresario," p. 46.

26: TEAMING UP WITH NORMAN, BIDDING BIRD GOOD-BYE

1. Liner notes to the 3-LP set *Stan Getz*, Book of the Month Club Records 40-5510, 1980, p. 12.

2. Norman Granz, "How LP Changed Methods of Waxing Jazz Sessions," *Downbeat*, September 23, 1953, p. 2.

3. Burt Goldblatt, *Newport Jazz Festival—the Illustrated History* (New York: Dial, 1977), p. 5.

4. George Wein with Nate Chinen, *Myself Among Others* (New York: Da Capo Press, 2004), p. 140.

5. *The Definitive Kenton*, Artistry Records Mono AR-2-102, February 28, 1954.

6. Lalo Schifrin, interview by author, August 17, 1998.

7. Hentoff, "Uncompromising Impresario," p. 46.

8. Dizzy Gillespie, interview by author, December 13, 1990.

9. Norman Granz, interview by Nat Hentoff, for the liner notes to *The Complete Jazz at the Philharmonic on Verve, 1944–1949*, (all rights reserved by Verve Records), p. 15.

10. Ibid., pp. 18–19.

11. Dizzy Gillespie, interview by author, December 13, 1990.

12. Hentoff, "Uncompromising Impresario," p. 79.

13. "U.S. Government to Send Jazz as Its Ambassador," *Downbeat*, December 28, 1955, p. 6.

27: GOODWILL AMBASSADOR

1. Carol Polsgrove, *"Divided Minds"* (New York, W. W. Norton, 2001), p. 7.

2. William Faulkner, *New York Herald Tribune*, September 9, 1955.

3. Quincy Jones, *Q—the Autobiography of Quincy Jones* (New York: Doubleday, 2001), p. 115.

4. *Pittsburgh Courier*, June 2, 1956.

5. Lalo Schifrin, interview by Dave Usher, from the CD *Dizzy in South America*, vol. 3, CAP Records 935 2001, and author interview of Lalo Schifrin, August 17, 1998.

6. Dave Usher, interview by author, August 14, 1999.

7. Dizzy Gillespie, interview from *Dizzy in South America*, vol. 3, disc 1, track 10, CAP Records 935, 2001.

8. Dizzy Gillespie, interview by author, December 13, 1990.

9. Jones, *Q*, p. 118.

28: SMALL GROUPS AGAIN

1. Linda Dahl, *Morning Glory—a Biography of Mary Lou Williams* (New York: Pantheon, 1999), p. 258.

2. Dizzy Gillespie and Ralph Ginzburg, "Jazz Is Too Good for Americans," *Esquire*, June 1957, pp. 55, 56.

3. Ibid., p. 55.

4. Dahl, *Morning Glory*, p. 263.

5. NBC News Research Office, New York, NY, 2002.

6. Howard Lucraft, "West Coast Jazz Festival, Predictable Performance and Huge Crowds Spelled Social Success," *Metronome*, December 1958, p. 16.

7. John Tyman, "Take Five," *Downbeat*, November 27, 1958, p. 45.

8. Whitney Balliett, "Jazz Records, the Great Gillespie," *New Yorker*, November 7, 1959, p. 162.

9. Ekkehard Jost, *Free Jazz* (New York: Da Capo Press, 1981), p. 50.

10. Nat Hentoff, "An Afternoon with Miles Davis," *Jazz Review*, December 1958, p. 12.

11. Dizzy Gillespie, interview by author, December 13, 1990.

29: ENTER LALO

1. Lalo Schifrin, interview by author, August 18, 1998.

2. Ibid.

3. Gunther Schuller, liner notes to *Gillespiana, Dizzy Gillespie and His Orchestra*, Verve LP V-8394, 1961.

4. Lalo Schifrin, interview by author, February 3, 2003.

5. Ibid.

6. Lalo Schifrin, liner notes to *The New Continent*, Limelight LP LS 86022, September 1962.

30: FILM STAR/PRESIDENTIAL CANDIDATE

1. Dizzy Gillespie, interview by author, December 13, 1990.

2. Ibid.

3. Gary Giddins, "The Genius and the Goddess," *Village Voice*, June 20, 1995.

4. Ross Firestone, liner notes to the CD *Dizzy for President*, Knit Classics KCR-3001, 2000.

5. Dialogue from track 2 of the CD *Dizzy for President*, Knit Classics KCR-3001, 2000.

6. Statement from track 8 of the CD *Dizzy For President*, Knit Classics KCR-3001, 2000.

7. Harry Frost, "Dizzy and the Heckler," *Downbeat*, October 10, 1963, p. 24.

31: A NEW FAITH IN DIFFICULT TIMES

1. Figures from the research department of the Recording Industry of America.

2. Gillespie with Fraser, *To Be, or Not . . . to Bop*, p. 379.

3. I conducted this interview on January 31, 2003.

4. Dizzy Gillespie, interview by author, December 13, 1990.

5. Yvonne Ervin, "Paquito d' Rivera," *Hot House*, March 2003, p. 17.

6. Charles "Whale" Lake, interview by author, April 1, 2000.

7. Crow, *Jazz Anecdotes*, pp. 142–43.

8. Nat Hentoff, "Conversations with Dizzy Gillespie," *Village Voice*, February 9, 1993; Nat Hentoff, "Dizzy in the Sunlight," *Village Voice*, February 16, 1993.

32: DANGEROUS APPETITES

1. Mike Longo, interviews by author, April 7 and May 10, 2003.

2. Jeffery Gettleman, "A Cherished Civil Rights Site Faces Its Doom," *New York Times*, July 26, 2003.

3. Jon Faddis, "Jon Faddis Talks to Martin Richards," *Jazz Journal*, March 1986, p. 11.

4. Mike Longo, interview by author, April 7 and May 10, 2003.

5. Earl May, interview by Paul Mathews, *Cadence*, November 2002, p. 8.

6. Dan Morgenstern, "Giants," record review, *Downbeat*, November 25, 1971, p. 18.

7. George Wein with Nate Chinen, *Myself Among Others: A Life in Music* (Cambridge, MA: Da Capo Press, 2003), p. 227.

8. Dan Morgenstern, "The Giants Of Jazz," record review, *Downbeat*, April 26, 1973.

9. Mike Bourne, "Mickey Roker: Flexibility and Sensitivity," *Downbeat*, May 25, 1972.

10. Mike Longo, interview by author, April 7 and May 10, 2003.

11. Ibid.

12. Ibid.

13. Dizzy Gillespie, interview by author, December 13, 1990.

33: RENEWAL IN THE SEVENTIES

1. Nat Hentoff, "Norman Granz: Impresario of Recorded Jazz," *New York Times*, February 8, 1976.

2. Ira Gitler, "Norman Granz: One of Jazz's Leading Iconoclasts," *Radio Free Jazz*, November 1977, pp. 10–12.

3. Oscar Peterson, *A Jazz Odyssey* (London and New York: Continuum, 2002), p. 264.

4. Dan Morgenstern, "Oscar and Dizzy," record review, *Radio Free Jazz*, November 1975, p. 11.

5. Charles "Whale" Lake, interview by author, April 1, 2000.

6. Arturo Sandoval, interview by author, September 19, 2003.

7. Ira Sabin, "Cuban Jazz '77,'" *Radio Free Jazz*, July 1977, pp. 5–6.

8. Ibid., p. 6.

9. Richard Servo, "Jazz Provides High Note of Cruise to Cuba," *New York Times*, May 22, 1977.

10. Gary Giddins, "It's Dizzy Again," *New York Times Magazine*, June 25, 1978.

11. Ibid.

34: SUMMING UP AND LOOKING FORWARD

1. Charles "Whale" Lake, interview by author, April 1, 2000.

2. Gary Giddins, "Licks: Spoiled Dream," *Village Voice*, February 25, 1981.

3. Michael Zwerin, "Unpredictable Gillespie, Bebop's Founder Clown," *International Herald Tribune*, July 9, 1985.

4. Charles "Whale" Lake, interview by author, August 14, 1999.

5. Dizzy Gillespie, interview by author, June 7, 1987.

6. John Lee, interview by author, October 30, 2003.

35: A CREATIVE RENAISSANCE

1. Dave Usher, interview by author, August 15, 1999.

2. Max Roach, interview by author, March 22, 1999.

3. Gary Giddins, "Weatherbird—Kings of the Blues," *Village Voice*, June 5, 1990.

4. Max Roach, liner notes to the CD, *The Paris All-Stars—Homage to Charlie Parker*, A&M Records, 75021 5300–2, 1990.

5. Gene Lees, liner notes to the CD *Rhythmstick*, CTI Records, R279477, 1990.

6. Dany Gignoux, *Dizzy Gillespie* (Kiel, Germany: Nieswand Verlag, 1993).

7. Charles Fishman, interview by author, August 12–13, 2003.

8. Ibid.

9. Charles "Whale" Lake, interview by author, April 1, 2000.

10. Gignoux, *Dizzy Gillespie*.

11. James Jones IV, "Dizzy Gillespie, the Working Man," *Downbeat*, August 1990, p. 16.

12. Mike Zwerin, "Gillespie and Makeba: A Meeting of Music," *International Herald Tribune*, April 24, 1991.

13. Charles Fishman, interview by author, August 12–13, 2003.

14. Charles "Whale" Lake, interview by author, April 1, 2000.

36: FINALE

1. Charles "Whale" Lake, interview by author, April 1, 2000.

2. Mike Longo, interview by author, January 18, 2003.

3. Mike Longo, interview by author, May 5, 2003.

4. Peter Watrous, "Dizzy Gillespie Tribute," *New York Times*, November 30, 1992.

5. Mike Longo, interview by author, May 5, 2003.

6. Affidavit of Dr. Harris B. Stratyner in the case of *Jean Bryson Tomas, Plaintiff v. Lorraine Gillespie and Dizlo Music Corporation*, December 27, 2000.

ACKNOWLEDGMENTS

I could not have written this book without the help of my indispensable assistant, Anthony Brown—a tireless organizer, talented researcher, and whiz with the computer. Tom Bruce, who preceded Anthony at the beginning of this endeavor, and Jill McManus, who made difficult research assignments seem easy, also made important staff contributions.

Of the scores of people who have helped me, I wish to single out three friends and a nephew of Dizzy who were especially dedicated to the task:

- *Mike Longo comes first. His contributions to my understanding of Dizzy's life, music, and spirituality cannot be overestimated.*
- *Max Roach, whose love of Dizzy extends back to the 1940s, gave unstintingly of his memories and knowledge.*

- *Boo Frazier, Dizzy's nephew, never tired of answering the multitudes of questions I put to him over many, many months.*
- *Virginia Wicks was always there. She made essential contacts, provided valuable documents, and offered sage advice at all hours of the day and night.*

Special thanks go to Dan Morgenstern and his entire staff at the Institute of Jazz Studies at Rutgers University, and particularly to his associate Tad Hershorn. I spent hundreds of hours studying recordings, book, periodicals, and videos at the institute, the greatest and friendliest jazz research center in the world. I am especially indebted to Charlie Fishman, Dizzy's personal manager during the last years of his career, who gave so generously of his time and his archives and who greatly enriched my text.

And in Dizzy's hometown of Cheraw, South Carolina, I wish to thank Wilbert and Gloria Motley, generous hosts during my two visits there, and Sarah Spruill of the Cheraw Visitors Bureau, who provided invaluable information about the town and Dizzy's youth there.

I am grateful to Mrs. Cynthia McDuffie, principal, and Frank Bishop McDuffie Jr., the president of the Laurinburg Institute in Laurinburg, North Carolina, for the knowledge they generously provided concerning the school which affected Dizzy's life so deeply and so positively. Also to Gene Davis, producer of an outstanding documentary about Dizzy for the A&E cable network, who allowed me generous use of materials from his archives.

Finally, kudos to my editors, Mauro DiPreta and Joelle Yudin; their encouragement, sense of balance, and expert guidance made this a much better book.

INDEX